SO YOU THINK YOU KNOW

ROCK AND ROLL?

SO YOU THINK YOU KNOW

ROCK AND ROLL?

Peter E. Meltzer

An In-Depth Q&A Tour of the Revolutionary Decade 1965-1975

Skyhorse Publishing

Skyhorse Publishing books may be purchased in bulk at special discounts for sales promotion, corporate gifts, fund-raising, or educational purposes. Special editions can also be created to specifications. For details, contact the Special Sales Department, Skyhorse Publishing, 307 West 36th Street, 11th Floor, New York, NY 10018 or info@ skyhorsepublishing.com.

Skyhorse® and Skyhorse Publishing® are registered trademarks of Skyhorse Publishing, Inc.®, a Delaware corporation.

Visit our website at www.skyhorsepublishing.com.

10 9 8 7 6 5 4 3 2 1

Library of Congress Cataloging-in-Publication Data is available on file.

Cover design by Rain Saukas
Cover photo credit: iStock

Print ISBN: 978-1-5107-1766-4
Ebook ISBN: 978-1-5107-1768-8

Printed in the United States of America

To Thomas and Charlotte, once more with love

CONTENTS

Introduction

As 1965 began, Lyndon Johnson had just been elected President in a landslide victory over Arizona Senator Barry Goldwater. The Second Vatican Council had not occurred. America's involvement in Vietnam had begun but not a single ground troop had been sent over and thus it had not yet registered as a major political or social issue. The Voting Rights Act had not yet been enacted into law. The legal voting age was 21. There had been no be-ins, sit-ins, campus takeovers, or war protests.

As 1965 began in terms of music, the British Invasion was well underway. Male performers wore their hair short and all bands generally appeared wearing the same outfit as one another, typically dresses for women and coats and thin ties for men. There was no such thing as rock operas, double albums or rock festivals. Bob Dylan had not yet angered folk purists by "going electric" at the Newport Folk Festival. Before 1965, major rock artists or bands who wrote their own material were so rare (the Beatles and Bob Dylan being notable exceptions), the term "singer-songwriter" did not exist. Death of musicians from drug overdose was almost unheard of.

In terms of the breadth and scope of what was about to transpire over the following decade, politically, socially and musically, the years 1965-1975 (which are referred to in this book as the "Decade") may as well have lasted several generations. When we refer to "the '60s", we are really not referring to the years 1960–1964 because almost nothing that we think of about that decade occurred in those years. Indeed, I submit that the years 1965-1975 capture the essence and spirit of "the '60s" much better than does the period from 1960–1969.

Between 1965 and 1975, Richard Nixon was elected twice and resigned. Man not only landed on the moon, but it became somewhat routine—until the last one in 1972. The last of the American troops had left Vietnam. (The Decade from 1965–1975 almost perfectly circumscribes America's involvement in the Vietnam War.) The appearance and clothing of America's youth in 1965 bore almost no resemblance to what it would look like a mere two years later and the same could be said of the quantum change in styles that would occur again between 1967 and 1969, as it would continue to evolve over the next six years. While hundreds of musical artists either became famous during the Decade or saw the end of their careers during that time, very few were successful at both ends of the spectrum. (Indeed, it could be argued that the Rolling Stones were the only artist or band releasing hit records at both the start and the end.)

In all respects, but especially musically, the era bookended by 1965 and 1975 was sui generis. When *Rolling Stone* magazine released its list of the 100 greatest albums in rock music history, a period spanning more than 50 years, nearly 60 percent of those albums were released in that one era.

Though set up in question-and-answer format, this book is not intended as a "trivia book," but rather as a wide-ranging portrait of that transformative and remarkable time, which began at the dawn of the singer-songwriter era and ended just before the disco era began. It is also intended to be catnip on steroids for all people who are fans of rock and roll during the period from 1965–1975 and hopefully filled with many "I never knew that!" moments.

This book took about two years to research and write. Regardless of how much readers know (or think they know) about rock music from 1965–1975 before reading this book, I expect that not only will they know a whole lot more after, but that the journey itself will be extremely enjoyable. The book is intended (as the Beach Boys would say) to be fun, fun, fun, but also challenging.

ANALYSIS OF THE MUSIC FROM 1965 TO 1975—FEW RECORDBREAKERS, BUT THE GREATEST DECADE FOR MUSIC IN ROCK HISTORY

The music of the Decade looms large over our consciousness more than 50 years after it ended. Why is this so? I will posit a few possible reasons that may seem logical but that are *not* the correct explanations in my view, leaving only the one reason that I consider to be the real one.

One possible explanation is that the first baby boomers were coming of age as the Decade started (the baby boom started in 1946 and continued until 1964). In other words, it's merely a demographic phenomenon. However, that is not a satisfactory explanation. It is safe to say that when we first start becoming interested in music—say during our end of the teenage years—we are always up to date with new releases. This constitutes the music each of us "grew up with." So baby boomers became teenagers from 1959 until 1977 (when the oldest and youngest boomers turned 13) and stayed teenagers from 1966 until 1984 (when the oldest and youngest boomers turned 20). So the overlap of the "Decade" I have chosen and the period from 1959–1984 is far from exact. If the baby boom theory was correct, then all 10-year periods starting each year from 1959 through 1974 ought to be equal in terms of popularity, but that is not the case.

In 2013, Wray Herbert wrote an article extoling 1960s music (especially late-1960s music) and then wondering whether or not his fondness for that music may be for the exact same reason I postulated, namely that it was simply the music he grew up with: "I had the good fortune to come of age during the richest musical epoch—well, ever. . . . The '60s witnessed an unparalleled burst of musical creativity, ranging from Cream to CCR to Hendrix and to Neil Young and Paul Simon and Joni Mitchell. There is simply no match—not before or since—for this outpouring of enduring song. [But my friends] say that '60s music *seems* incomparable to me because I was a young man when I encountered it."[1]

Are his friends right? Is his love for 1960s music simply a function of his age and nothing else? If yes, there is actually a scientific term for that—a "reminiscence bump," which is a peak in personal memories that comes in late adolescence and early adulthood. Herbert suggests that that is one explanation, but "the interpretation I favor—it could simply be that the music of Led Zeppelin and Dylan is better music, unparalleled before or since." In other words, he believes that his friends are wrong, and so do I. Also, I include the first half of the 1970s in that "unparalleled" period. That includes a prime portion of the careers of the Who, the Rolling Stones, Led Zeppelin, Bruce Springsteen, Queen, Neil Young, the Eagles, the Allman Brothers, Lynyrd Skynyrd, Stevie Wonder, Elton John, Linda Ronstadt, Pink Floyd, David Bowie, Billy Joel, Paul Simon, Marvin Gaye, James Taylor, Carole King, Aretha Franklin, Lou Reed, Carly Simon, Laura Nyro, Todd Rundgren and many others.

My own situation further belies the theory that my focus on the particular years of 1965–1975 is simply because that time period corresponds with my own musical coming of age, or my own "reminiscence bump." At the start of the Decade, I was only six years old. By the end of the Decade, I was still a junior in high school. Music held no real appeal for me until I was about 13, and most of the Decade was already over. Therefore, if everyone's favorite era is based solely when they first became truly interested in music, then mine would have been from 1972–1982.

Another possible explanation is that there were fewer acts (and fewer genres) during the Decade, so that each one played a larger part of the music scene. Thus, at least in theory, it may have been much easier to have blockbuster songs during the Decade because of the relative absence of competition. By way of analogy, it was much easier to have a hit TV series back when there were only three channels (NBC, ABC, and CBS) than it is today, when there are hundreds if not thousands of choices. However, this explanation doesn't work either, at least based on sales records. For example, based on the *Billboard* Hot 100 charts, it was far more difficult to dominate the charts during the Decade than it was thereafter, either in terms of artist domination or specific songs.

There are several ways to show this. For one, Wikipedia has a site called *List of Billboard Hot 100 Chart Achievements and Milestones for the U.S.* It contains a lengthy list of Guinness-type records, such as song, album and artist milestones. Except for Elvis and the Beatles, songs and artists from the Decade are startlingly absent from virtually every list and record.

Consider: There have been 34 songs which held the #1 spot for 10 weeks or longer. None of them was released during the Decade. In fact, all but five were released after 1990. Of the 14 songs which spent at least 25 weeks in the top 10, none were released during the Decade. This is also the case with the 26 singles which debuted at #1 (none by the Beatles!) In terms of most #1 singles, only the Beatles had the prime of their career during the Decade. How about three singles by one artist in the top 10 at the same time? That never happened during the Decade, but it has happened 13 times since. Most top 10 singles from one album? Once again, none were released during the Decade.

An examination of the top-selling singles of all time similarly reflects a puzzling absence of songs released during the Decade. Wikipedia lists all of the singles which have sold more than seven million copies. It is readily apparent which decade is conspicuously absent, especially when focusing on established stars as opposed to novelty songs or one-hit wonders.

Sales	1965–1975	Before	After
15 million copies or more (The one song from the Decade is a one-hit wonder)	1	6	6
10–14.9 million copies (Four of the six songs from the Decade are one-hit wonders)	6	9	14
8–9.9 million copies (Two of the three songs from the Decade are one-hit wonders)	3	3	7
7–7.9 million copies (All three songs from the Decade are one-hit wonders)	3	4	7

Thus, of the 69 songs which have sold more than seven million copies, there are only 13 from the Decade, and of those, only three of those are not novelty songs or one-hit wonders. Those would be "I'm a Believer" by the Monkees, "Whiter Shade of Pale" by Procol Harum (close to being one-hit wonders), and "Hey Jude" by the Beatles.

The higher difficulty of dominating the charts during the Decade is shown not only by single chart performance but by album chart performance as well. For example: Of the 60 albums that produced at least four top 10 hits, all but one is from after the Decade (the exception being *Introducing the Beatles* from 1964 which comes with an asterisk because it is basically a reconfigured American version of *Please Please Me* from the previous year).[2]

The situation in the U.K. is the same as in the U.S. For example, of the eight songs holding the top spot for 10 weeks or more, only Queen's "Bohemian Rhapsody" is from the Decade. That song is also the only song from the Decade among the top 10 best-selling singles of all time. The other songs on both lists are from after *and before* the Decade. In other words, as with the U.S., it is not simply a case of newer songs holding all the records.

The syndicated radio show, *American Top 40*, hosted by Casey Kasem, started in 1970, smack in the middle of the Decade. The songs that topped the chart in those early days were recognizable to all, just as many of them are recognizable to all today. When Kasem passed away in 2014, Will Bunch of the *Philadelphia Daily News* penned a column entitled *Casey Kasem and the Death of American Mass Culture*. He wrote:

> As FM stations proliferated and then finally the Internet [there was] a home for every musical niche (and non-musical) niche imaginable, and no one could any longer see the purpose of a shared "Top 40 radio." Why would anyone on the planet listen to Wayne Newton if he didn't have to? In 2014, there's a good chance that die-hard fans of Kendrick Lamar, the Parquet Courts or Lucero have never even heard the other two. Something is gained in the libertarian-ism of 21st century pop culture, perhaps, but something has been lost, a sense of community and shared feelings and emotions that many of us feel difficult to even express in words.[3]

When people go to a sporting event and hear "Sweet Caroline" by Neil Diamond, or "Rock and Roll Part 2" by Gary Glitter, or "Hang on Sloopy" by the McCoys or "Na Na Hey Hey Kiss Him Goodbye" by Steam, or any Beatles or Stones songs, these tunes—and many others from the Decade—are instantly recognizable to the entire audience, regardless of age, race or gender. There are far fewer songs of which that can be said since then, especially in the last 25 years. While there are obviously many songs that have been released since the end of the Decade that have been huge hits, most of the newer songs don't linger in our minds. I believe that a younger person is far more likely to recognize big hits from the Decade than an older person is to recognize current hits, except by the very top acts.

A third theory for the popularity of songs from the Decade is based on the assumption that older songs have an inherent advantage over newer songs simply because they have had a longer time to settle into our national consciousness. However, that theory is belied by an examination of the songs which *preceded* the Decade, because, with a few exceptions, those are relatively unremembered by anyone, young or old.

Since we know that people always love the songs from the time they first start becoming interested in music, what is more interesting therefore is to examine which era's music is of interest *aside from* the music they grew up with. The chart below shows the top five songs for selected weeks, starting in 1955 and continuing until the end of the Decade, and then at 10-year intervals after the Decade. This allows us to take three snapshots of top five songs in the beginning, middle and end of the Decade, and four snapshots after, through 2015. I suggest that songs from the Decade are much more recognizable to, say, a current 15–35-year-old demographic than more recent songs are to the current 55–75 demographic. While #1 or #2 songs are often recognizable to everyone, after that . . . not so much, *except for the music during the Decade*. In addition, I believe that the music *before* the Decade is less familiar to both old and young people alike, so it cannot be said that the older songs are always the most recognizable songs merely by virtue of being older.

In short, putting aside the music we each grew up with, I would wager that the percentage of top five songs people recognize from the Decade is far higher than for any period after *or before*. Moreover, as shown below, once we move beyond the very top songs, I believe that the difference in familiarity between songs from the Decade and those before or after, is even greater. In other words, the songs below actually understate the difference in overall recognizability and popularity of songs from the Decade versus other eras.

From 1955
1. "Love Is a Many-Splendored Thing" by The Four Aces
2. "Autumn Leaves" by Roger Williams
3. "Moments to Remember" by The Four Lads
4. "The Yellow Rose of Texas" by Mitch Miller
5. "The Shifting Whispering Sands (Parts 1 and 2)" by Billy Vaughn and His Orchestra

From 1960
1. "Are You Lonesome Tonight" by Elvis Presley
2. "Wonderland by Night" by Bert Kaempfert and His Orchestra
3. "Last Date" by Floyd Kramer
4. "A Thousand Stars" by Kathy Young and the Innocents
5. "Exodus" by Ferrante & Teicher

From the Decade #1 (1965)
1. **"Help!" by The Beatles**
2. **"Like a Rolling Stone" by Bob Dylan**
3. **"California Girls" by the Beach Boys**
4. **"Unchained Melody" by the Righteous Brothers**
5. **"It's the Same Old Song" by The Four Tops**

From the Decade #2 (1970)
1. **"Let It Be" by the Beatles**
2. **"ABC" by the Jackson Five**
3. **"Instant Karma" by John Lennon**
4. **"Spirit in the Sky" by Norman Greenbaum**
5. **"Bridge Over Troubled Water" by Simon and Garfunkel**

From the Decade #3 (1975)
1. "Get Down Tonight" by KC and the Sunshine Band
2. "Fallin' in Love" by Hamilton, Joe Frank & Reynolds
3. "Rhinestone Cowboy" by Glen Campbell
4. "One of These Nights" by the Eagles
5. "How Sweet It Is (To Be Loved by You)" by James Taylor

From 1985
1. "Say You Say Me" by Lionel Richie
2. "Broken Wings" by Mr. Mister
3. "Party All the Time" by Eddie Murphy
4. "Alive and Kicking" by Simple Minds
5. "Separate Lives" by Phil Collins

From 1995
1. "Kiss from a Rose" by Seal
2. "Waterfalls" by TLC
3. "Boombastic" by Shaggy
4. "Colors of the Wind" by Vanessa Williams
5. "I Can Love You Like That" by All-4-One

From 2005
1. "Don't Forget About Us" by Mariah Carey
2. "Run It!" by Chris Brown
3. "Grillz" by Nelly
4. "Laffy Taffy" by D4L
5. "Stick Witu" by the Pussycat Dolls

From 2015
1. "Uptown Funk!" by Mark Ronson
2. "Blank Space" by Taylor Swift
3. "Take Me to Church" by Hozier
4. "Thinking Out Loud" by Ed Sheeran
5. "I'm Not the Only One" by Sam Smith

Can there really be any question as to which groups of songs would be recognizable to the greatest number of people? Moreover, as noted, the farther down the list one goes, the greater the contrast in familiarity. For example, let's consider songs 6–10 from 1965 and 1975 from the same weeks for the songs above from those years and compare them to songs 6–10 for 1985 and 1995:

From the Decade #1 (1965); #6–#10
6. "I Got You Babe" by Sonny & Cher
7. "You Were on My Mind" by We Five
8. "Papa's Got a Brand New Bag" by James Brown
9. "Eve of Destruction" by Barry McGuire
10. "Hold Me, Thrill Me, Kiss Me" by Mel Carter

From the Decade #2 (1975); #6–#10
6. "Jive Talking" by The Bee Gees
7. "At Seventeen" by Janis Ian
8. "Someone Saved My Life Tonight" by Elton John
9. "Why Can't We Be Friends?" by War
10. "Fame" by David Bowie

From 1985
6. "Election Day" by Arcadia
7. "I Miss You" by Klymaxs
8. "That's What Friends Are For" by Dionne Warwick
9. "Small Town" by John Mellencamp
10. "Sleeping Bag" by ZZ Top

From 1995
6. "Gangsta's Paradise" by Coolio
7. "He's Mine" by MoKenStef
8. "Don't Take it Personal" by Monica
9. "Run-Around" by Blues Traveler
10. "One More Chance/Stay with Me" by Notorious B.I.G.

Without running through all of the 6–10 songs from the other weeks above that are outside the Decade, suffice it to say that most of them would not be recognized except by die-hard fans of the music of those particular years. Stated differently, if you didn't easily recognize songs 2–5 from those weeks, you would probably not recognize 6–10 either.

Here is another way to judge the music of the Decade as compared to other eras: In 2008, *Rolling Stone* magazine released its list of the 500 Greatest Songs of All Time. If we break the rock era down into four 11-year periods—since my "decade" is an 11-year period (1954–1964, 1965–1975, 1976–1986, 1997–2007), and if the there was no overall difference in the greatness of songs during those periods, then, at least in theory, each of those periods would have 25 percent of the songs released within them. However, that is emphatically not the case. Look at the disproportionate distribution:

Percentage of songs ranked 401–500 released between 1965–1975: 36 percent
Percentage of songs ranked 301–400 released between 1965–1975: 47 percent
Percentage of songs ranked 201–300 released between 1965–1975: 47 percent
Percentage of songs ranked 101–200 released between 1965–1975: 43 percent
Percentage of songs ranked 1–100 released between 1965–1975: 51 percent!

Similarly, in 2009 *Rolling Stone* released its list of the 500 Greatest Albums of All Time, which is perhaps even more telling because the list obviously covers more music.

Percentage of songs ranked 401–500 released between 1965–1975: 28 percent
Percentage of songs ranked 301–400 released between 1965–1975: 32 percent
Percentage of songs ranked 201–300 released between 1965–1975: 47 percent
Percentage of songs ranked 101–200 released between 1965–1975: 54 percent!
Percentage of songs ranked 1–100 released between 1965–1975: 59 percent!

In sum, assuming that one agrees with my premise that the music from the Decade is better remembered and more loved by most people than music from any other 10-year period before or after, despite being a down decade for record-breakers in terms of sales or chart dominance, then (aside from reminiscence bumps!), there is only one possible explanation: the music from the Decade was simply *better* than music from any other era. That's my conclusion and I'm sticking to it.

NOTES ABOUT THE BOOK AND THE QUESTIONS

Virtually all of the questions in the book are objective rather than subjective. In other words, there are no questions such as "who is the most underrated guitarist," or "who is undeservedly not in the Rock and Roll Hall of Fame," or "who was the most influential band," or the like.

Speaking of objective and subjective, some may have qualms with both the title and subtitle of the book because they are both a bit misleading. The objective issue is that a "decade" is of course a 10-year period, and yet the focus of this book, 1965–1975, while "sounding like" a 10-year period, is of course an 11-year period. Nevertheless, because I wanted to specifically include the years 1965 and 1975 in my book, I did so, while still retaining the word "decade."

The subjective issue involves "rock and roll." What exactly constitutes rock and roll? Dictionary.com defines it as "a style of popular music that derives in part from blues and folk music and is marked by a heavily accented beat and a simple, repetitive phrase structure." However, regardless of definition, people will always argue about what does and does not constitute "rock music." For example, the music produced by the Rolling Stones or Led Zeppelin or Lynyrd Skynyrd would be considered rock and roll by everyone. However, few would consider music by say, the Carpenters or Frank Sinatra or Johnny Cash as rock music. Then there are artists that might be considered more middle ground, such as the Byrds or the Grateful Dead. Also, the meaning of the term can change each new decade and each new generation. The types of artists who are considered rock musicians in 2015 may be different from 1995 or 1975.

To avoid getting bogged down in the morass of such esoteric questions, for purposes of this book, I am using a much simpler (and more objective) definition of rock and roll: Any song that is eligible for inclusion in the *Billboard* Hot 100 (in terms of singles) or the *Billboard* 200 (in terms of albums) is fair game for purposes of this book. As it happens, the majority of the artists, fans, singles and albums discussed in this book would likely be considered as within the rock and roll genre, but certainly not all of them. (The word "albums" itself seems charmingly anachronistic in the present day, but, during most of the Decade, before 8-tracks, cassettes and CDs, if buyers wanted one song, they purchased a 45, and if they wanted a collection of songs, they purchased an album.)

Even if some of the music discussed in this book might not be considered rock music to purists, that doesn't trouble me because the reality is that all of the songs discussed in the book are famous. For example, virtually everyone who has an interest in music from the Decade would probably recognize and could sing along with a song like "Sugar Sugar" by the Archies, even they who would disdainfully sneer at such a song as not remotely resembling "real" rock music.

In the interest of disclosure, while I do love true rock n roll, almost without exception, if there is any artist, band or song mentioned in this book, I'm a fan. I am not one who would ever say: "How can you possibly like such a song which is so sappy/corny/hokey/stupid/inane/bubblegum/grating/cloying/phony/horrible (pick your synonym) as that one?" Also, even though history obviously renders varying verdicts on some songs, they still hit the *Billboard* charts when they were originally released for a reason: America liked them.

In some instances, I provide hints to the answers, together with a warning beforehand that there is a "hint to follow." For the reasons discussed above, it was my intent for all of the questions in this book to be "fair"—i.e. to be tip-of-the-tongue type questions that that are too neither easy nor too hard. Therefore, in reading the book, it is my hope that readers will actually pause at the end of each question and make the effort to figure out the answer, rather than immediately jumping to the answer.

All chart information is either taken directly from *Billboard* or from Wikipedia, which in turn takes its figures from *Billboard*.

This book is both narrower and yet broader than other general rock and roll books. It is narrower in the obvious sense that it focuses on one specific period rather than on the entire 60-year history of rock and roll. Let's face it: most people who are interested in, say, the doo-wop group of the 1950s are likely not going to be interested in singers or rappers such as Britney Spears and Jay-Z (as both referenced in "Party in the U.S.A." by Miley Cyrus). Therefore, as to any book that attempts to cover the entire history of rock and roll, most readers are not going to be interested at all in huge chunks of it. By contrast, if one is interested in the music of the Decade, then they will like this whole book. To my knowledge, this is the first rock and roll book written that focuses specifically on the music of this particular period.

While narrower than other books in terms of the era covered, it is broader than other books in that it explores *every* aspect of music for this particular time period (as evidenced by the diversity of the chapters), whereas other books often focus on just a few of the subject matters of this book. That is not to say that there is no information or facts included about rock music before and after the Decade when I thought it was particularly interesting. However, all of the questions themselves strictly relate to the Decade.

With respect to every question, I tried to accomplish two goals. First was to strike the right balance between too easy and too hard—i.e. to make the questions of the "tip of the tongue" variety. For example, readers of this book would not be challenged by questions such as: Who was the drummer for the Beatles? What band released the song "Stairway to Heaven"? What is the name of Bruce Springsteen's backup band? Name a rock and roll musician who died of a drug overdose or a plane crash. Second was to avoid questions as to which readers not only have no idea as to the answers, but more problematically, *do not care*. The fact that the readers may have no clue as to the answer is not necessarily a bad thing, but what *is* a bad thing is that the answer is of no interest. For example:

- Name the original members of Procol Harum.
- Who was the manager of Carl Douglas?
- What group appears in the movie *Bunny Lake is Missing*?
- Who produced "Rock the Boat" by the Hues Corporation?
- What label did the group the Knickerbockers record for?

I believe that the reaction of most people to every one of these questions would be the same: I have no idea and I don't care. (The answers are not interesting, trust me.) So, if a reader knows the answer to a question, great. If not, that's OK too, so long as they find the question interesting. In short, a question that is too easy will bore the reader and a question that is too hard and uninteresting will have the same effect. So, the reaction I am shooting for on all of my questions is either (1) best characterized by the name of the popular quiz/game show on National Public Radio: "Wait, wait. Don't tell me!" or (2) "I don't know the answer but I'm intrigued to know."

I hope everyone who reads this book enjoys it.

CHAPTER 1

On The Chart with a Bullet! (*Billboard* Chart Phenomenons and Curiosities)

Since 1936, *Billboard* magazine has been advising us as to the popularity of American music. It is today, and always has been, the bible by which singles and albums have been officially ranked. Where rankings are concerned, this book will focus on two charts in particular, namely the *Billboard* Hot 100, which is a weekly listing of the 100 most popular singles in America, and the *Billboard* 200, which is a weekly listing of the 200 most popular albums in America. The *Billboard* Hot 100 has been in place since 1958. The first number-one song of the Hot 100 was "Poor Little Fool" by Ricky Nelson on August 4, 1958.

Billboard premiered a weekly Best-Selling Popular Albums chart in 1956. The first #1 album was "Belafonte" by Harry Belafonte. Beginning in 1959, *Billboard* split the ranking into two charts, Best-Selling Stereophonic LPs for stereo albums and Best-Selling Monophonic LPs for mono albums. In 1963, the stereo and mono charts were combined into a 150-position chart called Top LPs. The albums chart was expanded to 200 positions on May 13, 1967.

Originally, the charts were based on sales and radio play, but in this day and age they also take into account digital downloads and streaming activity. Of course, from 1965 to 1975, that was not a concern.

One of the things that makes rock and roll analysis fun, especially for those who enjoy statistics, is the ability to chart the performance of our favorite singles and albums. Perhaps not surprisingly, the *Billboard* charts contain many surprises and anomalies, and this chapter examines the performance of some of our favorite songs, albums and artists.

This song peaked at #2 in 1965. It was the only song of the Decade to be the *Billboard* #1 Record of the Year that year despite never hitting #1 on the weekly charts. (In fact, it remained the only one for 35 years until Faith Hill's "Breathe" and Lifehouse's "Hanging by a Moment" in 2000 and 2001 respectively.) It did however have staying power: it lingered on the Hot 100 for 18 weeks, the most weeks for any single within the calendar year 1965, 14 of which were in the top 40. The lead singer of the group was Domingo Samudio.

His appearance on stage and the name of his band was inspired by a character played by Yul Brynner in *The Ten Commandments*. What is the song and what was the name of the band?

"Wooly Bully" by Sam the Sham and the Pharaohs. Brynner played Pharaoh Ramses II.

The following year, the same group had another #2 hit. However, due to contractual disputes, the only member remaining from the band's lineup the year before was Sam the Sham himself. What song was that?

"Little Red Riding Hood."

This artist is the only person who has had a #1 song (either solo or not) on a *Billboard* chart (the Hot 100, Adult Contemporary or Hot Dance Club Songs) in six consecutive decades. Who is it?

Cher. In the 1960s, it was "I Got You Babe" (with Sonny) (Hot 100), in the 1970s, it was "Gypsies, Tramps and Thieves," "Half Breed," and "Dark Lady" (all Hot 100), in the 1980s, it was "If I Could Turn Back Time" and "After All" (Adult Contemporary), in the 1990s, it was "Believe" (Hot 100), in the 2000s, it was "Song for the Lonely" (among others) (Dance Chart), and in the current decade, it was "Woman's World" (among others) (also Dance Chart). As to the Dance Chart, unless one is an expert, who knew that Yoko Ono—going by the name Ono—has had *13(!)* #1 songs on that chart just since 2003?

This artist is the only person who has had a #1 album on the *Billboard* Hot 100 in six consecutive decades. Who is it?

Barbra Streisand. They include *People* (1964), *The Way We Were* (1974), *Guilty* (1980), *Higher Ground* (1997), *Love Is the Answer* (2009) and *Partners* (2014).

There have been a number of occasions where different songs with the same titles have reached #1 on the *Billboard* Hot 100 (not remakes, but actually different songs). However, there is only one such title which reached #1 twice during the Decade. One was by Petula Clark in 1966 and one was by Paul McCartney and Wings in 1973. As a hint, the same title reached #5 on the Billboard Hot 100 in 1983 for Lionel Richie (and #1 on the adult contemporary chart) and #1 again in 2006 with Justin Timberlake. What is the title that reached the top of the charts for four different artists?

"My Love."

This artist had an unusual divergence between album chart success—which was tremendous—and singles chart success—which was (relatively) mediocre in comparison. In the Decade alone, he released 13 albums, one of which was live. Of those, every one was top 20, 11 of them were top 10, seven of them were top five and two hit #1. Adding the first three albums released after the Decade brings the total to 16 albums, all top 20, and of those, there were 13 top 10s, eight top fives and three #1s. For all that fantastic chart success, one would think that there would be a correspondingly high number of singles represented on the chart, but that is not the case. There were "only" four top 10 songs, two of which reached #2 and two of which reached #7. That was it. In addition, the last 13 of the 16 albums referenced above, despite their success on the album chart, yielded only one top 10 song in total, and that hit #7. Who was the artist?

Bob Dylan. His only top 10 singles in the Decade were "Like a Rolling Stone" (#2 in 1965), "Positively 4th Street" (#7 in 1965), "Rainy Day Women #12 and 35" (#2 in 1966) and "Lay Lady Lay" (#7 in 1969).

Even though Dylan had no #1 singles of his own compositions, his songs have been covered so many times by so many artists that one would think that multiple covers of his songs have hit #1. It has happened, but only once. What is the only cover of a Dylan song to hit #1 on the *Billboard* Hot 100? As a hint, both the original and the cover were released in 1965.

"Mr. Tambourine Man" was #1 for the Byrds. Their version of the song was released just a few weeks after Dylan's original. This is one of three songs to appear twice on the 2004 *Rolling Stone* list of 500 Greatest Songs (Dylan's version at #107, the Byrds' version at #79). The others are "Blue Suede Shoes" by Carl Perkins (1956 original at #95) and Elvis Presley (1956 cover at #430) and "Walk This Way" by Aerosmith (1975 original at #346) and Run-DMC (1986 cover at #293).

True or false: Elvis Presley had no #1 singles in the U.S. during the Decade.

False. In 1969, "Suspicious Minds" reached #1.

Elvis had only three other top 10 songs during the Decade (as opposed to 31 in the previous decade, 13 of which reached #1). What were they?

"Crying in the Chapel" reached #3 in 1965, "In the Ghetto" reached #8 in 1969, and "The Wonder of You" reached #9 in 1970. "Crying in the Chapel" and "The Wonder of You" both reached #1 in the U.K.

Lists of best-selling artists, albums and singles can be notoriously inconsistent since they are of course dependent on the methodology of the surveys and compilation of the statistics. Sources include *Billboard*, the Recording Industry Association of America, Nielsen SoundScan and others. Nevertheless, virtually all sources agree that of the best-selling albums of all time by a female, only one of them was released during the Decade. Which album, and who was the artist?

Tapestry by Carole King, released in 1971. Remarkably, this album was put together in just five three-hour sessions in January 1971 and, just as remarkably, when it was recorded, King (real name Carol Klein) had never before performed live. It was recorded at A&M Studio B at the same time that the Carpenters were recording their eponymous third album in Studio A and Joni Mitchell was recording *Blue* in Studio C, all three studios located in a building on Hollywood Boulevard that was once the home of Charlie Chaplin Studios.

By 1973, it was the best-selling album of all time, overtaking *The Sound of Music*, which was released in 1965. It is generally agreed that the album has sold over 10 million copies and several sources claim that the album has sold over 25 million copies. In 2003, *Tapestry* was ranked #36 on *Rolling Stone's* list of the 500 greatest albums of all time. The album consists of one classic track after another including "I Feel the Earth Move," "So Far Away," "It's Too Late," "You've Got a Friend," "Will You Love Me Tomorrow?" and "(You Make Me Feel Like) A Natural Woman." Today, it seems almost impossible to imagine that a record could be recorded in less than two working days by a person who no one had ever seen perform live, and then have it become one of the best-selling records ever.

The list of songs written or cowritten by Carole King (many with her first husband Gerry Goffin) which were hits for other artists is astonishing. A small sampling: "Will You Love Me Tomorrow" by the Shirelles (which she wrote when she was only 18 and which is the first song in history by an all-female group to reach #1), "Take Good Care of My Baby" (Bobby Vee), "Some Kind of Wonderful" (The Drifters), "The Loco-Motion" by Little Eva (who was King's babysitter), "Crying in the Rain" (the Everly Brothers), "Go Away Little Girl" (Steve Lawrence), "Chains" (The Beatles), "One Fine Day" by the Chiffons, "Up on the Roof" (The Drifters), "I'm Into Something Good" (Herman's Hermits), and "Pleasant Valley Sunday" (The Monkees).[1]

There has only been one song in history by a British artist to reach #1 on the *Billboard* Hot 100 (and in fact it stayed there for five weeks) and yet not chart at all in the U.K. As

hints, it was released in 1967 and the singer was female. What is the song and who was the artist?

"To Sir With Love" by Lulu (born Marie McDonald McLaughlin Lawrie). The song is the theme from the movie of the same name starring Sidney Poitier. The song, with lyrics by Don Black and music by Mark London, was the *Billboard* Year-End Top Single for 1967.

Lulu also performed the theme song to a James Bond movie released during the Decade. Which one? As a hint, it starred Roger Moore as James Bond.

"The Man with the Golden Gun."

This song, released in 1967, is kind of the reverse of "To Sir With Love." It did not crack the top 100 in the U.S. but hit #1 in the U.K. The singer was the oldest singer to have a #1 song in the U.S., when he hit the top spot three years earlier when he was 62 years old. Despite its lack of chart success in the U.S. when released, the song has since become a classic in this country. What is the song and who is the singer? For extra credit, what was his #1 song in the U.S.?

"Wonderful World" by Louis Armstrong. His earlier #1 was "Hello Dolly."

Six singles released during the Decade sold over ten million copies worldwide. Of those six, one is by Roger Whittaker and another is by a Scottish band called Middle of the Road. The songs were both released in 1971 although the Whittaker song didn't become a hit until 1975. The Middle of the Road song was #1 or #2 in many countries around the world, but barely made a dent in the U.S. It is about as bubblegum as they come and is sometimes played on oldies stations today. What are the titles of the two songs?

The Roger Whittaker song was "The Last Farewell," and the Middle of the Road song was "Chirpy Chirpy Cheep Cheep."

There were three singles in the Decade that were #1 for more than six consecutive weeks. One was by the Beatles, one was by Marvin Gaye (both released in 1968) and one was by the Monkees (released in 1966). Two of them held the top spot for seven weeks and for one nine weeks. What are the three songs and which one was the nine-week song?

"Hey Jude" by the Beatles (nine weeks), "I Heard It Through the Grapevine" by Marvin Gaye and "I'm a Believer" by the Monkees (seven weeks each). "Hey Jude" and "I Heard It Through the Grapevine" are separated by only one song at the end of 1968, namely "Love Child" by Diana Ross and the Supremes, which held the top spot for two weeks.

Peter, Paul and Mary had only one #1 song and it was during the Decade. What was it?

"Leaving On a Jet Plane," written by John Denver.

How many top 10 songs in the U.S. did Crosby, Stills & Nash or Crosby, Stills, Nash & Young have during the Decade?

Surprisingly, none, especially considering that *Déjà Vu* was a #1 album that sold seven million copies in the U.S. alone. One of the ironies of that album is that, despite the tight-knit harmonies, relationships among the band members were anything but tight, even though this was the first studio album they made together and the only one they made during the Decade. While Crosby, Stills and Nash sang their trademark harmony vocals on most of the tracks, Neil Young sang only on his two compositions, "Helpless" and "Country Girl." As for playing the instruments, on most of the tracks the principal songwriter used his bandmates only on an as-needed basis. For example, Stephen Stills played most of the instruments himself on his song "Carry On" (including electric and acoustic guitar, organ, bass and percussion), with the only exception being percussion added by Graham Nash. David Crosby played on only five of the tracks, as did Young. David Browne wrote: "*Déjà Vu* was a sonically enveloping and powerful illusion, but it was an illusion nonetheless. The group hug of *Crosby, Stills & Nash* was replaced by the sound of four men each in his own space."[2]

There is only one song on *Déjà Vu* on which all four band members played instruments (and all but Young sang). As a hint, it is a classic song and the only one of the nine songs on the album which one of the band members did not write (which perhaps explains why there was greater collaboration on the song).

"Woodstock" by Joni Mitchell.

There has been only one time when an artist has reached #1 with a song and then reached the top 10 again with a completely reworked version of the same song. The first version, released in 1962, was an uptempo pop song. The second version, released in 1975, was a slow ballad with a very different arrangement. Who is the artist and what is the song?

The artist is Neil Sedaka and the song is "Breaking Up is Hard to Do." Howard Greenfield wrote the lyrics.

Sedaka also had two #1 songs in 1975. One was "Laughter in the Rain," which held the top spot for one week. The other was his most successful song, holding the top for three weeks. Although the lyrics were written by his sometime collaborator Philip Cody, the subject matter of this song was very atypical for a Sedaka song. The narrator is commiserating with a friend who got dumped by a woman who is referred as "the bitch." What is the song?

"Bad Blood." To watch Sedaka perform the song live presents an odd juxtaposition between what he is singing about and his ebullient mood. Perhaps he is thinking about the money he has made from the song as opposed to his jilted friend.

Who was the uncredited backup singer on "Bad Blood"?

Elton John.[3]

There is only one group in history who had #1 songs on the *Billboard* Hot 100 before, during and after the time span covering the "Beatles era" of 1963–1970. It is an American group, whose #1 songs were in 1962 (two), 1963 (one), 1964 (one) and 1975 (one). Who is it?

The Four Seasons. Their #1 songs were "Sherry," "Big Girls Don't Cry," "Walk Like a Man," "Rag Doll," and "December 1963 (Oh What a Night)." The Four Seasons released a number of singles on the Philips label from 1964–1970. Some of these were hits such as "Let's Hang On!" and "Working My Way Back to You." However, based on the record labels on their singles, they were actually billed as "The Four Seasons Featuring the 'Sound' of Franki Valli."

True or false: Franki Valli never had a solo #1 song.

False, but with an asterisk. He had one. "My Eyes Adored You" hit #1 in March 1975. However, though billed as a Franki Valli release, his Four Seasons bandmates sang on it with him. In this respect, it was really no different from other many other Four Seasons records. However, it is still considered a Franki Valli song.

There is a reference in "My Eyes Adored You" to a place in New Jersey. What is it?

There are actually two, although one does not technically exist by the name given to it in the song. Valli sings about "Barnegat Bridge and Bay." There is of course a Barnegat Bay. There are also three bridges which span the bay from the mainland to the peninsula, although none of them are called Barnegat Bridge.

This man had an incredible 96 songs in the *Billboard* Hot 100, some before the Decade but most during. This is more than any solo artist other than Elvis Presley (Lil Wayne also has more if one counts singles on which he is a "featured artist") and he certainly had the most songs in the Hot 100 during the Decade. Yet, despite this success, he never had a #1 song. Who is he?

James Brown.

This artist or group had the most #2 hits (five) without ever hitting #1. All of them were in 1969 and 1970. This was during a phenomenally productive two-year period in which the artist or group released five top 10 albums and four of those were top five and two of those were #1. Who was it?

Creedence Clearwater Revival.

This woman released six consecutive top five albums (two in the Decade, four after) and three of them reached #1. Who is she?

Linda Ronstadt.

There was only one time in the Decade when two singers were both in the top 30 with the same song at the same time. It happened on June 12, 1971 and both singers were female. The song is from a rock opera. What was the song and who were the artists?

The song is "I Don't Know How to Love Him" from *Jesus Christ Superstar*. Yvonne Elliman's original hit #28 while Helen Reddy's cover reached #13.

There is been only one occasion where a mother and her son both wrote or cowrote (but not with each other) songs which reached #1. The mother's song reached #1 for Elvis Presley. The son's song reached #1 for Three Dog Night. Who are they?

Mae Axton cowrote "Heartbreak Hotel," which became Elvis's first #1 song in 1956. Her son Hoyt wrote "Joy to the World," which held the #1 spot for six weeks in 1971. Although Axton was a prolific singer-songwriter, most of his famous compositions were performed by others. These include "Greenback Dollar" (The Kingston Trio and Trini Lopez), "The No-No Song" (a #3 song for Ringo Starr in 1973), "Never Been to Spain" (Three Dog Night) and "The Pusher" (Steppenwolf).

When Axton performed "Joy to the World" for Three Dog Night, two of the three main vocalists—Danny Hutton and Cory Wells—rejected the song, but Chuck Negron felt that the band needed a "silly song to help bring the band back together as a working unit." The record was ranked by *Billboard* as the year-end #1 pop single of 1971. The single went on to sell five million copies worldwide, making it one of the best-selling singles of all time.

As for the name of the band, Hutton's then-girlfriend June Fairchild suggested the name after reading a magazine article about indigenous Australians, in which it was explained that on cold nights they would customarily sleep in a hole in the ground while holding onto a dingo, a native species of wild dog. On colder nights they would sleep with two dogs and if the night was really freezing, it was a "three dog night."[4]

There has been only one group who released two hit songs that were covered by two other performers and the two covers both reached #1 in consecutive weeks (in 1987). As a hint, the covers were by Tiffany and Billy Idol respectively. Who was the group and what were the songs?

The group was Tommy James and the Shondells. The songs were "I Think We're Alone Now" by Tiffany and "Mony Mony" by Billy Idol. Tommy James cowrote "Mony Mony," but his version only reached #3 in 1968, while his version of "I Think We're Alone Now" reached #4 in 1967. The week before the group was to appear on *The Ed Sullivan Show* in January 1969, Ed closed his program by announcing "and next week, for all the youngsters . . . Tony Jones and the Spondells."[5]

Why is "Mony, Mony" called what it is? A clue to the answer appears several times in the 1969 Oscar winner *Midnight Cowboy*, including a scene in which Jon Voight is playing Scrabble with a woman (Brenda Vaccaro) and he thinks that the word "money" is spelled "mony" and he proceeds to explain why, to her amusement.

James was inspired by the letters M-O-N-Y, which appeared at the top on the Mutual of New York Insurance Company building for many years. James could always see it from his

Manhattan apartment. (The words "Mutual of New York" all appeared but the letters MONY were in red neon lighting twice the size of the other letters.) Said James:

> "We had most of the words to the song, but we still had no title. And it's just driving us nuts, because we're looking for like a 'Sloopy' or some crazy name— it had to be a two-syllable girl's name that was memorable and silly and kind of stupid sounding. . . . So Ritchie Cordell, my songwriting partner and I are up in my apartment up at 888 Eighth Avenue in New York. And finally we get disgusted, we throw our guitars down, we go out on the terrace, we light up a cigarette, and we look up into the sky. And the first thing our eyes fall on is the Mutual of New York Insurance Company. M-O-N-Y. True story. With a dollar sign in the middle of the O, and it gave you the time and the temperature. I had looked at this thing for years, and it was sitting there looking me right in the face. . . . We said, 'That's perfect! What could be more perfect than that?' Mony, M-O-N-Y, Mutual of New York." James later said that "if I had looked the other way, it might have been called 'Hotel Taft.'"

Accordingly, in the song, Mony is a girl's name and it is pronounced moe-ni. In *Midnight Cowboy*, Voight's character had noticed the letters atop the skyscraper as well. In fact, as we find out later in the movie when he is playing Scrabble, Voight's none-too-bright character thought that it spelled the word "money."

In December, 2007, the new owners of the building took down the Mutual of New York lettering and replaced it with "1740," reflecting the address of the property at 1740 Broadway.[6]

After the Beatles, who had the most # 1 songs during the Decade?

The Supremes, with nine. They had three additional #1 songs in 1964.

This song had an unusual chart history. In the U.K., it was released in 1967, and peaked at #19 on the charts. The same version was then re-released in 1972 and charted again, this time at #9, and then re-released a *third* time in 1979 and charted yet again, this time at #14. It is the only song in British history where the original version hit the top 20 on three separate occasions. In the U.S., on the other hand, its chart peak was higher than with any of the British versions. It hit #2 in 1972 and stayed there for several weeks. Yet, it also holds the dubious distinction of the highest complete Hot 100 disappearance from the pre-digital download era, vanishing entirely from the chart after sitting at #17 on

December 2, 1972. It is considered the signature song of this well-known British quintet. What is the song?

"Nights in White Satin" by the Moody Blues. This song was written by Justin Hayward when he was only 19 years old.

The song "Unchained Melody," recorded by the Righteous Brothers, also charted in the top 20 three times, once when released in 1965 and twice more in 1990, when it was featured in the movie *Ghost*. In the U.K., it hit #1 on *four* different occasions. One would think that one of those occasions was in 1965 when the Righteous Brothers version was originally released, but that is not the case even though that version did hit #1 in 1990. The four times are: Jimmy Young (1955), the Righteous Brothers (1990), Robson and Jerome (1995) and Gareth Gates (2002).

This British band had nine top 10 songs in the U.S. between January 1965 and April 1966. They played their own instruments but did not write any of those songs. Their lead singer was only 17 in January 1965 when the run started. What is the group?

Herman's Hermits. Lead singer Peter Noone was born in November 1947.

This was the first group (and only one in the Decade) whose first four singles all reached #1. As a hint, all four of them hit #1 in 1970 (although one of those was released in 1969). Who was the artist or group? For extra credit, name the songs.

The Jackson 5. The four songs, in order, were "I Want You Back" (released in 1969), "ABC," "The Love You Save" and "I'll Be There."[7] Mariah Carey's first five singles all hit #1 in 1990 and 1991.

The Beatles had six #1 songs in 1964 and five more in 1965. Aside from them and the aforementioned Jackson 5 however, there was only one time during the Decade that an artist or group had four #1 singles in the same calendar year. As a hint, the year was 1965. Who was the artist or group? For extra credit, name the songs.

The Supremes: "Come See About Me," "Stop! In the Name of Love," "Back in My Arms Again" and "I Hear A Symphony."

There were only two groups in the 1960s whose first seven singles were all top 10. As hints, they were both American (somewhat unusual, given the huge success of the British bands). The lead singer of one of them—a drummer (also unusual)—was *Cash Box*

magazine's 1965 "Male Vocalist of the Year," winning against nominees Elvis Presley and Frank Sinatra. He has a famous father. That group's first five singles were all top five. The other band's name was inspired by some lyrics in the song "Coffee Blues" by Mississippi John Hurt which was a tribute to Maxwell House Coffee—just a little bit of it did the trick. The first group did not write their own music and the second group did (or more precisely, one of them did). The name of the second group was also unusual for the era in that it began with "the" but did not end with a plural, despite being a group. Who were the two bands?

Gary Lewis and the Playboys and the Lovin' Spoonful respectively. Gary Lewis is the son of actor/comedian Jerry Lewis. The first seven singles of the former were "This Diamond Ring" (#1), "Count Me In" (#2), "Save Your Heart For Me" (#2), "Everybody Loves a Clown" (#4), "She's Just My Style" (#3), "Sure Gonna Miss Her" (#9), and "Green Grass" (#8). The first seven singles of the latter (written or cowritten by John Sebastian) were "Do You Believe in Magic" (#9), "You Didn't Have to be So Nice" (#10), "Daydream" (#2), "Did You Ever Have to Make Up Your Mind" (#2), "Summer in the City" (#1), "Rain on the Roof" (#10), and "Nashville Cats" (#8).[8]

This performer is the third top-selling singles artist in British history behind only Elvis and the Beatles. He is the only act in British history to have had #1 songs in five consecutive decades, the '50s through the '90s. While most of his success was before the Decade, he did have 12 top 10 songs during the Decade (which, while impressive, is a pittance compared to his pre-decade chart success). In total, he had 14 #1 songs and 69 top 10 songs in the U.K. He had more top 75 hits (131), more top 40 hits (120), more top 20 hits (95) and more top 10 hits (66) than anyone except Elvis, topping even the Beatles. Little wonder that he is the most successful British male solo artist of all time. Yet, for all that success, he was comparatively invisible in the U.S. His highest charting studio album in the U.S. only hit #75. He did have three top 10 hits in the U.S., all of them released after the Decade. Who is he?

Cliff Richard. His top 10 songs in the U.S. were "Devil Woman" (#6, 1976), "We Don't Talk Anymore" (#7, 1979) and "Dreamin'" (#10, 1980). [9]

Cliff Richard's backup band was the most successful backup band in British history. Their first seven studio albums (four released before the Decade and three released during the Decade) all went top 10 in the U.K. Their success is even more unusual considering that they were an instrumental band. What was the name of this group?

The Shadows.

Continuing with acts having far greater success in the U.K. than in the U.S., the act that spent the most weeks on the British chart in 1966 was not the Beatles or the Stones, but rather a group that is almost unheard of here, with no top 50 singles here ever. However, between 1966–1968, they had eight top 10 singles in the U.K. Their unusual name consisted of the nicknames of their five members. What was the name of the group?

Dave Dee, Dozy, Beaky, Mick and Tich, also known as DDDBMT. A name that hardly rolls off the tongue.

Who was the first Australian group or artist to have a top five hit in the U.S. and U.K. and what was the song? As a hint, it happened in February 1965.

The group was the Seekers and the song was "I'll Never Find Another You," which reached #1 in the U.K and #4 in the U.S (not to mention #1 in Australia).

Many of the Seekers' hit songs, including "I'll Never Find Another You," "A World of Our Own," "The Carnival is Over" (lyrics), and their biggest seller, "Georgy Girl" (music), were written by this man. As a hint, he is the brother of the woman known as the White Queen of Soul.

Tom Springfield, brother of Dusty Springfield.

Name every top 10 single by Pink Floyd during the Decade.

There were none. Their only top 10 hit was "Another Brick in the Wall," which reached #1 in 1979.

Name every top 10 single by Led Zeppelin.

There is only one, "Whole Lotta Love," which reached #4 in the U.S. in 1969. "Stairway to Heaven" was never officially released as a single. As is the case with Pink Floyd and a number of other bands, singles chart performance is not necessarily an indicator of either album sales or influence as a band.

There have been only two times that an artist has hit #1 on the *Billboard* Hot 100 pop chart with both a vocal tune and an instrumental. Who were the artists and what are the four songs? As hints, Artist 1 is known primarily as the founder of a major record label and Artist 2 is known for his distinctive bass-baritone voice and romantic image.

Answers: The first artist is Herb Alpert. His vocal is "This Guy's in Love with You," written by Burt Bacharach and Hal David and his instrumental is "Rise," co-written by Randy Badazz Alpert. The second artist is Barry White. His vocal is "Can't Get Enough of Your Love, Babe," which he wrote and his instrumental is "Love's Theme" by The Love Unlimited Orchestra, which was a 40-piece orchestra formed by White.

Rolling Stone magazine ranked this album as #2 on its list of the 500 greatest albums of all time. Yet, it never reached higher than #10 on the *Billboard* 200 albums chart and there were no #1 or #2 singles on it. What album is it and who is it by?

Pet Sounds by the Beach Boys, released in May 1966. The only top 10 singles were "Sloop John B" (#3) and "Wouldn't It Be Nice" (#8). Although all of the Beach Boys other than Mike Love usually played instruments in concert, the band as musicians took almost no part in the creation of this album. The only exceptions were "That's Not Me," on which Carl Wilson played guitar, Dennis Wilson played drums, and Brian Wilson played organ, and "Sloop John B," "I'm Waiting For the Day" and "God Only Knows," on which Carl Wilson again played guitar. On most of the other tracks, the boys simply added vocals. On one song, "Caroline, No," the only Beach Boy on the track is Brian Wilson, who sang vocal. On two other songs, none of the Beach Boys participated at all. These were both instrumentals composed by Brian Wilson, one called "Let's Go Away for Awhile," as well as the title track. (If a band puts a song on an album in which its members neither sing nor play instruments, is that song "by" the band or one of its members?)

Pet Sounds was clearly Brian Wilson's vision and creation. He wrote and arranged nearly all of the songs, with Tony Asher supplying the lyrics on several, including "God Only Knows" (where Carl Wilson supplies the lead vocal) and "Caroline, No." The actual title of the latter song was "Carol I Know." Asher's high school sweetheart had moved to New York to become a dancer and he had not seen her for a year. When he went to visit her, he was surprised at how much she had changed. Said Asher:

> I had in mind a song in which the girl had undergone these changes and was perhaps trying to explain to the former lover the inevitability or maybe the unavoidability of growing up. And I was going to have him answer "Oh, Carol, I know," as a way of acknowledging that unavoidability, but then going on to

say that even though he knew it had to happen, he missed the old "her." Brian, understandably, heard it as "Caroline, No" which struck me as a far more interesting line than the one I originally had in mind.

Despite the fact that the Beach Boys collectively contributed almost nothing to *Pet Sounds* in terms of playing instruments, that is not to say that Brian Wilson did not have a lot of help. In fact, there were over 70 musicians who played on the album.[10]

This highly successful British band had 10 albums in the top 10 in the U.K. of which six were top five and one reached #1. They also had eight top 10 and five top five albums in the U.S. This does not even count live or compilation albums. In terms of singles, they had 13 in the top 10 in the U.K., of which six were top five. Yet, for all that success, they never had a #1 single in the U.S. or the U.K. pop chart. Who is this iconic British band?

The question gives the answer—The Who. (One song, "You Better You Bet," reached #1 in 1981 but that was on the recently established rock chart, which did not exist during the Decade.)[11]

The Who is rightfully considered one of the greatest rock bands in history. As noted above however, they never had a #1 single in the U.S. or the U.K. during the Decade (which was their most prolific period). Which of the following singles released by the band during the Decade ever reached the top 10?

   a. "I Can't Explain"
   b. "My Generation"
   c. "Substitute"
   d. "The Kids Are Alright"
   e. "Happy Jack"
   f. "I Can See for Miles"
   g. "Magic Bus"
   h. "Pinball Wizard"
   i. "The Seeker"
   j. "See Me, Feel Me"
   k. "Won't Get Fooled Again"
   l. "Baba O'Reilly"
   m. "5:15"
   n. "Squeeze Box"

Remarkably, only one, "I Can See for Miles," which barely edged in at #9 in 1967.

This foreign-born artist released a greatest hits album that reached #5 on the *Billboard* 200. The album was ranked number 46 on *Rolling Stone* magazine's list of the 500 greatest albums of all time. Despite the fact that it "only" reached #5, as of April, 2016, it has spent a total of 413 nonconsecutive weeks on the *Billboard* 200, a period of longevity on the chart surpassed by only a few albums. It has sold over 11 million copies, making it one of the best-sellers of all time. Yet this popular and critical acclaim is somewhat surprising in that the artist never had any singles in the *Billboard* Hot 100, except for one song that got to #51. As a hint, the album was released in 1984, posthumously. What is the album and who is it by?

Legend by Bob Marley (and the Wailers).

Who is the only member of Congress to have written and performed a #1 hit song (not while a member of Congress), and what is the song? As a hint, the song was released in 1965.

Sonny Bono. The song is "I Got You Babe." Bono was a congressman for California's 44th district from 1994 until his death in 1998 in a skiing accident while still in office. Another songwriter-musician turned Congressman is John Hall of the group Orleans. He wrote "Dance with Me," which reached #5 and cowrote "Still the One" with his (then) wife Joanna, which reached #6. He was a congressman for New York's 19th Congressional district, serving from 2007 to 2011. Bono was a Republican, Hall a Democrat.

One of the best-selling albums in history appears on the top five of every list, yet never reached #1 on the *Billboard* Hot 200. It stalled at #2. What album is it? As a hint, it was released in late 1971. As a further hint, there are no words on the cover.

Led Zeppelin IV.

True or false: Frank Sinatra never had a solo #1 song during the Decade.

False. The song was "Strangers in the Night." Sinatra had not had a #1 song in 11 years. As the song recording sailed towards its conclusion, Sinatra realized that the musicians were playing for another 30 seconds after his vocal and he was used to cold endings on most of his songs. "What the hell am I supposed to do when the orchestra keeps on playing?" he said to the producer Jimmy Bowen. "Well Frank just scat your way out. You're the king of that." Frank first tried a parade of "tra-la-la's," which sounded very pedestrian. Bowen, not wanting to embarrass Frank and therefore trying to be very diplomatic and with close to 100 VIPs looking on, asked him to give it another shot. Then, as written by Kent Hartman, "with cigarette in hand and a take-no-prisoners attitude etched on his face, he came through on the third take with an inspired flurry of 'dooby-dooby-doos' that took the song's fade to an entirely different level."

Guitarist Glen Campbell was especially excited about the seating arrangement because he was going to be sitting only six feet away from Sinatra. He kept staring at Sinatra while Ol' Blue Eyes was laying down his vocal. After the session, Campbell saw Bowen and Sinatra talking to one another while looking his way. With his curiosity getting the better of him, he asked Bowen, "Was Mr. Sinatra talking about me out there tonight?" Bowen replied yes and, assuming that Sinatra was probably complementing his guitar-playing abilities, Campbell asked what Sinatra had to say. Bowen replied, "Frank said he wanted to know who was the fag guitar player that kept staring at him."

The song reached #1 and it remained on the charts for 15 weeks. It won the 1967 Grammy for Record of the Year. However, Sinatra hated the song, calling it "the worst fucking song I've ever heard" and he had no problem expressing that sentiment whenever he played it in concert, which he was of course forced to do, given its success. (At other concerts he said "I just cannot stand this song, but what the hell" and "I hated this goddamn song the first I've heard it. And I still hate it! So sue me, shoot bullets through me. Shoot."

The song had a surprising legacy for children. Television executive Fred Silverman had been working on development of a Saturday morning cartoon for CBS. It was to be focused on a dog called Too Much, but Silverman was not satisfied with the name. However, after hearing Sinatra scat at the end of Strangers in the Night, he decided to rename the dog "Scooby-Doo" and re-rechristen the show *Scooby-Doo, Where Are You!*[12]

Frank Sinatra did have a non-solo #1 hit song during the Decade. What was the song and who else sang on the track?

"Something Stupid," sung with his daughter Nancy. It reached #1 in 1967, and stayed there for four weeks.

This group had by far more #1 singles on the *Billboard* adult contemporary chart during the Decade than any other artist or group (12) and more than any other artist or group in history (15) other than Elton John (16). The group also had more top 3 singles (10) on the *Billboard* Hot 100 between 1970 and 1973 than any artist or group in the world. As a hint, it is a duo. Who is it?

The Carpenters.[13]

Having a #1 hit song is obviously not easy and it usually means lasting fame. Today, there are very few songs that hit #1 during the Decade by artists or groups who are not still famous now, and most people who are fans of music from the Decade can readily identify the performers of almost all #1 songs from that era. There are a few (relatively) obscure ones however. Name the performers of the following #1 songs from the Decade.

1965	I'm Telling You Now
1965	Game of Love
1967	Kind of a Drag
1971	Want Ads
1972	Oh Girl
1973	Show and Tell

1965	I'm Telling You Now	Freddie and the Dreamers
1965	Game of Love	Wayne Fontana and the Mindbenders
1967	Kind of a Drag	The Buckinghams
1971	Want Ads	The Honey Cone
1972	Oh Girl	The Chi-Lites
1974	Show and Tell	Al Wilson

Although the feat has been repeated a number of times since, the first album to debut at #1 was released in 1975. Who is the artist or group and what is the album title?

Elton John—*Captain Fantastic and the Brown Dirt Cowboy*. The only single on that album is "Someone Saved My Life Tonight."

The longest song to reach #1, lasting over eight minutes, was released in 1971. When asked to interpret what the song means, the singer/songwriter said "it means that I don't ever have to work again if I don't want to." What is the song and who is the artist?

The song is "American Pie" and the singer and composer is Don McLean. The song was 8:43 in length which was too long for one side of a 45 rpm record in use at the time. Therefore, DJs were given a special unbroken version to play on the air. The song was #5 on the "Songs of the Century" list created in 2001 by the Recording Industry Association of America (RIAA).

In 2011, McLean stated for the first time that the song was written and first performed publicly in Philadelphia in 1971. This refuted a longstanding claim by a Sarasota Springs, New York, tavern called the Tin & Lint that it was written there. (There is even a gold-faced plaque, fading with age, that is on the wall over one of the wooden tables and reads: "American Pie, written by Don McLean, summer 1970.")

In 2015, the original handwritten lyrics and accompanying notes to the song were sold at auction by Christies for $1.2 million.[14]

There has been only one group in history whose only album went to #1 in the U.S. Who is it? As a hint, it was released in 1969 and was by a British group.

Blind Faith, one of the first "supergroups," consisting of Eric Clapton, Ginger Baker, Steve Winwood and Rick Grech. Their album was of the same name.

Dark Side of the Moon **by Pink Floyd was on the** *Billboard* **charts for 741 weeks from 1973 to 1988. According to some estimates, it has sold over 40 million copies, and by any measure, is one of the best-selling albums of all time. How many weeks was it #1?**

    a.   0
    b.   1
    c.   7
    d. 14

Answer: b. It occurred on April 28, 1973.

When the Doors formed in 1965, they decided to name themselves after Aldous Huxley's book, *The Doors of Perception,* **that detailed the author's experiences with taking mescaline. The title was inspired by a William Blake quotation: "If the doors of perception were cleansed, everything would appear to man as it is, infinite." Which of the following songs by the Doors hit the top 10 on the** *Billboard* **Hot 100?**

1. "Break On Through (To the Other Side)"
2. "People are Strange"
3. "Love Me Two Times"
4. "Hello, I Love You"
5. "Roadhouse Blues"
6. "L. A. Woman"
7. "Riders on the Storm"

8. "Love Her Madly"
9. "The Unknown Soldier"
10. "The End"

Only one, "Hello, I Love You," which reached #1 in August 1968.[15]

When "Hello, I Love You" was #1, another Doors song, recorded by another artist, was a top five song at the same time. What is the song and who is the artist?

"Light My Fire" by Jose Feliciano.

Besides "Hello, I Love You" and "Light My Fire," the Doors had one other top 10 hit. It reached #3 in early 1969. What song was it?

"Touch Me." Guitarist Robby Krieger wrote "Touch Me," "Love Her Madly" and "Love Me Two Times." Although the whole band was credited with "Light My Fire," it was primarily written by Krieger. The band's biggest hit that was solely written by Morrison was "Hello, I Love You."

There were eight songs by Canadian artists or bands which reached #1 in the U.S. during the Decade. One man wrote or cowrote three of them. Who was he? As a hint, two of the songs were the A and B sides of the same single released by one famous group he was with and the third was with another famous group he was with.

Randy Bachman. The first two were "American Woman" backed with "No Sugar Tonight/New Mother Nature" by the Guess Who. Bachman wrote "American Woman" with band members Burton Cummings, Garry Peterson and Jim Kale. Because of its supposed anti-American sentiment, Pat Nixon requested that this song not be performed when the band played at the White House on July 17, 1970 where they were performing because her daughter Tricia was a big fan of the group. The third song was "You Ain't Seen Nothing Yet" by Bachman Turner Overdrive.

Burton Cummings has given somewhat differing explanations of how "American Woman" came about, but what they share in common is that he was up on stage (either alone or having just rushed onto the stage at the beginning of a set) and essentially improvised the entire song, words and music.

I started singing whatever came into my head. It was all stream-of-consciousness, at the moment stuff. And no one would have ever heard it again but there happened to be a kid bootlegging the show that night. This was way back in the '60s and he had a cassette machine and those machines were a relatively new invention at the time. . . . We noticed this on stage. Our road manager got the cassette tape and we listened to it later and heard this jam about American woman stay away from me. So we actually learned it from that tape. Otherwise no one would have heard it again. . . . And that was a monstrous song for us; it was #1 on *Billboard* for three weeks. So it was all an accident . . . The music gods probably sent us that kid with the cassette machine.

Despite the inspiration for the song, all of the band members at the time, including Bachman, were given songwriting credit.

As for "No Sugar Tonight/New Mother Nature," the first part of the song was written by Bachman. He said that the inspiration for the song arose when he saw a couple arguing and he heard the woman say: "And one more thing, you're getting no sugar tonight." When he presented the song to bandmate Burton Cummings and his record company, Bachman was told that the song was too short. As it happened, Cummings had been working on a song of his own, "New Mother Nature," which was also not considered a finished product. It was decided to put the two songs together and the result was a #1 hit, credited to both Bachman and Cummings.

Incidentally, Bachman's surname is pronounced like "back-mən." The more common pronunciation of "bock-mən," especially on American radio, became so widespread, especially after BTO became popular, that he did not bother correcting anyone.[16]

There have been nine songs which have reached #1 for two different artists. Interestingly, in each case, one version of the song was released during the Decade and one was not. The artists who released the various songs outside the Decade are listed below. Try to identify the song title as well as the other artist who also had a #1 hit with the song during the decade. By way of example, the answer to the first question below would be *Go Away Little Girl* and Donny Osmond, since he had a #1 hit with that song in 1971. For extra credit, there has only been one instance where the first #1 version was actually written by the artist who sang it. Name that one instance.

	Artist	Year	Writer(s)
1.	Steve Lawrence	1962	Carole King and Gerry Goffin
2.	Little Eva	1962	Carole King and Gerry Goffin

3.	Christina Aguilera, Lil' Kim, Mýa and Pink	2001	Bob Crewe and Kenny Nolan
4.	Mariah Carey	1992	Berry Gordy, and others
5.	Bananarama	1986	Robbie van Leeuwen
6.	Club Nouveau	1987	Bill Withers
7.	Michael Bolton	1991	Calvin Lewis and Andrew Wright
8.	The Marvelettes	1961	Georgina Dobbins
9.	Kim Wilde	1987	Holland-Dozier-Holland

Answers:

	Song	Artist	Year
1.	Go Away Little Girl	Donny Osmond	1971
2.	The Loco-Motion	Grand Funk Railroad	1974
3.	Lady Marmalade	Labelle	1974
4.	I'll Be There	The Jackson Five	1970
5.	Venus	Shocking Blue	1970
6.	Lean on Me	Bill Withers	1972
7.	When a Man Loves a Woman	Percy Sledge	1966
8.	Please Mr. Postman	The Carpenters	1975
9.	You Keep me Hangin' On	The Supremes	1966

The only instance where the first #1 version was written by the artist who sang it was *Lean on Me* by Bill Withers.

There were four songs from the Decade that reached #1 that were theme songs from movies or which had the same title as the movie. One is an instrumental. What were they?

"To Sir With Love" (#1 for five weeks in 1967), "Love Theme From Romeo and Juliet" (#1 for two weeks in 1969), "Theme from Shaft" (#1 for two weeks in 1972), and "The Way We Were" (#1 for two weeks in 1974). "Aquarius/Let the Sunshine In" from *Hair* was #1 for six weeks in 1969 and a movie version of the Broadway show was made in 1979, but that was not a theme song or title song.

This famous movie soundtrack did not chart at all on the *Billboard* 200 and peaked at "only" #49 in 1978—"only" because virtually every song on the soundtrack is known to millions. Yet, the soundtrack had been released three years earlier, in 1975. The gap was occasioned by the fact that it took some time for word of mouth—or perhaps more precisely, word of oversized, disembodied female lips with bright red lipstick overdubbed with a male voice. What was the movie?

Rocky Horror Picture Show, produced by Lou Adler.

In addition to "The Way We Were," Barbra Streisand had another top 10 song in the Decade. It reached #6 in 1971. What was it?

"Stoney End."

There have been six songs which reached #1 which were not instrumental and not sung in English. The music (if not necessarily the titles) to all of them are instantly recognizable. True or false: Every one of those songs was released during the decade.

False. In fact, none of them were. There were three before, three after, and none during. (Perhaps that says something about the music of the decade, but I don't know what.) They are:

"Nel Blu Dipinto Di Blu (Volare)"—Domenico Modugno (Italian—1958)
"Sukiyaki"—Kya Sakamoto (Japanese—1963)
"Dominique"—The Singing Nun (French—1963)
"Rock Me Amadeus"—Falco (German—1986)
"La Bamba"—Los Lobos (Spanish—1987)
"Macarena (Bayside Boys Mix)"—Los del Río (English/Spanish—1996)

Psy's 2012 worldwide hit, "Gangnam Style," only reached #2 on the *Billboard* Hot 100.

This artist or group has had the most consecutive top 10 albums in history, 23, more than half of which were released during the Decade. Who is it?

The Rolling Stones.

CHAPTER 2

What's the Story Behind that Song?
(Derivations of Songs)

Every song (even those which are banal) obviously has *some* derivation, though some are more interesting than others. This chapter will examine the stories behind a few of the iconic songs from the Decade, often explained by the songwriters themselves.

Which song was written about the artist's impending breakup with Judy Collins?

"Suite: Judy Blue Eyes," written by Stephen Stills and performed by Crosby, Stills & Nash. Collins and Stills had met in 1967 and dated for two years. In 1969, she was appearing in the New York Shakespeare Festival musical production of *Peer Gynt* and had fallen in love with her costar Stacy Keach, eventually leaving Stills for him. Stills was devastated by the possible breakup and wrote the song as a response to his sadness and possibly to win her back. When Collins was asked if it worked, she said, "No. It just made me feel more regret."

The title of the song is a double entendre because, while the first word can be heard as "sweet," the song itself is actually a "suite" in the sense that it is four short songs put together. The first section is a traditional pop song. The lead vocal is performed by Stills, with Crosby and Nash providing harmonies. The second section is performed in half time relative to the first section, and features three-part harmony from the band, with Stills performing a brief vocal solo. The third section is more upbeat and features poetic lyrics ("chestnut brown canaries," "ruby-throated sparrows"). Each phrase is initially sung by Stills, with Nash then joining, and finally Crosby rounding out the harmonies. The final section (the coda) includes the famous "doo-doo-doo-doo-doo" sung by Crosby and Nash, with Stills singing Spanish lyrics in the background.

Stills plays all of the instruments on the track except for the drumming, which is by Dallas Taylor.

The first time that the band ever performed the song live was at Woodstock in 1969, which was in fact only their second live appearance together. On the question of precisely where they first got together, memories diverge: Stills recalls the occasion being an evening at Cass Elliot's, while Crosby and Nash remember the fateful moment as taking place at Joni Mitchell's. All three, however, agree on what happened. Crosby and Stills were playing "You Don't Have to Cry," and Nash asked them to sing the song again, then twice more. On the third round Nash joined in, adding a pure, high harmony over the top of Stills' low part and Crosby's middle. "As our three voices intertwined, it was a slightly scary moment," Nash recalls. "Nothing had ever been so right, musically, in my life. Everybody in the room froze. When the song was over we all just looked at each other, then laughed. I was physically, psychically, and musically linked with David and Stephen from that point onwards."[1]

An artist explained his song as follows: "I wrote about slave trade from the view of the recruiter from the slave trade. He is talking, you know, come to America. I mean, you could say the slave trade is bad, horrendous or a great crime of the nation, but I chose to do differently." Who is the artist and what is the song he is talking about?

Randy Newman talking about "Sail Away." The slaver attempts to convince his listeners to climb aboard his ship and "sail away" with him to America (specifically Charleston, South Carolina), which he portrays as a land of happiness and plenty.[2]

Jim Weatherly describes how he came to write a certain song as follows: "The song actually came about after a phone call I had with Farrah Fawcett. Lee Majors was a friend of mine. . . . He had just started dating Farrah. One day I called Lee and Farrah answered the phone. We were just talking and she said she was packing. She was gonna take a plane to Houston to visit her folks. So, it just stayed with me. After I got off the phone, I sat down and wrote the song probably in about 30 to 45 minutes. . . . A girl that comes to L.A. to make it and doesn't make it and leaves to go back home. The guy goes back with her. Pretty simple little story, but it felt real to me."

Weatherly recorded the song himself to no great acclaim. However, the song became a #1 hit for another artist on the *Billboard* Hot 100 and R&B charts in 1973. What is the song? (As a hint, both the destination and the mode of transportation changed from Weatherly's original version, and the genders of the two characters were reversed.)

"Midnight Train to Georgia" by Gladys Knight and the Pips. The original title was "Midnight Plane to Houston." By the way, a "pip" is a spot on a die.[3]

One of the more famous protest songs was written by a 19-year-old named P.F. Sloan. It had been recorded by the Turtles, Jan and Dean and the Grass Roots to not much fanfare. It was offered to another artist. According to Sloan, "[the artist] didn't like the song

that much. He liked a few other songs of mine better. One in particular called "What's Exactly the Matter With Me," which originally was the A-side of the record. When he was ready to record, he picked four songs and [this song] was the fourth to be recorded, if there was time. If you listen to the recording he's rushing singing through the lyric because of the time constraints and he was reading it for the first time off a piece of paper I had written the lyric on!"

The singer sang the song only once and his raspy voice is evident. The vocal track was a rough mix and was not intended to be the final version, but a copy of the recording leaked out to a DJ, who began playing it. The song was an instant hit, reaching #1 on the *Billboard* Hot 100. The more polished vocal track that was at first envisioned was never recorded. What is the song and who is the singer?

"Eve of Destruction" by Barry McGuire. McGuire concurs with Sloan's version of the recording session:

> The band was playing and I'm reading the words off this wrinkly paper. I'm singing, "Well, my blood's so mad feels like coagulatin," that part that goes, "Ahhhhhh, you can't twist the truth," and the reason I'm singing "Ahhhhhh" is because I lost my place on the page! People said, "Man, you really sounded frustrated when you were singing." Well, I was. I couldn't see the words. I wanted to re-record the vocal track, and [producer Lou Adler] said, "We're out of time. We'll come back next week and do the vocal track." Well, by the next weekend, the tune was released. The following Monday, it was being played on the #1 rock music station in Los Angeles, and it was incredible what happened. It all just exploded.

According to McGuire's website, the success of the song actually hurt his career because it became successful without any help from the radio industry or the DJs because it all happened before it caught the attention of most radio stations. "I don't know if it's true or not," said McGuire, "but I heard that the word was that no matter what I came out with next, nobody was gonna play it because I was a loose cannon in the music business. They didn't have control of the last one, and they weren't gonna let the next one get away from them." As it turned out, he was a one-hit wonder, at least as a solo performer. He also cowrote and sang *Green, Green* when he was a member of the New Christy Minstrels in 1963.

Sloan also wrote "Secret Agent Man" which was a hit for Johnny Rivers. He also played the guitar introduction on "California Dreamin'" by the Mamas and the Papas.

If you want to know what McGuire looks like today, picture either G. Gordon Liddy of Watergate infamy or the actor who plays Dr. Yen Lo in the 1962 version of *The Manchurian Candidate*: totally bald (or shaved) head and very prominent mustache (although not in 1965 when he recorded "Eve of Destruction").[4]

This song started as a poem written by Sandra "Sandy" Gaston, the wife of the singer-songwriter who recorded it. She describes the inspiration for the poem as follows: "My [first] husband was going to New York to be a lawyer. . . . His father was borough president of Brooklyn at the time . . . They did not have any relationship or communication because they had been so busy until his son went off to college and was gone. . . . So I had observed something that gave me the idea for the song." Once Ms. Gaston married the singer-songwriter, they had a son, which gave him the idea to turn the poem into a song. On a YouTube video, he says that it's about his son Josh and "frankly, this song scares me to death." What is the song and who is the artist?

"Cat's in the Cradle" by Harry Chapin. Chapin has said that it took the birth of his son Josh to turn his wife's poem into a song. However, even though Sandy said that he sometimes introduced the song at concerts by saying, "This is a song my wife wrote to zap me because I wasn't home when our son Josh was born," the genesis of the song actually occurred long before Josh was born, in that Sandy was really pondering the relationship between her ex-husband and his father at the time. The song topped the *Billboard* Hot 100 in December 1974. It is Chapin's only #1 song.

Chapin died in a car crash at age 38 on July 16, 1981 on the Long Island Expressway. Either due to a mechanical or medical problem (possibly a heart attack), his Volkswagen ended up in the path of a tractor-trailer truck. Even though Chapin's license had been revoked for a long string of traffic violations, his widow Sandy won $7.2 million in a negligence lawsuit against Supermarkets General, the owner of the truck, based on the $12 million Chapin would have earned over the next 20 years.[5]

This Denver-based band fronted by Jerry Corbetta had a #3 hit in 1970 on the Liberty Records label. Liberty folded, as did the group's next label, Brut Records. Corbetta then cowrote a song (on Claridge Records) about the group's frustration after CBS Records had turned them down for a recording contract. It became a #9 hit for the band in 1975. The song contains the sounds of dialing two different phone numbers; one was an unlisted number at CBS Records and the other was the White House. It also contains riffs from "I Feel Fine" by the Beatles and "Superstition" by Stevie Wonder. What is the song and who is the group? For extra credit, what was their earlier #3 hit, which is also referenced in the song?

The song is "Don't Call Us, We'll Call You" by Sugarloaf and their earlier hit was "Green-Eyed Lady." The song likely resonates with every music hopeful who has been turned down by a label. In this one, the "A&R" (artists and repertoire) person tells the band that they sound too much like "John Paul and George" (followed immediately by the "I Feel Fine" riff).[6]

Mel Tillis described the genesis for a song he wrote as follows: "[The song] is based on a true story of a man [who] was injured during World War II in Germany and was sent to England to recuperate. While he was in England, he met a nurse that helped nurse him back to health. He married her and brought her back home. His wounds kept recurring, and he'd have to go to the veteran's hospital to get treated. Then one day he went to the hospital and became temporarily paralyzed. During this time, his problems started increasing. His wife stood by him till she could stand it no longer." She starts getting herself dolled up and going out every night, causing understandable frustration with the vet. In the song, the singer states that he would kill her if he could move. In real life, he did kill her in a murder-suicide. The song was recorded by another artist who had a big hit with it. What is the song and who is the artist?

The song is "Ruby, Don't Take Your Love to Town" and the artist is Kenny Rogers who recorded the song with the First Edition. Rather than World War II, Tillis wrote that the narrator was injured in an "Asian war." This led many to assume that the soldier was injured in Vietnam since it became a hit for Rogers in 1969 (though originally in 1967 recorded by Johnny Darrell, who had a #9 country hit with it that year). However, Tillis has stated that he was referring to the Korean War and not to Vietnam.[7]

The creator of this song said it was based on a true story: "I was just hanging around downtown when I was about nine years old and heard the story and got to know this lady. I was fascinated by her grit. To see this very insignificant, socially disenfranchised lady—a single mother—who was willing to march down to the local aristocracy and read them the riot act so to speak, was fascinating." The song was released in 1968. It won the 1968 Grammy Award for Best Country and Western Vocal Performance and was voted as the Single of the Year by the Country Music Association. It was also a huge crossover hit and was first song ever sung by a woman (she didn't write it) that rose to #1 on both the *Billboard* Hot 100 and country charts, a feat that would not occur again until Dolly Parton's "9 to 5" in 1981. What is the song and who is the artist?

"Harper Valley P.T.A.," written by Tom T. Hall and performed by Jeannie C. Riley.[8]

The lyrics of this song tell a true story: On December 4, 1971, the band who recorded it was in Montreux, Switzerland, where they had set up camp to record an album using a mobile recording studio. On the eve of the recording session, a Frank Zappa and the Mothers of Invention concert was being held in a casino theatre. The place suddenly caught fire when somebody in the audience fired a flare gun into the rattan-covered ceiling. The resulting fire destroyed the entire casino complex, along with all the Mothers' equipment. Everyone had to be evacuated. Bass guitarist Roger Glover, watching the fire from an adjacent hotel, noticed a layer of smoke hovering just over Lake Geneva, which the casino overlooked. What is the song and who is the band?

"Smoke on the Water" by Deep Purple. All of the details above are mentioned in the song, including the Mothers, Zappa, the town, Lake Geneva, and "some stupid with a flare gun" burning the place down.

Some artists and bands have an influence and a legacy which cannot be measured by their chart success (or lack thereof). Todd Rundgren, the Velvet Underground, the Grateful Dead, Jimi Hendrix, Black Sabbath, Laura Nyro, Patti Smith and Randy Newman are some who come to mind. Another is Deep Purple. They are considered to be among the pioneers of heavy metal and modern hard rock, although their musical approach changed over the years. Originally formed as a progressive rock band, the band's sound shifted to hard rock in 1970. Deep Purple, together with Led Zeppelin and Black Sabbath, have been referred to as the "unholy trinity of British hard rock and heavy metal in the early- to mid-Seventies." Similarly, Joe Elliot, lead singer for Def Leppard, said that they were the only three bands that mattered in 1971. Deep Purple did have two songs which reached #4 on the *Billboard* Hot 100: "Hush" in 1968 and "Smoke on the Water" in 1973.[9]

Speaking of Deep Purple, their lead singer Ian Gillian sang an important part in a famous rock opera. Which one and what part did he sing?

He sang the role of Jesus in the original recording of *Jesus Christ Superstar*. Released in 1970, this was the second collaboration of Andrew Lloyd Webber and Tim Rice, after *Joseph and the Amazing Technicolor Dreamcoat*.

On the classic 1970 album *Bridge Over Troubled Water*, Paul Simon wrote two songs that in part directly address Art Garfunkel—rather wistfully—about the possibly impending breakup of their partnership. (Garfunkel sings lead on one of the songs.) What are the two songs and in what way are they referencing Artie?

One is "The Only Living Boy in New York" on which Paul Simon has the lead vocal. In the opening lines, Simon tells "Tom" to get his plane on time and assures him that his acting part will go fine. "Tom" is a reference to the fact that in the '50s, they called themselves Tom and Jerry after the cartoon characters. (Garfunkel named himself Tom Graph, a reference to his math proficiency and tendency to keep detailed records of hit singles' chart positions on graph paper. Simon called himself Jerry Landis, after the surname of a girl he had dated, Sue Landis. Their 1957 song "Hey Schoolgirl" was released as Tom and Jerry.) These lines refer to the fact that Art was flying to Mexico to film *Catch-22*, leaving Paul alone in New York to continue working on the album. Simon had ambivalent feelings at best about Garfunkel seeming to give priority to his acting career. In 2011, he called it "a disappointment I was trying to block out."

The second song, on which Art sings lead vocal, is "So Long Frank Lloyd Wright." Garfunkel always had a passion for architecture and initially majored in it at Columbia University. Simon is therefore writing about him as if he was the famous architect, or a wannabe, fondly (or perhaps in a melancholy way) remembering the nights they would harmonize together. In his book *Fire and Rain*, David Browne wrote that just before introducing the song at a concert in Amsterdam, Garfunkel said that he asked Paul to write a song about Wright, and Simon said that he didn't know anything about Wright at the time.[10]

As for the song "Bridge Over Troubled Water" itself, in 1959, the Swan Silvertones released their cover version of a vintage gospel tune, "Oh Mary, Don't You Weep." Lead singer Claude Jeter included an improvised line about being a bridge over deep water if you trust in Him. Simon said that the song and the title to his song were inspired by Jeter's improvised line (although as Simon told the *New York Times* in 2016, just because someone hears that line "doesn't mean they're going to write 'Bridge Over Troubled Water,'" like he did). Simon later personally went to Jeter's apartment and gave him a check for $1,000 for inspiring the song and also had Jeter sing the falsetto background vocal on "Take Me to the Mardi Gras." Simon keeps a framed copy of the string arrangement for "Bridge Over Troubled Water"—its title, misheard from the demo by the arranger, is "Like a Pitcher of Water."

Simon generously gave the vocal on his masterpiece song to Art Garfunkel, a move that he occasionally said he later regretted. [11]

The inspiration for this song came from an incident where the songwriter was jailed in New Orleans in 1965 for public intoxication. While in the cell, he fell into a conversation with a homeless man and they talked about the man's life. At one point, one of the other men in the cell asked him to dance and he obliged. What is the song and who made it famous? For extra credit, name the songwriter.

The song is "Mr. Bojangles," and it was made famous by the Nitty Gritty Dirt Band's cover version, released in 1970. It was written by Jerry Jeff Walker. Some people have thought that the song referred to Bill "Bojangles" Robinson, the famous stage and movie personality, who is perhaps best remembered today for his dancing with Shirley Temple in a series of films during the 1930s. However, that was not the case. Rather, the man Walker met referred to himself as "Mr. Bojangles" to conceal his true identity from the police. In his autobiography, Walker wrote: "On a night when the rest of the country was listening to The Beatles, I was writing a 6/8 waltz about an old man and hope. [Walker wrote the song in 1968 and it appeared on an album released that year of the same title.] It was a love song. In a lot of ways, Mr. Bojangles is a composite. He's a little bit of several people I met for only moments of a passing life. He's all those I met once and will never see again and will never forget."[12]

In what autobiographical Elton John song does he express gratitude for being talked out of a possibly disastrous marriage to a woman to whom he was engaged, as well as possible suicide?

"Someone Saved My Life Tonight." Bernie Taupin's lyric refers to a time in 1969, before John was a popular musician, when John was engaged to be married to his girlfriend, Linda Woodrow. While having serious doubts about the looming marriage, John contemplated suicide. He took refuge in his friends, especially Long John Baldry, who convinced John to abandon his plans to marry in order to salvage and maintain his musical career. Baldry is both the "someone" in the title and is also referred to as "Sugar Bear" in the song. Said Baldry: "Apparently I gave Elton some very good advice when he was in a pickle, and he wrote a song about it."[13]

CHAPTER 3

The FAB Four (Or the FAB 1+1+1+1): Beatles and Ex-Beatles

Peple have made entire careers specializing in the music and lives of the Beatles, and if I was so inclined, this book could have been entirely about the Beatles. But it's not. Nevertheless, for those who are fans of the band, both as a unit and later as solo artists, this chapter is for you.

What is the only Beatles #1 song not credited to Lennon-McCartney?

"Something" by George Harrison. Paul McCartney said that this song was Harrison's best and John Lennon said it was the best track on *Abbey Road*. It is the second most widely covered Beatles song after "Yesterday." When Frank Sinatra performed this song in concert, he occasionally would introduce it as his favorite Lennon-McCartney composition, but he gave proper attribution to Harrison on stage at Caesars Palace in 1978 before performing the song.[1]

There was only one Beatles single ever released (including the A-side and a B-side) which includes another artist on the credit (i.e "The Beatles with _____"). What are the two songs and who is the artist?

The songs are "Get Back" and "Don't Let Me Down" and the artist is Billy Preston. Preston was recruited by George Harrison to ease the growing tensions in the band, and played electric piano on both songs, which were recorded in January of 1969. The band members thought that Preston brought a whole new energy to "Get Back," and Ringo appreciated how, when Preston joined the session, "the bullshit went out the window." McCartney appreciated his contributions as well. "It was like having a guest in the house," said McCartney, "someone you put your best manners on for. It might've helped us all behave better with one another on the sessions."

However, according to Beatles biographer Bob Spitz, Preston's welcome eventually wore thin on McCartney: "As with any guest, as time wore on, Paul felt Preston overstayed his welcome. Billy turned up at the studio day after day, participating in everything from the direction of the music to deciding where, or even whether, they would stage a concert. Paul found this intrusion 'a little bit puzzling,' to say nothing of presumptuous. Sitting in with the Beatles was one thing; joining them was another."

Regarding "Get Back," in 1980, Lennon said that "there's some underlying thing about Yoko in there," and that McCartney looked at her in the studio every time he sang "Get back to where you once belonged."[2]

In what is likely the shortest gap in history between the release of a song and its covering by another artist who had never previously heard the song, in 1967, Jimi Hendrix opened one of his shows with a Beatles song which had only been released three days earlier. Hendrix yelled "Watch out for your ears!" and then launched into it. Unknown to him, the Beatles were in attendance and were delighted by the performance. What is the song?

"Sgt. Pepper's Lonely Hearts Club Band," from the album of the same name, which was released in the U.S. on June 1, 1967. Commenting on the occasion, McCartney stated:

I remember him opening at the Saville on a Sunday night, 4 June 1967. . . . Jimi opened, the curtains flew back and he came walking forward, playing "Sgt. Pepper," and it had only been released on the Thursday so that was like the ultimate compliment. It's still obviously a shining memory for me, because I admired him so much anyway, he was so accomplished. To think that that album had meant so much to him as to actually do it by the Sunday night, three days after the release. He must have been so into it, because normally it might take a day for rehearsal and then you might wonder whether you'd put it in, but he just opened with it. It's a pretty major compliment in anyone's book. I put that down as one of the great honors of my career.

Hendrix did not know that they were in attendance. Hendrix's performance can be seen on YouTube.

When *Sgt. Pepper's* was released, the band had not released an album in 10 months, which was an eternity considering they had released an album every three months in the U.S. between their first release, *Meet the Beatles*, in January 1964 and their most recent release, *Revolver*, in August 1966. The notion of releasing an album of new songs every three months for nearly three years—especially of the remarkable quality of all of the Beatles albums—seems unthinkable today.

Highly unusual for the time, there were no singles on the album and the songs could only be heard in the early days on lowly FM radio, which was the poor stepsister of AM; few people even had FM reception at the time. This may explain why there are no rankings or *Billboard* chart action on any song from the album, which is often considered the best album from the greatest band in rock history.[3]

Because of the seemingly interminable delay in the release of *Sgt. Pepper's*, Capitol Records decided to release two singles that were recorded during the sessions and were intended to be on the album. Accordingly, on February 13, 1967, a "double A-sided" single was released. However, the songs never made their way onto the album, to George Martin's regret. They did later appear on *Magical Mystery Tour* however. One is classic Lennon and the other is classic McCartney. What are the two songs?

"Strawberry Fields Forever" and "Penny Lane" respectively.

There is only one Beatles song in which one of the members is mentioned by (first) name in the actual lyrics of the song (as opposed to informal references such as when Ringo says "rock on George, one time for me" in "Honey Don't" or when he says "alright George" in "Boys" or when George Harrison says "Go Johnny go" on "For You Blue") or spoken references (such as when Ringo is mentioned by the lounge MC in "You Know My Name"). What is the song and what is the line? (As a hint, it appears on the White Album. As a further hint, the Beatle mentioned is Paul.)

The song is "Glass Onion." John sings, "The walrus was Paul."

Wikipedia ranks sales of Beatles singles in 10 countries, namely the U.S., the U.K., Austria, Australia, Belgium, Canada, Germany, Switzerland, New Zealand and Norway. Only two Beatles songs reached #1 in every one of those countries, both released during the Decade. They were released in 1968 and 1969 respectively and both were written by Paul McCartney. What were they?

"Hey Jude" and "Get Back." The only other songs which reached number three or higher in all 10 countries are "Let It Be" and, surprisingly, "Hello, Goodbye."

True or false: the Beatles wrote all of their top 10 hits released during the Decade.

True. In fact, their only top 10 hit that they did not write was the Phil Medley and Bert Russell song "Twist and Shout" which was on the band's first U.K. album *Please Please Me*, released in 1963.

George Harrison wrote two songs complaining about how he was short-shrifted on his earnings, one by the private sector (more specifically his record company) and one by the public sector. What were they?

The more well-known song is "Taxman," which led off the Beatles' 1966 album *Revolver*. Harrison said, "'Taxman' was when I first realised that even though we had started earning money, we were actually giving most of it away in taxes. It was and still is typical." As their earnings placed them in the top tax bracket in the United Kingdom, the Beatles were liable to a 95 percent supertax introduced by Harold Wilson's Labor government (hence "there's one for you, nineteen for me").

The backing vocals' references to "Mr. Wilson" and "Mr. Heath", suggested by Lennon, refer to, respectively, the leader of the Labor Party and the leader of the Conservative Party, the two largest parties in British politics at the time. Wilson, then Prime Minister, had nominated all four of the Beatles as Members of the Order of the British Empire just the previous year.

As the lead track on *Revolver*, "Taxman" represents the only time a Beatles album opens with a George Harrison song or lead vocal. "Here Comes the Sun" opens the second side of "Abbey Road" and "Within You Without You" opens the second side of *Sgt. Pepper's*.

The less well-known song is "Only a Northern Song." Northern Songs was a music publishing company formed in 1963 primarily to exploit Lennon-McCartney compositions. In 1965, the company went public. While Lennon and McCartney each owned 15 percent of the public company's shares, Harrison owned only 0.8 percent, as did Ringo Starr. (Company founder Dick James and Chairman Charles Silver owned a combined 37.5 percent.) Harrison was contracted by Northern Songs as a songwriter only, and because Northern retained the copyright of its published songs, this meant Lennon and McCartney, as major shareholders of Northern, would earn more from Harrison's own songs than he did." As Harrison said, "the song was copyrighted to Northern Songs Ltd. which I didn't own." The lyrics reflect this frustration when he thinks that it doesn't matter what his words are or what chords he plays because: "it's only a Northern Song."

After Brian Epstein's death on August 27, 1967, Lennon and McCartney sought to renegotiate their publishing deal with James. There was no deal struck and the relationship between the two Beatles and James became very icy. Early in 1969, James and Silver abruptly sold their shares in Northern Songs to ATV Music for £1,525,000, giving the four Beatles no notice or the chance to buy them out. Lennon learned of the sale from a morning newspaper during his honeymoon with Yoko Ono.[4]

What is the first Beatles recorded song on which only one member sings and plays an instrument? (As a hint, it was released in 1965 and there are other instruments played on the song but not by the Beatles.)

"Yesterday." Besides Paul on acoustic guitar, it had two violins, a viola and a cello. The song was considered so different from other works by the Beatles that the band members vetoed the release of the song as a single in the United Kingdom and so it never charted at all while the band was together. (It did reach #8 in the U.K. when re-released in 1976.)

There are two songs, one by the Beatles and one by Rod Stewart, which have the same title, at least homophonically (i.e. they are pronounced the same but the spelling is different), although the Beatles version is just a 40-second snippet. What songs are they?

"Maggie Mae" by the Beatles and "Maggie May" by Rod Stewart. The Beatles' version is a traditional Liverpool folk song about a prostitute who robbed a "homeward bounder": a sailor coming home from a trip. The song appears on *Let It Be*.

For diehard Beatles fans: There are only two songs written and released by the Beatles during the Decade on which all four band members were given writing credit. One of those two is also an instrumental song, in fact, the only song written and released by the Beatles during the Decade that was an instrumental. As much as any Beatles songs released during the Decade can be called obscure, these both qualify. What are the songs? (As a hint, the instrumental appears on *Magical Mystery Tour* and the other appears on *Let It Be* and lasts only 51 seconds.)

The instrumental song is "Flying" and the other is "Dig It." (Longer versions of "Dig It" exist, one of which can be heard on the *Let It Be* documentary.) The reason for the "released during the Decade" qualifier is because the group cowrote another instrumental in 1965 called "12-Bar Original," but it did not appear on an album until *Anthology Two* in 1996. The song mentioned in the previous question, "Maggie Mae," was also credited to all four band members but because it is in the public domain, they were simply the arrangers of the song.

Also for diehard Beatles fans: Name the only Beatles song released during the Decade that is credited to Lennon, McCartney ... and Starkey, and the only one that is credited to

Lennon, McCartney ... and Ono. The first appears on *Rubber Soul* and the second appears on the White Album. (You were expecting Yoko's name to appear on perhaps *Meet the Beatles*?)

"What Goes On" and "Revolution 9" respectively.

Excluding "Maggie Mae," how many songs of other artists did the Beatles cover from *Rubber Soul* onwards (i.e. *Rubber Soul, Revolver, Sgt. Pepper's, Magical Mystery Tour, The Beatles, Yellow Submarine, Abbey Road* and *Let It Be*)?

None. Until 1965, before the band became famous, it was fairly common for them to cover other artists both on their albums and when performing live. For example, *Please Please Me, With the Beatles!* and *Beatles for Sale* all contained six covers each.

Excluding "Maggie Mae" and albums released after the Beatles broke up, the last two covers they did both appeared on *Help!* in 1965. What were they? As a hint, on one, Ringo sings lead.

"Act Naturally" by Johnny Russell and Voni Morrison (where Ringo sings lead) and "Dizzy Miss Lizzy" by Larry Williams.

John Lennon had only one solo #1 in the U.S. while he was alive. What was the song? As a hint, it's not what you think.

"Whatever Gets You Thru the Night," released in 1974. Classics such as "Give Peace a Chance" (topping out at #14), "Instant Karma" (#3) and even "Imagine" (#3) never reached the top spot. "(Just Like) Starting Over" did reach #1, but that was after he was murdered.

Which performance closed with the following line: "I'd like to say thank you on behalf of the group and ourselves, and I hope we passed the audition," and who said it? As a hint, it was the Beatles' last public performance together.

This was how John Lennon closed the January 30, 1969 concert played on the roof of Apple headquarters at 3 Savile Row in London on a bitterly cold day. The rooftop concert was cut short after only 42 minutes when police arrived on the roof to stop it because of building traffic below and complaints from neighborhood merchants. Since the event was being filmed, Ringo was hoping for a dramatic showdown, but it was not to be: "I always feel let down about the police. When they came up, I was playing away and I thought, 'Oh great, I hope they drag me off.' We were being filmed and it would've looked really great, kicking the cymbals and everything. Well, they didn't of course. They just came bumbling in: 'You've got to turn that sound down.' It could have been fabulous."[5]

What artist played with the Beatles at the rooftop concert?

Billy Preston, who played the organ.[6]

Given that George Harrison was one of the great guitar players of his era and given that he wrote a classic song *about* his guitar, namely "While My Guitar Gently Weeps" from the White Album, one would think that he would have played lead guitar on that song. He didn't. Who did? (As a hint, the guitar player was not a Beatle.)

It was Eric Clapton. As would again be the case several months later when Billy Preston was brought in by Harrison to play on "Get Back" and "Don't Let Me Down," Clapton gave the group (and this track) a needed shot of adrenaline. In particular, while working on the song on August 16, 1968, Harrison felt that Lennon and McCartney were showing a distinct lack of enthusiasm for his song and not "taking it seriously." Harrison therefore asked Clapton to play lead guitar while Harrison played acoustic guitar.

While on the subject of who played what instrument on *The Beatles*, there were a number of combinations and substitutions that would have been unthinkable on earlier Beatles albums where each of the Beatles played their accustomed instruments and no one else was involved. One of the primary reasons for this was that, as tensions within the band increased in 1968, each of them became more interested in their own compositions and less interested in those of their bandmates. As producer George Martin recalled: "I was recording not a band of four, but three fellows who had three accompany us each time."

So for example, on "Back in the U.S.S.R.," the drums were played not by Ringo but by each of the other three Beatles. This was because Ringo temporarily quit the band during the recording sessions for this track. For the same reason, Paul was the drummer on "Dear Prudence." He was also the sole performer on his songs "Blackbird," "Wild Honey Pie" and (except for a brass arrangement added by George Martin) on "Mother Nature's Son." While there are numerous instruments played on McCartney's song "Martha My Dear" (written in honor of his sheepdog Martha), none of them are played by the other three Beatles. The entire track is played by him backed with many session musicians.

Paul McCartney made several "solo" recordings, meaning that he was either the only musician on the track or that no other Beatles performed, starting with his song

"Yesterday," written in 1965. However, there is only one Beatles track which John Lennon played and sang unaccompanied by the other Beatles or anyone else. What song is it? (As a hint, it appears on the White Album.)

"Julia," written in homage to his mother.[7]

Although Ringo Starr handled lead vocals on a total of 11 Beatles songs, he wrote only two. Which ones are they? As a hint, one appeared on the White Album and one appeared on *Abbey Road*.

The first is "Don't Pass Me By" and the second is "Octopus's Garden."

There are at least three Beatles songs on which none of them played any instruments. That's not to say that they were a cappella, but rather that the instruments were played by others. One of them appeared on *Revolver* and one of them appeared on *Sgt. Pepper's* and they were both primarily written by Paul McCartney. The third was written by George Harrison and released in 1968 and did not appear on any album until *Past Masters, Volume Two*. Name them.

"Eleanor Rigby" and "She's Leaving Home" are the McCartney tunes. "The Inner Light" is the Harrison song. Eleanor Rigby employs a classical string ensemble consisting of an octet of studio musicians—four violins, two cellos and two violas, all performing a score composed by producer George Martin. There was a similar string arrangement on "She's Leaving Home," this time with a double bass and harp added in. The wonderful harp intro was played by Sheila Bromberg, who was paid nine pounds for her work.[8]

The day before, McCartney wanted to work on the song's score, and he learned that Martin was unavailable, so he contacted Mike Leander, who did it in Martin's place. It was the first time a Beatles song was not arranged by Martin (and the only time it was done with the Beatles' consent; Phil Spector's orchestration of *Let It Be* was done without McCartney's knowledge). Martin was hurt by McCartney's actions, but he produced the song and conducted the string section.[9] On "The Inner Light," the exotic Indian instruments included a shehnai, bansuri, sarod, pakhavai and harmonium.[10]

There is a song on *Sgt. Pepper's Lonely Hearts Club Band* about a Mr. Kite. What is the exact title of the song—with proper punctuation?

"Being for the Benefit of Mr. Kite!" and not "For the Benefit of Mr. Kite" as is often thought. Before the start of the first take of the song, which can be heard on Beatles *Anthology*

Two, engineer Geoff Emerick announces, "'For the Benefit of Mr. Kite!' This is take 1." Lennon immediately responds, "*Being* for the Benefit of Mr. Kite!'", reinforcing the exact title of the 1843 poster from which the title (and many of the song lyrics) were taken.

The Beatles wrote songs for others that were very successful. For example, "A World Without Love" went to #1 for Peter and Gordon in 1964. "Bad to Me" was a hit for Billy J. Kramer and the Dakotas, and "Come and Get It" by Paul McCartney was a top 10 hit for Badfinger in 1969. However, there are only two instances where songs that the Beatles released themselves were covered by other artists and where those cover versions went to #1, once in the U.K. (for three different artists!) and once in the U.S. What are they? As a hint, neither song was released by the Beatles as a single. As a further hint, not only do the two songs appear on the same album, but they appear consecutively.

One is "With a Little Help from My Friends" which went to #1 for Joe Cocker in the U.K. in 1968. Cocker's cover was ranked #2 in UpVenue's top 10 best music covers of all time in 2009. In a 2014 BBC poll, it was voted the seventh best cover version ever.

The other song is "Lucy in the Sky with Diamonds" which went to #1 for Elton John in the U.S. in 1975. Both tracks of course appear on *Sgt. Pepper*. The two Beatles covers that reached the top 20 are Richie Havens's version of George Harrison's song "Here Comes the Sun" (#16 in 1971) and Stevie Wonder's cover of "We Can Work It Out" (#13 in 1971). Other notable covers include Wilson Pickett's version of "Hey Jude" (#23 in the U.S. and #16 in the U.K in 1968) and Aretha Franklin's rendition of "Eleanor Rigby" in 1969.[11]

True or false: For all of the Beatles' accomplishments, awards and honors, they never won an Academy Award.

False, although in a somewhat surprising way. When most people think about the Beatles and movies, they think of *A Hard Day's Night* (1964) and *Help!* (1965). Perhaps some may also think of the 1968 cartoon *Yellow Submarine*. (*Magical Mystery Tour* was not a movie, but a 52-minute television film which was only aired on BBC1.) What many people forget however (or perhaps never knew in the first place) is that a documentary was made about the making of the album *Let It Be*, resulting in a 1970 film of the same name. That film won the group an Academy Award for Best Original Song Score. The documentary was shot over a four-week period in January 1969, often at a sound stage at Twickenham Film Studios. It was intended to simply chronicle the evolution of an album, but instead it captured the prevailing tensions between the band members, and in this respect it unwittingly became a document of the beginning of their breakup.

Every day of the week is mentioned in at least one Beatles song. Match the song with the day of the week mentioned. One or more of the songs may contain references to more than one day of the week.

1.	Sunday	a.	"Lady Madonna"
2.	Monday	b.	"I Am the Walrus"
3.	Tuesday	c.	"Being For the Benefit of Mr. Kite!"
4.	Wednesday	d.	"When I'm 64"
5.	Thursday	e.	"She's Leaving Home"
6.	Friday		
7.	Saturday		

1.d. (Sunday morning) 2.a. (Monday's child); 3.b. (bloody Tuesday); 4.e. (Wednesday morning); 5.a. (Thursday night); 6.a. (Friday night); 7.c. (feat performed on Saturday). "Lady Madonna" actually mentions every day of the week except for Saturday.

The following questions deal with Beatles songs recorded during the Decade that have a woman's name in the title.

Two titles consist of nothing but a woman's first name. Which are they?

"Julia" and "Michelle."

Two of the titles refer to actual women. Which are they?

First is "Julia," which is the name of John's mother. She died at age 44 in 1958 when she was hit by a car driven by a drunk off-duty police officer when John was 17. When John was 5, she moved away and was taken in by his aunt, Mimi. While John and his mother were distant for a time, they grew closer again when John became a teenager. He was devastated by her death. "I lost her twice," he said. "Once as a five-year-old when I was moved in with my auntie. And once again when she actually physically died."[12]

Second is "Dear Prudence." The subject of this song is Prudence Farrow, actress Mia Farrow's sister, who was present when the Beatles went to India to study with Maharishi Mahesh Yogi. Farrow became so serious about her meditation that she turned into a near recluse and rarely came out of the cottage she was living in. "She went completely mental,"

John recalled. "If she'd been in the West, they would have put her away." As a result, Lennon wrote a song for her, encouraging her to join the others by asking her to come out and play. The song was "a simple plea to a friend to 'snap out of it.'"[13]

Name eight other Beatles songs with women's names in the title.

"Eleanor Rigby," "Lady Madonna," "Lovely Rita," "Lucy in the Sky with Diamonds," "Maggie Mae," "Martha My Dear" (Martha being McCartney's sheepdog), "Polythene Pam," and "Sexy Sadie."

The last of these songs was written by John Lennon about Maharishi Mahesh Yogi. Lennon was disillusioned because the Maharishi had allegedly made a sexual advance toward one of the women there. Lennon later told *Rolling Stone* that when the Maharishi asked why he was leaving, he replied, "Well, if you're so *cosmic*, you'll know why." Mia Farrow has occasionally been identified as the object of the Maharishi's desires, including by Lennon, but McCartney and Harrison as well as others deny that the incident ever occurred at all, and claim that Lennon's information was based on a false rumor started and spread by John's friend Alexis "Magic Alex" Mardas. The original title of the song was "Maharishi" but it was changed to "Sexy Sadie" at Harrison's request.

Finally, the song "Hey Jude" could theoretically be on the list to the extent that Jude could be short for Judith or a variant of Judy. However, in this case, it was written by Paul McCartney for John's son Julian who was suffering from the divorce of John and his first wife Cynthia. It was originally called "Hey Jules" but he changed it to Jude because that was easier to sing. But where did Jude itself come from? According to Beatles biographer Bob Spitz, he took it from a character in the show *Oklahoma!*, although that character's name is actually Jud Fry.

Incidentally, even though everyone has heard "Hey Jude" a thousand times, it is unlikely that too many people have noticed that Paul McCartney (or possibly John Lennon) can faintly be heard saying "Fucking hell" at 2:58. In *Here, There and Everywhere* written by the band's recording engineer Geoff Emerick, John Lennon was quoted as saying "Paul hit a clunker on the piano and said a naughty word. I insisted we leave it in, just low enough so that it can barely be heard. Most people won't ever spot it but *we'll* know it's there." Others however have attributed it to Lennon himself. For example, Malcolm Tofy, the mix engineer on the recording, recalled that when Lennon was overdubbing his harmony vocal, and in reaction to the volume being too loud in his headphones, he first called out "Whoa!" then, two seconds later, swore as he pulled the headphones off. In any event, during the recording of the master take, just after the line "the minute you let her under your skin" Lennon shouts "Oh!" (or "Whoa!") at 2:56, followed by McCartney (or Lennon) saying "Fucking hell!" at 2:58, underneath the next line "then you begin."[14]

What Beatles song alludes to or contains the title of five other Beatles songs and what are the songs? As a hint, it is on the White Album.

"Glass Onion." The five songs are "Strawberry Fields Forever," "I Am the Walrus," "Lady Madonna," "The Fool on the Hill" and "Fixing a Hole."

Another song on the White Album mentions a Beatles song from the same album! What is the song?

"Savoy Truffle" by George Harrison mentions "Ob-La-Di, Ob-La Da."

Again, for hardcore Beatles fans: There are two Beatles songs where they actually sing snippets of two of their other songs. Once is at the end of the live performance of "All You Need is Love," played before a worldwide audience on June 25, 1967 (but not on the studio recording of that song) and once is at the end of "Revolution 9," which no one has ever actually heard, at least all the way through. In this case, it was a distorted version of the actual recording of a well-known Paul McCartney tune. What are the two songs?

The first is "She Loves You" and the second is "Get Back."

What was the time gap between the Beatles' first and last live performances in America (the last also being their final performance ever before a paying audience)?

a. 2.5 years
b. 3.5 years
c. 4.5 years
d. 5.5 years

The answer is a. The brevity of the Beatles' live-playing career, especially in America, is astonishing. The time span from their first live performance in America to their last was less than 2½ years, namely from February 1964 to August 1966. (They had been performing in England and Germany since January of 1961.) When the Beatles gave their last live performance ever (at least to a paying audience), George Harrison was only 23 years old and Paul McCartney was only 24 years old. It is difficult to imagine another band ever vying for the title of the greatest rock group in history with such an incredibly short live playing career and with the band members still being so young at the time they stopped.

The first Beatles performance in America was on the *Ed Sullivan Show* in February 1964. Their last concert before a paying audience was at Candlestick Park in San Francisco on August 29, 1966. The park's capacity was 42,500, but only 25,000 tickets were sold. Fans paid between $4.50 and $6.50 for tickets, and the Beatles' fee was around $90,000. The Beatles took to the stage at 9:27 PM and were on stage for only 33 minutes, performing only 11 songs, the last one of which was "Long Tall Sally." That means it lasted nine minutes shorter than the rooftop concert, which was itself cut short by the police due to complaints about noise. Although a 33-minute performance for a headlining act seems ridiculously short today, that was not unusual for the Beatles during the era they performed.

Many critics were unkind, to put it mildly, in their assessment of the band during their first month in America in February 1964. *Newsweek* wrote: "Visually they are a nightmare, tight, dandified Edwardian-Beatnik suits and great pudding bowls of hair. Musically they are a near disaster, guitars and drums slamming out a merciless beat that does away with secondary rhythms, harmony and melody. Their lyrics (punctuated by nutty shouts of "yeah, yeah, yeah") are a catastrophe, a preposterous farrago of Valentine-card romantic sentiments."

William F. Buckley concurred, in his inimitable way:

> An estimable critic writing for *National Review*, after seeing Presley writhe his way through one of Ed Sullivan's shows ... suggested that future entertainers would have to wrestle with live octopuses in order to entertain a mass American audience. The Beatles don't in fact do this, but how one wishes they did! And how this one wishes the octopus would win. ... The Beatles are not merely awful; I would consider it sacrilegious to say anything less than that they are god awful. They are so unbelievably horribly [sic], so appallingly unmusical, so dogmatically insensitive to the magic of the art that they qualify as crowned heads of anti-music, even as the imposter popes went down in history as "anti-popes."

And finally, the *New York Times* piled on: "The Beatles' vocal quality can be described as hoarsely incoherent, with the minimal enunciation necessary to communicate the schematic texts. Two theories were offered in at least one household to explain the Beatles' popularity. The specialist said: 'We haven't had an idol in a few years. The Beatles are different, and we have to get rid of our excess energy somehow.' The other theory is that the longer parents object with such high dudgeon, the longer children will squeal so hysterically."[15]

Another noteworthy Beatles concert during their short touring career was their first Shea Stadium concert on August 15, 1965 before more than 55,000 screaming fans. This was the first time in history that a rock band had ever performed at a stadium. (Elvis Presley did play six shows at the Cotton Bowl in Dallas in 1956 and 1957 but his largest audience was "only" 26,000 fans, far under Cotton Bowl capacity.) The Beatles' set lasted only 30 minutes. Tickets ranged from $4.50 to a "top dollar" price of $5.65. A documentary was made of the event called, naturally, *The Beatles at Shea Stadium*. Less well remembered was their second performance at Shea on August 23, 1966, where there were 11,000 unsold seats. At that time, the popularity of the band was in temporary decline in America partly because of John Lennon's recent comment that the Beatles were more popular than Jesus.[16]

The Beatles did perform live and "in public" (meaning not in the studio) three times after their August 29, 1966 performance in Candlestick Park. Once was the rooftop concert atop Apple headquarters on January 30, 1969. However, because only a handful of people (mostly "insiders") were on the rooftop with them and actually saw them perform, that would not really be considered a "public performance." The other two also involved a select few group of people who actually saw them live, but there were millions more who saw the other two on television. On both of these occasions, they performed only one song. Name the two occasions and the two songs.

The first occurred on June 25, 1967, when the Beatles appeared on *Our World*, the first live, international, satellite television production. Creative artists, including the Beatles, opera singer Maria Callas, and painters Joan Miró and Pablo Picasso—representing nineteen nations— were invited to perform or appear in separate segments featuring their respective countries. The Beatles performed "All You Need is Love" which, according to George Martin and Ringo Starr, was written by John Lennon specifically for the occasion. Keith Moon of the Who played brush sticks for the performance. It was preceded by just one rehearsal. The performance includes bits of other songs including "La Marseillaise" (the French national anthem), "In the Mood" by Glenn Miller, "Greensleeves" by Bach, and the Beatles' own "She Loves You."[17]

The second song was "Hey Jude," performed on *Frost on Sunday* (in multiple takes) on September 4, 1968.[18]

The Beatles released seven songs in which the titles are not part of the lyrics. Two of these songs are on *Revolver*, one is on *Sgt. Pepper's*, one is on the White Album, one is on *Let It Be* and two were not on any album while the Beatles were still together, although they were released later on *Past Masters*, *Volume Two*. What are the songs? Three of them are by George Harrison. I would speculate that only two of them would be familiar to the casual Beatles fan by title and the other five would not. However, all of them should be recognizable upon hearing the words and music.

On *Revolver*, it is "Love You To." This was written and sung by Harrison and features Indian classical instrumentation including a tabla, hand-drums, sitar and a tambura. It was the first Beatles song to fully reflect the influence of Indian classical music. This song is extremely unusual for the Beatles in that Harrison and Ringo Starr were the only Beatles musicians on the song, with Ringo playing tambourine.

The second *Revolver* song is one primarily written and sung by John Lennon, "Tomorrow Never Knows." (Lennon sings about turning off one's mind and floating downstream.) The title of the song came from one of Ringo's malapropisms, as did the song "A Hard Day's Night." In a 1964 interview, Ringo is discussing the fact that the previous day his hair was supposedly cut while he was being interviewed and without his knowledge. He said, "I was talking away and I looked 'round, and there was about 400 people just smiling. So, you know—what can you say?" John then says, "What can you say?" Ringo responds, "Tomorrow never knows," and John starts laughing. A video of the 32-second exchange with the interviewer can be seen on YouTube.

The *Sgt. Pepper's* song is "A Day in the Life." On the White Album, it is "Yer Blues." This one, another Lennon composition, begins with Lennon talking about being lonely and wanting to die.

On *Let It Be*, "For You Blue," another Harrison number. (Harrison sings that the girl is sweet and lovely.) On *Past Masters, Volume Two* is "The Ballad of John and Yoko." This is one of the few compositions on which only John and Paul played and sang. George was on holiday and Ringo was filming *The Magic Christian* and John did not want to wait for them to return to record the song. John was on lead vocal and guitars and percussion, while Paul played bass, drums, piano and maracas. Mark Lewisohn, who went through all the Beatles recordings, wrote that just before take four (of 11 in all), you hear them joking:

John (on guitar): Go a bit faster, Ringo!
Paul (on drums): Okay, George!

The final song is the third Harrison-penned tune, "The Inner Light," which appears on *Past Masters, Volume Two*.

There are obviously only 50 state songs. One of those songs, which names the state (and that is also the state slogan), is quoted in a Beatles song. The odd thing is, the song is not actually referring to that state. In fact, it's not referring to any place in the U.S. at all. What is the Beatles song, what is the state song included in that song, and why is it not referring to that state? (As a hint, it appears on the White Album.)

The song is "Back in the U.S.S.R." (written by Paul McCartney), and the State song is "Georgia On My Mind." The "Georgia" being referred to the Soviet Republic of Georgia, part of the former Soviet Union. In a tribute to "California Girls" by the Beach Boys, McCartney sings of the Ukraine girls who knock him out and the Moscow girls, who make him sing and shout, before paying homage to Georgia.

Paul McCartney wrote the song while the Beatles were in Rishikesh, India. The title is a tribute to Chuck Berry's "Back in the U.S.A." Mike Love of the Beach Boys also attended the retreat in Risikesh at the same time and told McCartney that, in order to make the song sound more like a Beach Boys number, "you ought to put something in about all the girls around Russia," and he did.[19]

There is only one Beatles song which mentions a city and the state in which it is located. As a hint, the song was released in 1969 and was played by the band during the rooftop concert. What is the song and what is the city and state?

The song is "Get Back" and the city and state is Tucson, Arizona.

Tara Browne was a socialite and an heir to the Guinness fortune. On December 18, 1966, he drove his Lotus Elan through a traffic light at the intersection of Redcliffe Square and Redcliffe Gardens in London, colliding with a van. He was instantly killed. He was only 21 at the time. Although he was already married with two kids, he had separated from his wife and in fact was driving with 19-year-old model Suki Potier when the crash occurred. She was not injured (though she later died in a car crash at age 34). An article about the crash appeared in the January 17, 1967 issue of the *Daily Mail*. John Lennon said that he wrote about this tragedy in a Beatles song. What is the song?

"A Day in the Life," the final song on *Sgt. Pepper's*, which Lennon started working on immediately after the article appeared. Lennon did take some liberties with the actual facts. However, (1) there was an article about the crash in the paper, (2) there was a photograph of the gruesome crash and (3) it is very true that Browne didn't notice the light changing.

As it turned out, on the very next page of the *Daily Mail* issue was an article about the poor condition of the roads in the town of Blackburn, Lancashire. The article was entitled "The Holes in Our Roads" and it began: "There are 4,000 holes in the road in Blackburn, Lancashire, or one twenty-sixth of a hole per person, according to a council survey." Lennon made reference to that in the song too.

In a *Playboy* interview just before he was assassinated, Lennon said:

I was reading the paper one day and I noticed two stories. One was the Guinness heir who killed himself in a car. That was the main headline story. He died in London in a car crash. On the next page was a story about 4,000 holes in Blackburn, Lancashire. In the streets, that is. They were going to fill them all.

In a separate interview, he stated: "I knew the line had to go: 'Now they now how many holes it takes to—something—the Albert Hall.' It was nonsense verse, really, but for some reason I couldn't think of the verb. What did the holes do to the Albert Hall? It was Terry [Doran, a friend of the Beatles] who said 'fill' the Albert Hall. And that was it."

And what of the final piano chord, which has been called "the most famous finale in all of rock"? That was created by having Lennon, McCartney, Ringo Starr and roadie Mal Evans share three different pianos, with George Martin on the harmonium, and all played an E-major chord simultaneously. It took nine takes to perfect because the four players were rarely able to hit the keys at precisely the same time. The wall of sound which can be heard on the album lasts about 42 seconds.[20]

Other Beatles songs besides "A Day in the Life" are also based loosely on actual events that appeared in the paper. Another one that appears on *Sgt. Pepper's* involved a 17-year-old girl named Melanie Coe. The article again appeared in the *Daily Mail* and in this case the headline read "A-Level Girl Dumps Car and Vanishes." (A-level is the higher of the two main levels of standardized examinations in secondary schools in the U.K., with O-level being the lower level). In this case, the accompanying article did not merely form the basis for a snippet of the song (as with "A Day in the Life") but for the entire song. What is the song? (And no, Ms. Coe was not the girl who Paul McCartney "saw standing there," even though that girl was "just 17" as well.)

"She's Leaving Home." When she ran away from home in February 1967, Ms. Coe was pregnant. In the song, Melanie leaves a note for her parents as she steals away at 5:00 a.m. and meets "a man from the motor trade." In reality, she left in the afternoon when her parents were out and went off not with the father of her unborn child but with a croupier. Her father found out and she was back home 10 days later. She later ran off again. She then got married and divorced a year later. Then she moved to California to live in an ashram. She wound up on the Hollywood scene, dating several celebrities, including Burt Ward, who played Robin in the original ABC-TV *Batman* series. Today she lives in Spain.

As for the parents' role, John came up with the Greek chorus, showing their confusion, in that her parents thought that they had bestowed financial luxury on her. This was also referenced in the article, and Ms. Coe confirmed that they did give her everything—except their affection. "As a 17-year-old I had everything money could buy—diamonds, furs, a car—but my father and mother never once told me they loved me." More recently, she said: "It was nice to be immortalized in a song but it would have been nicer if it had been for doing something other than running away from home."

In a remarkable coincidence, in 1963, McCartney had appeared as a judge on the British television show *Ready Steady Go!* to decide which of four young women did the best job of miming Brenda Lee's song "Let's Jump the Broomstick." One of the contestants was Coe, then only 13. Paul judged her to be the best mimer, which meant she got to dance on the show for the next year. A clip of Paul judging her performance can be seen on YouTube.[21]

In 2010, *Rolling Stone* picked the 100 greatest Beatles songs of all time. Two of the top 10 are by George Harrison. What were they?

"Something" (#6) and "While My Guitar Gently Weeps" (#10).[22]

What was the first live album released either by the Beatles or by one of its members (whether solo or as part of another band)? (Hint: It was released in the 1960s.)

Live Peace in Toronto 1969 by the Plastic Ono Band which was recorded at the Toronto Rock and Roll Festival on September 13, 1969 and released in December 1969 before the Beatles even broke up. Side one consisted of "Blue Suede Shoes," "Money (That's What I Want)," "Dizzy Miss Lizzy," "Yer Blues," "Cold Turkey" and "Give Peace a Chance." As for side two, as written by Richard Grinnell of AllMusic: "Side two, alas, was devoted entirely to Ono's wailing, pitchless, brainless, banshee vocalizing on "Don't Worry Kyoko" [4:48] and "John John (Let's Hope for Peace)" [12:38]—the former backed with plodding rock rhythms and the latter with feedback. No wonder you see many used copies of the LP with worn A-sides and clean, unplayed B-sides—and Yoko's 'art' is just as irritating today as it was in 1969. But in those days, if you wanted John you had to take the whole package."[23]

This man likely spent more time in the physical presence of the Beatles, both collectively and individually, than any person in history, including George Martin (i.e. it's not George Martin!). Among many other connections with the group:

- **Though not a trained singer or musician, he sang in the chorus of "Yellow Submarine."**
- **He played harmonica on "Being for the Benefit of Mr. Kite!" Paul McCartney showed him where the notes were on the organ, nodded his head when he wanted him to play, and shook it when he wanted him to stop.**

- On "A Day in the Life," he controlled an alarm clock; counting the measures in the original 24-bar pause, and was one of the five piano players simultaneously hitting the last chord of the song.
- He played tambourine on "Dear Prudence," and trumpet on "Helter Skelter," where he played a double solo with Lennon, even though neither was proficient on the instrument.
- He hit an anvil on "Maxwell's Silver Hammer," because Ringo Starr could not lift the hammer high enough to get the right sound and keep in time with the song.
- According to his diary, he helped Paul McCartney write the lyrics for "Fixing a Hole" (or as he referred to it, "Where the Rain Comes In"), which appears on the *Sgt. Pepper's* album and was promised royalties by McCartney but never received them.
- He appeared in four (out of five) Beatles films, namely *A Hard Day's Night, Help!* (where he played a confused channel swimmer who pops up through an ice-hole in Austria, and on a beach in the Bahamas), *Magical Mystery Tour*, and *Let It Be.*
- He can be seen talking to police officers on the Savile Row rooftop when they came to stop the January 30, 1969 rooftop concert. Before the concert, he placed a camera and a microphone in a corner of Apple's reception area, so that when the police came in to complain about the noise—which was expected—they could be filmed and recorded. He can also be seen appearing to negotiate with the police on the rooftop towards the end of the concert.
- He was the only member of the Beatles' entourage who attended (and was a witness) at the marriage of Paul McCartney and Linda Eastman in 1969.
- He was the cowriter, along with George Harrison, of the song "You and Me (Babe)" that appears on the 1973 album *Ringo.*
- He was the one who discovered Badfinger (then known as the Iveys) and recommended them to the Beatles, who signed them to Apple Records.

Who was he?

Mal Evans. While officially their road manager, he was a constant presence in their lives, both in the studio and outside the studio, whether they were on the road or not, acting as a general factotum in their lives. Even though they stopped touring in 1966, and thus technically did not need a "road manager" any further, he remained a presence within their inner circle. A large man (6 feet, 6 inches tall), he was originally a bouncer at the Cavern Club and was hired by Brian Epstein to be the Beatles' road manager back in 1962.

In January 1976, Evans was depressed about the separation from his wife who had asked for a divorce around Christmas. He had some friends over who later said that he was "really doped-up and groggy." He picked up an air rifle. One of his friends then called the police and told them that Evans was confused, had a rifle, and was on Valium. The police arrived and as soon as Evans saw them, he pointed a rifle at them. They told Evans to put it down, not knowing it was an air rifle. He refused and the police fired six shots, four hitting Evans, killing him instantly. He was only 40 years old. Evans was cremated on January 7, 1976, in Los Angeles. None of the former Beatles attended his funeral, but Harry Nilsson and other friends did. George Harrison arranged for Evans's family to receive £5,000, as Evans had not maintained his life insurance premiums, and was not entitled to a pension.

One of the reasons that Evans was so broke when he died was because, whatever love the Beatles felt for him, he certainly was not generously paid. His weekly salary never rose above £38 and he repeatedly (and heartbreakingly) wrote in his diary that he could not live on such a paltry sum. Yet he still had sympathy for the band members and the problems they were facing towards the end. For example, on April 24, 1969, he wrote: "Had to tell George [Harrison]—'I'm broke.' Really miserable and down because I'm in the red, and the bills are coming in, poor old Lil [his wife] suffers as I don't want to get a raise. Not really true don't want to ask for a raise, fellows are having a pretty tough time as it is."[24]

Aside from John Lennon on guitar and Andre Perry on percussion, who is the only person playing an instrument on "Give Peace a Chance"? (As a hint, he is playing the guitar and is usually thought of as a television star rather than as a musician.)

Tommy Smothers. He is seated on the bed next to Lennon and Timothy Leary is seated just next to Yoko.[25]

What non-Beatle member of the Rock and Roll Hall of Fame was in the first incarnation of the Plastic Ono Band?

Eric Clapton.

True or false: The Beatles never recorded a Christmas song which they wrote.

False: They wrote the song "Christmas Time (Is Here Again)," which was credited to all four Beatles. It was recorded for their 1967 fan club Christmas record but was not released until 1995. There are different versions of the song, one lasting 9:13, one lasting 6:07 and one lasting 3:03, but what they all have in common is that the lyrics consist of little more than an endless repeating of the song title throughout the song. It is not well remembered that the group released a Christmas record for their fan club every year from 1963–1969. Most consisted of a little jocular singing, followed by Christmas wishes from each of the band members. The John Lennon song "Happy Xmas (War is Over)" reached #4 in the U.K. in 1972 and #2 in 1980 after Lennon was assassinated.

Paul McCartney described this song as "probably my favorite Beatles track." The extended version is one of the longest Beatles songs. As a hint, the only words sung in the entire song consist essentially of the words in the title. What is the song?

"You Know My Name (Look Up the Number)." The song is a music hall comedy number. Lennon came up with the lyric/title after seeing a phone book. He said: "That was a piece of unfinished music that I turned into a comedy record with Paul. I was waiting for him in his house, and I saw the phone book was on the piano with 'You know the name, look up the number.'" McCartney went on to explain: "It's so insane. All the memories . . . I mean, what would you do if a guy like John Lennon turned up at the studio and said, 'I've got a new song.' I said, 'What are the words?' and he replied, 'You know my name, look up the number.' I asked, 'What's the rest of it?' 'No, no other words, those are the words. And I want to do it like a mantra!'" While there are various versions of this song, the version which appears on *Anthology 2* is 5:43. While there are other words in this song, they are spoken and not sung.[26]

The Beatles have a song which is even longer than "You Know My Name (Look Up the Number)" and yet it has only 14 words in the entire song. What is the song? As a hint, it appears on *Abbey Road* and has a parenthetical in the title.

"I Want You (She's So Heavy)." The only other words besides the six in the title are it's, driving, me, mad, so, bad, babe and yea. John Lennon wrote this song about his love for Yoko Ono. The final master lasted 8:04, but Lennon decided on a surprise ending. During the final edit with the guitars, drums and white noise climaxing endlessly, he told recording engineer Geoff Emerick to "cut it right there" at the 7:44 mark, bringing the song (and side one of the *Abbey Road* album) to an abrupt end. It's a mass of overdubbed guitars, with a slow-building wall of white noise generated by Harrison's brand-new Moog synthesizer ("I had to have mine made specially," he said, "because Mr. Moog had only just invented it"). In explaining his minimalist lyrics, Lennon commented, "When you're drowning, you don't say, 'I would be incredibly pleased if someone would have the foresight to notice me drowning and come and help me.' You just *scream*."[27]

At the other end of the length spectrum, there is a Beatles song that also appears on *Abbey Road* which is only 23 seconds long. What song is it? There is a longer version of the song which was recorded (and which can be heard on YouTube), which was 2:10, but it does not appear on a Beatles album.

"Her Majesty," which is the last track of the *Abbey Road* album, written by Paul McCartney.

Eric Burdon, of the Animals fame (later known as Eric Burdon and the Animals), claims that there is a reference to him in the John Lennon composition, "I Am the Walrus." What is that alleged reference?

Burdon claimed that he was the Eggman. Burdon was known as 'Eggs' to his friends, the nickname originating from his fondess for breaking eggs over naked women's bodies. Burdon's biography mentions such an affair taking place in the presence of Lennon, who shouted "Go on, go get it, Eggman . . ."

"I Am the Walrus" was the first Beatles song recorded after the death of their manager, Brian Epstein, from a sleeping pill overdose on August 27, 1967. The recording of this song came mostly in early September 1967. Incidentally, many people don't realize that Epstein was only 32 years old when he died.[28]

There are quite a number of real and fictional people mentioned in Beatles songs. Perhaps not surprisingly, virtually all of these songs come from the latter half of the band's career when they had started to spread their wings lyrically and musically. It would be difficult to imagine Lennon and McCartney putting people's names in their songs back when they were writing songs such as "She Loves You" or "Love Me Do."

Here are a few questions which focus on songs in which people are named by both first and last name. We'll start with real people. I will name the song and you name the person whose full name(s) is/are mentioned in the song.

"The Ballad of John and Yoko."

Peter Brown. Brown was part of the group's management team, he was witness to the wedding of Paul and Linda McCartney and best man at the wedding of John and Yoko in 1969. Brown was trying to assist John and Yoko find a country where they could get married. It was Peter Brown who told Lennon that he and Yoko could get married in Gilbraltar. The song was the 17th and last U.K. #1 single for the band. It has been said that Brown was never referred to by his first name or last name only, but rather always the full "Peter Brown."[29]

"Dig It" which is on the album *Let It Be* (three people)

B.B. King, Doris Day and Matt Busby. Busby was a Scottish football player and manager, who managed Manchester United between 1945 and 1969.

"Being for the Benefit of Mr. Kite!" (Hint: He ran the circus.)

Pablo Fanque. Mr. Fanque (1796–1871) was a black circus performer and later proprietor of his own circus, which was the most successful circus in England for 30 years. The inspiration and a number of the words and phrases for this song came from an 1843 poster that John Lennon found at an antiques shop in London. Besides the title itself, the poster also makes reference to "21 somersets on the solid ground" and "a hogshead of real fire!" In the song however, the horse is named Henry rather than Zanthus, as in the poster.[30]

"Two of Us" (Spoken words at the start of the song.)

Charles Hawtrey. Hawtrey was an English actor and musician.

"I Am the Walrus"

Edgar Allen Poe.

And now for *fictional* people. I will name the song; you come up with the fictional person's name.

"Maxwell's Silver Hammer"

Maxwell Edison

"Ob-La-Di, Ob-La Da"

Desmond Jones and Molly Jones (although, as discussed elsewhere herein, "Desmond" is actually a reference to a real person).

"Get Back"

Loretta Martin

"Eleanor Rigby"

Duh!

"Sgt. Pepper's Lonely Hearts Club Band"

Billy Shears

"Dig It"

Georgie Wood

"You Know My Name (Look Up the Number)"

Dennis O'Dell

What was the last song the Beatles recorded together?

Fittingly enough, "The End." Recording began on July 23, 1969, when the Beatles recorded a one-minute, thirty-second master take that was extended via overdubs to two minutes and five seconds. At this point, the song was called "Ending." The first vocals for the song were added on August 5, additional vocals and guitar overdubs were added on August 7, and bass and drums on August 8, the day the *Abbey Road* cover picture was taken. Orchestral overdubs were added August 15, and the closing piano and accompanying vocal on August 18.[31]

What was the last song the Beatles released and the only one which they ever worked on after January 1, 1970?

Paul McCartney's classic "Let It Be."[32]

The last album the Beatles recorded was not the last one they released. What was the last album recorded and what was the last album released?

The last album in which most of the songs were recorded was *Abbey Road* (February through August 1969) but the last album released was *Let It Be* (May 1970). *Abbey Road* was released shortly after its completion in September 1969 but *Let It Be* was recorded primarily in January and February of 1969. *Let It Be* (which was originally going to be titled *Get Back*) was intended for release in July 1969, but its release was pushed back to September to coincide with the planned television special and the theatrical film about the making of the album. In September, the release was pushed back to December, because the Beatles had just recorded *Abbey Road* and wanted to issue that album instead. It then got pushed back again. There were actually two songs on *Let It Be* which were recorded in 1970, one being "Let It Be" itself and the other being George Harrison's "I Me Mine," so purists could argue that *Abbey Road* was the final "album" recorded, if judged by the final song. (It was stated above that "The End" was the last song that the Beatles recorded together and that is because John Lennon did not play on "I Me Mine" and because, on the song "Let It Be," other than vocal overdubs on January 4, 1970, all of the rest of the recording was done in January and April 1969.)

What song was the first post-Beatles #1 song in the U.S. for Paul McCartney?

"Uncle Albert/Admiral Halsey." Writing credit on this song is actually attributed to both Paul and Linda McCartney. One would think that there could be two reasons for Linda's inclusion as a cowriter on this song. One is that she actually helped him write it, which seems unlikely. A second is perhaps as a kind of gift or expression of love or thanks due to his deep devotion to her. But there is a third possible reason as well: money. According to Songfacts, "Under a deal he signed with the Beatles, songs he wrote until 1973 were owned by Northern Songs Publishing and Maclen Music. By splitting the credits with his wife, he could keep half the royalties in the family." That sounds logical but it would not explain why she was also given cowriting credit for the following Wings songs, because they were all released in 1973 or later: "Live and Let Die," "Jet," "Band on the Run," "Junior's Farm," "Listen to What the Man Said," "Silly Love Songs," and "Let 'Em In." All of these songs reached the top 10.

Which song is described here: (a) It was a #1 song in January 1974 for an ex-Beatle. (b) It was written by two men who, according to Wikipedia, "wrote more motion-picture musical song scores than any other songwriting team in film history," but who are certainly not associated with rock music in any way. In fact, most of their movies were Disney films, one being *Mary Poppins*.

"You're Sixteen" by Ringo Starr, and written by the Sherman brothers, Robert and Richard. It is probably safe to say that most people do not realize that the writers of

"Supercalifragilisticexpialidocious" had a #1 song on the *Billboard* Hot 100. However, this certainly was not a case of the brothers trying to write a hit song for an ex-Beatle. The song was first recorded by Johnny Burnett in 1960 and that version reached #8 on the *Billboard* Hot 100.

Which ex-Beatle had the most solo top 10 singles during the Decade?

Perhaps surprisingly, it was Ringo, with 8: "It Don't Come Easy" (#4; 1971); "Back Off Boogaloo" (#9; 1972); "Photograph" (#1; 1973); "You're Sixteen" (#1; 1973); "Oh My My" (#6; 1974); "Only You (and You Alone)" (#5; 1974); "Snookeroo" (#3; 1974); and "No No Song" (#3; 1975). Paul McCartney had a total of 10, two with Linda McCartney, and eight with Wings.

Two of the above songs were actually cowritten by Ringo and George Harrison, one officially credited and one not. What were they?

"Photograph" and "It Don't Come Easy" respectively. Ringo acknowledged that he had substantial assistance from George on the latter. For example, in an episode of *VH1 Storytellers* in 1998, right before performing the song, Starr said: "I wrote this song with the one and only George Harrison."[33]

After the Beatles broke up, who was the first to have a #1 single and the first to have a #1 album?

The first #1 single was George Harrison's "My Sweet Lord," in January 1971. (Its album, *All Things Must Pass*, also reached #1.) The first #1 album was *McCartney* by Paul McCartney in April 1970. Each of the Beatles had solo #1 songs. The first #1 single by McCartney was "Uncle Albert/Admiral Halsey" in August 1971. John Lennon's first #1 album was *Imagine* in October 1971. His first #1 single was "Whatever Gets You Thru the Night" in October 1974. Ringo Starr's first #1 single was "Photograph" in October 1973.

True or false: There were never any albums released by former Beatles on which all four band members participated.

False, and in fact, it happened twice, both times on albums of Ringo Starr. The first was his eponymous 1973 album, produced by Richard Perry. In fact, not only did they all play on the album, but they also each composed material. John Lennon wrote and played piano on "I'm the Greatest." George Harrison also played electric guitar on that track. Paul McCartney wrote and played piano on "Six O'Clock." Harrison cowrote and sang on "Photograph" with Starr. All three other Beatles also played on contributed songs on Ringo's 1976 album *Ringo's Rotogravure*.

In many respects, it is not so surprising that Ringo is the one Beatle with whom all of the others would be willing to work with after the breakup of the band. At one point or another, Paul and John were obviously at swords' points with each other and George was frustrated with both over their unwillingness to allow him to include more of his own compositions on Beatles albums. Ringo, on the other hand, in addition to his generally genial nature, was probably seen by the others as less threatening.

Last but not least: Who was better, Lennon or McCartney?

This is of course not really a fair or even a serious question because it is obviously so subjective (which is not to say that this very question has not been endlessly debated for many decades). It has often been suggested that McCartney wrote better melodies and Lennon wrote more interesting lyrics (and that same suggestion has been criticized as being either wrong or overly simplistic almost as often). There is no denying McCartney's gifts however. He was a more talented (and certainly more versatile) musician than Lennon. His amazing flair for melody is undeniable.

In a 2016 review of (yet another) biography of the band in the *New Yorker*, Adam Gopnik wrote:

> McCartney has worked so hard at seeming an ordinary bloke that it is easy to miss the least ordinary and least bloke-ish thing about him: the magnitude of his melodic gift. A genius for melody is a strange, surprisingly isolated talent, and doesn't have much to do with a broader musical gift for composition; Mozart certainly had it, Beethoven not so much. Irving Berlin could barely play the piano and when he did it was only in a single key (F-sharp major: all the black keys), and yet he wrote hundreds of haunting tunes. [McCartney] had the gift in absurd abundance.

On the other hand, McCartney's lyrics were rarely memorable and often downright banal, especially when untethered from Lennon after the breakup. It's just that the music he wrote was so tuneful that the words rarely mattered.[34]

Despite McCartney's varied talents, I still favor Lennon as between the two, for the simple reason that on balance, I tend to favor the songs he composed slightly more than McCartney's songs. He was mercurial and had many rough edges (which is a good thing), while McCartney, possibly because he was such a nice and "normal" guy, had about as many rough edges as a bowling ball. Also, while Lennon's worst efforts (both during and after his association with the band) were generally just not good, McCartney's could be downright embarrassing. I wonder if, without Lennon's influence, we might have been subjected to a steady diet of sappiness such as "Silly Love Songs" and "Ebony and Ivory" and "My Love" far earlier in McCartney's career. Dave Barry even wondered how the Beatles McCartney and the post-Beatles McCartney could even be the same person. "Did Paul's brain get taken over by aliens from the Planet Twinkie? I mean, he was a Beatle for goshsakes, a certified genius, a man who wrote dozens of truly great songs, including such butt-kicking rockers as 'I'm Down,' and then for some mysterious reason he began cranking out songs such as 'Uncle Albert/Admiral Halsey,' 'Listen to What the Man Said' and 'Let 'Em In.'" [35]

While McCartney rarely pushed the envelope lyrically, he certainly had the capacity to do so musically, especially during his Beatle days, as evidenced by such innovative and hard-rocking songs as "Helter Skelter," "Why Don't We Do It in the Road?," "Birthday" and "The End." Indeed "Birthday" is a good example of McCartney's capacity for gritty, almost heavy metal, music and inane lyrics (a la "Hello, Goodbye") at the same time.

In late 2014, Matt Schichter created a half-hour documentary which consisted simply of 551 artists (primarily singers, songwriters and musicians) being interviewed over many years and answering a single question: Lennon or McCartney? Some answered quickly and some agonized about the "right" answer for them. The final tally was Lennon: 282; McCartney: 196; No answer/can't decide: 50, George Harrison: 15; Ringo Starr: four; others: four. [36]

Also, in 2010, *Rolling Stone* picked the 100 greatest Beatles songs of all time. Three of the top 20 songs on the *Rolling Stone* list are attributed by the magazine to "Lennon-McCartney," but by virtually all accounts, each of those three songs were written entirely or at least primarily by John Lennon. Certainly he is the lead or sole singer on all of them. Those songs are "Norwegian Wood," "In My Life" and "A Day in the Life." If those songs are considered Lennon compositions, as they should be, then 11 of the top 20 are Lennon songs and only four are McCartney songs. (Two are by George Harrison and three really are by "Lennon-McCartney." The #1 song was "A Day in the Life.") Long before I was even aware that most Lennon-McCartney songs are not really "Lennon-McCartney songs," I made a list of my favorite 50 Beatles songs. I know now that about two-thirds of them were primarily Lennon songs.

Regardless of who was "better," one thing is quite clear: they both produced far superior product as Beatles, both in quantity and quality, than either of them did afterwards. The magical chemistry that Lennon and McCartney had as Beatles, even when they were writing their own songs (which occurred with more and more frequency during the second half of the band's existence) is perhaps best shown by looking at their post-Beatles output. While they each certainly created some masterpieces, they were relatively few and far between and counterbalanced (especially in Paul's case) with a fair amount of dreck. Even when they could hardly abide each other's company as Beatles—such as during the tension-filled making of the White Album—the songs they wrote equaled or exceeded almost everything they created as solo artists. They apparently needed the disparate gifts that each brought to the band, not to mention the competitive juices that flowed between them.

What is so remarkable about the *Rolling Stone* list is not that such a list could be put together in the first place—plenty of other acts could have been chosen for such a "100 greatest" list—but that most of the songs on the list would be recognizable not just to diehard Beatles fans, but to even casual fans of music from the Decade. Consider: the #100 song on the list (i.e. the "worst" song on the list) was a #1 song (!), "Hello, Goodbye." Admittedly, this is not one of their masterpieces (indeed, Lennon scoffed at the fact that it was released as the A-side to his composition "I Am the Walrus"), but still. How many other groups or solo artists would have a #1 song and one as well-known as "Hello, Goodbye" as their #100 song? Other examples of classic Beatles songs way down the list: #90 is another #1 song, "The Long and Winding Road," #87 is "Love Me Do," #84 is "Across the Universe," #80 is "Mother Nature's Son." And so on. Even though the list is obviously subjective, the point is still clear.

The fact that the Beatles had such a short career—relative to any other act that could have a "100 greatest" list bestowed on them—makes the list even more amazing. The only other band that comes close to the Beatles on this score is the Rolling Stones, and in fact *Rolling Stone* made an identical list for them.[37] Suffice it to say that—even aside from the fact that the Stones have a nearly 50-year body of work to choose from (as opposed to about seven for the Beatles)—the vast majority of the songs on the bottom half of their list would only be recognizable to true Stones fans. That's really the difference between the Beatles and everyone else who released enough music to have a 100 greatest list: all of the other such acts have plenty of true-blue fans who would recognize all or most of their particular 100 songs (the Grateful Dead or Elton John or Billy Joel for example), but only the Beatles would have such a high percentage of their songs that are instantly recognizable even to the casual fan.

Finally, if *Rolling Stone* can pick their top Beatles songs so can I. I tend not to favor such top-of-the-mind "obvious" choices such as "Hey Jude," "Let It Be" or "Yesterday," but rather less frequently heard songs. (I would never call any of them "obscure" because an "obscure Beatles" song is practically an oxymoron.) In keeping with the theme of this book, these songs are from the Decade only, which of course rules out some of their earlier masterpieces that may have otherwise made the list. The list is alphabetical so as not to play favorites.

Song	Main Writer
"Across the Universe"	Lennon
"A Day in the Life"	Lennon
"Blackbird"	McCartney
"Eleanor Rigby"	McCartney
"For No One"	McCartney
"Girl"	Lennon
"Help!"	Lennon
"Here, There and Everywhere"	McCartney
"I Am the Walrus"	Lennon
"I've Just Seen a Face"	McCartney
"In My Life"	Lennon
"Mother Nature's Son"	McCartney
"Norwegian Wood"	Lennon
"Revolution"	Lennon
"She's Leaving Home"	McCartney
"Strawberry Fields Forever"	Lennon
"Two of Us"	McCartney
"While My Guitar Gently Weeps"	Harrison

CHAPTER 4

Only the Good Die Young
(Premature Deaths)

As is well known, there is no shortage of stars who have died long before their time, often, anomalously, at age 27. Often the cause of death was drug overdose, but there have been a myriad of other causes, including plane crashes, motorcycle crashes and suicide. This section focuses on artists who died prematurely (often during the Decade), whose heyday was during the Decade, or on songs recorded by these artists.

This woman was a key member of a group that is in the Rock and Roll Hall of Fame. By age 24, she was a vocalist (but not lead vocalist) on 10 #1 hits by the group. She began to suffer from weight gain, alcoholism and depression. Her home was foreclosed. She died at age 32 from cardiac arrest. Who was this woman?

Florence Ballard of the Supremes. She was with the group from their formation in 1959 until she left the group (or was ousted) in 1967. Ballard was actually responsible for forming the group and also chose the name "Supremes." They had previously been known as the Primettes, but Berry Gordy required them to change their name, and she chose Supremes over several other alternatives offered, even though Diana Ross and Cindy Wilson didn't like it because they thought it sounded too masculine. After Gordy made Ross the lead singer and the star of the group (officially changing their name to Diana Ross and the Supremes in 1967), Ballard resented it. She began to gain weight, miss rehearsals, and appear inebriated on stage. Berry replaced her with Cindy Birdsong. She was given only $150,000 to walk away from the group and had no royalty rights to any of the Supremes' hits. She embarked on a solo career, but it was unsuccessful and ended quickly. It has been written that she died in poverty, but this is not the case. While she certainly did live through a period of poverty, and lived on welfare for a time, she received an insurance settlement in 1975 and was getting back on her feet when she died in 1976. Of the Supremes' 12 #1 hits, nine came out during the Decade.[1]

Which song is being described here:

- It is one of only three songs in the Decade, and only the second song ever, to be a posthumous #1 song on the *Billboard* Hot 100.
- The title has a person's first and last name in it. The song was written by two men who intended that person as a woman. However, the artist who made the song famous was a female who changed around a few pronouns (but not the name itself) to make that person a man.
- This song was the only one which even reached the top 10 for this artist. However, other artists had recorded it beforehand. Roger Miller was the first artist to have a hit with the song, which peaked at #12 on the U.S. country chart in 1969.
- The artist died only a few days after recording the song.

"Me and Bobby McGee," written by Kris Kristofferson and Fred Foster and made famous by Janis Joplin. The song was released on her album *Pearl* which was released after she died of a heroin overdose at age 27 on October 4, 1970. In talking about the title and the creation of the song, Kristofferson said: "The title came from [producer and Monument Records founder] Fred Foster. He called one night and said, 'I've got a song title for you. It's "Me and Bobby McKee."' I thought he said 'McGee.' Bobby McKee was the secretary of Boudleaux Bryant, who was in the same building with Fred. Then Fred says, 'The hook is that Bobby McKee is a she. How does that grab you?' (*Laughs*) I said, 'Uh, I'll try to write it, but I've never written a song on assignment.' So it took me a while to think about."

When asked about how he came up with the famous line about freedom being synonymous with having nothing left to lose, Kristofferson told *Esquire* magazine: "I was working in the Gulf of Mexico on oil rigs, flying helicopters. I'd lost my family to my years of failing as a songwriter. All I had were bills, child support and grief. And I was about to get fired for not letting 24 hours go between the throttle and the bottle. It looks like I'd trashed my act. But there was something liberating about it. By not having to live up to people's expectations, I was somehow free." On YouTube, Janis can be heard delivering a beautiful first take of the song in the studio.

A website, toponehitwonders.com, called the song (and thus Janis) a one-hit wonder, but regardless of her success judged by chart performance, she certainly does not seem like a one-hit wonder, especially when her influence on other artists is taken into account.[2]

"Me and Bobby McGee" was the second song to reach #1 posthumously. What was the first? A few hints:

- Like "Me and Bobby McGee," *it* was also recorded just a few days before the artist's death.
- The performer was a cowriter of the song who died in a plane crash.
- His cowriter was his guitarist, Steve Cropper.

"(Sittin' On) The Dock of the Bay," by Otis Redding and Steve Cropper. In 1967 Otis lived in Bill Graham's boathouse right across the bay from San Francisco. He would literally sit and watch the ships on the bay coming and going, and that was the genesis of his most famous song. Although the song is written in the first person, many of the lyrics were written by Cropper about Otis, such as about leaving his home in Georgia and heading for the San Francisco Bay.

Recording of the song started on November 22, 1967 and recording was finished on December 8, 1967. Two days later, the plane in which Redding and his road band were flying crashed. Otis and all but one of the band members died. He was just 26 years old. The record company rushed final production on the song, and when it was released early in 1968, it shot to the top of the charts.

Interestingly, Otis's famous whistling ending to the song was never intended to be left in. At the end of the December 8 recording session, Otis and Cropper were still trying to figure out a lyric with which to end the song. So Otis did the whistling just as a place-holder until he could return and sing the final fade out. That, of course, never happened, and Otis's poignant whistling was kept in the recording.

The song won the 1968 Grammy Award for Best Rhythm and Blues Performance and Best Rhythm and Blues Song for Redding and Cropper.[3]

The third and final posthumous song to hit #1 during the Decade was by Jim Croce. It first appeared on an album released in 1972 but did not reach #1 until 1974, although Croce recorded two albums subsequent to that one. What was the song?

"Time in a Bottle." It appeared on his album *You Don't Mess Around with Jim*.

All of the following people died during the Decade. Which one (or more) did not die at age 27:

a. Malcolm Hale of Spanky and Our Gang
b. Brian Jones of the Rolling Stones
c. Alan Wilson of Canned Heat
d. Jimi Hendrix
e. Janis Joplin

f. Mama Cass Elliot of the Mamas and the Papas
g. Jim Croce
h. Duane Allman of the Allman Brothers Band
i. Jim Morrison of the Doors
j. Ron "Pigpen" McKernan of the Grateful Dead
k. Dave Alexander of the Stooges
l. Pete Ham of Badfinger
m. Gary Thain of Uriah Heep

All of them were 27, except for f. Mama Cass, who died at 34, g. Jim Croce (30), and h. Duane Allman (24).[4]

There has likely been only one time that *two* members from the same band have committed suicide. In both cases, they felt that they were being taken financially advantage of by their business managers or record label, although other factors were involved as well, including the fact that the second was allegedly depressed over the suicide of the first. One of them, who was the main songwriter for the band and who penned two top 10 songs in the U.S. and U.K, is listed above and he died in 1975. His bandmate died in 1983 at age 36. Who is the band and who were the two who committed suicide?

Pete Ham and Tom Evans of Badfinger. Formerly known as the Iveys, Badfinger was discovered by Beatles road manager Mal Evans, who in turn recommended them to the Beatles. They were signed as one of the first non-Beatles acts to newly formed Apple Records. Paul McCartney wrote their first big hit, "Come and Get It," a top 10 hit for the band in 1969. After leaving Apple as it was crumbling in the early 1970s, the band signed with Warner Brothers. However, between 1973 and 1975, the band became embroiled in many financial and managerial problems, especially with their manager Stan Polley who was accused of mishandling their finances, leaving Ham broke and unable to make mortgage payments on a newly acquired house. On April 24, 1975, he hanged himself in the garage of his Surrey home. He left behind a pregnant girlfriend, who gave birth to their daughter one month after his death. His suicide note read in part, "I will not be allowed to love and trust everybody. This is better. P.S. Stan Polley is a soulless bastard. I will take him with me."

As for Evans, he too had severe financial troubles and hung himself from a tree. Although he did not leave a suicide note, he was apparently never able to get over the suicide of Ham, his friend and writing partner. His wife quoted him as saying, "I want to be where Pete is. It's a better place than down here."

In 1998, Dan Matovina wrote a book entitled *Without You: The Tragic Story of Badfinger*. In that book, he agreed that Stan Polley was indeed a "soulless bastard," as Ham called him. By way of example, a financial statement prepared by Polley's accountants for the period from December 8, 1970 to October 31, 1971 showed Polley's income from the band: "Salaries and advances to client, $8,339 (Joey Molland), $6,861 (Mike Gibbins), $6,211 (Tom Evans), $5,959 (Pete Ham). Net corporation profit, $24,569. Management commission, $75,744 (Stan Polley)." According to Matovina's website: "When prompted, he [Stan Polley] had often bragged that anyone under his wing would be so broken emotionally and financially that if they challenged him, they'd never even attempt to sue him."[5]

Besides "Come and Get It," Badfinger's other biggest hits—at least for them—were "No Matter What," "Baby Blue," and "Day After Day." The reason for the qualification is that Ham and Evans wrote a song that become a bigger hit for another artist than any of their own songs were for them. It was a #1 song for four consecutive weeks in 1972 and was named the #4 song for all of 1972. It has been covered more than 180 times. Paul McCartney called it "the killer song of all time." In an eerie foretelling of future events, the despondent singer in the song appears to be contemplating his own suicide, albeit over the possible loss of a girl. As a hint, the song was made famous by a singer who sometimes went by one name. As another hint, Mariah Carey's 1994 cover of the song reached #3 in the U.S., but it was her first #1 song in Germany, Sweden and the U.K. What is the song and who made it famous?

"Without You" by (Harry) Nilsson. The singer appears devastated that he may have lost his girlfriend. The song actually resulted from the combining of two separate songs, one written by Ham and one written by Evans, but neither was totally happy with their own compositions. Ham's was called "If It's Love," but he felt the song was missing a good chorus. That came from Evans' song "I Can't Live." Despite the song's later huge success, neither Ham nor Evans considered the song to have much potential at the time Badfinger recorded it, and so it was never released as a single. Of course, the two arrangements were quite different. As Rob Smith wrote on Popdose.com, "To say that Badfinger's jaunty, acoustic-based original version of "Without You" differs from Harry Nilsson's hit 1972 cover is to say a pleasantly bright day at the beach differs from a billion-ton cloud of solar plasma launched by the sun that's coming to wipe out life on this planet as we know it."[6]

Amazingly, two of the most famous (or infamous) deaths in rock history both occurred in the same London apartment (or, as the Brits would say, flat) located at 9 Curzon Street.

One was a singer and one was a musician. Both performers died at age 32 although the events occurred four years apart, in 1974 and 1978. The same person owned the unit at both times and he was famous in his own right. Who were the two performers and who owned the apartment? For extra credit, name the falsely rumored cause of death of one of them and the actual cause of death.

Cass Elliot and Keith Moon both died in the apartment owned by Harry Nilsson. Elliott was staying at Nilsson's flat while headlining at the London Palladium. She died on July 29, 1974. For a long time, it was rumored that she had choked on a ham sandwich, a cause of death which may have seemed logical to some because she was overweight. This rumor originated with Dr. Anthony Greenburgh, the first physician to examine Elliot after her death. He told the press that it appeared to have been a simple case of asphyxia. "From what I saw when I got to the flat, she appeared to have been eating a ham sandwich and drinking Coca-Cola while lying down—a very dangerous thing to do. This would be especially dangerous for someone like Cass who was overweight and who might be prone to having a heart attack. She seemed to have choked on a ham sandwich."

In the initial installment of the Austin Powers movie trilogy, he references the death of people who died while he was frozen for 30 years: "Jimi Hendrix. Deceased—drugs; Janis Joplin. Deceased—alcohol; Mama Cass: Deceased—ham sandwich."

As it turned out, Greenburgh overlooked the fact that the ham sandwich by Cass's bed had not in fact been touched. The official findings of the coroner's inquest were that Cass Eliot died from "fatty myocardial degeneration due to obesity" (i.e., a heart attack brought about by fatty degeneration of the heart muscle fiber), and nothing was found to have been blocking her mouth or throat. Her crash diets to lose a large amount of weight in a relatively short period of time, and the prolonged, combined effects of obesity and severe dieting had weakened her heart to the point of failure.[7]

Four years later, on September 7, 1978, the Who's drummer Keith Moon returned to the same room in Nilsson's flat after a night out. He died that day, also at age 32, from an overdose of Clomethiazole, a prescribed anti-alcohol drug. Nilsson then sold the flat to Moon's bandmate, Pete Townshend.

The primary causes of early death of musical artists from the Decade are plane crashes, drug/alcohol/pills abuse and gunshot. This woman died at age 24 from brain cancer. She had four top 10 songs on the *Billboard* Hot 100 and five top five songs on the R&B chart. Who was she? (As a hint, all the songs were duets with the same person and she was African-American.)

Tammi Terrell. All of the above hits were performed with Marvin Gaye, including "Ain't No Mountain High Enough," "Ain't Nothing Like the Real Thing," "Your Precious Love," "If I Could Build My Whole World Around You," and "You're All I Need to Get By."

Each of these songs, other than "If I Could Build My Whole World Around You," were written by the same songwriters. Who?

Nickolas Ashford and Valerie Simpson. On "Ain't No Mountain High Enough," their vocals were recorded separately and then mixed together. Diana Ross had a #1 hit with the song in 1970, her first post-Supremes #1 song.[8]

Who was the cofounder of the band Chicago and singer of "Colour My World" (yes, the British spelling of "Colour" is correct) who died from an accidentally self-inflicted gunshot wound?

Terry Kath. It happened on January 23, 1978, just before Kath turned 32. The only witness to the incident was Chicago's keyboard tech, Don Johnson, whose account of what happened was later summarized by trombonist James Pankow.

> Evidently, he had gone to the shooting range, and he came back to Donny's apartment, and he was sitting at the kitchen table cleaning his guns. Donny remarked, "Hey, man, you're really tired. Why don't you just put the guns down and go to bed." Terry said, "Don't worry about it," and he showed Donny the gun. He said, "Look, the clip's not even in it," and he had the clip in one hand and the gun in the other. But evidently there was a bullet still in the chamber. He had taken the clip out of the gun, and the clip was empty. A gun can't be fired without the clip in it. He put the clip back in, and he was waving the gun around his head. He said, "What do you think I'm gonna do? Blow my brains out?" And just the pressure when he was waving the gun around the side of his head, the pressure of his finger on the trigger, released that round in the chamber. It went into the side of his head. He died instantly.

Kath was an accomplished guitarist. According to the band's saxophonist Walter Parazaider, after watching Kath play in 1968, "this guy came up very quietly and tapped me on the shoulder. He says, 'Hi, I'm Jimi Hendrix. I've been watching you guys and I think your guitarist is better than me.'"[9]

Who was the lead singer and harmonica player of the Yardbirds who died from electrocution in the basement of his home by playing an improperly grounded guitar?

Keith Relf. He was only 33 years old at the time. He sang lead on their hits such as "For Your Love," "Heart Full of Soul" and "Shapes of Things."

CHAPTER 5

We're Having a Party (Rock Festivals and Benefit Concerts)

The first, the biggest, and, some would say, the greatest rock festivals all occurred during the Decade. This chapter will focus on four rock festivals in particular, namely Woodstock, Altamont, a concert that was even bigger than Woodstock, but seldom remembered today, and one sometimes known as the British Woodstock.

WOODSTOCK

Woodstock was not the largest rock festival ever held. It was not the first multi-day star-filled concert either. Almost nothing went as planned. It was a financial disaster for the promoters. The weather was often horrible with intermittent downpours creating a sea of mud. There were problems with the sound system, critical shortages of food, drinking water, and toilet facilities. Yet, nearly 50 years later, it remains the most unforgettable rock concert ever held. There have been attempts to "recreate" Woodstock over the years (both at the original site and elsewhere), but none of them have matched the original in terms of memory-searing images and musical performances.

Most of the attendees got in for free. It was not supposed to be that way however. Tickets for the three-day event cost $18 in advance and $24 at the gate. There were supposed to be fences to ensure orderly entrance into the event, but because of the last-minute change of venue, the fences were never completed and people could just walk in, and it soon became clear that there was no way to stop that. There were safety concerns as well, in part because so many more people came than were ever anticipated. (The promoters had assured township officials that no more than 50,000 people would attend.) So, as was famously announced from the stage early on in the concert: "It's a free concert from now on. That doesn't mean that anything goes. What that means is we're going to put the music up here for free. What it means is that the people who are backing this thing, who put up the money for it, are going to take a bit of a bath. A big bath. That's no hype, that's truth. They're going to get hurt."

Perhaps if there had been some merchandising, it would have helped the promoters, but as hard as it is to believe today, there was nothing for sale at the concert other than programs. No t-shirts, no hoodies, no trinkets, no music being sold, no nothing. As for the festival programs, they went largely undistributed, and many of them were thrown away, still in their boxes after the festival. Today those programs cost about $600 on eBay.

Despite everything, the festival has always been considered to be a huge success and its impact was undeniable. Even financially, the losses suffered by the promoters from the event itself were more than recouped once revenues from the highly successful documentary and soundtrack album came in. Shortly after the event in 1969, rock critic Ellen Sander wrote: "No longer can the magical multicolored phenomenon of pop culture be overlooked or underrated. It's happening everywhere, but now it has happened in one place at one time so hugely that it was indeed historic. . . . What happened was that the largest number of people ever assembled for any event other than a war lived together, intimately and meaningfully and with such natural good cheer that they turned on not only everyone surrounding them but the mass media, and, by extension, millions of others."[1] There were many iconic performances at Woodstock, many of which were captured in the four-hour documentary about the concert. Some of the most memorable include the following six in particular: "Freedom (Motherless Child)" (Richie Havens), "The 'Fish' Cheer/I Feel Like I'm Fixing to Die Rag" (Country Joe and the Fish), "Suite: Judy Blue Eyes" (Crosby, Stills & Nash), "See Me, Feel Me" (The Who), "With a Little Help from My Friends" (Joe Cocker) and "The Star Spangled Banner" (Jimi Hendrix).

The Woodstock concert lasted from August 15-18, 1969. Where was it held? This may sound like asking who is buried in Grant's Tomb or when was the War of 1812, but, since the answer is not Woodstock, that's not the case (although Woodstock is a town in New York).

It was actually held near the hamlet of White Lake in the town of Bethel, New York, which is about 60 miles southwest of Woodstock. The iconic poster for the event called it "an aquarian exposition in White Lake, NY."

Was the concert originally supposed to be held in Woodstock? If not, why was it called Woodstock?

The concert was never going to be in Woodstock. However, Bethel was not the first location. Woodstock was originally scheduled to take place in in the town of Walkill, New York, which the organizers had leased for $10,000 in the spring of 1969. Town officials were assured that no more than 50,000 would attend. Town residents immediately opposed the project. In early July, the town board passed a law requiring a permit for any gathering over 5,000 people. This law was passed with the express purpose of banning Woodstock. On July 15, 1969, the Wallkill Zoning Board of Appeals officially banned the concert on the basis that the planned portable toilets would not meet town code.

The reason the concert was known as Woodstock (which is actually short for its full title, the Woodstock Music and Art Fair) is because the organizers called their company "Woodstock Ventures."[2]

The most famous song about Woodstock is probably the song of that title by Joni Mitchell. Ironically however, she did not actually appear at the concert. She was invited however. Why did she not appear?

Because her manager expressed concern that if she performed at the concert, she would miss her scheduled appearance on *The Dick Cavett Show* scheduled for the day after the concert ended. However, Jefferson Airplane, David Crosby and Stephen Stills all performed at Woodstock and yet all appeared on the same Cavett show on August 19, 1969 (the concert ended the day before). Joni looked on rather forlornly as the remaining guests described what an amazing experience Woodstock was. Not being there, she said, gave her an intense perspective on what was happening during the landmark concert, and in fact she wrote the song while in her hotel room in New York City watching televised reports about the event. David Crosby, was did perform at the concert later said: "She captured the feeling and importance of the Woodstock festival better than anyone who'd been there."[3]

The story of Joni Mitchell's non-appearance at Woodstock is probably the most famous because of the irony of a non-performer—who wanted to attend the event—writing the most iconic song about the event. However, there were numerous other bands who were asked to appear who didn't, either because they didn't want to attend or couldn't attend or because they didn't understand what they were missing. For many artists, including the Beatles and Bob Dylan, there are no known reasons given by the artists or their managers, only fan theories. Therefore, they are just that: theories only. The artists or managers who actually gave the reason their bands did not appear include the following:

Jethro Tull: Leader Ian Anderson was put off by naked women and hippies. In an interview on the subject of why the band skipped Woodstock he said: "I knew it was going to be a big deal. The reason I didn't want to play Woodstock is because I asked our manager, Terry Ellis, 'Well, who else is going to be there?' And he listed a large number of groups who were reputedly going to play, and that it was going to be a hippie festival, and I said, 'Will there be lots of naked ladies? And will [they] be taking drugs and drinking lots of beer, and fooling around in the mud?' Because rain was forecast. And he said, 'Oh, yeah.' So I said, 'Right. I don't want to go.' Because I don't like hippies, and I'm usually rather put off by naked ladies unless the time is right. Well, indeed, unless the money's right."

The Doors: It was known that Morrison did not like performing outdoors. In an interview with *Hullabaloo* magazine in 1968 he said: "We've never done too well in those outdoor daytime concerts. I think that we need the night and sort of theater-type atmosphere and mood in which to work. There's something about the daylight and the open spaces that just sort of dissipates the whole magic." However, in 1996 interview, guitarist Robby Krieger said "we never played at Woodstock because we were stupid and turned it down. We thought it would be a second-class repeat of Monterey Pop Festival."

Tommy James and the Shondells: James would later say "We could have just kicked ourselves. We were in Hawaii, and my secretary called and said, 'Yeah, listen, there's this pig farmer in upstate New York that wants you to play in his field.' That's how it was put to me. So we passed."

Led Zeppelin: Their manager, Peter Grant, did not want them to be just another act on the bill. Instead, they played three shows that weekend, all within driving distance of the festival. Two on Saturday, August 16, took place at the Convention Hall in Asbury Park, N.J., with Led Zeppelin headlining over Woodstock act Joe Cocker. The next day, they performed at the Oakdale Musical Theatre in Wallingford, Connecticut, as the only band on the bill.[4]

Joni Mitchell's classic song "Woodstock" makes reference to the exact location in Bethel where the concert was held and to the owner of the land. What was that reference?

She sings of "Yasgur's farm," in reference to Max Yasgur's 600-acre dairy farm where the concert was held. Many of his neighbors turned against him after the festival, and he was no longer welcome at the town general store, but he never regretted his decision to allow the concert on his farm. He was paid $75,000 for the use of the farm. Sadly, Yasgur died of a heart attack less than four years after the festival, at age 53.[5]

What do the bands Sweetwater, Quill, Keef Hartley Band, and the Incredible String Band and the singer Bert Sommer all have in common?

They all performed at Woodstock. Though we often think of Woodstock as one headliner act performing after another, a number of artists have not only long since been forgotten, but were not necessarily even big stars at the time, including the above. Sommer's face (and more importantly his hair) is the image for the cover of the original playbill for the Broadway show *Hair*, so far more people have seen him that way than at Woodstock, even if they didn't know it was him.[6]

This man, along with Michael Lang, was one of the main organizers of Woodstock, and is sometimes referred to as "the Father of Woodstock." He also arranged for the financing of the *Woodstock* documentary directed by Michael Wadleigh, which won the 1970 Academy Award for Best Documentary. Interestingly, he also cowrote three hit songs, namely "Dead Man's Curve" by Jan and Dean (Brian Wilson was also a cowriter), "The Pied Piper" by Crispian St. Peters (#4 in the U.S.) and "The Rain, The Park and Other Things" by the Cowsills (#2 in the U.S.). Who is he?

Artie Kornfeld.[7]

One of the most famous performances at Woodstock was a number which was actually improvised on the spot by the performer because he had run out of songs to play. Who was the artist and what was the song?

Richie Havens, and the song is "Freedom." Havens was the festival's first performer. Because many artists were delayed in reaching the festival location, he was told to keep playing long after his scheduled set was over. Once he ran out of tunes, he took an old spiritual, "Motherless Child," added some lyrics, came up with his own arrangement, and turned it into what is now known as the classic "Freedom." "'Freedom' came from a totally spontaneous place," he said.

The first major act signed for Woodstock was Creedence Clearwater Revival. Yet, although they performed there, no numbers from their set were included in the original Woodstock movie. Why not?

Because bandleader and writer John Fogerty felt that the band's performance was subpar. (Several tracks from the event were eventually included in the 1994 commemorative box set.) Also, the band complained that they had to take the stage at three in the morning because the Grateful Dead had jammed so far past their scheduled time (what a shock) that by the time CCR began playing, many in the audience had gone to sleep. Band bassist Stu Cook held an opposing view, saying "the performances are classic CCR and I'm still amazed by the number of people who don't even know we were one of the headliners at Woodstock '69." He added: "There were probably no great performances. But in our set I think we probably played

75, 80 percent on the money. We definitely should have been included in the film. It was a huge mistake."

One might think that, as of 1969, rock and roll was not yet old enough to have an "oldies band" perform at Woodstock, but there was one there. Who was that band?

Sha Na Na. The band had been formed by two Columbia University students, John "Jocko" Marcellino and Joe Witkin. The band's name comes from the 1957 song "Get a Job" by the Silhouettes which begins "Sha na na na - sha na na na na." Unlike every other act that played at the festival, Sha Na Na didn't even have a record deal, let alone a commercially available recording. In fact, the 12-man group, which specialized in 1950s doo-wop and vintage rock and roll, had only formed a few months earlier. "Woodstock was just the seventh or eighth time we'd played in concert," Marcellino noted.

The group's fast-paced, 12-song set immediately preceded Jimi Hendrix's festival-concluding performance, which culminated with his visionary reinvention of "The Star Spangled Banner." Sha Na Na was paid $350 to play, but the check bounced, Marcellino recounted. And the group received just $1 for the film rights to its performance in the Oscar-winning *Woodstock* film documentary. "There were 12 of us, so that was 8 cents apiece. But I'm so grateful, because this whole career with Sha Na Na wouldn't have happened without Woodstock. We were in the most important music film documentary ever, even if we didn't get paid." Or, as Witkin noted: "We were starting off as nothing, so how could you rip us off?"

Even for 1969, the band was unabashedly anachronistic and especially so at Woodstock.

There were only four female performers at Woodstock, two of whom were solo artists, and two of whom were in bands. All of them are famous. Who were they?

The solo artists were Joan Baez (who was six months pregnant at the time) and Melanie. The other two were Grace Slick of Jefferson Airplane and Janis Joplin, who appeared with her Kozmic Blues Band. Although she is probably associated most frequently with Big Brother and the Holding Company, she had parted ways with them by the time of Woodstock.

There was only one song that was performed by two different artists, one of them being an iconic performance. It was a well-known Lennon-McCartney tune (as if any aren't well-known). One of the performances was by Richie Havens, who admitted that he didn't know any of the lyrics to the song. Therefore, he basically just sang doo-doo-doo and

da-da-dum throughout the whole song. Still, it was a beautiful performance. What was the song and who was the other performer, whose version is probably more famous than the original? (As a hint, Ringo Starr sang the original.)

"With a Little help from My Friends." The other singer was Joe Cocker, whose soulful rendition was one for the ages.

Several songs that were relatively unknown at the time became famous as a result of being performed at Woodstock. One was Richie Havens's improvised version of the old spiritual "Motherless Child," which became known as "Freedom" after Havens closed out his opening set with that tune. Another was the anti-war song by Country Joe McDonald which starts with the chant "Give me an F!" Anyone who was at Woodstock or saw the film or has a recorded version of the music knows the song well. Two questions: First, what is the actual name of the song? Second, the "F-word" spelled out by McDonald at Woodstock is not the usual word he spelled out when he performed that song. What is that word?

The actual name of the song is the "I-Feel-Like-I'm-Fixin'-to-Die Rag" (hyphens included). The usual word he spelled out was F-I-S-H, since the full name of his band was Country Joe and the Fish. A few other points of interest about Country Joe:

- Notwithstanding his obvious opposition to the Vietnam War, at the age of 17, he enlisted in the United States Navy for three years and was stationed in Japan.
- He was dating fellow performer Janis Joplin at the time.
- Both of his parents were Communist Party members in their youth and they named their son after Joseph Stalin.
- He was the only artist to perform twice at Woodstock, once on his own on Saturday, August 16, and the next day with his band, on Sunday, August 17.
- He is likely the only performer ever who was paid *not* to appear on the *Ed Sullivan Show*. During the summer of 1968 the band played on the Schaefer Music Festival tour. It was the band's drummer, Gary "Chicken" Hirsh, who suggested before one of the shows that they should spell out the word "fuck" instead of "fish," which they did. Although the crowd loved it, executives from the Sullivan show heard about what happened. They then canceled a previously scheduled appearance by the band, telling them to keep the money they had already been paid in exchange for never playing on the show. Depending on the source, the amount paid was either $2,500 or $10,000.[8]

Which song is described here:

- It is often referred to as the "unofficial anthem of Woodstock" and is featured in Michael Wadleigh's documentary about the festival. (AllMusic.com calls it the "rural hippie anthem.")
- The distinctive instrument in the song is the flute. The music is closely derived from "Bull Doze Blues," recorded in 1928 by Texas bluesman Henry Thomas. In that version (which can be heard on YouTube), Thomas accompanies himself on a quill, which is a type of pan flute. On the Woodstock song, the quill parts were played with a flute.
- Alan Wilson, the singer of the song, was one of the many rock stars who died at age 27, shortly before Hendrix (who died two weeks later) and Joplin (who died four weeks later).

"Goin' Up the Country" by Canned Heat. In the film, *Woodstock*, Canned Heat's spoken introduction to their performance of the song is heard, but the movie then cuts to the studio recording played over a montage of festival attendees. The 1970 soundtrack album and the director's cut of the movie feature the festival performance of the song, but without the spoken intro. Not surprisingly, the studio version sounds much cleaner, while the concert performance was, by the band's own admission, somewhat ragged.[9]

There was an incident at Woodstock in which a fairly well-known person jumped on stage between songs of the band that was performing. He grabbed a microphone and yelled "I think this is a pile of shit! While John Sinclair rots in prison!" One of the band members immediately yelled, "Fuck off! Fuck off my fucking stage!" and then proceeded to conk the intruder on the head with his guitar. Name the guitar-wielding person and the party crasher. (For a hint, the guitarist was the songwriter for a famous English rock band and the "victim" was one of the leading social activists of the time.)

Pete Townshend and Abbie Hoffman. Townshend was never one to tolerate sharing the stage with anyone who didn't work with the Who, was already in a bad mood because he didn't think the set was going well. The incident took place during a camera change, and was not captured on film. The audio of this incident, however, can be heard on The Who's box set, *Thirty Years of Maximum R&B* (Disc 2, Track 20, "Abbie Hoffman Incident"). It can also be heard on YouTube. In his 1969 book *Woodstock Nation*, Hoffman wrote that he was on a bad LSD trip at the time.

John Sinclair was the manager for the Detroit rock band MC5 and a founding member of the White Panther Party, a militantly anti-racist socialist group and counterpart of the Black Panthers. Arrested for possession of marijuana in 1969, Sinclair was given ten years in prison. The sentence was criticized by many as unduly harsh, and it galvanized a noisy protest movement. Sinclair was eventually freed in December 1971. John Lennon wrote a song called "John Sinclair," which urged the judge to set Sinclair free.

Most of our aural remembrances from Woodstock come from the music—but not all. Who said the following:

"This is the second time we've played in front of people man. We're scared shitless."

Stephen Stills.

"The New York State Freeway is closed, man."

Arlo Guthrie. In fact, it never closed.

"To show that our hearts are in the right place let's sing a song for the Governor of California, Ronald Ray-guns!"

Jeffery Shurtleff just before beginning his duet, "Drug Store Truck Drivin' Man" with Joan Baez.

"The brown acid that is circulating around us is not specifically too good. It's suggested that you do stay away from that. Of course, it's your own trip so be my guest but please be advised that there is a warning on that one, OK."

One of the stage announcers, Chip Monck (safe to say, likely not his real name. Ditto Wavy Gravy). It is often thought that he said "stay away from the brown acid," which is close, but not what he actually said.

There were several classic songs written about Woodstock, perhaps none more famous than Joni Mitchell's song of the same name. Another one was written by a female artist who, unlike Joni, did perform there. Who was the artist and what was the song?

"Lay Down (Candles in the Rain)" by Melanie (last name Safka). As written on the superseventies.com website:

She came onstage as evening fell, just after a particularly horrendous squall, and watched amazed as the hills slowly lit up with thousands upon thousands of candles. From her vantage point, it must have been one sight to see, particularly from the perspective of an amateur folk artist who happened to be the focal point of their attention. Moved by the experience, Melanie authored "Lay Down (Candles in the Rain)" in which she attempted to capture the spirituality and magic of that moment. To convey a sense of the warm crowd, she envisioned hundreds of voices joining her on the chorus. The Edwin Hawkins Singers had recently hit the charts with "Oh Happy Day" so she asked the gospel group if they would be interested in accompanying her. She auditioned the song before the group, and once they decided that it was sufficiently spiritual in content, they agreed.

Melanie was not a big star at the time of her Woodstock performance. In fact, the security guards did not know who she was and initially refused to issue her a performer's pass. She had to sing her song "Beautiful People" to prove to them that she was a scheduled performer. She was paid only $750 for her set. (Jimi Hendrix was the top earner at $18,000 and Blood Sweat and Tears was second, receiving $15,000 for their set. Miscellaneous other artists were paid as follows: Joan Baez—$10,000; Creedence Clearwater Revival—$10,000; the Band— $7,500; Janis Joplin—$7,500; the Who— $6,250; Arlo Guthrie—$5,000; Crosby, Stills, Nash & Young—$5,000; Grateful Dead— $2,500; Joe Cocker—$1,375.)[10]

Another band was scheduled to play but did not make it because they were stuck in New York City. They demanded helicopters to the concert which tour organizers refused to provide. Which band was it?

Iron Butterfly. The routine shorthand answer about how the band missed Woodstock is that they got "stuck at the airport" and couldn't travel the traffic-choked 100 miles of highway from New York City to upstate New York in time. According to drummer Ron Bushy:

Basically, we were in New York City at the Americana Hotel, waiting and waiting. Our semi with all of our equipment was in the parking lot, but we couldn't get it onto that little highway up to Woodstock. So we spoke to the Who, and they said we could use their equipment. But what happened was, because so many babies were being born and with all the health problems, they commandeered all the helicopters, which was the only way for us to get up there. We were scheduled to play on the last day, but we couldn't get up there. We went down to the Port Authority three times and waited for the helicopter, but it never showed up.

While Bushy's recollection may be accurate as far as it goes, other sources provide the real reason for *why* the helicopter never showed up, namely the arrogant attitude of their agent. Festival cocreator Michael Lang, in his book *The Road to Woodstock,* wrote that "Iron Butterfly was booked for Sunday afternoon, but John Morris [production coordinator and stage MC] told me that their agent had called with a last-minute demand for a helicopter to pick them up.... Apparently the agent had a real attitude, and we were up to our eyeballs in problems." According to Morris: "They sent me a telegram saying, 'We will fly to LaGuardia. You will have helicopters pick us up. We will fly straight to the show. We will perform immediately, and then we will be flown out.'" Upon hearing about this telegram, Lang recounted: "I told John to tell him to forget it; we had more important things to deal with." Morris then sent his own reply telegram to the band's agent:

F or reasons I can't go into
U ntil you are here
C larifying your situation
K nowing you are having problems
Y ou will have to find
O ther transportation
U nless you plan not to come.[11]

One of the most famous performances at the concert—and indeed one of the most famous live performances of any song in history—was seen by only a small fraction of the audience size compared to its peak. Who was the artist, what was the song? (As a hint, the artist was the last performer of the concert and his set was played on Monday morning after most attendees had already left.)

The artist was Jimi Hendrix and the song was "The Star-Spangled Banner." Here are a few interesting facts about Hendrix's seminal performance, courtesy of Joel Brattin, professor of literature at Worcester Polytechnic Institute, who has made an extensive study of the life and music of Hendrix:

- *Hendrix performed with a temporary band.* The Jimi Hendrix Experience, with which he had recorded three smash albums and electrified crowds at the Monterey Pop Festival two summers before, had broken up. Hendrix assembled a group he called Gypsy Suns and Rainbows, which included two musicians he had played with at the start of his career on the Chitlin' Circuit in Nashville: bassist Billy Cox and guitarist Larry Lee. Neither had ever performed in front of a large crowd before. Drummer Mitch Mitchell, who was part of the Experience, and two percussionists rounded out the band, one of the largest Hendrix ever appeared with. The group performed just twice more before disbanding.
- *It was the only Hendrix band that included a second guitarist.* Larry Lee backed up Hendrix on a number of songs, played some lead on "Jam Back at the House," and contributed several lead choruses to the 12-bar blues "Red House."
- *It was the only major performance that Hendrix gave in the morning.* By 1969, Hendrix was a major star who had earned the traditional headliner's position: playing last. Technical and weather delays caused the festival to stretch into Monday morning. The organizers had given Hendrix the opportunity to go on at midnight, but he opted to do it in the morning. One benefit of the delay: the morning light made for excellent filming conditions, which may be part of the reason this particular Hendrix performance is so well known.
- *Hendrix did not perform for half a million people.* In fact, when he took to the stage at 9:00 a.m., the crowd, which once numbered 500,000, had dwindled to fewer than 200,000—perhaps considerably fewer. When the crowd is panned on several occasions during his performance, it is evident that it has shrunk to a fraction of its original size.
- *"The Star Spangled Banner" was not played on its own.* It was part of a medley lasting over half an hour, one of the longest such medleys. The medley also included hits like "Voodoo Child (Slight Return)" and "Purple Haze," and an unaccompanied improvisation lasting nearly five minutes. Hendrix performed the national anthem as a solo in the midst of this medley.
- *It was not the first time Hendrix had performed "The Star Bangled Banner"—by a long shot.* In fact, there are nearly 50 live recordings of Hendrix playing the national anthem, 28 made before Woodstock. They range from about a minute to more than six minutes; the Woodstock version was three minutes and 46

seconds. It was among the best, Brattin says. "And, certainly, no other version is so iconic."

- *Hendrix performed an encore, a rarity.* He almost never performed encores, but at Woodstock, despite the vanishing crowd, he did. On recordings, he can be heard considering "Valleys of Neptune," which he never performed publicly, before or after Woodstock. He opted, instead, for "Hey Joe," his first hit song.
- *Hendrix was not supposed to close Woodstock.* Steeped in childhood memories of the song, Woodstock organizer Michael Lang wanted Roy Rogers to come on after Hendrix and play "Happy Trails." The cowboy crooner declined.[12]

BIGGER THAN WOODSTOCK

Interestingly, the largest rock concert of the Decade was not Woodstock but rather a one-day event that is almost completely forgotten today. It took place on July 28, 1973 and there were only three bands performing: The Grateful Dead, the Band and the Allman Brothers. An estimated 600,000 people attended. What was the name of the event? (As a hint, the name of the event makes reference to the location where it was held, and that location is normally known for something else entirely.)

The Summer Jam at Watkins Glen. The event was held at the Watkins Glen International Raceway. Similar to Woodstock, there was an enormous traffic jam for those attempting to make it to the concert site. Long and narrow country roads forced fans to abandon their cars and walk for miles to the concert. 150,000 tickets were sold for $10 each, but for all the other people, the concert was free. The promoter was Bill Graham. During the Band's set, there was a drenching rainstorm, and in a scene reminiscent of Woodstock, people were covered with mud.

Commenting on the event several years later, Robert Santelli wrote that there was little magic to the event considering the size of the crowd—i.e., it was no Woodstock:

Each of the three groups at Watkins Glen played unusually long sets. The Grateful Dead performed for five hours, the Allman Brothers for four, and the Band for three, including a thirty-minute break due to a thunderstorm. . . . At Watkins Glen a feeling of monotony and tedium constantly challenged the viewers' interest in the music and the proceedings onstage. Long, winding solos were frequent. The heat, the lack of comfort, and the crowded conditions dulled otherwise stirring moments. Many of the 600,000 could barely see the stage, let alone the musicians. . . . Woodstock also had had two sets of LPs and a movie to carry on its significance. No such enduring properties came out of Watkins Glen. . . . Watkins Glen did not register with the political portion of the youth culture as had some festivals in the past. To have 600,000 young people at one time in one place would have been the ultimate dream for any sixties radical. But that was just it—the sixties were over.

Although there were no reports of violence at the concert, the day was marred by the death of Willard Smith, 35, a skydiver from Syracuse, New York. He dove from an airplane carrying flares. However, one of the flares ignited his body suit and he was engulfed in flames.[13]

ALTAMONT

The December 6, 1969 Altamont rock concert (officially known as the Altamont Speedway Free Festival) is indelibly associated—not without justification—with three things: the Rolling Stones, Hells Angels and a death. Three hundred thousand people attended the free concert. Perhaps Altamont was an indication that the major multi-artist rock concert, and the peace and love atmosphere which had pervaded the 1967 Monterey pop festival and even Woodstock, which occurred only four months previously, was a thing of the past. What is clear is that almost everything went wrong and that it brought the 1960s to a violent end. Writing for *Rolling Stone* shortly after the event, John Burks called it "rock and roll's all-time worst day." Although intended as a "Woodstock West," it certainly didn't turn out that way. Perhaps for obvious reasons, the details and minutiae of the event are not nearly as well remembered today as they are with Woodstock.

What and where is Altamont?

Altamont was a motor speedway located in Alameda County in Northern California between the towns of Tracy and Livermore. It first opened on July 22, 1966 and closed in October 2008. In a very lengthy and detailed narrative which appeared in *Rolling Stone* six weeks after the event, entitled "The Rolling Stones Disaster At Altamont: Let It Bleed," the authors wrote that

It was as if Altamont's organizers had worked out a blueprint for disaster. Like:

1)   Promise a free concert by a popular rock group which rarely appears in this country [the Stones]. Announce the site only four days in advance.

2) Change the location 20 hours before the concert.
3) The new concert site should be as close as possible to a giant freeway.
4) Make sure the grounds are barren, treeless, desolate.
5) Don't warn neighboring landowners that hundreds of thousands of people are expected. Be unaware of their out-front hostility toward long hair and rock music.
6) Provide one-sixtieth the required toilet facilities to insure that people will use nearby fields, the sides of cars, etc.
7) The stage should be located in an area likely to be completely surrounded by people and their vehicles.
8) Build the stage low enough to be easily hurdled. Don't secure a clear area between stage and audience. [Photos and video of the concert show that the performers are only a few feet away from the audience with no barrier or security separating them.]
9) Provide an unreliable barely audible low fidelity sound system.
10) Ask the Hells Angels to act as 'security' guards.

Legend has it that the Hells Angels motorcycle gang was hired to provide general security for the event in exchange for $500 in free beer. While the free beer part of the story is true, the principals involved claim that the only security the Hells Angels were supposed to provide was to protect the generators and the stage. According to the road manager of the Stones' 1969 U.S. Tour, Sam Cutler, "The only agreement there ever was . . . the Angels would make sure nobody tampered with the generators, but that was the extent of it. But there was no way they were going to be the police force or anything like that. That's all bollocks." According to Cutler, the arrangement was that all the bands were supposed to share the $500 beer cost, "[but] the person who paid it was me, and I never got it back, to this day."

Whatever their intended role, the Angels did act as a self-appointed security force. As night fell, the Angels had been drinking their free beer all day in front of the stage, and most were very drunk. The crowd had also become antagonistic and unpredictable, attacking each other, the Angels, and the performers. Marty Balin of Jefferson Airplane was punched in the head and knocked unconscious by an Angel during the band's set. Mick Jagger had been punched in the head by a concertgoer within seconds of emerging from his helicopter.

During the Stones' set, Jagger was visibly intimidated by the unruly situation and urged everyone to "Just be cool down in the front there, don't push around." During the third song, "Sympathy for the Devil," a fight erupted in the front of the crowd at the foot of the stage, prompting the Stones to pause their set while the Angels restored order. After a lengthy pause and another appeal for calm, the band restarted the song and continued their set with less incident until the start of "Under My Thumb."

At that point, some of the Hells Angels got into a scuffle with Meredith Hunter, an 18-year-old African American male. He was dressed in a bright lime-green suit. He attempted to get onstage with other fans. One of the Hells Angels grabbed Hunter's head, punched him, and chased him back into the crowd. Hunter was reportedly enraged, irrational and so high he could barely walk. Hunter drew a long-barreled .22 caliber revolver from inside his jacket. Hells Angel Alan Passaro, seeing Hunter drawing the revolver, drew a knife from his belt and charged Hunter from the side, parrying Hunter's pistol with his left hand and stabbing him twice with his right hand, killing him. Passaro was himself only 21 at the time.

The incident was captured in the 1970 documentary about the 1969 Stones tour culminating in the Altamont concert, *Gimme Shelter*. The grainy footage lasts about 2 seconds. In the film sequence, the silhouette of a revolver is clearly seen against the grey-crocheted sweater and white shirt of Hunter's girlfriend Patty Bredahoft, who was trying to restrain him. Passaro is reported to have stabbed Hunter five times in the upper back, although only two stabs are visible in the footage. Witnesses also reported Hunter was stomped on by several Hells Angels while he was on the ground. Hunter's autopsy confirmed he was high on methamphetamine when he died. Passaro was arrested and tried for murder in the summer of 1971, but was acquitted after a jury viewed concert footage showing Hunter brandishing the revolver and concluded that Passaro had acted in self-defense.

The Stones were not aware of the stabbing when it occurred (although Jagger did stop the song to plead for calm) and finished their set. It was not known that the incident had been captured on film until the raw footage was screened more than a week later. The video of the incident can be seen on YouTube as well as Jagger watching the video for the first time.[14]

One of the bands who—along with the Rolling Stones—actually helped organize the event was supposed to come on stage to perform but did not, once the violence and mayhem increased. Who was that band?

Not surprisingly, given the location of the concert, the Grateful Dead. The Dead had been scheduled to play between Crosby, Stills, Nash & Young and the Rolling Stones, but after hearing about the Balin incident, they decided not to play and left the venue, citing the quickly degenerating security situation.

BRITISH WOODSTOCK

Commenting on Altamont, Keith Richards concluded that the real problem was young Americans versus the Brits: "I think it illustrates the difference between the two countries.... You can put half a million young English people together and they won't start killing each other. That's the difference." What was Richards referring to when he talked about "putting a half million young English people together"?

A free outdoor festival held in Hyde Park, London on July 5, 1969, headlined by the Stones and featuring various bands including King Crimson, in front of a crowd estimated at between 250,000 and 500,000 fans, rivaling Woodstock in attendance. The concert was called The Stones in the Park. The Stones were nervous about their performance for several reasons. First, it is little remembered that they had not performed in public for over two years. Second, Brian Jones had been fired by the remaining group members less than a month previously. He was to be replaced by guitarist Mick Taylor. Third, Jones had drowned in his pool, only two days before the Hyde Park concert.

For the first part of the show, Jagger was dressed all in white, including a dress, which looked like a Seinfeld puffy-shirt above the waist. The Stones played a 14-song set, and Jagger delivered a eulogy for Brian Jones. Some of the songs had never been performed live before, and by their own estimation, their performance was ragged. In 1971, in an interview with *Rolling Stone*, Richards said, "We played pretty bad until near the end, because we hadn't played for years.... Nobody minded, because they just wanted to hear us play again." Security was provided by none other than the Hells Angels, though there was little resemblance to their American counterparts. They performed their duties in exchange for a cup of tea. There were only twelve arrests on the day.[15]

BENEFIT CONCERTS

Benefit concerts are a different species of musical gathering than the above megaconcerts in the sense that their originating motivation is a charitable purpose, often a humanitarian crisis. Their objective can be to raise funds (Live Aid), influence legislation (Farm Aid), raise awareness of a particular issue (Live 8, not to be confused with Live Aid) or uplift a nation after a disaster (America: A Tribute to Heroes). While the motivation for these spectaculars may be different from other all-star rock concerts, the vibe at the two kinds of events is typically very similar.

It would not be accurate to suggest that rock benefit concerts were nonexistent during the Decade, but they certainly did not hit their stride until after the Decade was over.

Some of the biggest benefit concerts in the early years following the Decade included the following:

Year	Name	Cause	Stars Appearing
1979	Gift of Song	UNICEF	ABBA, Bee Gees, Olivia Newton John, John Denver, Earth Wind & Fire, Rita Coolidge, Rod Stewart, Donna Summer
1979	No Nukes	Oppose nuclear energy	Crosby, Stills and Nash, Bruce Springsteen, James Taylor, Carly Simon, Doobie Brothers, Tom Petty
1985	Live Aid	Ethiopian Famine	Queen, Elvis Costello, U2, the Who, Paul McCartney (London), Bob Dylan, Tom Petty, Madonna, Duran Duran (Philadelphia)
1986	Farm Aid	Relief to farmers	There have been 30 Farm Aid concerts since 1985. Willie Nelson, John Mellencamp and Neil Young have been staple performers.

The first major rock benefit concert did occur during the Decade however. What was the concert and who organized it?

The Concert for Bangladesh organized by George Harrison and Ravi Shankar. The event consisted of two concerts held at 2:30 and 8 pm on August 1, 1971, playing to a total of 40,000 people at Madison Square Garden in New York City. The shows were organized to raise international awareness and fund relief efforts for refugees from East Pakistan (now Bangladesh), following the Bangladesh Liberation War-related genocide. The concerts were followed by a best-selling live album, a boxed three-record set, and an Apple Films concert documentary, which opened in theaters in the spring of 1972. Performers included Ringo Starr, Bob Dylan, Eric Clapton, Billy Preston, Leon Russell, and the band Badfinger. The concert was Harrison's first live appearance before a paying audience since the Beatles' last live performance at Candlestick Park in San Francisco in 1966.[16]

While Starr appeared and performed, John Lennon and Paul McCartney did not. McCartney felt that there were still bad feelings among his ex-Beatle bandmates resulting from their breakup. Lennon, unlike McCartney, was originally scheduled to appear. He did not, however, and there were conflicting reasons why. According to one version, Harrison had insisted that Yoko Ono not perform with him and Lennon agreed to that. However, when Yoko heard about this arrangement, she and Lennon had an argument about it and so he declined to appear. According to a second version, Lennon was upset at Harrison that Yoko was not invited to perform at all. This was Yoko's version. According to a third, this coming from Lennon himself after the fact, "I just didn't feel like it. We were in the Virgin Islands and I certainly wasn't going to be rehearsing in New York, then going back to the Virgin Islands, then coming back up to New York and singing." Nevertheless, the event marked the first time that two Beatles played together onstage since 1966.

The concerts raised close to $250,000 for Bangladesh relief, which may not seem like a lot today but was far in excess of the $25,000 that Shankar was hoping to raise.[17]

CHAPTER 6

I'm with the Band (Groupies)

The focus of this book is more on the singers, songwriters and musicians than on those whose lives may intersect with these performers. Nevertheless, many who fall into that category have led fascinating lives in their own right. One such group is groupies, or less pejoratively (if one considers that pejorative), women who have dated multiple rock stars. The most famous ones were often immortalized in song. **Here are profiles of six notable women and their names. Identify which woman fits which profile.**

1. *High Times* magazine wrote that "if there was such a thing as a female Forrest Gump of rock 'n roll, she would be it." As the dust jacket of her autobiography states: she "wasn't famous. She wasn't even almost famous. But she was there." She was one of the few people who was up on the roof with the Beatles watching their January 30, 1969 rooftop concert (besides Yoko Ono and Mo Starkey, Ringo's wife at the time). She was in the studio when the Beatles recorded the White Album, *Abbey Road* and *Let It Be*. She sang in the chorus when Paul McCartney recorded "Hey Jude." She is the subject of Leon Russell's song "Pisces Apple Lady," which he wrote to woo her. She is also the subject of a George Harrison song which actually has her last name in the title. She worked with the Rolling Stones as their personal assistant on their 1972 tour and made a drug run for Keith Richards. She is "the woman down the hall" in Joni Mitchell's song "Coyote." She is pictured on the back of the Rolling Stones album *Exile on Main Street*. She had intimate relationships with Ringo Starr, Mick Jagger, Bob Dylan and others. However, unlike some women who had no professional connection with the men they slept with, she actually worked for the Beatles as a kind of general factotum. She was also employed by virtually every group and artist with whom she associated thereafter, including the Rolling Stones, Eric Clapton, Crosby, Stills, Nash & Young, Bob Dylan, Linda Ronstadt, Fleetwood Mac, John Denver, Jennifer Warnes and others.

2. This woman's Wikipedia bio describes her as "an occasional backup singer, rock groupie, drug dealer and legal secretary who served 15 months in the California

state prison system for injecting John Belushi with a fatal dose of heroin and cocaine in 1982." She was intimate with multiple members of the Band, including Rick Danko and Levon Helm. Richard Manuel offered to marry her but she turned him down. She became pregnant with a child who was called "the Band baby" because its paternity was unclear. She then had a tumultuous affair with Gordon Lightfoot and he commented that his #1 song "Sundown" was written with her in mind. Though married at the time, he had a 3-year relationship with her and when she went out without him, he was extremely jealous.

3. This woman had a reputation for having sex (and especially oral sex) with every rocker who passed through Little Rock, Arkansas. Her list includes stars both from the Decade and after. By her own acknowledgment, her list of conquests includes Don Henley, Eddie Van Halen, David Lee Roth, Sammy Hagar, Mick Fleetwood, John McVie, Lindsey Buckingham, Gene Simmons, Paul Stanley and Peter Criss of Kiss, Huey Lewis, Neil Diamond, Peter Frampton, Stephen Stills, Graham Nash, Willie Nelson, Frank Zappa, Paul Schaffer, Leslie West of Mountain, the entire Chicago band, all of ZZ Top, all of the Allman Brothers Band, and many drummers including Keith Moon, John Bonham, Alex Van Halen, Steppenwolf drummer Jerry Edmonton, and Three Dog Night drummer Floyd Sneed. Most famously, she is mentioned by name in the 1973 #1 song "We're An American Band" by Grand Funk Railroad in reference to her doing "her act" when the band was passing through Little Rock.

4. According to Wikipedia, this woman is an "artist and self-described 'recovering groupie' who creates plaster casts of famous persons' penises and breasts. [She] began her career in 1968 by casting penises of rock musicians." She was with Jimi Hendrix, Frank Zappa, Noel Redding of the Jimi Hendrix Experience, Zal Yanovsky of the Lovin' Spoonful, Eric Burdon and others. In "Five Short Minutes," Jim Croce sings: "She casted me in plaster while I sang her a tune." Kiss wrote a song about her called Plaster Caster.

5. This woman has been called "perhaps the most well-known groupie of all time." She had affairs with Mick Jagger, Jimmy Page, Keith Moon, Gram Parsons, Waylon Jennings, Chris Hillman, Noel Redding, and Jim Morrison. She has written five books, several of which are memoirs about her exploits and her life, including I'm with the Band: Confessions of a Groupie; Backstage Secrets of Rock Muses and Supergroupies; Take Another Piece of my Heart: A Groupie Grows Up, One Night Bands; and Rock Bottom: Dark Moments in Music Babylon.

6. This woman dated Paul Cowsill of the Cowsills, Mick Jagger, Iggy Pop, David Bowie, Elvis Costello, Jimmy Page, Steven Tyler and Todd Rundgren. She is

the mother of Liv Tyler, Steven Tyler's daughter. She was the November 1974 Playmate of the Month.

a. Cynthia Albritton; b. Cathy Smith; c. Pamela Des Barres; d. Connie Hamzy; e. Bebe Buell; f. Chris O'Dell

Answers: 1.f; 2.b; 3.d.; 4.a; 5.c; 6.e. Hamzy is the "sweet sweet Connie" mentioned in "We're An American Band." As for Buell, unlike some women who have been with countless rock stars (and often seem proud of it), she told *New York* magazine that that is not the case with her. "My reputation is so overblown. I can count the number of men I've been with on two hands; it just seems like a lot because you recognize their names. I was a free agent. When I got a paycheck, I went to Bergdorf and I bought my own clothes. There were no rock stars buying me my clothes." The George Harrison song mentioned is called "Miss O'Dell."[1]

CHAPTER 7

That's Not a Real Band! (Manufactured or Fictitious Bands)

Many of our favorite songs from the Decade come not from organically formed bands, but rather bands that were either "manufactured" by studio executives or fictitious, in that there was no real band behind the songs that made them famous. This chapter will examine some of these bands and their famous songs.

The intended A-side of this song was called "Sweet Laura Lee." There is likely not one person in a million to whom that song would mean anything. As for the intended B-side, it became the #1 song in the country for two weeks in 1969 and was the last song of the 1960s to be #1 for more than one week. When the song was recorded, there was no band involved, so as with other "manufactured bands," once the song became a surprise hit ("surprise" being an understatement), one had to be quickly created (and named) both to create an album and tour behind the song. As a first hint, the name of the band created was called Steam. As a second hint, the song is often heard at sporting events. What is the name of this intended B-side song?

"Na Na Hey Hey Kiss Him Goodbye." How did this song come about? Unusually. In the early 1960s, Paul Leka, Gary DeCarlo and Dale Frashuer were in a band called the Chateaus and wrote a primitive version of the song called "Kiss Him Goodbye." (Leka later cowrote and coproduced *Green Tambourine*, which was a big hit for the Lemon Pipers.) In 1968, DeCarlo decided to record "Sweet Laura Lee," a ballad written by Larry Weiss, who wrote *Rhinestone Cowboy*. Frausher suggested that they use "Kiss Him Goodbye" as the B-side. According to Leka, "I said we should put a chorus to it to make it longer. I started writing while I was sitting at the piano going 'na, na, na, na, na, na, na, na' . . . Everything was 'na na' when you didn't have a lyric." Someone else added "hey hey." While intended as the B-side to "Sweet Laura Lee," when the Mercury executives heard the song, they loved it and decided to issue it as an A-side song and it was credited to the then non-existent band Steam.

It has been written that the three songwriters were totally embarrassed by the song and that they created the band name Steam to hide their identities. However, DeCarlo told Songfacts that this was not the case.[1]

In 1967, the Beatles released *Sgt. Pepper's Lonely Hearts Club Band* **and** *Magical Mystery Tour.* **The Rolling Stones released** *Between the Buttons* **and** *Their Satanic Majesties Request. Sgt. Pepper's* **was the #1 selling album for 15 consecutive weeks. Despite that, one band sold more albums then both of those groups** *combined* **in that year. Who was that band?**

The Monkees. *More of the Monkees*, their second full-length album, was released on January 9, 1967 and displaced the band's debut album, *The Monkees*, from the top of the *Billboard* 200 chart and remained at #1 for 18 weeks. Combined, the first two Monkees albums were at the top of the *Billboard* chart for 31 consecutive weeks. The Monkees are the only band in history to have four #1 albums in the same year (1967), namely *The Monkees* (released in 1966 but still #1 on the charts in 1967), *More of the Monkees*, *Headquarters* and *Pisces, Aquarius, Capricorn & Jones, Ltd.*

The Monkees are often remembered as a "fake band." There is some evidence to support this. For example, the band was not formed organically, but rather, each of its members was recruited to star in a television show about a band. In that sense, they were a manufactured band who didn't know each other before they were formed, and therefore some called them "The Prefab Four," a nod to the Beatles being the original Fab Four. The show's producers already had Davy Jones in mind as one of the band members. On September 8–10, 1965, *Daily Variety* and the *Hollywood Reporter* ran an ad to cast the remainder of the band/cast members for the TV show: "Madness!! Auditions. Folk & Roll Musicians-Singers for acting roles in new TV series. Running Parts for 4 insane boys, age 17–21. Want spirited Ben Frank's types. Have courage to work. Must come down for interview." Out of 437 applicants, the other three chosen for the band/cast of the TV show were Michael Nesmith, Peter Tork and Micky Dolenz. One of the ones not chosen was Stephen Stills, who nevertheless mentioned the opportunity to Tork.

Besides being recruited to play a band in a TV show, none of the Monkees wrote or played any of the instruments on either of their first two albums, *The Monkees* and *More of the Monkees*.

Nevertheless, there is also unfairness to the charge of being a fake band. First, they sang vocals on all of their songs. Second, they all had musical ability. Peter Tork played keyboard and bass guitar. Nesmith was an accomplished guitarist and songwriter. Most notably, he wrote "Different Drum," which became a hit for Linda Ronstadt. Mickey Dolenz learned to play the drums for the band, and was also the lead singer on many of their songs, including their #1 hits "Last Train to Clarksville" and "I'm a Believer," and also on "Pleasant Valley Sunday," which reached #11 on the *Billboard* charts. Nesmith said it was Dolenz's voice that gave the group their distinctive sound. While Jones was not as accomplished musician as Tork and Nesmith, he too played a variety of instruments and handled lead vocals on a number of songs, including the #1 hit "Daydream Believer."

The Monkees were irritated that all of their first two albums had been issued with no input from them, save their vocals. They were especially unhappy about the release of their second album, *More of the Monkees*. First, they were not even aware that was going to be released and they had no input as to the songs selected. Second, they had to buy their copies at a record store. Third, they were offended by the liner notes, which praised the team of songwriters before mentioning, almost as an afterthought, the names of the group members themselves. Mike Nesmith said it was "probably the worst record in the history of the world." Obviously the record-buying public did not agree. They lobbied Don Kirshner, who was the supervisor both for their television series and their record releases, for more involvement in all aspects of the record-making process on future albums. Kirshner was uninterested in meeting their demands and tensions between him and the group worsened. He was dismissed in 1967. In any event, the group eventually did play instruments on the albums released thereafter, starting with *Headquarters*, released in May 1967.

Perhaps the real moneymaker among those having a connection with the group was Mike Nesmith's mother, Bette Nesmith Graham. She invented a typewriter correction fluid later known commercially as Liquid Paper. Over the next 25 years she built the Liquid Paper Corporation into a multimillion dollar international company, which she sold to Gillette in 1979 for $48 million.[2]

There was a song released by a band in 1969. The singers were Ron Dante and Toni Wine. The song was written by Dante and Jeff Barry. The musicians on the song were Ron Ron Frangipane (keyboard), Chuck Rainey (bass), Gary Chester (drums), Dave Appell (guitar), Harry Amanatian (guitar), and Ray Stevens (handclaps). The song spent four weeks at the top of the *Billboard* Hot 100 chart and was the #1 single of the entire year, beating out the Rolling Stones, the Beatles, Creedence Clearwater Revival and everyone else. The song lists at number 73 on *Billboard's Greatest Songs of All Time*. What is the name of the song and what is the name of the band that recorded it? (As a hint, the "band" was comprised of fictional characters.)

The song is "Sugar, Sugar" and the band is the Archies, based on the comic book. This song has been covered by some surprising artists given its very bubble-gummy nature, including Bob Marley and the Wailers, Gladys Knight and the Pips and Wilson Pickett (whose version actually hit #25 on the *Billboard* Hot 100 and, even more surprisingly, #4 on the R&B chart).

And now for the truly important question: among the characters in the *Archie* comic book series, who played what role in the band?

Archie: lead vocals/lead guitar
Reggie: bass guitar/backing vocals
Jughead: drums
Betty: tambourine
Veronica: organ
Hot Dog: mascot/conductor

The original 1969 cartoon video of the song can be seen on YouTube.[3]

There is actually a direct link between the Monkees and the Archies and that link was Don Kirshner. As noted above, Kirshner, known as "The Man with the Golden Ear," wanted to keep a good thing going with the Monkees, which was essentially that they would sing the songs and not have much input beyond that, whether in terms of playing instruments or songwriting. They all bristled at Kirshner pulling all the strings and having them acting as hired puppets, especially Mike Nesmith. In reflecting on the breakup years later, Kirshner was bitter, but gloating at the same time: "I had a song in my possession called 'Sugar, Sugar' which I felt after 'I'm A Believer' could be one of the biggest songs of all time. I gave the boys [$1 million in four royalty checks for 'I'm a Believer'] which they took and I gave them the gold records Mike and Peter said ['Sugar, Sugar' is] a piece of junk. We're never going to do this song. Mike proceeded to put his fist through the wall at the Beverly Hills Hotel and as we say, they rest is history." As for the beauty of "managing" the Archies, Kirshner said: "I [wound] up with a group that didn't talk back. I don't have to take any nonsense. I can do it my way. It sold over 10 million copies and outsold 'Honky Tonk Women.'"

Songwriter Jeff Barry was also proud of the song: "The song was based purely on the music. There wasn't any supporting act there bumping and grinding and being cute and sexy or appealing in any way. They didn't exist. It was sold totally through the ears."[4]

On "Sugar, Sugar," Ron Dante sang lead vocals and Toni Wine sang "I'm gonna make your life so sweet!" Wine's name is not familiar to most people even if her voice is familiar, based on this song. However, in addition to being a background singer (Gene Pitney's "It Hurts to Be In Love" and Willie Nelson's "Always On My Mind"), she is also a talented songwriter in her own right. She wrote "A Groovy Kind of Love" with Carol Bayer Sager when she was only 17 years old and the Mindbenders had a #2 hit with it. She also cowrote the hit song

"Candida," by the group Dawn. However, just as there was no actual band called the Archies, there was also no actual band called Dawn, at least at first.

In 1970, Hank Medress was producing a song called "Candida," written by Toni Wine and Irwin Levine for Bell Records. Medress believed that "an ethnic feel" would suit the song well. He asked his friend Tony Orlando, whose heritage is Puerto Rican and Greek, to perform the lead vocal. However, Orlando was managing the music publishing division of Columbia Records and he was concerned that performing on a Bell Records single could be a conflict of interest that could jeopardize his job at Columbia. Medress reassured him by saying they would make up a band name for the release, and that nobody would know who the singer was. Orlando finally agreed, partly because he believed the song would be unsuccessful and would not attract any attention. He sang his lead vocal over previously recorded tracks background vocal by Wine, Jay Siegel of the Tokens ("The Lion Sleeps Tonight"), and others.

Wine picks up the story from there:

> So there we were, Tony put his lead on, and the record was released by this group called Dawn which had been named after one of the Bell Records promotion men's daughter. So Dawn came out with "Candida" and just incredibly, it was this huge record. And we then wound up doing the album. And of course, there was no Dawn, meaning Telma and Joyce. The entire first album, really, was Tony and myself [and a few other singers]. It was after the first album, which included "Knock Three Times" . . . that Dawn became a true reality, Joyce and Telma and Tony, and they became Tony Orlando and Dawn. At that point, after "Candida" and "Knock," Tony was not worried about losing his day job.

With Telma Hopkins and Joyce Vincent Wilson singing backup, the group was officially first called Dawn featuring Tony Orlando before becoming Tony Orlando and Dawn. They had two #1 hits and a #3 hit after that during the Decade, namely "Tie a Yellow Ribbon Around the Ole Oak Tree" (#1, 1973), "Say, Has Anybody Seen My Sweet Gypsy Rose" (#3, 1973), and "He Don't Love You (Like I Love You)" (#1, 1975).[5]

Continuing with the bands who were not necessarily what they represented, we have the Partridge Family. The Partridge Family television show consisted of Shirley Jones playing keyboards, David Cassidy playing guitars and banjo, Susan Dey on piano and Hammond organ, Danny Bonaduce on bass guitar, Jeremy Gelbwaks on drums (later Brian Forster) and Suzanne Crough on percussion. Who if any among the Partridge Family actually played instruments on their recordings?

None of them.

Who if any among the Partridge Family actually sang on their recordings?

David Cassidy sang lead vocal and Shirley Jones was a background vocalist. Cassidy was Jones's stepson in real life.

The Partridge Family had a #1 song. What was it?

"I Think I Love You," released in 1970. Incidentally, the only actual mother and son to have sung on #1 hit sings (as opposed to a TV mother and son like Jones and Cassidy on *The Partridge Family*) are Jones (on this song) and her son Shaun Cassidy, who had a #1 hit in 1977 with "Da Doo Ron Ron."

A real family band was the inspiration for the Partridge Family. This band had a #2 song which was first heard in a Broadway musical. What was the song and who was the band?

"Hair" by the Cowsills. The group consisted of six brothers and a sister and their mother Barbara (although no more than five of the brothers were ever with the band at once). They had a second song that also reached #2 entitled "The Rain, The Park and Other Things." Because the song title is not heard in the song lyrics, the title may be unfamiliar to many. However, this would qualify as one of those "if you heard the song you would recognize it" songs. It is also sometimes known as "Flowers in her Hair."

The 1967 Grammy winner for Best Contemporary Recording was recorded by studio musicians. When it became a surprise international hit (reaching #1 on two separate occasions on the *Billboard* Hot 100), an actual group was assembled and then toured as the New Vaudeville Band, which was totally different from the session players. What was the name of the song?

"Winchester Cathedral." The song was written by producer/songwriter Geoff Stephens. The singer was John Carter, who sang through his hands to simulate the sound of a megaphone (as on old Rudy Vallee records). "Winchester Cathedral" was an enormous hit. The song hit #1 on December 3, 1966, displacing "You Keep Me Hangin' On" by the Supremes. After a one-week stay there, it was knocked off the summit by the Beach Boys' "Good Vibrations," only to rebound to the top spot the following week. After two additional weeks, it was knocked off the top for good by "I'm a Believer" by the Monkees. Stephens suddenly needed a band for touring purposes and put together a brand-new group, the New Vaudeville Band, for that purpose. They did release several albums under that name, with the first naturally being titled *Winchester Cathedral*. (Although the recorded version of the song that became a hit is also attributed to the New Vaudeville Band on the 45, there was no actual band by that name at the time.)[6]

CHAPTER 8

A Poll Not Worth Winning (Worst Songs)

From a singer's or songwriter's standpoint, the good thing about singing or writing a song that shows up on many "worst song" lists is that the song was almost assuredly a hit song. A forgotten song or one that was never noticed in the first place is never going to "win" (if that's the right word) a worst song poll. For this reason, I suspect that if many singers or songwriters were told that a song they were about to release would forever be considered a strong contender in future worst song polls, that would make them more excited about the prospects of the song, not less.

Of course, determining what songs are considered the "worst" of any particular period is obviously a subjective (and often a somewhat tongue-in-cheek) exercise. Nevertheless, there are certain songs that appear over and over both in polls of public opinion (including the *Rolling Stone* Readers Poll of the Worst Songs of the 1960s and 1970s) and in the eyes of music critics. Here, we will look at a few.

This song "won" a 2006 CNN poll for worst song of all time and apparently the vote was not close. A major reason is that many considered the lyrics offensive to women. Matthew Wilkening of AOL Radio, who ranked the song at #48 on his list of the 100 Worst Songs Ever, wrote: "Way to make 'your' woman instantly regret deciding to embark on this wonderful adventure with you, buddy!" Of course, the song was a huge smash and hit #1 on the *Billboard* Hot 100 in 1974. What was the song?

"You're Having My Baby" by Paul Anka. In addition to referring to the baby as "my" instead of "our," Anka also praises the woman's choice to not have it aborted, because that was "a lovely way" of expressing her love for him. The National Organization for Women gave Anka the "Keep Her in Her Place" award during "its annual putdown of male chauvinism" on Women's Equality Day, and *Ms.* magazine "awarded" Anka their "Male Chauvinistic Pig of the Year" award.

Notwithstanding the burgeoning women's liberation movement and songs such as "I Am Woman" by Helen Reddy and "Harper Valley PTA" by Jeannie C. Riley, there were some other songs from the Decade where the attitudes of the (generally male) songwriters towards women seem hard to believe from a remove of many decades. These songs might at least be eligible for a "worst lyrics" category. In the 1969 song "Take a Letter Maria," R.B. Greaves dictates a letter to his secretary Maria. He tells his wife that he is going to be leaving her. (As if his secretary wasn't busy enough doing actual work! Although in fairness, his wife was having an affair.) In the 1971 Cornelius Brothers song "Treat Her Like a Lady," the title itself sounds great, but we are reminded that "strange as it seems, you know you can't treat a woman mean." In the 1967 hit song "It Must Be Him" by Vikki Carr, the singer's man has repeatedly done wrong by her. Yet, when the phone rings, she will be suicidal if he is not the one calling.

Some of the pre-decade songs are even worse, such as the 1962 Crystals song where the title says it all: "He Hit Me (and It Felt Like a Kiss.)" Amazingly this song was cowritten by Carole King and her then husband Gerry Goffin. It is hard to imagine Carole King, circa the *Tapestry* album from 1971, writing such a song. On the other hand, maybe Goffin penned those lyrics himself. He was also the cowriter (this time with Jack Keller) of the 1962 song by the girl group Cookies, "Girls Grow Up Faster Than Boys," in which the girls proudly advise us that they are everything girls should be: "36–21–35."[1]

This very successful song also appears on many worst song lists. It is in the top 10 of the *Rolling Stone* Readers Poll of the Worst Songs of the 1970s, with *Rolling Stone* writer Andy Greene calling it "an incredibly, stunningly crappy song." It is included on the 1998 Rhino Records compilation album '70s Party Killers, consisting of what Rhino considered the worst songs of the Decade. Matthew Wilkening of AOL Radio also had this song on his list of the 100 Worst Songs Ever, writing: "The whiny, caterwauling vocals on this chorus must be heard once (never twice!) to be believed." It has been "a target of parody and ridicule for embodying what are perceived by many as the most insipid lyrical and musical qualities of 1970s soft rock music."[2]

As a more specific hint to the song, in an interview, Julie Andrews said that she was once asked to sing this song, but she couldn't do it, and had to ask for something else. She then sang a few bars of the song anyway, with its famous "whoa, whoa, whoa" chorus, to the audience's great amusement. Later, during the question and answer period, when someone from the audience claimed to be the creator of the song, Andrews crossed her forearms across her face. What is the song?

"Feelings" by Morris Albert. When the song was first released, songwriting credit was attributed to Albert himself (born Maurício Alberto Kaisermann). However, the melody to the song was lifted directly from a 1956 song by Loulou Gasté. When Gasté first heard Albert's song, he promptly sued Albert for copyright infringement. A jury agreed with Gasté that there was "striking similarity" between the music of the two songs and awarded him seven-eighths of all royalties (with Albert getting the rest for writing the lyrics). The jury's finding was affirmed by the Second Circuit Court of Appeals.[3]

The words "worst song" and "Beatles" are rarely heard together, but within the band's own oeuvre, obviously some songs are considered better than others. While any "worst song" designation is obviously subjective, it is fair to say that one or both of two songs in particular show up consistently on most lists of the Beatles' worst songs. As a hint to start, both tracks appear on the White Album.

The first song was voted the voted worst song of all time in a 2004 online poll in England. *New Musical Express* website editor Luke Lewis has argued that the Beatles recorded "a surprising amount of ropy old toss," singling out this song in particular. Tom Rowley in the *Telegraph* named the track as a "reasonable choice" for derision. It was also included in *Blender* magazine's 2004 list, "50 Worst Songs Ever!" The *Houston Press* named it one of the 10 worst Beatles songs. CNN journalist Todd Leopold reported in 2006 that John Lennon "loathed" the song (which gives a hint that Lennon did not write it).

As for the second song, while some critics praised it for its cutting-edge nature, most did not, and fans have been almost unanimous in their dislike of the song. In his book *Can't Buy Me Love*, Jonathan Gould wrote that the song "is an embarrassment that stands like a black hole [on] the White Album. . . . It is a track that neither invites nor rewards close attention." The *New Rolling Stone Album Guide* called the song "justly maligned." The toptens.com website lists this song as the worst Beatles song, as do ultimateclassicrock.com, ranker.com and others. It also appears on the top 10 worst Beatles song lists of the *Independent*, the CBS radio station Q105 and others. Interestingly, just as John Lennon said he "loathed" the first song, Paul McCartney lobbied (obviously unsuccessfully) to keep the second song off of the White Album, which gives you an idea as to who it might be by.

As a final hint, while the first song above was a very recognizable hit, reaching #1 in several countries, the second song is virtually never played on the radio and would not be recognized except by diehard Beatles fans. What are the two songs?

The first song is "Ob-La-Di, Ob-La-Da," a McCartney composition, and the second is "Revolution 9," written by Lennon.[4]

This song was written in 1929, but this singer's cover, accompanying himself on the ukulele, hit the top 20 in 1968.

"Tiptoe Through the Tulips" by Tiny Tim. *Vanity Fair* called his marriage to Miss Vicki on the *Tonight Show* "the moment reality television was born." It was the most-watched event in the history of late-night television until Carson's final show, on May 22, 1992. While of course known for his distinctive falsetto, Tiny Tim also occasionally sang in his normal baritone register. An example would be his rendition of Irvin Berlin's anti-war song "Stay Down Here Where You Belong" on his debut album *God Bless Tiny Tim*. He also performed "I Got You Babe" both on that album and in concert, singing both Sonny's part in a lower voice and Cher's part in his falsetto.[5]

Rolling Stone **rated this song the second worst song of the '60s, calling it "a shitty, shitty, saccharine love song about a dead girl that America fell in love with in 1968." In 2006, CNN.com called it "the worst song of all time." It has placed similarly high (or low depending on one's perspective) in a number of other polls as well. However, that did not prevent it from being a massive hit. It was released as a single in the U.S. in 1968 and spent five weeks at #1 the *Billboard* Hot 100, from April 7 to May 11, and three weeks atop *Billboard's* Hot Country Singles chart. It was written by Bobby Russell, who also wrote O.C. Smith's "Little Green Apples" and Vicki Lawrence's "The Night the Lights Went Out in Georgia." Who is the singer and what is the song?**

"Honey" by Bobby Goldsboro. The song was covered by many artists although virtually all of them were within the year following the release of the song, at which point the covers essentially came to an abrupt halt. Those who covered the song include Björn Ulvaeus, later of ABBA, who sang a Swedish-language version called "Raring," Gary Puckett and the Union Gap, Andy Williams and Tammy Wynette.[6]

For those who don't care for bubblegum music, virtually any of those songs could be considered among the worst '60s songs. According to the *Rolling Stone* poll however, this one from 1968 "won." As was often the case with these kinds of songs, though purportedly performed by a "group," that group was in reality simply a collection of studio musicians brought together to record the song. The song was cowritten by Joey Levine, who sang "Life Is a Rock (But the Radio Rolled Me)" by Reunion. The song ranked #2 in *Dave Barry's Book of Bad Songs*. *Rolling Stone* called it "absolutely terrible." Even if one is a fan of bubblegum music, it's easy not to care for this song. It is however a favorite of Homer Simpson. What is the song and who is it by?

"Yummy Yummy Yummy" by the Ohio Express.

This song is #1 in Dave Barry's "Book of Bad Songs." It is #3 on the *Rolling Stone* poll of the worst songs of the 1960s (although the editors defend it as "not a terrible song").

Time magazine included it in its 2011 list of Top 10 Songs with Silly Lyrics. The lengthy song reached #2 on the *Billboard* Hot 100 in 1968 and is performed by someone who is thought of as an actor far more than as a singer (especially remembered for playing King Arthur in the 1967 film *Camelot*). Oddly, he sang the words wrong by always adding a possessive plural to the title. As a further hint, the song was written by Jimmy Webb. What is the song and who made it famous?

"MacArthur Park" by Richard Harris (or, as Harris sings it, "MacArthur's Park"). The musicians on the original studio recording included Wrecking Crew members Hal Blaine on drums, Larry Knechtel on keyboards, Joe Osborn on bass guitar, and Mike Deasy on guitar, along with Webb himself on harpsichord.

Perhaps the reason that the song gets so much negative (or satirical) attention is because of the oddity of the lyrics, especially the verse that refers to the cake being left out in the rain and at the singer's anguish that it took so long to make it and that he will never have the recipe again! If the lyrics were sung perhaps in a jaunty manner, or otherwise gave some indication that the singer was aware of the goofiness of the words (or if the music was light-hearted), that would be one thing, but in Harris's melodramatic (one might say overwrought) rendition, there is no sense of that at all, thereby creating an odd juxtaposition between the actual words and the tone of the song. The same is true of Donna Summer's 1978 version of the song, which did even better than Harris's version, by topping the *Billboard* Hot 100. Of all of Webb's hit songs, Summer's version of this song was the only one that reached the top.[7]

This song is an English-language adaptation of the song "Le Moribond" by Belgian singer-songwriter Jacques Brel, with lyrics by American singer-poet Rod McKuen. The original French-language song is a rather bitter sardonic ballad, in which the singer, as he is dying, gives backhanded farewells to his adulterous wife and her various lovers. (There is a great subtitled video on YouTube of Brel performing this song in 1964.) However, this Canadian artist's English language reworking of the song was turned into a sentimental farewell (some say cloyingly so) to friends and family, with all references to adultery removed. On the positive side (at least for the artist), the song became one of the biggest selling singles of all time, with sales estimates ranging from six million to 14 million. It was also a #1 song on the *Billboard* 100 in 1974. On the negative side, it is often held up as an example of bad music, and according to a 2006 CNN poll, it was voted the fifth worst song of all time. What is the song and who is the artist?

"Seasons in the Sun" by Canadian artist Terry Jacks. Jacks claimed that he became aware of the song not in its original French version but from an earlier English-language version recorded by the Kingston Trio in 1963. The Trio's version is somewhat of a middle ground between the darkness and bitterness of the McKuen version and Jacks's maudlin version, although it clearly makes reference to the singer's cheating wife. James Sullivan called Jacks's song "an unsurpassed nadir of pop music." In *Dave Barry's Book of Bad Songs*, he wrote that he "would rather undergo a tax audit" than listen to this song.[8]

This song was written by Willis Alan Ramsey and was first recorded by him in 1972. It was then recorded by America in 1973 and their cover was successful enough to be included on their greatest hits album. However, the most successful version of this song hit #4 in 1976 for Captain and Tenille and it is that version that gets particular scorn. The song appears on a number of worst song lists, including the 2006 CNN poll, undoubtedly due to its bizarre subject matter. In a 2012 interview Gerry Beckley of America said: "It's a polarizing little number. After concerts, some people tell us they can't believe we didn't play it, while others go out of their way to thank us for not performing it."[9] What is the song?

"Muskrat Love." The original title of the song was "Muskrat Candlelight." When the Captain and Tenille performed the song at a White House dinner for Queen Elizabeth II, according to *People* magazine, "they somehow grossed out a few guests while singing their cutesy ditty about anthropomorphic muskrats. One woman, Lady Keith ... took it upon herself to sniff that the song 'was not suitable for the Queen.'" but the idea of a song about muskrats making love did not bother Toni Tenille: "Only a person with a dirty mind would see something wrong. It's a gentle Disneyesque kind of song."[10]

The last "worst song" might have "won" all of the worst song surveys except that it is not nearly as well remembered as the other songs we have considered. It does however appear on Dave Barry's list. That said, it was on the *Billboard* charts for eight weeks in 1971, peaking at #17. It was written by Rupert Holmes who wrote and performed the #1 hit "Escape (The Piña Colada Song)" in 1979 and the song "Him," which reached #6 in 1980. It was recorded by a group called the Buoys. The song is about cannibalism. Three men are trapped in a mine that caved in. Two of them survive by eating the third. As a hint, the name of the song is the first name of the one who was eaten. What is the name of the song?

"Timothy." In the last verse, the singer notes that he and his friend were rescued the next morning, that his stomach was full, and that no one ever found Timothy. In fairness to Holmes, he was actually trying to write a song that would get banned, and since the song became a hit, it was mission accomplished. He wrote the song when he was 20. He had a friend who worked as an engineer for Scepter Records and he got the executives there to agree to let them record one song, but they would not promote it. Holmes therefore decided to write a song that would get banned to promote controversy.

Holmes added that kids knew what the song was about and would request radio stations to play it, which they did. Once stations figured out the subject matter, they pulled it, which led to a kind of ongoing tug of war: Says Holmes: "The kids would call in and say 'Why'd you pull the song off the air,' and they'd say, 'Because it's disgusting, you shouldn't be listening to stuff like that.' Well, all you have to do is tell a teenage kid that he shouldn't be listening to something because it's disgusting and vile and loathsome, and he'll demand it. So the record, unlike 'Piña Colada,' which vaulted up the charts, went up like one or two digits every week. It was on the charts forever. Stations were playing it, kids were clamoring for it, it would move up the charts, then the station would pull it, the kids would clamor more and some other station would go on it to satisfy that demand. It just kept going up the charts."[11]

CHAPTER 9

Name that Act (Specific Artists)

This chapter will focus on interesting aspects of the lives of specific bands and solo artists who achieved success during the Decade.

This songwriter achieved stardom in an unusual way. The initial album by him and his partner, released in late 1964, flopped and he moved out of the country. A year later, without his permission or even his knowledge, a record producer on his label took an acoustic song that appeared on that initial album and overdubbed the recording with drums, electric guitar and electric bass. The modified version of the song was then re-released on the next album of the songwriter and his partner, released in 1965. Within months of its re-release, it was the #1 song in the country and the rest, as they say is history. Who is the artist and what is the song? For bonus points: The name of the song which is the answer to the above question is *almost* the same as the name of the album on which it appears (the second time), but not exactly. What is the name of the album?

The artist is Paul Simon, the song is "The Sound of Silence" and the album is *The Sounds of Silence.* The song originally appeared on the debut album of Simon and Garfunkel, entitled *Wednesday Morning, 3 AM,* which was released in 1964. It did not sell well upon its release and Simon moved to England. In New York, a record producer noticed that "The Sound of Silence" off that album had been attracting listener attention at stations along the East Coast. On a whim, he decided to capitalize on the interest by fortifying the track with a rock combo. There was only one small problem: though still contracted to Columbia, for the time being, Simon & Garfunkel were no longer a working entity. That didn't deter the producer. One night, while in the studio working on "Like a Rolling Stone" by Bob Dylan, he asked the studio musicians present to stay in the studio for one more song. It was then they added the additional instruments and breathed new life into Simon's acoustic classic, unknown to Simon himself. In 1999, BMI named "The Sound of Silence" as the 18th-most performed song of the 20th century.[1]

In a 2000 interview with Terry Gross of National Public Radio, Simon explained how it came to pass that he owned the rights to all of his songs, which was very unusual in that era: "It was just when I was coming out of college. They offered to pay me $150 a week which seemed like so much money that I really couldn't refuse it but I was probably never more miserable. My job was to take the songs that this huge publishing company owned and go around to record companies . . . and see if any of their artists wanted to record the [songs]. I worked for them for about six months and never got a song placed, but I did give them a couple of my songs that I was writing because I felt so guilty about taking their checks. . . . Then I got into an argument with them and I said, 'Look, I quit, I don't want to work here anymore and I'm not giving you my new song. See ya.' And the song that I had just written was 'The Sound of Silence.' I thought, 'I'll just publish this myself,' and from that point on I owned my own songs, so that was a lucky argument."[2]

This band had five consecutive U.S. top 10 albums released between 1971 and 1975 (one per year). Despite that impressive accomplishment, they never had one top 10 single in the U.S. In fact, other than one song which reached #12 in 1974, nothing else reached the top 50 during the Decade—largely because their best-known songs were not released as singles. One of their songs starts with a reference to an apparently homeless man "eyeing little girls with bad intent." Who is the band and what is that song?

The band is Jethro Tull and the song is "Aqualung." Despite the repulsive image conjured by the opening lyrics, singer and songwriter Ian Anderson has said that the song was in part to draw attention to the plight of the homeless: "It's about our reaction, of guilt, distaste, awkwardness and confusion, all these things that we feel when we are confronted with the reality of the homeless. You see someone who's clearly in desperate need of some help, whether it's a few coins or the contents of your wallet, and you blank them out."

Incidentally, Jethro Tull was a real person, and a famous one at that, at least in his day. He was an English agricultural pioneer (1674–1741) who perfected a horse-drawn seed drill in 1701 that economically sowed the seeds in neat rows. He later developed a horse-drawn hoe. His methods helped to provide the basis for modern agriculture.[3]

The Grateful Dead is rightfully considered one of the great rock bands in U.S. history, yet they never had a top 10 album. Which one or more of the following tracks released by the band during the Decade reached the top 10?

a. **"The Golden Road (to Unlimited Devotion)"**
b. **"Truckin'"**
c. **"Rosemary"**
d. **"Sugar Magnolia"**
e. **"St. Stephen"**

f.   "Uncle John's Band"

g.   "Casey Jones"

h.   "Mexicali Blues"

i.   "Turn on Your Love Light"

j.   "One More Saturday Night"

k.   "Friend of the Devil"

None of them. In fact, none of them even reached the top 50, although in fairness, the only ones actually released as singles were "Truckin'," "Sugar Magnolia," "Uncle John's Band," "Casey Jones" and "One More Saturday Night." The Dead eventually had a #1 hit with "Touch of Grey" in 1987. Clearly, the band's renown was based on its live performances rather than album or singles sales.[4]

A website has tracked the setlist for every Grateful Dead concert between 1965 and 1995. According to that site, their most-played song is not one of their own compositions, but a song written by John Phillips of the Mamas and the Papas (although he wrote it in 1963 before that band had formed). What is the song?

"Me and My Uncle." The top eight: "Me and My Uncle" (607 times), "Sugar Magnolia" (591), "Playin' in the Band" (587), "The Other One" (585), "China Cat Sunflower" (546), "I Know You Rider" (546), "Not Fade Away" (531), "Truckin'" (519).[5]

Of course, the Dead's concerts did not consist solely of heir preplanned set list. They played a lot of requests as well. On the album *Ladies and Gentlemen . . . The Grateful Dead*, Bob Weir introduces this song as the Dead's "most requested number." It was sung by Weir himself. It is a Marty Robbins tune from 1959 which the Dead played in concert 389 times. What song is it?

"El Paso."

How many top 10 songs did Neil Young have as a solo artist during the Decade?

Only one, but it was a #1 song. "Heart of Gold" reached #1 in April 1971. Other than that song, there were no other singles in the top 30. (Some of his classic tracks like "After the Gold Rush," "Southern Man," and "Love Is a Rose," and others were never released as singles. "The Needle and the Damage Done," and "Old Man," now considered two of his best-known singles, only reached #31 and #61 respectively.)

While having only modest success on the singles front, Young's 1972 album *Harvest* was the best-selling album in the United States in 1972, beating out such mega-sellers as *Tapestry* by Carole King, *Honky Château* by Elton John, *Exile on Main Street* by the Rolling Stones and *Chicago V.* Crosby, Stills and Nash all contributed backing vocals on various songs and Linda Ronstadt and James Taylor added background vocals to both "Heart of Gold" and "Old Man."[6]

John Denver (born Henry John Deutschendorf, Jr.) died at age 53 while flying his personal plane in 1997. Which one or more of the following songs was written solely by him? Which, if any, were not written by him at all?

  a. "Annie's Song"
  b. "Leaving on a Jet Plane"
  c. "Rocky Mountain High"
  d. "Take Me Home, Country Roads"
  e. "Thank God I'm a Country Boy"

Denver is the sole composer of a and b only. Bill Danoff and Taffy Nivert cowrote "Take Me Home, Country Roads" with Denver, and Mike Taylor cowrote the music to "Rocky Mountain High." The only one Denver did not write at all was "Thank God I'm a Country Boy," which was by John Martin Sommers.

Most people consider Jimmy Buffet to be a post-decade artist and it is true that most of his hits came afterwards, starting with *Margaritaville* in 1977, which reached #8 on the *Billboard* Hot 100 and #1 on the Adult Contemporary chart. That was his most successful song. However, his second most successful song was written and released in 1974, reaching #30 on the Hot 100 and #3 on the Adult Contemporary chart. What is the song? (As a hint, the third line references Hush Puppies.)

"Come Monday." Surprisingly, these are his only two solo songs that ever hit the top 10 on either chart.

This band appeared on *The Ed Sullivan Show* more times than the Beatles or Rolling Stones *combined*. Andrew Loog Oldham, former manager of the Rolling Stones, once said: "During that first 18 months of the British invasion, every time [the Beatles] looked over their shoulders, it was not the Stones, yet, or the Kinks or Who. It was [this band]." Who was the band?

The Dave Clark 5. The band was unusual for its day in that Clark, the drummer, was the leader of the band and sometimes literally the front man in concert, placing his drums stage front with the guitarists and keyboards off to the side. The height of their career straddled the start of the Decade, especially 1964 and 1965, during which they had 11 top 20 hits, and seven top 10 hits (including "Glad All Over," "Bits and Pieces," "Because," "I Like It Like That" and "Catch Us If You Can"). The band was inducted into the Rock and Roll Hall of Fame in 2008 by Tom Hanks. Hanks joked that "the Dave Clark 5 was one of the few British bands of the day that never replaced their drummer. What would they have been called?"

It is well known that many artists from the Decade were naïve when it came to finances and their business affairs and many of them suffered greatly as a result, especially when under contract with less than scrupulous managers or record companies. Dave Clark had no such misfortune. He retained all of the rights to the band's music and became (and stayed) a multimillionaire.

Most of the band's hit songs ⬛ **nd lead vocalist and keyboard player Mike Smith (who passed a** ⬛ **Hall of Fame induction ceremony). However, their lone #1 sin** ⬛ **s not written by them. What song was it?**

"Over and Over," by Robert Jam⬛

Interestingly, in Eric Clapton's stellar career, he had only one #1 song in the U.S., either with a band or on his own. It was during the Decade and he did not write the song. What song was it and what famous person wrote it and originally recorded it?

"I Shot the Sheriff" from 1974. The song was written by Bob Marley and appeared on the Wailers album *Burning* released in 1973. There is a verse in that song whose meaning was not revealed until decades after the song came out. In a documentary about Marley made by his girlfriend Esther Anderson, she explains that she was on birth control pills, and he thought the pills were sacrilege. According to Anderson, her doctor who prescribed the pills became sheriff John Brown and the lyrics, which Anderson helped write, include the line about killing a seed before it grows.[8]

In one remarkable year in the late 1960s, this band released three albums that contained a total of nine singles that reached the top 10 on the *Billboard* Hot 100. In fact, in 1969–1970, they were the most successful band in the world. Despite that success,

the leader of the band decided to go out on his own. In explaining his decision, he told a Swedish magazine in 1997:

> I was alone when I made that music. I was alone when I made the arrangements, I was alone when I added background vocals, guitars and some other stuff. I was alone when I produced and mixed the albums. The other guys showed up only for rehearsals and the days we made the actual recordings. . . . The other guys in the band insisted on writing songs for the new album, they had opinions on the arrangements, they wanted to sing. . . . That's when I understood I had a choice to make. . . . And of course I was the one who should [create the songs on my own]. I don't think the others really understood what I meant, but at least I could manage the situation the way I wanted. The result was eight million-selling double-sided singles in a row. . . . And *Melody Maker* had us as the best band in the world. That was after the Beatles split, but still. . . . And I was the one who had created all this. Despite that, I don't think they understood what I was talking about. . . . They were obsessed with the idea of more control and more influence. So finally the bomb exploded and we never worked together again.

Who was speaking and what was the band?

John Fogerty talking about Creedence Clearwater Revival. One of the other band members was Fogerty's brother Tom. Their hits included "Suzie Q" (#11, 1968), "Proud Mary" (#2, 1969), "Bad Moon Rising" (#2, 1969), "Green River" (#2, 1969), "Down On the Corner" (#3, 1969), "Travelin' Band" (#2, 1970) backed with "Who'll Stop the Rain" (#2-B, 1970), "Up Around the Bend" (#4, 1970) backed with "Run Through the Jungle" (#4, 1970), "Lookin' Out My Back Door" (#2, 1970) backed with "Long as I Can See the Light" (#2, 1970) and "Have You Ever Seen the Rain" (#3, 1971). Other hits, B-sides and LP cuts like "Born On the Bayou," "Lodi," "Commotion," "Run Through the Jungle," "Someday Never Comes," "Sweet Hitch-Hiker," "I Put a Spell On You," and their version of "I Heard It Through the Grapevine" also continue to receive a fair amount of airplay.

Where did the band name come from? They had been called the Blue Velvets and then the Golliwogs and had been performing for years together. What about CCR? Tom Fogerty had a friend, Credence Nuball. The band believed that his first name, when stretched out to "creed," had connotations of believability and integrity. "Clearwater" came from a TV commercial for Olympia beer. Though it doesn't use the phrase "clear water," it does show a clear running stream, and the voiceover says that it's the water that makes the right beer. As for Revival, it was John Fogerty's aspiration that, after four years as the Golliwogs, after ten years of playing together, it was time to go in a new direction: "I was in the mood for a revival for ourselves," he said.

One (of many) reasons the band broke up is because of tensions between John Fogerty and the rest of the band. In particular, bassist Stu Cook and drummer Doug Clifford felt that they were shunted to the side and not permitted to write songs for the group. As Cook said, they were "tired of that riff about John Fogerty's back-up band." To accommodate them, John agreed to release an album with contributions from both Cook and Clifford (Tom Fogerty had left the band by then). It came out in 1972 and was called *Mardi Gras*. It was a commercial and critical flop, although the one hit on the album, "Sweet Hitch-Hiker," was written by Fogerty. Commenting on the album for *Rolling Stone* magazine, Jon Landau called the album "Fogerty's Revenge," and said that Cook's three songs were "bad enough to qualify as offensive."

Finally, on the subject of CCR, while it is not at all uncommon for successful bands to have more compilation albums than actual studio albums, in the case of this band, the ratio is comical: six studio albums (excluding *Mardi Gras*) and 38 compilation albums. That's what happens when a band releases few studio albums with a large number of hits on them. By comparison, even the Beatles (about whom the same can be said), have "only" 48 compilation albums, but that is in comparison to 23 studio albums released in the U.S. and U.K.[9]

The Band was one of the iconic groups of the Decade. They were inducted into the Rock and Roll Hall of Fame in 1994. *Rolling Stone* ranked them #50 on their list of the 100 Greatest Artists of All Time. Some of their classic songs—mostly written by guitarist Robbie Robertson—include "The Weight," "Up on Cripple Creek," "The Shape I'm In," "It Makes No Difference," "Life Is A Carnival," "Don't Do It," "Stage Fright," and "Ophelia." How many top 10 songs did the Band have?

None. In fact, they didn't have any top 20 singles either—at least not when recorded by them.

However, in 1971, another artist or band had a #3 hit with one of their songs (which also reached #1 on the adult contemporary chart). What song and who was it? (As a hint, this song is not in the list above.)

"The Night They Drove Old Dixie Down" by Joan Baez (written by Robbie Robertson). This was Baez's only top 30 single, but then, like her contemporaries Joni Mitchell and Judy Collins, her fame and her influence was not based on being a "singles artist" in the first place.

In a career spanning more than 50 years, she only ever released 13 singles, the last one being her own composition "Diamonds and Rust" in 1975.

Interestingly, there are a number of differences in the lyrics between the way Baez recorded "The Night They Drove Old Dixie Down" and the way they were written and performed by The Band. The reason is because, as she told *Rolling Stone*, she initially learned the song by listening to the recording on the Band's album, and had never seen the printed lyrics at the time she recorded it, and thus sang the lyrics as she had (mis)heard them—and there were quite a few. So, for example whereas Robertson's version tells us that on May 10, the Confederate capital of Richmond, Virigina, fell, Baez, apparently confusing May 10 with "train," sings that the narrator took a train to Richmond that fell (which makes no sense, unless the train fell off a bridge).

Similarly, in Robertson's version, the narrator says that his wife calls for him to come quickly, because she sees Gen. Robert E. Lee. Baez however, adds the word "the" before his name, which makes a significant difference because, rather seeing the man himself, as with The Band's version, Baez is referring something named after him. As it turns out, there *was* a boat called the *Robert E. Lee*, which was a blockade runner for the Confederacy that was launched in 1862—whether Baez was aware of that or not is anyone's guess. (The *Robert E. Lee* was captured by the U.S. Navy on November 9, 1863 and was rechristened as USS *Fort Donelson* on June 29, 1864.)

Despite the changed lyrics, Baez's version is great, as is the original. In more recent years, in her concerts, Baez has performed the song as originally written by Robertson.

The original configuration of the Band ended its touring career in 1976 with an elaborate live ballroom performance on November 25 at the Winterland Ballroom in San Francisco that featured numerous musical celebrities. This performance was immortalized in Martin Scorsese's 1978 documentary *The Last Waltz*. After that, they dis-"band"-ed, until 1983, when all group members other than Robertson put "the band" back together (there are just too many possible puns here). However, pianist Richard Manuel died at age 40 in 1986, in an apparent suicide by hanging.

The only original member who left the group for good in 1976 was Robertson, who hated life on the road. "I understand why the Eagles get together and say, 'I really don't like the rest of you guys, but the money is too good to pass up because next year nobody may be offering me that,' but this isn't about prostitution for me," Robertson said in 2002 of his ongoing indifference to a Band reunion.

Robertson also had a feud with drummer Levon Helm about songwriting credits. Robertson is credited as writer or cowriter for the majority of the Band's songs, but in his 1993 autobiography *This Wheel's on Fire—Levon Helm and the Story of the Band*, Helm disputes the validity of the official songwriting credits as listed on the albums, and explains that the Band's songs were often honed and recorded through collaboration between all members. However, in 2002, Robertson denied that Helm had written any of the songs attributed to Robertson:

> I know that Levon's had a tough time, he's had health problems [in 1998, Helm was diagnosed with throat cancer, which caused him to lose his singing voice], but it's not my fault and I wish him the best. To say that it was an issue [while they were together in the Band] is just nonsense, utter nonsense, after all these years. Who did the work? I tried, I begged Levon to write songs or help me write songs—all the guys. I always encouraged everybody to write. You can't make somebody do what they don't want to do or can't do, and he's not a songwriter.

In 2008, Robertson's daughter Alexandra defended her father in a letter to the *Los Angeles Times*, commenting that Helm's solo work consisted almost entirely of songs written by others.[10]

Harry Nilsson (who performed professionally as Nilsson) wrote and performed a song which has no chord changes at all. The entire song is played in the C7 chord. It reached #8 in 1971. As a hint, the song features three distinct characters (the narrator, the sister who has an upset stomach, and the doctor), all sung in different voices by Nilsson. What is the song?

The song is "Coconut," which appears on *Nilsson Schmilsson*. Nilsson was an interesting and enigmatic fellow and certainly his music defies easy categorization. He was one of the few major pop-rock recording artists of his era to achieve significant commercial success without ever performing major public concerts or undertaking regular tours. Although a talented singer and songwriter, the songs that made him famous were mostly written by others, while some songs that he did write *were* hits for others. In the former category is "Everybody's Talkin'," written by Fred Neil in 1966. Nilsson's great cover of "Everybody's Talkin'" went to #6 on the *Billboard* Hot 100, won a Grammy in 1970 for Best Pop Male Vocal Performance, and was featured in *Midnight Cowboy*. (That movie remains the only X-rated movie ever to win Best Picture.) Also in the former category is his only #1 hit, "Without You," written by Pete Ham and Tom Evans of the British band Badfinger. Nilsson again won a Grammy for Best Pop Male Vocal Performance for this song in 1973.

On the other hand, Nilsson wrote the song "One," which was famously covered by Three Dog Night and reached #5 on the *Billboard* chart, even though Nilsson's own version was not successful. He also wrote the 1972 song "You're Breaking My Heart," in reference to his marital difficulties with his second wife Diane Clatworthy.

All of the Beatles were huge fans of his. When John Lennon and Paul McCartney held a press conference in 1968 to announce the formation of Apple Corps, Lennon was asked to name his favorite American artist. He replied, "Nilsson." McCartney was then asked to name his favorite American group. He replied, "Nilsson."

In 1991, Nilsson found himself in a dire financial situation and had to file for bankruptcy after it was discovered that his financial adviser Cindy Sims had embezzled all the funds he had earned as a recording artist. She pleaded guilty to three counts of grand theft but only served two years in state prison as a result, and never made restitution. "We went to bed one night a financially secure family of eight and woke up the next morning with $300 in our checking account," Nilsson wrote in a letter filed in court (he thought he was worth $5 million). According to Nilsson's letter, Sims took away foreclosure notices from his home so he wouldn't see them. "I'm scared," Nilsson wrote in the letter. "I never believed this could happen. It was my greatest fear growing up and it's still my greatest fear." He died of heart failure at age 52 in 1994.[11]

This Canadian man did not become a singer-songwriter until age 34. He has never released a single in the U.S. and has had very little success anywhere else in the world. His first album was released in 1967. Although in 2012, at age 77, he released an album which hit the top five in 11 countries (#3 in the U.S.), prior to that, his highest charting album in the U.S. only reached #63. Aside from one song from the 1960s and one from the 1980s (both of which are well-known through covers by other artists, though neither of which would be considered "smash hits"), many people would not recognize any of his other songs. Yet, the critic Bruce Eder assessed his overall career in popular music by asserting that

[he is] one of the most fascinating and enigmatic—if not the most success-ful—singer/songwriters of the late '60s, [and] retained an audience across five decades of music-making interrupted by various digressions into per-sonal and creative exploration, all of which have only added to the mystique surrounding him. Second only to Bob Dylan (and perhaps Paul Simon), he commands the attention of critics and younger musicians more firmly than any other musical figure from the '60s who [was] still working in the 21st century, which is all the more remarkable an achievement for someone who didn't even aspire to a musical career until he was in his thirties.

His first studio album was released in 1967 and his last in 2016, and he only released 12 studio albums in between.

He has won countless awards (including a 2010 Grammy Lifetime Achievement Award) and has been inducted into the American Rock and Roll Hall of Fame and both the Canadian Music Hall of Fame and the Canadian Songwriters Hall of Fame. He is also a Companion of the Order of Canada, the nation's highest civilian honor.

One sad thing he shares in common with Harry Nilsson is that they are both the victims of massive embezzlement by their managers/advisors (unusually, both women), they both lost virtually all of their money, and neither received any restitution from their embezzlers. He died on November 7, 2016 at age 82. Who is this man?

Leonard Cohen. The songs referenced above are "Suzanne," which appeared on his 1967 debut album *Songs of Leonard Cohen* and covered by Judy Collins the same year, and "Hallelujah" from 1984, which, like "Suzanne," has been covered by numerous artists, notably John Cale.

Part of the reason that Cohen continued to release new music until his death in 2016 at the age of 82 was financial necessity. Like Harry Nilsson and so many other artists, he was swindled out of most of his life savings. Since the mid–1960s, Cohen had relied on his manager Kelley Lynch to handle all of his financial affairs. However, Cohen's daughter Lorca suspected Lynch of financial improprieties and urged her father to review his finances more closely. He checked his bank account and noticed there was a $75,000 withdrawal by Lynch to pay a credit card bill, and then he discovered that most of his money was gone (including money from his retirement accounts and charitable trust funds). Lynch's malfeasance had actually begun as early as 1996 when she started selling Cohen's music publishing rights without his knowledge. (Talk about a trusting client!)

In 2005, Cohen sued Lynch in California, alleging that she had misappropriated over $5 million from his retirement fund. In 2006, he won the case by default and was awarded $9 million. However, reportedly, he was never able to collect any of that money. Cohen was remarkably sanguine about the experience: "You know, God gave me a strong inner core, so I wasn't shattered. But I was deeply concerned." However, at the time the suit was filed, he also spoke of his need to keep producing music in view of the theft: "What can I do? I had to go to work. I have no money left. I'm not saying it's bad; I have enough of an understanding of the way the world works to understand that these things happen." As for Lynch, after entry of the judgment, Lynch began harassing Cohen and as a result, in 2012, she was sentenced to 18 months in prison. Said Cohen: "It gives me no pleasure to see my onetime friend shackled to a chair in a court of law, her considerable gifts bent to the service of darkness, deceit and revenge."[12]

In 1974, Cohen—who looks a little like Dustin Hoffman and sounds a little like Lou Reed—released a song called "Chelsea Hotel #2" on his fourth studio album, *New Skin for the Old Ceremony*. In mentioning about how the song came about, Cohen has told the story of how one day, a number of years prior, there was a young woman in the elevator in his building who "commanded huge audiences." He gathered his courage and asked her: "Are you looking for someone?" She said "Yes. I'm looking for Kris Kristofferson." He replied: "Little lady, you're in luck—I'm Kris Kristofferson." Even though she of course knew that he was not Kristofferson, they nevertheless had a sexual encounter. According to the song, the woman told Cohen that she had a rule about sleeping only with handsome men, but that she was prepared to make an exception in Cohen's case. Though not considered attractive, she was able, according to one writer, to "use her celebrity to sleep with men who ordinarily would have been out of her league." She seems to acknowledge as much herself when, according to the song, she tells Cohen "we are ugly, but we have the music." While not mentioning the woman's name in the actual song, he used to identify her before performing the song in concert. Who was this woman?

Janis Joplin. In later years, Cohen came to regret his kiss and tell, or at least the graphic nature of it: In a 1994 BBC radio interview, he referred to it as "the sole indiscretion in my professional life. Looking back, I'm sorry I did because there are some lines in it that are extremely intimate." He was no doubt referring not only to some of the comments above that she presumably told him in confidence, but also to the line "giving me head on the unmade bed."[13]

Before the Bee Gees turned to disco in 1975 and started saturating the airwaves and the *Billboard* charts with their string of #1 hits from the soundtrack to *Saturday Night Fever*, they had an extremely successful "first act" to their career. Notwithstanding all of their success however, they only had one #1 song in America. Which one of the following songs was it?

a. "To Love Somebody"
b. "I Gotta Get a Message to You"
c. "Massachusetts"
d. "I Can't See Nobody"
e. "Words"
f. "How Can You Mend a Broken Heart?"

The answer is f, which reached #1 in the U.S. in June 1971. Interestingly, that song was not a big hit in the U.K. even though "Massachusetts" and "I Can't See Nobody" both reached #1 there. "Massachusetts" was actually written for the Australian band the Seekers, but the

Bee Gees were never able to get the song to them, so they recorded it themselves. The Bee Gees had never been to Massachusetts when they recorded this song, notwithstanding the lyrics about going back to Massachusetts and Massachusetts being one place they had seen. They just liked the sound of the name. This is the first Bee Gees song on which Robin Gibb sang lead vocal. (Incidentally, though the Bee Gees are usually thought of as an Australian band, they were all born in England and did not emigrate to Australia until 1958, when Barry was 12 and the twins Robin and Maurice were 9.)

According to the group's 1997 Hall of Fame citation "Only Elvis Presley, the Beatles, Michael Jackson, Garth Brooks and Paul McCartney have outsold the Bee Gees."[14]

Before San Francisco bands such as the Jefferson Airplane, the Grateful Dead and Moby Grape, there was this band. About them, Richie Unterberger of AllMusic.com wrote: "While they only had two big hits, [they] were one of the most important and underrated American groups of the 1960s. They were the first U.S. unit of any sort to successfully respond to the British Invasion. They were arguably the first folk-rock group, even predating the Byrds, and also anticipated some key elements of the San Francisco psychedelic sound with their soaring harmonies and exuberant melodies." Because of their name, people at first thought they were British. In the same vein, according to legend (later denied by a band member), they chose a name so that their records would be placed immediately behind those of the Beatles in record-store bins. Who is the band? For extra credit, name their two biggest hits.

The band was the Beau Brummels (named after George Bryan "Beau" Brummell, 1778–1840, the British arbiter of men's fashion). Their two biggest hits were "Laugh, Laugh" and "Just a Little," both of which were top 20 hits in 1965. As for whether they wanted a name that was close to the Beatles in the alphabet, lead singer Sal Valentino said in 2008: "That's a total myth. We just needed a name, and that sounded good. We didn't even know how to spell it. Everybody now has a notion of what people were thinking back then, but we never thought of those kinds of things."[15]

This psychedelic rock band never had a single which rose above #30 on the *Billboard* Hot 100. It released only six albums. One of them however, released in 1968, sold over 30 million copies. The B side of the album contains only one song, which has the same name as the album. It lasts 17:03 and contains a famous drum solo. Who is the band and what is the name of the album?

The band is Iron Butterfly and the album is of course *In-A-Gadda-Da-Vida*. It has been written that the album was the first ever to be certified as platinum (over 1 million sold) by the Recording Institute Association of America but that distinction appears to belong to *The Eagles Greatest Hits (1971–1975)*.

Sources differ as to the derivation of the name of the song, but most versions mention that it relates to a mishearing or slurring of "In the Garden of Eden." For example, in the liner notes to the 1995 reissue of the album it states: "[While] Doug Ingle (keyboards) . . . wrote the song around the "Garden of Eden" hook, he was working his way through a gallon bottle of Red Mountain wine. By the time he committed the idea to tape, he was quite a bit drunk. Later, when Ron Bushy (drums) got home from working at the Galaxy Club, Ingle had consumed ⅔ of the bottle. Bushy asked Ingle what the title of [the] new song was and Ingle slurs out "In-A-Gadda-Da-Vida." Bushy says, "I thought it was catchy so I wrote it down." The recording of "In-A-Gadda-Da-Vida" that appears on the album was meant to be a soundcheck while the band waited for the arrival of their producer. When the rehearsal was completed, it was agreed that another take was not needed.[16]

Paul Revere and the Raiders had five top 10 hits in the Decade but only one #1 song. What was it?

"Indian Reservation (The Lament of the Cherokee Reservation Indian)," by John D. Loudermilk, a very successful country songwriter. The Raiders were not the first to have a hit with this song, but their version was certainly the most successful. The song refers to the forcible removal and relocation of "Five Civilized Tribes" (Cherokee, Chickasaw, Choctaw, Creek and Seminole) from several southeastern states to the southern Indian Territory in present-day Oklahoma. The removal of these tribes throughout the 1830s is often referred to as the "Trail of Tears." The removal came on the heels of President Andrew Jackson's Indian Removal Act of 1830.

Songfacts states: "Isn't it ironic that a song like this, brimming with simmering rage and an implied threat to retake the land for the natives, was written by a white country songwriter, recorded by a band named after the white European patriots whose colonization of the U.S. took the land from the Cherokees in the first place, and sold by Columbia Records, a company originating as 'Columbia Graphophone Company' in the U.K.?"

Because Mark Lindsay was the leader singer for the band, people sometimes thought he was Revere, who actually played keyboards, and it led to some bitterness between them. Said Lindsay: "There were too many concerts where after the show people would come up to me and go 'Gee Paul! I really love your music,' and I'd say, 'I'm not Paul. I'm Mark Lindsay.' And they'd say 'Well who's Paul?' I'd point over to Paul's keyboards and they'd say 'Oh, he's just a piano player.' He heard that too many times and I think it kind of bruised his ego, which I can totally understand."

Lindsay lived for a time with Raiders producer Terry Melcher at 10050 Cielo Drive in Los Angeles, which was the house in which actress Sharon Tate and others were murdered in August 1969 by members of Charles Manson's family at his direction.[17]

Another top five hit for Paul Revere and the Raiders came out in 1966. That was the year that Barry Sadler's pro-military song, "Ballad of the Green Berets," swam fiercely against the tide of all the anti-Vietnam songs in vogue at that time. This was also the case with the Paul Revere song, although this time in the case of drugs. At a time when many songs seemed to be about drugs and arguably casting them in a positive light (Bob Dylans's "Rainy Day Women #12 and #35" and the Byrds' "Eight Miles High" being two contemporary examples), this hit song was clearly anti-drug. What was its title?

"Kicks" (which, according to the song, were getting harder to find). This song was written by Barry Mann and Cynthia Weil. Mann said that the song was written about their friend, fellow songwriter Gerry Goffin, whose ongoing drug problems were interfering with his career and his relationship with then wife Carole King.

Rolling Stones bassist Bill Wyman said of this man: "He formed the band. He chose the members. He named the band. He chose the music we played. He got us gigs." To whom was he referring?

Stones guitarist Brian Jones. Keith Richards agreed that "the Rolling Stones was Brian's baby." In simplified version, and omitting band members who joined and left the group before they attained stardom, Jones started the band in 1962 and recruited Jagger, who then brought on his childhood friend Richards. Bill Wyman was then recruited, followed by Charlie Watts in 1963. Richards says that Jones came up with the name the "Rollin' Stones" (later with the "g") while on the phone with a venue owner. "The voice on the other end of the line obviously said, 'What are you called?' Panic. *The Best of Muddy Waters* album was lying on the floor—and track five, side one was "Rollin' Stone."

Jones was an incredibly talented and versatile musician. In addition to guitar, he played harmonica, marimba, keyboards, percussion, saxophone, sitar, Appalachian dulcimer, and recorder. Problems developed for Jones when Andrew Loog Oldham started managing the band in 1963. This had previously been the primary province of Jones. In addition, Oldham encouraged Mick Jagger and Keith Richards to start writing their own songs, whereas Jones had preferred covers of blues songs, and in fact had no talent whatsoever for songwriting himself. As Richards wrote in his autobiography: "Between June 1964 and August 1966 . . . was the period where everything—songwriting, recording, performing—stepped into a new league, and the time when Brian started going off the rails. . . . He lost his status and then lost interest. Having to come to the studio and learn to play a song Mick and I had written would bring him down." Essentially, the pairing of Jagger and Richards by Oldham was the beginning of the end for Jones. Incidentally, Oldham was only 19 years old when he started managing the band and he guided them through five of their most important years, 1963–1967.

Jones' drug use began to escalate as did the hostilities between him and the other band members. In June 1969, he was advised that the band was going to continue on without him. Only a few weeks later, at around midnight on the night of July 2–3, 1969, Jones was discovered motionless at the bottom of his swimming pool. The coroner's report stated "death by misadventure" and noted his liver and heart were heavily enlarged by drug and alcohol abuse. He was 27 years old.[18]

This country rock band started in San Francisco in 1969. Its members included Jerry Garcia, Phil Lesh, and Mickey Hart. Robert Hunter was also associated with this band. What is its name? You're thinking Grateful Dead, right? Wrong. (As a hint, one of the group's more successful songs was "Panama Red.")

New Riders of the Purple Sage. Garcia, Hart and Lesh all played with the band in its early days and Garcia played pedal steel guitar on the band's self-titled debut album. Its main members during the Decade were founder and band leader John Dawson (nicknamed "Marmaduke"), David Nelson and Dave Torbert.

Who are the only "main members" of the E Street Band who performed on *Greetings from Asbury Park*?

Clarence Clemons and Garry W. Tallent. Steven Van Zandt did add sound effects on "Lost in the Flood." The other band members at that time were Vini "Mad Dog" Lopez and David Sancious. As of 2012, Tallent was the only original E Street Band member still alive. Danny Federici died in 2008 and Clarence Clemons died in 2011. The first album on which drummer Max Weinberg and keyboardist Roy (the Professor) Bittan played was *Born to Run*. As for the title track itself, however, Weinberg did not play the drums; former drummer Ernest "Boom" Carter did. As Springsteen wrote in his 2016 autobiography, this was Carter's only recorded E Street appearance and "he picked a good one." Both Weinberg and Bittan played on several tracks on Meat Loaf's *Bat Out of Hell*, including the title track, "You Took the Words Right Out of My Mouth," and "Paradise by the Dashboard Light."

What was the first album released by Bruce Springsteen with his backing band in which it was officially called the E Street Band?

Born to Run. Although many of the same band members played with him on *Greetings from Asbury Park* and *The Wild, the Innocent, & the E Street Shuffle*, the band was not officially named when those albums were released.[19]

In the song "Blinded by the Light," Bruce Springsteen's first song on his first album, he refers to a "deuce." What is a deuce?

A 1932 Ford hot rod. When the Manfred Mann Earth Band recorded this song in 1976, it sounded like they were singing "wrapped up like a douche, another rotor in the night." The song went to #1. When he appeared on *Storytellers*, the misheard lyric caused Springsteen to joke that the success of Manfred Mann's version was because people thought they were singing about a feminine hygiene product. This was the only Springsteen song covered by another artist whose version reached #1. However, "Because the Night" reached #13 for Patti Smith in 1978, "Fire" reached #2 for the Pointer sisters in 1979, and Natalie Cole had a hit with "Pink Cadillac" in 1988.[20]

In 1967, two men, independently of one another, answered an advertisement for talent placed in the *New Musical Express* by Liberty Records A&R man Ray Williams who was searching for new talent. Neither of them passed the audition for Liberty Records or even met one another during the process. Nevertheless, Williams recognized their talents and put them in touch with each other. They have since collaborated on 30 albums. Who are these two men? As a hint, one of the two does not sing or play any instruments on any of those albums.

Elton John (born Reginald Dwight) and Bernie Taupin. As the music writer and lyric writer respectively, the two have an unusual style of collaboration, or perhaps more accurately, non-collaboration. In fact, they are generally not physically together and in fact do not work together in any way on the creation of the songs. First, Taupin writes the lyrics, with no involvement by John. They are usually inspired by some event in his life or something he has read. He works on them at his horse ranch in Southern California (where he moved to in the mid–1970s) and delivers the lyrics fully formed to John. Elton then goes into a studio, props the papers on the piano and churns out melodies and harmonies to fit the words without any further input from Taupin. John does this at breakneck speed. "It's kind of spooky," he said. "I get bored if it takes more than 40 minutes."

In an interview, Elton acknowledged his debt to Bernie: "He's more important than I am because he has to write the words before I write the music. . . . Without Bernie, basically, there would never have been an Elton John. I mean, without that stroke of good fortune and kismet as it were, Elton John probably wouldn't have happened. I'm just a purveyor of Bernie's feelings, Bernie's thoughts."[21]

There are some British acts about whom there is significant buzz in America before they have ever set foot here. The Beatles would be an obvious example. However, in those cases, the artists or bands normally have one or more hit songs under their belt first, whether in the U.K. or the U.S. before they begin to tour here. Elton John was an exception. His debut in the U.S. was on August 25, 1970. At that time, he had no hit singles in either country. He had released one album in the U.K. a year earlier, *Empty Sky*, which attracted no attention in the U.K. and wasn't released in the U.S. until 1975, well after he had become famous. His next album, *Elton John*, had only been released in the U.S. less than a month earlier and was certainly not yet a hit album. Nevertheless, the buzz about his talent had begun to circulate among the music cognoscenti.

His U.S. debut was at the Troubador in West Hollywood and was not for one night but for six nights, with the entire run sold out. In attendance were Quincy Jones, Gordon Lightfoot, Leon Russell, the Beach Boys' Mike Love and Three Dog Night's Danny Hutton. Before his first show, Neil Diamond introduced him: "Folks, I've never done this before, so please be kind to me. I'm like the rest of you; I'm here because of having listened to Elton John's album. So I'm going to take my seat with you now and enjoy the show." After the first night, Robert Hilburn, music critic for the *Los Angeles Times*, wrote: "Tuesday night at the Troubadour was just the beginning. He's going to be one of rock's biggest and most important stars." And as Hilburn predicted, in 1990 *Rolling Stone* magazine declared these shows to be among the 20 most important concerts in the history of rock and' roll.[22]

True or false: Elton's first #1 song was "Your Song."

False. It was "Crocodile Rock."

The Young Rascals (later the Rascals) had three #1 hits and three more top 10 hits. The two members of the group who wrote five of those songs are both in the Songwriters Hall of Fame. Name the three #1 songs and the two songwriters. For extra credit, name the other three songs.

The three #1 songs were "Good Lovin'" (written by Rudy Clark and Arthur Resnick), "Groovin'" and "People Got to Be Free," both by Felix Cavaliere and Eddie Brigati. Cavaleri's and Brigati's other top 10 hits were "A Beautiful Morning" (#3), "A Girl Like You" (#10), and "How Can I Be Sure" (#4). They also wrote "I've Been Lonely Too Long," which, although it only reached #16 in 1967, is a well-known song today. Cavaliere handled lead vocals on all of these songs (other than "How Can I Be Sure," where Brigati sang lead), which is likely why he became more famous than Brigati.

This band had six top 10 hits during the Decade. After their eponymous initial album, the next seven (including one greatest hits album) all began with the letter H. What is the band?

America. The albums are *Homecoming, Hat Trick, Holiday, Hearts, History* (the greatest hits album), *Hideaway,* and *Harbor.* The name of the band is actually anachoristic because Dewey Bunnell was born and raised in England and Gerry Beckley and Dan Peek were both living in England when the band was formed. The trio called themselves America because they did not want anyone to think they were British musicians trying to sound American.[23]

This band was probably the most successful of the white bands signed by the Motown label. In fact, Motown named its subsidiary label after this band. The band had three top 10 songs, two of which were covers of Temptations songs that actually charted higher than the Temps' originals. The third song was written for the group. Name the band and the three top 10 songs. As a hint the three top 10 songs were "(I Know) I'm Losing You," "Get Ready: and "I Just Want to Celebrate."

The band was Rare Earth, as was the Motown subsidiary label. While Motown created the label to expand its audience, based on the vocals of drummer and lead singer Peter Hoorelbeke (especially on the Temps' covers), one listening to their songs on the radio would never know that Rare Earth was not a traditional black Motown band. Indeed, while it seems odd to create an all-white band to perform Temps covers and sound like the Temps, the success of the covers cannot be questioned. Gil Scott-Heron was apparently not a fan. In his song "The Revolution Will Not Be Televised," he sings that the theme song to the revolution will not be sung by the Rare Earth.

Another white artist who recorded for Motown until 1981 was Teena Marie. She was known for her distinctive soulful vocals and her success in the R&B and soul genres earned her the title of the Ivory Queen of Soul (as opposed to Dusty Springfield who earlier was known as the White Queen of Soul). She referred to herself as "a black artist with white skin." When she passed away in 2010, newsone.com titled her obituary "The Life, Legacy and (Yes) Blackness of Teena Marie."[24]

CHAPTER 10

Name that Tune (Specific Songs)

This chapter will focus on interesting aspects certain songs that became huge hits during the Decade.

It is reasonably well known that Eric Clapton cowrote "Layla" regarding his unrequited (at the time) love for Pattie Boyd, the then-wife of George Harrison. Here are a few questions regarding other aspects of the song that are not so well known.

Derek and the Dominos consisted of four members. However, a fifth musician played lead guitar and slide guitar on "Layla." Who was it?

Duane Allman.

Where does the word "Layla" come from?

This is a hard one. It comes from the story of *Layla and Majnun*, by the 12th-century Persian poet Nizami Ganjavi. In the story, Qays and Layla fall in love with each other when they are young, but when they grow up, Layla's father doesn't allow them to be together. Qays becomes crazy about her and that's why he is later given the name *Majnun* (lit. "possessed") in his community. He eventually goes mad. He never gives up his love for Layla.

Interestingly, the song was unsuccessful when released in 1970. While it later did become a hit in 1972, it never reached higher than #10 on the *Billboard* Hot 100. As for Clapton's desire to be with Boyd, he eventually got his wish. Boyd divorced Harrison in 1977 and married Clapton in 1979 during a concert stop in Tucson, Arizona. Harrison was not bitter about the divorce and attended Clapton's wedding party with Ringo Starr and Paul McCartney. During their relationship, Clapton wrote another love ballad for Pattie called "Wonderful Tonight" (1977). Clapton and Boyd divorced in 1988 after several years of separation.

Commenting on the song, Clapton said: "'Layla' is a difficult one, because it's a difficult song to perform live. You have to have a good complement of musicians to get all of the ingredients going, but when you've got that . . . I love to hear it. It's almost like it's not me. It's like I'm listening to someone that I really like. Derek and the Dominos was a band I really liked—and it's almost like I wasn't in that band."[1]

Who are the six artists mentioned (along with hit songs by them) in the song "Rock and Roll Heaven," which reached #3 on the *Billboard* **Hot 100 for the Righteous Brothers in 1974? For extra credit, what are the references for each of these artists?**

1. Jimi Hendrix ("rainbows" refers to the Hendrix song "Rainbow Bridge").
2. Janis Joplin (reference to "Piece of My Heart" by Big Brother and the Holding Company).
3. Otis Redding (reference to "The Dock of the Bay").
4. Jim Morrison (reference to "Light My Fire").
5. Jim Croce (reference to "Bad Bad Leroy Brown").
6. Bobby Darin (reference to "Mack the Knife").

"Rock and Roll Heaven" was cowritten by Alan O'Day. He wrote and performed a #1 song in 1977, "Undercover Angel." He also wrote a song which reached #1 for an Australian performer in December 1974. What was the song and who is the artist?

"Angie Baby" by Helen Reddy.

In 2014, Chuck Klosterman wrote a book of funny essays entitled *I Wear the Black Cat.* **In one of them he writes: "I was intrigued by the math: The main character ... Is flee-ing from seven women. Four of these females are possessive, so he finds them unappealing; two others hate him ... which comes across as neutral; the seventh is (I think) the one he likes, but she can't reciprocate. It's clearly the problem of the young man, as no one over 35 could sustain interest in seven simultaneous relationships unless they're biracial and amazing at golf."**

What song lyrics and what song is he referring to?

"Take it Easy" by Glenn Frey and Jackson Browne which was released in May 1972 and is the first cut on the Eagles' first album.

In another verse of the song, Frey mentions a city and state and portrays a scene at a street corner in that city. Many years later, the city in question erected a life-size bronze statue and mural commemorating the song. What is the city and state?

Winslow, Arizona. In 1999, the city of Winslow (which is located on Interstate 40, between Flagstaff and the New Mexico border) installed a statue and mural—called "Standin' on the Corner Park"—at the corner of Second Street and Kinsley Avenue. The statue is of a man holding an acoustic guitar that is resting on the shoe of his right foot. He stands near a lamppost. Above his head, a metal sign, crafted in the style of U.S. Route shields, displays the words "Standin' on the corner." The trompe-l'œil mural on the wall behind the statue is that of a storefront, and includes the reflection of a red flatbed Ford pickup truck driven by a blonde-haired woman. The second floor of the mural features an eagle perched on one window sill on the left and a man and woman (apparently the man on the corner and woman in the truck) embracing in another window on the right. If the name of the park was going to match the song lyrics exactly, it would be called "Standin' on *a* Corner Park."[2]

The title of the first song on the first side of the eponymous first solo album by Paul Simon was inspired by the name of a chicken and egg dish he saw on a Chinese menu in New York. What was the song?

"Mother and Child Reunion." Simon revealed this in a 1972 interview with *Rolling Stone.* In Jaime Geller's book *The Joy of Kosher*, she provides a recipe for a mother and child reunion which, in her version, is a chicken and corn egg drop soup. "Mother and Child Reunion" has been described (including by Simon himself) as one of the earliest attempts by a non-Jamaican white musician to play reggae music. To get the right feel, Simon recorded the song in Jamaica with Jimmy Cliff's backing vocal group. Whitney Houston's mother, Cissy Houston, also sang background vocals on the recording. A VH1.com article on the history of white musicians trying their hand at reggae stated that "[this] was probably the first time many Americans heard a proper reggae groove, even if it was backing up a 5-foot-tall Jewish kid from Queens, NY."[3]

This band had 17 top 10 hits in the U.K. (some before the Decade) and 6 in the U.S. However, their highest ranking song in the U.S. (reaching #2), never got higher than #32 in the U.K. The "plot" of that song involves an FBI agent who is scouting a nightclub prior to a raid. There are some unsavory characters there. He comes across a tall beautiful woman, who he later protects in an ensuing shootout at the club. Afterward, the District Attorney congratulates him on his fine work and the agent gets the girl. Who is the band and what is the song? For extra credit, name the band member who cowrote the song, sang the song, and yet had left the band by the time the song made it big in America.

The band is the Hollies, the song is "Long Cool Woman in a Black Dress," and the cowriter is Allan Clarke. Clarke rejoined the group in 1973, shortly after the success of this song.

Here's a silly little question: Name what is undoubtedly the only song in history (a huge hit) which rhymes the words "yacht", "apricot" and "gavotte"?

"You're So Vain," the 1972 song from Carly Simon which appears on her album *No Secrets*, is an interesting song on several fronts. A few other questions about that song follow.

One of the most famous rock stars in the world sings some of the backing vocals, which are uncredited. Nevertheless, his distinctive voice can still be discerned in the choruses, especially on the "don't you's." Who is it?

Mick Jagger. When asked how she was able to get him, Simon said: "I guess it was kind of chance in a way. I was in London, it was 1972 and he happened to call at the studio while I was doing the background vocals with Harry Nilsson. Mick said, 'Hey, what cha doin'?' and I said, 'We're doing some backup vocals on a song of mine. Why don't you come down and sing with us?' So Mick and Harry and I stood around the mic singing 'You're So Vain' and Harry was such a gentleman—he knew the chemistry was between me and Mick; in terms of the singing, so he sort of bowed out saying, 'The two of you have a real blend—you should do it yourselves.'"[4]

In another part of the song, Carly sings that the person whom she is addressing is watching himself "gavotte." What does "gavotte" mean?

Though used as a verb by Simon, it is actually a French folk dance, popular in the 18th century. It is somewhat majestic and pose-y, long before "vogue"ing came into . . . well, vogue. Simon has stated in interviews that she pictured the character in her song making a dramatic entrance, one hand raised and the other on his hip, much like those elegant pantaloon-wearing Baroque folks did back in the day.

As for the reference to seeing clouds in her coffee, Simon said: "It came from an airplane flight that I took with Billy Mernit, who was my friend and piano player at the time. As I got my coffee, there were clouds outside the window of the airplane and you could see the reflection in the cup of coffee. Billy said to me, 'Look at the clouds in your coffee.' I liked the phrase and used it to illustrate the illusion of having a relationship with the subject of the song."

Finally, the ultimate question: Who is the song about? There have been myriad possibilities and rumors mentioned over the years as to who the song is about, many of which were started by Simon herself. They include James Taylor, Mick Jagger, Warren Beatty, David Cassidy, David Bowie, Cat Stevens and, as she stated before the song became a hit, the possibility that the song may be about no one person in particular. (There was also speculation that it was about David Geffen, but Simon has specifically denied that.) Simon clearly seems happy to stoke the controversy and mystery herself, as evidenced by the fact that her own website used to list virtually every comment she has ever made on this subject. In 2015 however, while publicizing her memoir, *Boys in the Trees*, she finally revealed a little of the answer to *People* magazine, stating that the second verse (of three total verses, excluding the chorus) was about Warren Beatty and added that while "Warren thinks the whole thing is about him," he is the subject only of that verse, while the remainder of the song refers to two other, still-unnamed men.[5]

This song was released on Apple Records and was one of the few big hits on that label *not* by the Beatles. It was #1 in many countries around the world and reached #2 on the *Billboard* Hot 100 (and #1 according to *Cash Box* and *Record World*). It was originally a Russian romance song, composed by Boris Fomin (1900–1948) with words by the poet Konstantin Podrevskii. The earliest recording of the song was made in 1925 by Tamara Tseretel and this charming version can be heard on YouTube (as can a number of Russian versions of the song). A musician and playwright named Gene Raskin made an English language version of the lyrics and then illegally put a copyright on both the tune and the lyrics. What is the song and who is the artist? (As a hint, the performer of the song is female.)

"Those Were the Days" by Mary Hopkin. In 1962, the Limeliters released an English language version of Raskin's song which closely matches Hopkin's, although it was never released as a single. It was her version which became a worldwide hit. The song was produced by Paul McCartney and was released on August 30, 1968, only three months after Apple was formed. It was the second Apple release ever, the first being "Hey Jude," released the same day.[6]

This 1972 song begins with what has been called "the mother of all bass lines." Each verse of the song makes reference to one of the "superstars" at Andy Warhol's New York studio, the Factory, including Holly, Candy and Little Joe. The bass line was played by a British session musician named Herbie Flowers, who overdubbed an electric bass on top of a double bass. He came up with the riff himself. He was paid 24 pounds for his contribution. (Some sources have said it was only 17 pounds, but Flowers himself said he was normally paid 12 pounds and received double the rate as a result of the overdub.) Flowers' participation lasted all of 20 minutes. What is the song?

"Walk on the Wild Side" by Lou Reed, coproduced by David Bowie and Mick Ronson. It is also Flowers' distinctive bass line that opens "Jump into the Fire" by Harry Nilsson, which is the song heard in the movie *Goodfellas* when Ray Liotta's character leaves his house on what proves to be his last day of freedom. Holly was Holly Woodlawn, a transgender actress, who moved to New York from Miami Beach. "Candy" was based on Candy Darling, also a transgender actress. The background vocals ("doo doo doo", etc.) are sung the British vocal trio the Thunderthighs, who are not actually "colored girls," despite the song's lyrics. The famous sax solo at the end was played by Bowie's own jazz tutor Ronnie Ross, who nailed the solo in just one take.[7]

Paul Simon's song "Mrs. Robinson" originally referenced a different "Mrs." Which one? (As a hint, she was a former First Lady of the United States.)

Mrs. Roosevelt. This was apparently a reference to former First Lady Eleanor Roosevelt. On an appearance on *The Dick Cavett Show* on April 4, 1970, when Simon mentioned Mrs. Roosevelt in connection with the making of the movie *The Graduate*, Cavett joked "that would change the plot of the movie a lot, wouldn't it?"

The upbeat infectious music on this Rolling Stones song belies its dark subject matter. Most people who have never read or thought about the lyrics of this song have no idea what it's about. The song is about (among other things) a slave owner raping his underage slaves in the middle of the night. Writing about the song on AllMusic.com, Ritchie Unterberger wrote: "The brilliance of the track is that it is so musically powerful and irresistible that the most PC-conscious listener will find it hard not to dance to it before getting around to pondering the lyrics. But it can't be denied that the words are among the most troubling evocations of evil and sexploitation Jagger and Richards devised, whether that was a conscious or subconscious effect." What is the song?

"Brown Sugar." Many people assume that this song is a paean to a black woman. However, like other songs that don't mean what people may think (such as Bruce Springsteen's 1984 hit "Born in the USA" or "(You Gotta) Fight for Your Right (To Party!)" by the Beastie Boys, or "Lucy in the Sky with Diamonds"), that is not the case. Besides slavery and interracial sex, the song touches on cunnilingus, lost virginity, sadomasochism and heroin (according to Richards, "brown sugar" is a slang term for Mexican heroin). In a 1995 interview with *Rolling Stone* magazine, Mick Jagger said: "It's such a mishmash. All the nasty subjects in one go . . . I never would write that song now." When Jann Wenner asked him why, Jagger replied, "I would probably censor myself. I'd think, 'Oh God, I can't. I've got to stop. I can't just write raw like that.'"

There has always been a question as to what exactly Jagger was singing in the words that sound like (and are usually written down as) "scarred old slaver." However pianist and producer Jim Dickinson has said Jagger was actually singing "Skydog slaver," Skydog being the nickname for Duane Allman, because he was high all the time. Jagger heard somebody say it and he thought it was a cool word so he used it. Keith Richards quotes Dickinson's explanation in his autobiography *Life*, but without comment. Because Skydog and "scarred old" sound so similar, especially when sung with Jagger's heavy accent, it is virtually impossible to know what he is actually singing. However, Dickinson's explanation seems logical because Allman was in fact known as Skydog and he did frequently record at the famous Muscle Shoals Sound Studio where "Brown Sugar" was recorded.

This song was the first single released on Rolling Stones Records, and is the opening track and lead single from their 1971 album *Sticky Fingers*. It was recorded over a three-day period from December 2 to December 4, 1969. However, it was not released until 1971 due to legal wranglings with the band's former label. It was performed live however at the infamous concert at Altamont on December 6, 1969, only two days after the song was finished.[8]

It might seem that rock and roll had not been around long enough during the Decade for there to be "oldies acts," but that's not the case. In 1971, a famous singer was part of a "rock and roll revival concert," which included Chuck Berry, Bo Diddley and Bobby Rydell. While he did play the old songs for which he was famous, the audience was displeased with his (then) modern appearance, as well as the fact that he also played his new compositions. They started booing him and he walked off the stage. He wrote a song about the experience which reached #6 on the *Billboard* Hot 100 in 1972. Who is the artist and what was the song?

The artist is Rick Nelson and the song is "Garden Party." Nelson's musical heyday was in the 1950s and the first few years of the 1960s. However, he had not had a hit since 1963 and so had basically disappeared from the nation's consciousness between 1963 and 1971. His appearance was also very different from the way his fans remembered him. Instead of the gel-filled pompadour he wore during his teen idol days, his hair had become much longer. He now wore bell-bottoms. Even his name had changed: he was no longer Ricky but now Rick. The audience was not happy that he played his newer country-tinged compositions, even though he did mix in many of his old hits. As with the song "American Pie," there are numerous veiled (or not-so-veiled) references to real-life people and events. For example, the title of the song itself refers to the fact that the concert took place at Madison Square Garden. "Yoko's walrus" refers to John Lennon and "Mr. Hughes" was apparently an alias of George Harrison. He mentions saying hello to Mary Lou, one of his biggest hits. Finally, he mentions Johnny B. Goode, a reference to Chuck Berry's song. "Garden Party" was Nelson's last song on the charts. He died in a plane crash on New Year's Eve 1985 when he was only 45 years old.[9]

This legendary song by this legendary band appeared on their first album, released in 1969. At the time, it garnered no attention at all. However, that changed when a live version of the song was released two years later. That version of the song lasts more than 22 minutes and is considered one of the most famous live performances in rock history.

If you're thinking that the answer is "Free Bird" by Lynyrd Skynrd, that would be an excellent guess, but wrong. That song did not come out until 1974 and did not become famous for its live version until after the Decade was over. One thing that the two songs have in common however (besides being iconic and long live performances) is that they both became known as the two songs that audience members yell out that they want to hear ("Play Free Bird man!"), not only for these two bands, but also, as sort of a joke, for other artists as well. While "Free Bird" eventually became more famous for it, this was the original "call out" song. It all started when one scratchy-voiced guy shouted out the name of the song just before the band launched into it. What is the song and what is name of the live album on which it appears? (Though not by Lynyrd Skynrd, the song is by another quintessentially Southern band.)

The song is "Whipping Post" by the Allman Brothers, written by Gregg Allman, and the album on which it appears is *At Fillmore East*. The album was recorded over three nights in March 1971 for which the band was paid $1,250 a night. In 2002, *Rolling Stone* called this album "the finest rock performance ever committed to vinyl." Despite being a double album, it contained a total of only seven songs on the four sides (can you say extended jam?).

In 2005, the august *Wall Street Journal* wrote an article entitled "Rock's Oldest Joke: Yelling 'Freebird!' In a Crowded Theater." While mentioning "Whipping Post" as being one of the original call-out songs, it begins:

> One recent Tuesday night at New York's Bowery Ballroom, the Crimea had just finished its second song. The Welsh quintet's first song had gone over fairly well, the second less so, and singer/guitarist Davey MacManus looked out at the still-gathering crowd. Then, from somewhere in the darkness came the cry, "Freebird!" It made this night like so many other rock 'n' roll nights in America. . . . Yelling "Freebird!" has been a rock cliché; for years, guaranteed to elicit laughs from drunks and scorn from music fans who have long since tired of the joke. Bands mostly just ignore the taunt. But one common retort is: "I've got your 'free bird' right here!"

This happened so frequently to Frank Zappa that he and his band eventually learned the song and made it part of their concert repertoire.

The Fillmore East itself has an interesting history. Located on the Lower East Side of New York, it was opened as a Yiddish theatre in 1925. It was purchased by promoter Bill Graham in 1967 to be a kind of East Coast companion to the Fillmore West located in San Francisco. Despite a deceptively small marquee and façade, it could seat almost 2,700. Because of its excellent acoustics, there were many live performances recorded there, including albums by the Chambers Brothers, Joe Cocker, Crosby, Stills, Nash & Young, Miles Davis, Derek and the Dominos, the Grateful Dead, Jimi Hendrix, Jefferson Airplane, John Lennon and Yoko Ono, Neil Young, and Frank Zappa. Given its fabled status, it is surprising that it was in existence for only three years, from 1968 to 1971.[10]

This song, released in 1966, was credited to a duo, but one of the two did not perform on it. Phil Spector, the producer and cowriter of the song, paid him $20,000 to stay away from the studio when it was being recorded. Even though the song reached no higher than #88 on the *Billboard* Hot 100, *Rolling Stone* ranked the song at #33 on its list of the 500 Greatest Songs of All Time, one of the few instances (among released singles) where the *Rolling Stone* ranking on this list was far higher than the highest ranking of the song during its original release. Despite the failure of the original version, it was covered by a number of other artists including Deep Purple and Eric Burdon and the Animals. However, the post-Diana Ross Supremes and the Four Tops (together) released the most successful cover version, which peaked at #7 on the soul chart and #14 on the *Billboard* Hot 100. What song is being described, who is the original by and who was paid $20,000 not to perform?

The song is "River Deep-Mountain High." Although credited to Ike and Tina Turner on an album of the same name, Ike is the one who was paid the money not to play or sing on the track because Spector did not want him to interfere with the production of the song. Spector used over 20 top session musicians for the recording, including Hal Blaine, Leon Russell, Carol Kaye and Glen Campbell. The completed record cost about $22,000, at the time an unbelievable price tag for a single. Not surprisingly for a Phil Spector production, the recording session was arduous. Tina Turner commented: "I must have sung that 500,000 times," Tina later said. "I was drenched with sweat. I had to take my shirt off and stand there in my bra to sing."

Spector was banking heavily on the song being a hit and was devastated that it wasn't. A biographer called it "the most appalling blow of his career—a sharp and vicious chop in the place where it hurt the most—his ego." His label, Philles Records, did not release another album until 1969.[11]

It is not uncommon for songs to be adopted from the music of earlier songs, sometimes even from prior centuries. What is extremely rare however is for a hit from the

Decade (or any period after the Decade) to be exactly taken from the music and words of a *recorded* song which actually predates public radio. The song in question was recorded in 1911 and was made famous by Harry Champion. During the Decade, it became a #1 song for Herman's Hermits. As a hint, it was one of the very few songs of the Hermits on which Peter Noone was not the lead singer. What is the song?

"I'm Henry VIII, I Am." Earlier sources usually spell the name "Henery" and the music requires the name "Henery" to be pronounced as three syllables (and with silent "h" at the start of Henry). The sheet music for the 1965 Herman's Hermits revival, however, presented the name as "Henry." While Champion's version contains additional verses, the Hermits' version is simply the chorus of Champion's, with identical music.

The lead solo on the Hermits' version was played by the group's lead guitarist Derek "Lek" Leckenby. In the *New York Times*, Colin MacInnes wrote that this song was the fastest-selling song in history to that point and that it "drove teen-agers wild and their parents mad." As to the origins of the group's name, sources differ, but they all have in common the fact that someone noticed a resemblance between Noone and Sherman from *The Rocky and Bullwinkle Show*, which somehow morphed into Herman.[12]

This song is often considered the unofficial national anthem of Cuba and one of its most patriotic songs. This is presumably not because of the lyrics but because those lyrics were part of a very long poem written by a famous Cuban poet and national hero, José Martí (1853–1895). Although there were several recorded versions of the song, the most successful was by the Sandpipers, whose rendition reached #7 in 1966. What is the song?

"Guantanamera."[13]

This song was written in 1963 by Chet Powers and was released on albums or performed live by a number of very well-known acts, including the Kingston Trio, We Five, Judy Collins, Joni Mitchell, the Chad Mitchell Trio, Jefferson Airplane, Linda Ronstadt, and the Carpenters. It was not a major hit for any of them (although the We Five cover did go to #31.) However, it did become a major hit in 1969 for a group that had no other hits. They originally released it in 1967, when it peaked at #62. However (and here is the hint), interest in their song was renewed in 1969, when it was used in a radio public service announcement as a call for brotherhood by the National Conference of Christians and Jews. The single was re-released, hitting #1 in *Cash Box* magazine, and reaching #5 on the *Billboard* Hot 100 chart. It also earned a million-selling gold single from the RIAA. What is the song and who is the band?

"Come Together" by the Youngbloods.

What famous 1972 song mentions T Rex, the Beatles (and their song "Revolution"), and the Stones?

"All the Young Dudes" by Mott the Hoople, which reached #3 in the U.K. in 1972 but, surprisingly, only reached #37 in the U.S. The name of the band comes from the 1966 Willard Manus novel of the same name about an eccentric who works in a circus freak show.

Speaking of "All the Young Dudes," that song was written specifically for Mott the Hoople by another artist because their bass player, Peter Watts, told him that the band was going to break up due to lack of commercial success and the songwriter was a fan who wanted to help them. Who was the songwriter?

David Bowie. He had previously offered them "Suffragette City" but they passed on that. But when drummer Dale Griffin first heard "All the Young Dudes," he said, "He wants to give us that? He must be crazy!'" It was ranked #256 on the *Rolling Stone* list of 500 Greatest Songs of All Time.

Which song was Bruce Springsteen referring to when he said, while writing it, "the rhyming dictionary was on fire!" (As a hint, it is the first song on his first album, *Greetings from Asbury Park*.)

"Blinded by the Light."

Which Simon & Garfunkel song consists of the singing of a tender very well-known traditional Christmas carol juxtaposed over a simulated TV newscast discussing depressing events of the day?

"7 O'Clock News/Silent Night," which appears on *Parsley Sage Rosemary & Thyme*. As the track progresses, the song becomes fainter and the news report louder. Although Simon "created" the newscast (voiced by a DJ at the time, Charlie O'Donnell), the events described are not only real, but they all occurred on the same day, August 3, 1966. Those events included: a report that President Johnson's hope of a full ban on discrimination for any type of housing had "no chance"; the death of comedian Lenny Bruce from an overdose of narcotics at the age of 42 [although he was actually 40]; the urging by Cook County Sheriff Richard Ogilvie of the cancellation of a civil rights march planned by Martin Luther King; the grand jury indictment of Richard Speck for the murder of nine [actually eight] student nurses; and a speech by "former Vice President Richard Nixon" to Veterans of Foreign Wars [actually to the American Legion] urging an increase in the war effort in Vietnam, and calling opposition to the war the "greatest single weapon working against the United States."

This song, written and performed by Peter Sarstedt, was released in 1969. It reached #1 in the U.K. and was a minor hit in the U.S., although the song is still played on old-ies stations today. The song is about a girl named Marie-Claire who is a member of the French jet set, but who—based on the title—may not be content, despite her glamorous lifestyle. The song mentions Marlene Dietrich, Zizi Jeanmaire (a French ballerina), Pierre Balmain (a French designer of elegant fashion), Boulevard Saint-Michel (a street in the Latin Quarter of Paris, Sasha Distel (a French singer), the Sorbonne University, Picasso, Juan-les-Pins (a fashionable beach resort on the French Riviera), Saint Moritz and Aga Khan (a world-travelling Islamic leader and racehorse owner). What is the song?

"Where Do You Go To (My Lovely)?" Eden Kane (real name Richard Sarstedt) and Peter Sarstedt are the first pair of siblings to score #1 songs as solo artists. Kane's #1 was "Well I Ask You," released in 1961. A third brother Robin Sarstedt (real name Clive Sarstedt) also made the Top 3 in 1976 with "My Resistance Is Low," making them the only set of three brothers to have separate solo top three singles.

CHAPTER 11

Odds and Ends (Or as the Who Would Say, Odds and Sods)

Not every interesting aspect of rock music during the Decade can be slotted neatly into the other 39 chapters that comprise the other parts of this book. This chapter is devoted to all of those "other" questions and answers!

The drummer of one of the most famous bands in the world befriended Charles Manson, and when he heard about Manson's desire to become a rock star, he arranged an audition for Manson with a highly respected record producer? Who was the drummer and what was his band?

Dennis Wilson of the Beach Boys. Manson wanted to become a musical artist more famous than the Beatles and he thought that he had the talent to match theirs. The long odds against him attaining that goal appeared to get shorter in 1968 when he met Wilson, who thought that Manson may have some musical talent. He even was able to arrange an audition for Manson with his friend Terry Melcher, a highly respected record producer in Los Angeles. Melcher, the only child of actress Doris Day, produced the Byrds' cover hits "Mr. Tambourine Man" and "Turn! Turn! Turn!"

How important was this audition to Manson? As his biographer stated: "Charlie had been keeping everyone busy preparing for Helter Skelter, but a cataclysmic race war paled compared to Charlie finally getting a record deal. All of his followers were ordered to drop everything else and prepare for Melcher's visit." Melcher heard a few of Manson's compositions but decided to pass on the opportunity to sign Manson. Was Melcher tempted to sign Manson? Apparently not. He recalled later that Charlie's songs were "below-average nothing, as far as I was concerned. Manson was like every other starving, hippie songwriter who was currently jamming Sunset Boulevard, 100,000 every day, who looked, dressed, talked and sang exactly like Charles Manson, sang about the same topics of peace and revolution, about the themes that were in the Beatles' albums."

Wilson however remained impressed with Manson's musical talents. He took one of Manson's songs called "Cease to Exist," reworked it by altering the lyrics and adding a new bridge, and changed the title to "Never Learn Not to Love." The song was released on the Beach Boys' 1969 album *20/20* and also as the B-side of the "Bluebirds over the Mountain" single in 1968, with Wilson being credited as the sole composer. Manson explicitly told Wilson that the words were not to be altered. When Manson heard about the release of the song by the Beach Boys, with the changed lyrics and no credit being given to Manson, he threatened Wilson with murder. The Manson incident gave everyone a scare in the Beach Boys' camp, especially after his well-known crimes came to light. Wilson then severed his ties with Manson. Melcher went on to cowrite the 1988 song "Kokomo" with John Phillips, Scott McKenzie and Mike Love of the Beach Boys, which reached #1 on the *Billboard* charts.[1]

Mike Love was the lead vocalist for the Beach Boys on many of their hits released during the Decade. However, he did not sing lead vocals on the only two Beach Boys songs which reached #1 during the Decade. What were the two songs and who were the lead singers?

The first was "Help Me Rhonda" (1965) and Al Jardine sang lead vocal. It was the first Beach Boys song to feature Jardine on lead vocal. The original title was "Help Me, Rhonda." Is there an actual Rhonda? In 2012, Brian Wilson, who composed the song along with Mike Love, said no. He also cited this as one song that he wished he could have improved: "I would've made a better rhythm—it wasn't in the pocket."

There is a fascinating 40-minute audio clip on YouTube in which a drunken Murry Wilson, the father of Brian, Dennis and Carl, and the uncle of Mike Love, can be heard interfering with the recording session for this song and basically berating all of the boys at one time or another. "You're so tight fellas, I can't believe it." He repeatedly told Jardine to "syncopate it a little" and to "loosen up." Murry was the band's original manager (and music publisher) until they fired him in 1964.

Though instrumental in getting the band signed with Capitol Records, it has been suggested that, as a frustrated songwriter himself, he was jealous of the ease with which Brian crafted beautiful hit songs, which led to Murry constantly belittling his son's talents (but referring to himself as a "genius"), which in turn supposedly led to much of the emotional and mental turmoil Brian experienced later on. A letter that Murry wrote to Brian in 1965 (just when "Help Me Rhonda" was topping the charts) was discovered in 2010 and it read in part: "No matter how many hit songs you write, or how many hundreds of thousands of dollars you may earn, you will find when you finish this short cycle of business success that you didn't do it honestly and for this reason you are going to suffer remorse." In 1969, Murry sold the Sea Of Tunes Publishing Company, which consisted of all of Brian's Beach Boys music, to Irving Almo Music for the paltry sum of $700,000. He kept the money.

The other Beach Boys song to reach #1 during the Decade was "Good Vibrations," and Carl Wilson sang lead vocal on that song, although Mike Love sang parts of the chorus. The various sections of the song were edited together by Wilson into numerous sound collages, and its production spanned seventeen recording sessions at four different recording studios. The recording is reported to have used over 90 hours of magnetic recording tape, with an eventual budget estimated between $50,000 and $75,000 ($360,000 and $550,000 today). The two other Beach Boys songs to reach #1 were "I Get Around" (1964) and "Kokomo" (1988) and Mike Love sang lead vocal on both of those. [2]

It is not of course uncommon for bands to experience a magical period during which they are seemingly blessed by the angels and produce one masterpiece after another, only to never again be able to replicate that success. Indeed, this can be said to be the experience of most bands who have hit it big. Eventually however, most of them break up once the new hits stop coming. Some linger on however long after their hitmaking era has ended, which is both a blessing and a curse. It is a blessing in the sense that they are still able to draw crowds and thus make a very comfortable living by touring and playing the oldies. However, it also forces them to be chained to their past and to be constantly reminded that their ability to create worthy new material that the public wants to buy has deserted them.

The Beach Boys are a prime example of this. All of Brian Wilson's magic came between 1963 and 1966 but the group released another 18 studio albums after that, several of them referring to summer, cars and surfing in the titles, just like in the old days. For the most part, the public didn't care about any of them. As David Hepworth writes: "It's important to bands that they feel they are moving forward. This is vital for their self-respect. But as one unmemorable album follows another from premature acclaim to the bargain bin of history, each auspicious beginning is followed by the familiar flatness, each round of press interviews and TV appearances gives way to faint embarrassment as the new songs are dropped from the set list never to return, we in the audience increasingly identify with the line that makes a popular T-shirt slogan at festivals—'Play some old.'" He was referring to the Beach Boys but could easily have been referring to numerous other groups. While the Rolling Stones of course had a far longer heyday than the Beach Boys, they continue to successfully tour more than 25 years after their last top 10 hit. [3]

Many of the Beach Boys' early hit songs were about surfing, including "Surfin' USA," "Catch a Wave," "Surfin'," and others. However only one of them actually surfed

(who was, for that matter, the only one who actually looked like a handsome "beach boy").
Which one?

Drummer Dennis Wilson.

Spell the last name of the guitarist for the Who who wrote most of their songs and whose first name is Pete.

Townshend.

Chip Taylor cowrote one of the few Supremes songs that reached #1 which was not written by the Motown songwriting team of Holland-Dozier-Holland. (When the song reached #1 in 1968, the group had changed its name to Diana Ross and the Supremes.) What was the song?

"Love Child," which was cowritten by Frank Wilson, Pam Sawyer and Deke Richards.

In 1999, BMI released its list of the most performed songs of the century in terms of number of radio and television airplays. There was only one song on the list with more than 8 million airplays, including cover versions. Although originally released just before the Decade began, it reached #1 in February 1965. What is the song and who originally recorded it? As a hint, it was written by Barry Mann, Phil Spector and Cynthia Weil.

"You've Lost That Lovin' Feelin'," by Bobby Hatfield and Bill Medley, better known as the Righteous Brothers. It was produced by Phil Spector. Hatfield reportedly expressed his annoyance to Spector upon learning that he would have to wait until the chorus before joining Medley's vocals. When Hatfield asked Spector just what he was supposed to do during Medley's solo, Spector replied: "You can go straight to the fucking bank." On the other hand, Medley doesn't sing at all on the group's hit "Unchained Melody." (As for who is who, in the group, Medley was the taller dark-haired one who sang the low parts with his bass-baritone voice, and Hatfield was the blond-haired one taking the higher register vocals with his countertenor voice.)

"You've Lost That Lovin' Feelin'" ran for nearly four minutes when released. This was much too long by contemporary AM standards but Spector refused to cut it shorter. Instead, on the label where the time is indicated, he also tricked the deejays into thinking it was a shorter song by printing "3:05" while the track actually ran 3:46. Among the background singers in the song's crescendo is a young Cher.[4]

The Righteous Brothers had a follow-up hit in 1966, also written by the great songwriting team of Mann and Weil. They were about halfway through composing the song but they decided to shelve it because they thought it sounded too much like "You've Lost That Lovin' Feelin'." Nevertheless, they played a bit of it for Bill Medley. Nothing came of that at the time. However, about six months later, after the group had parted ways with Phil Spector, Medley called up Mann, who recalled the conversation as follows: "[Medley asked] 'What ever happened to that song you played me?' And I said, 'We didn't want to complete it. It sounded like a poor man's 'Lovin' Feelin'.' He said, 'No, I love that song! Please, complete the song, we'd love to record it.' So we ended up completing the song, and they ended up recording it." The song hit the top of the *Billboard* Hot 100 chart and was ranked by Bilboard as the #3 song for all of 1966. What is the song, which is in fact reminiscent of "Lovin' Feelin'"?

"(You're My) Soul and Inspiration."[5]

"On the night of January 6, 1970 [Paul] McCartney settled into his seat at the Royal Albert Hall. Along with 5,000 others in the elegantly domed theater with boxed seats, he was about to witness the London debut of the band everyone was calling the 'American Beatles.'" Who was the band? (As a hint, the author added, "one of them was actually English, but a catchy press moniker couldn't be denied.")

Crosby, Stills, Nash & Young. The English one was of course Graham Nash.[6]

The following drummers are all on record as being influenced in their style by another drummer: John Bonham of Led Zeppelin, Peter Criss of Kiss, Neil Peart of Rush, Stewart Copeland of the Police, Ian Paice of Deep Purple, Tommy Aldridge of Thin Lizzy and other bands, Bill Bruford of Yes, Alex Van Halen of Van Halen and Nick Mason of Pink Floyd. Who was this British drummer?

Ginger Baker of Cream. AllMusic stated that "virtually every drummer of every heavy metal band that has followed since that time has sought to emulate some aspect of [his] playing." Peart said: "His playing was revolutionary—extrovert, primal and inventive. He set the bar for what rock drumming could be."[7]

This song is divided into the following six sections:

1. Intro (0:00–0:52)
2. Ballad (0:52–2:36)

3. Guitar solo (2:36–3:03)
4. Opera (3:03–4:07)
5. Hard rock (4:07–4:56)
6. Outro (4:56–5:55)

Because the opera part of the song was considered impossible to play live, the stage would go dark, the band would leave the stage and the recorded version of the song would play during this section. What song is it?

"Bohemian Rhapsody" by Queen.

In a 1968 song that is considered one of the earliest funk hits, the lead singer of the band starts the song by introducing himself, announcing what city he is from—Houston, Texas, and the name of a new dance his band started. After recording the song, he was drafted into the U.S. Army and began serving in Vietnam, where he suffered a leg wound. It was not until he was convalescing in a military hospital that he learned that his song had become the #1 song back in America. He tried to convince people in the hospital that the song was his. What is the song, who is the singer, and what is the name of his band?

The song is "Tighten Up," the singer is Archie Bell and the band is Archie Bell and the Drells. *Rolling Stone* ranked the song as #270 on the 500 greatest songs of all time.[8]

Two of the biggest Motown groups of all time have each been performing for more than 50 years. One of them had the exact same lineup for 45 years, until 1997. The other had 17 different lineups with 17 different members, also until 1997. Who are the two groups?

The first is the Four Tops. Their four-man lineup consisted of lead singer Levi Stubbs (born Levi Stubbles, a cousin of Jackie Wilson), and groupmates Abdul "Duke" Fakir, Renaldo "Obie" Benson and Lawrence Payton. The second is the Temptations. Their so-called "classic 5 lineup", in effect from 1964–1968, consisted of lead singer David Ruffin, tenors Otis Williams and Eddie Kendricks, baritone Paul Williams and bass Melvin Franklin. However, they continued to have tremendous success for the next seven years after Dennis Edwards replaced David Ruffin as lead singer.

James Taylor has had only one #1 hit on the *Billboard* Top 100. What song is it? As a hint, it was not written by him.

"You've Got a Friend," by Carole King which appeared on his album *Mud Slide Slim*. It reached #1 in 1971. His classic song "Fire and Rain" only rose as high as #3 and, surprisingly, "Carolina on My Mind" only reached #118.

One of Barry Manilow's biggest hits, released in 1974, was written under a different title by Scott English and Richard Kerr. It was a hit in 1971 for English in the U.K. and in 1972 for Bunny Walters in New Zealand. In the U.S. however, a band had a #1 hit with a song of the same title in 1972 which was a completely different song. Therefore, to avoid confusion with that song, Manilow changed the title from one girl's name to a rhyming girl's name. What was the original title of the song, what did Manilow change it to and who was the band who had a #1 hit with the original title in 1972?

"Brandy," "Mandy," and Looking Glass.

A. Bruce Johnston of the Beach Boys was only a very occasional songwriter.
B. Barry Manilow has been a very prolific songwriter over his career.
Why are A and B ironic when juxtaposed together?

Because one of Johnston's relatively few songs with which Manilow had a big hit was "I Write the Songs." Although originally released in 1975, it won the Grammy for Song of the Year in 1977. Johnston has stated that the "I" in the song refers to God. Meanwhile, Manilow was reluctant to record the song not only because he did not write that particular song but because the lyrics of the song generally (such as "I write the songs that make the whole world sing") "could be misinterpreted as a monumental ego trip." However, Clive Davis, President of Arista Records, convinced him to record it.[9]

Who or what is "The Corporation"? (As a hint, they have a connection to Berry Gordy.)

They were a team of songwriters and producers put together by Berry Gordy in 1969 to create songs for Motown's new act at the time, the Jackson 5. The four members were Gordy himself, Alphonzo Mizelle, Freddie Perrin and Deke Richards. They wrote and produced the #1 songs "I Want You Back" (1969), "ABC" and "The Love You Save" (both in 1970), as well as other Jackson 5 singles such as "Mama's Pearl" and "Maybe Tomorrow" (both in 1971). The group members were never billed individually on the original Jackson 5 releases they worked on. Even the songwriters' credit was listed as "The Corporation." The reason is because Gordy did not want any more of his Motown songwriters to become "back room superstars" à la the songwriting team of Holland-Dozier-Holland that had defected from the label two years earlier. The Corporation disbanded in 1972.[10]

This is the only group in history to have four guitarists on the *Rolling Stone* list of 100 Greatest Guitarists (not with the band at the same time). Two of the four were among the original members of the group, and one is a nephew of one of the original members.

The Allman Brothers. The two original members are Duane Allman and Dickey Betts. The nephew is Derek Trucks, whose uncle Butch Trucks was an original member. The fourth is Warren Haynes, who joined the group in 1989. The only original band members who are still with the band as of 2016 and who have never left the band are Gregg Allman and Butch Trucks. The same could also be said of drummer Jai Johanny "Jaimoe" Johanson, except that he was not with the band from 1980–1982. Dickey Betts left the band in 2000. Betts wrote the band's signature song *Ramblin' Man*, and it was their only top 10 song, peaking at #2 on the *Billboard* Hot 100. The band was highly unusual in having two drummers in their regular lineup, namely Butch Trucks and Johanson.[11]

The Cyrkle had two hits in the Decade both of which are frequently heard on oldies stations today. What were they?

In 1966, they had a #2 hit with "Red Rubber Ball," which was written by Paul Simon and Bruce Woodley of the Australian band the Seekers. Their other hit, "Turn Down Day," written by Jerry Keller and David Blume, reached #16 on the *Billboard* charts. The group opened for the Beatles on their final tour ever in 1966. The Cyrkle were managed by Beatles manager Brain Epstein, which presumably accounts for why they were the opening act on that tour. They were the only American group in Epstein's stable.

What do Chip Taylor, James Wesley Voight (actor Jon Voight's brother), the Troggs and Merliee Rush have in common?

Taylor and Voight are the same person. He wrote the biggest hit songs for both the Troggs and Merrilee Rush, namely "Wild Thing" and "Angel of the Morning," respectively.

In 2007, this album was named the #1 Canadian Album of All Time by Bob Mersereau in his book *The Top 100 Canadian Albums* [i.e. albums by Canadian-born artists]. What is the album and who was the artist? As a hint, it was released in 1972 and was the best-selling album in the U.S. that year.

Harvest by Neil Young. There was a legend about this album that had circulated more many years but was not actually confirmed by Young until 2016. Graham Nash was at Young's ranch near San Francisco and Young asked Nash if he wanted to hear the as-yet unreleased album. Nash said yes. However, rather than going into Young's studio, they rowed out into the lake in front of the ranch. Nash assumed Young brought a cassette player with him. Instead, according to Nash, "he has his entire house as the left speaker and his entire barn as the right speaker. And I heard 'Harvest' coming out of these two incredibly large loud speakers louder than hell. It was unbelievable. Elliot Mazer, who produced Neil, produced 'Harvest,' came down to the shore of the lake and he shouted out to Neil, 'How was that, Neil?'" Young shouted back, "More barn!" Young had never spoken about the incident before 2016 but he confirmed Nash's account: "I had the left speaker, big speakers set up in my house with the windows open. And I had the PA system . . . playing the right-hand channel." When asked if he truly did yell back, "More barn!" he said, "Yeah, I think it was a little house heavy."[12]

There have been a fair number of triple albums released over the years but virtually all of these have been either live performances or compilations of previously released material. Triple albums of original new material are rare indeed. This triple album is considered the first one in rock music history. It is not obscure either, spending seven weeks atop the *Billboard* 200. What is the triple album? (As a hint, it was released in 1971.)

All Things Must Pass by George Harrison, which contained hits such as "My Sweet Lord" and "What is Life." Harrison was always frustrated by his unofficial quota of one or two songs per Beatles album, and now, untethered, he was finally free to release all of his own material, some of which he had been stockpiling over the years (even though the third disc consisted only of studio jams). Commenting on the historical significance of the album, Jayson Greene wrote: "It was the heaviest and the most consequential Beatles solo album, the first object from the Beatles fallout to plummet from the sky and land with a clunk in a generation of living rooms. It is a paean to having too much ambition, too much to say, to fit into a confined space, and for this reason alone it remains one of the most important capital-A Albums of all time."

The album was heavy because, rather than being packaged in a triple gatefold cover, it was designed as a hinged thick box. As one Apple rep stated: "It was a bloody big thing. You needed arms like an orangutan to carry half a dozen." The packaging caused some confusion among retailers, who, at that time, associated boxed albums with opera or classical works.[13]

The Grass Roots had two top 10 hits, "Let's Live for Today" in 1967 and "Midnight Confessions" in 1968. Their lead guitarist on both of those songs was a regular on the

television show *The Office* throughout its nine-year run. His name on the show is the same as his name in real life. Who is he?

Creed Bratton.

What unusual method did Gregg Allman use to try and exempt himself from the draft and was it successful?

He shot himself in the foot and yes, it was successful. In 1965, the band was called the Allman Joys. Gregg's older brother Duane was exempt from the draft because he was the eldest son in the family without a father (who was murdered). Gregg told *Rolling Stone* columnist Gavin Edwards what happened: "My brother [Duane] said, 'I'll tell you what we're gonna do. Just shoot a bullet through your foot.' I thought he was joking. He wasn't."

So the night before his physical examination, Duane threw Gregg a "foot-shooting party," plying him with speed and whiskey, and inviting over some friends and some girls. Gregg painted a target on his left moccasin. "I didn't want to hurt myself," he said. "The long bones in your foot come to a V, and I wanted to hit it right there so it would crack two of them but not really upset anything permanently." Although understandably nervous at first, he eventually was goaded by Duane into doing the deed. "I was bleeding quite a bit because the speed and liquor had my blood pressure going." The next day, Gregg showed up at the induction center with a huge bandage and crutches—he was quickly disqualified.[14]

One wonders whether some tenuous connection might be drawn between this act and Duane's death a mere six years later. Say for example that Gregg had been drafted and served in Vietnam. This could have easily had an impact or the formation and history of the Allman Brothers band—or whether there even would have been one. However, Gregg did avoid the draft, the band was formed (in 1969), and by late 1971, the band and its members were becoming stars, especially because their landmark live album, *At Fillmore East*, had just been released 3 months previously. Duane was living the rock star life. However, on October 29, 1971, he was killed in a motorcycle accident in Macon, Georgia while riding at a high rate of speed. (Bandmate and bassist Berry Oakley died also in a motorcycle accident 13 months later, a mere three blocks from where Duane Allman died. Their graves are side by side in Macon's Rose Hill Cemetery.)

When Allman died, he was only 24 years old, a full three years younger than all of the members of the "27 club" (Jim Morrison, Jimi Hendrix, Janis Joplin, Brian Jones, etc. Berry was also 24 when he died.) Aside from Buddy Holly (who was only 22 when he died) and Selena (23), Allman is probably the most famous rock star to die at such a young age. Other stars who died when they were as young or even younger than Allman include Ritchie Valens

(17, on the same flight as Buddy Holly), Bobby Fuller (23), Tammi Terrell (also 24), Sid Vicious (21), and Biggie Smalls (24). Holly and Valens were both killed in a plane crash on February 3, 1959, which became "the day the music died" in Don McLean's "American Pie."

In regard to avoiding the draft, as Gregg Allman did, Phil Ochs wrote and sang a great song called "The Draft Dodger Rag." The song is sung from the perspective of a gung-ho and patriotic young man who has been drafted. When he reports for duty however, he recites a long list of reasons why he can't serve, including poor vision, flat feet, a ruptured spleen, allergies and asthma, back pain, addiction to multiple drugs, his college enrollment, his disabled aunt, his employment at a defense factory, and the fact that he carries a purse. As the song ends, the young man tells the sergeant that he'll be the first to volunteer for "a war without blood or gore." According to music journalist Jon Savage, Iggy Pop actually did avoid the draft by pretending to be gay and Lou Reed avoided it by exaggerating his mental instabilities.[15]

In 1966, this artist released the first rock double album ever. *Rolling Stone* ranks it as #9 of the 500 Greatest Albums of all time. What is the double album and who is the artist?

Blonde on Blonde by Bob Dylan. It just preceded the release of *Freak Out!*, the double album by the Mothers Of Invention. Ultimateclassicrock.com ranks *Blonde on Blonde* as the second best double album of all time (behind *Exile on Main Street* by the Stones).[16]

What internationally famous group was banned from touring in the United States from 1965-1969, during the height of their career?

The Kinks. The ban was instituted by the American Federation of Musicians. Though no specific reason was given, it was widely attributed to their rowdy onstage behavior. For example, during a 1965 concert in Wales, lead guitarist Dave Davies insulted drummer Mick Avory and kicked over his drum set. Avory responded by hitting Davies with his hi-hat stand, rendering him unconscious. Avory fled the scene, fearing that he had killed his bandmate. To placate the police, Avory later claimed that it was part of a new act in which the band members would hurl their instruments at each other. Many years later, frontman Ray Davies commented, "In many respects, that ridiculous ban took away the best years of the Kinks' career when the original band was performing at its peak." By the time the group was allowed to return in 1969, "the Woodstock generation had arrived and the Kinks were almost forgotten."[17]

Some of the greatest bands of the Decade (or of any era) released a surprisingly small number of studio albums in their original incarnation (excluding reunion albums after

band breakups). For example, Crosby Stills and Nash released only one, the self-titled album released in 1969. While they did release albums after that, starting with *CSN* in 1977, those must be considered as reunion albums.

How many studio albums were released by the following bands?
Cream

Four albums, namely *Fresh Cream* (1966), *Disraeli Gears* (1967), *Wheels of Fire* (1968) and *Goodbye* (1969).

Velvet Underground with Lou Reed

Four albums, namely *The Velvet Underground & Nico* (1967), *White Light/White Heat* (1968), *The Velvet Underground* (1969) and *Loaded* (1970).

Big Brother and the Holding Company with Janis Joplin

Only two, the self-titled debut album in 1967 and the classic *Cheap Thrills* in 1968.

MC5

Three albums, namely *Kick Out the Jams* (1969), *Back in the USA* (1970) and *High Times* (1971).

Faces

Four albums, namely *First Step* (1970), *Long Player* (1971), *A Nod Is as Good as a Wink . . . to a Blind Horse* (1971), and *Ooh La La* (1973).

Blind Faith

Only one, their self-titled album released in 1969.

Derek and the Dominos

Again, only one, *Layla and Other Assorted Love Songs*, released in 1970. During the Decade, Eric Clapton seemed to make a habit of being a member of classic bands which released only a few albums, or in the case of Blind Faith and Derek and the Dominos, only one album.

As for the derivation of the name of the band, there have always been conflicting stories, including among the band members themselves, but the most fun one comes from keyboardist Bobby Whitlock. Just before their very first gig, they decided to call themselves Derek and the Dynamics (Derek being a nickname for Clapton) and they told the name to the announcer. "He said, 'That's fine,' and went out on stage to introduce us—he said 'Ladies and gentlemen! Derek and the Dominos!' My heart went to the floor; I couldn't believe it. I could see myself in a zoot suit—we'd be wearing one color suit and Eric would be wearing another. Where I grew up, if the name was the Dominos, you were going to be wearing matching suits. That was the first thing that flashed through my mind, but it stuck, and that was that. That was the first time we were ever called Derek and the Dominos, but always after that."[18]

Buffalo Springfield

Three albums, *Buffalo Springfield* (1966), *Buffalo Springfield Again* (1967) and *Last Time Around* (1968). This band took their name from the side of a steamroller made by the Buffalo-Springfield Roller Company.

Crosby, Stills, Nash and Young

Only one studio album in the Decade—the great *Déjà Vu*, released in 1970. Later albums such as *American Dream* from 1988 and *Looking Forward* from 1999 are reunion albums.

Name a band from the Decade that had a punctuation mark in its name and their one big hit.

? and the Mysterians and "96 Tears." The song was written by frontman Question Mark, a/k/a Rudy Martinez. The song hit #1 in October 1966.

Jimi Hendrix had only one top 20 song and that song only reached #20. It was a cover of another song which was released only six months earlier. Both versions are considered classics. What is the song and who is the singer-songwriter on the original?

"All Along the Watchtower" by Bob Dylan.

There is only one song which falls within all of the following categories: (1) it was cow-ritten by John Lennon with another singer-songwriter, (2) who was not Paul McCartney, and (3) it was a #1 hit in America for the other singer-songwriter. What is the song and who is the artist who recorded it? (As a hint, it was released in 1975 and Lennons sings backing vocals on the track.)

"Fame" by David Bowie. Lennon's contribution to the song was not traditional in the sense of developing the music or the lyrics. However, he did contribute to the song in certain important ways. First, he came up with the title. Second, he provided the inspiration for the theme of the song—bemoaning the nature of celebrity because he had discussed this with Bowie. Third, he plays guitar on the song. Finally, it is Lennon who sang the repeated words "fame, fame, fame" with his voice heard at fast, normal, and slow playback speeds, until Bowie's vocal is heard singing the final lyrics of the song before the fade. This was Bowie's only #1 hit in the U.S. during the Decade.[19]

Rolling Stone magazine made a list of the 100 top music videos. Not surprisingly, almost all of them post-date the start of MTV, which was August 1, 1981. (The first video, appropriately enough, was *Video Killed the Radio Star* by the Buggles.) Surprisingly how-ever, one song (and only one song) is from the Decade and it came in at #7 no less. What song is it and who is the artist or group? There is also a reasonably famous person on the left side of the screen throughout the song (at least reasonably famous at the time). For extra credit, name that person. If any hints are necessary, here are a few. Try to answer the question with as few hints as possible because each one gives away more about the answer. A few hints:

- The title of the song is not in the lyrics.
- Although released in 1965, the "video" was first seen in 1967 in a film clip from a documentary about a 1965 tour by the artist or group called *Don't Look Back*.
- The clip features the singer flipping cue cards, each one containing the last words of each line of the song.

The answer is Bob Dylan, and the song is "Subterranean Homesick Blues."
Answer to extra credit question: Beat poet Allen Ginsberg.

On the subject of noteworthy or influential pre-MTV music videos, there is one song that did not make the *Rolling Stone* list of top videos, but perhaps it should have.

In *A Concise History of Rock Music,* Paul Fowles wrote that the song is "widely credited as the first global hit single for which an accompanying video was central to the marketing strategy." *Rolling Stone* itself, though leaving this song off list, wrote that "its influence cannot be overstated, practically inventing the music video seven years before MTV went on the air." As a hint, the song (released in 1975, along with the video) is the signature song on the signature album of one of most successful bands of the 1970s and 1980s.

The song is "Bohemian Rhapsody" and the album is *A Night at the Opera.* In 2012, the song was voted the favorite #1 single is British rock music history.[20]

How many albums did Bob Marley release solely under his own name?

None—they all mentioned his band, the Wailers. His first six albums were released strictly under their name, and the last seven were released by Bob Marley and the Wailers. *Natty Dread,* released in 1974, was the first album released as Bob Marley and the Wailers and the first recorded by Marley without former bandmates Peter Tosh and Bunny Wailer.

This Broadway musical had the most songs to reach the top five on the *Billboard* Hot 100 chart. It spawned a #1, a #2, a #3 and a #4. In every case, though, the versions of the songs which reached those levels were covers by other artists as opposed to the original cast recording. All four songs are well-remembered today. The questions are: what was the musical, what were the songs, and who were the artists. For extra credit, identify the peak position of each song.

The musical was *Hair* and the songs are as follows:

#1—"Aquarius/Let the Sunshine In"—The 5th Dimension
#2—"Hair"—The Cowsills
#3—"Good Morning Starshine"—Oliver
#4—"Easy to be Hard"—Three Dog Night

Though little remembered today, Oliver actually had a bigger hit than "Good Morning Starshine," which is well-remembered today. It was called "Jean" and it reached #2 in 1969. As for "Aquarius/Let the Sunshine In," it stayed at #1 for six weeks in the spring of 1969, it was listed at #66 on *Billboard*'s Greatest Songs of All Time and it won Grammys in 1970 for Record of the Year and Best Pop Vocal Performance by a Group.

There were two songs by Jamaican artists which reached #1 during the Decade. Who were the artists and what were the songs? The singer of one of the songs (which he cowrote) would be considered a one-hit wonder, although the song sold 11 million copies world-wide, making it one of the biggest-selling singles ever. It came out in 1975. The other song was #1 for four weeks in November 1974. (As a hint, neither artist is known as a reggae singer, so that rules out Bob Marley and Jimmy Cliff.)

The first is *Kung Fu Fighting* by Carl Douglas and the second is *I Can See Clearly Now* by Johnny Nash, which he also wrote.

Here's one for fans of the Boss. People often think his wife Patti Scialfa was the first woman in the E Street Band, but she wasn't. Instead, it was an Israeli woman who was with the band as a violinist and background singer from September 1974 to March 1975. She sang vocals on "4th of July, Asbury Park (Sandy)" from *The Wild, the Innocent & the E Street Shuffle*, and she played violin on "Jungleland" from *Born to Run*. Then she returned to Israel where she has had a successful career as a lyricist and screenplay writer. Who is this woman?

Suki Lahav.[21]

This man was born in Berlin to a Jewish couple who had emigrated from Russia. He was named Wulf Wolodia Grajonca. His father died two days after he was born. Due to the increasing peril to Jews in Germany, his mother placed her son and one of his sisters in a Berlin orphanage, which sent them to France in a pre–Holocaust exchange of Jewish children for Christian orphans. He was one of a group known as the One Thousand Children (OTC), those mainly Jewish children who fled the Nazis, but whose parents were forced to stay behind. Nearly all these OTC parents were killed by the Third Reich. This man's mother died at Auschwitz. He went on to become famous and influential in the rock world, though not as a singer, songwriter, producer or musician. He died at age 60 in a helicopter crash in 1991. Who was he?

Bill Graham.[22]

Jim Croce had five top 10 hits and he wrote all but one of them himself. What was that song?

"I Got a Name" written by Charles Fox and Norman Gimbel. It is featured in the 2012 Quention Tarantino movie *Django Unchained*, obviously anachronistically since the movie takes place just after the Civil War. Tarantino used the same technique in his prior movie *Inglorious Basterds* which takes place during World War II. "Chapter Five" of that movie, called "Revenge of the Giant Face," opens with David Bowie's song "Cat People (Putting Out Fire)."

Name four famous songs from the Decade in which there is stuttering. One reached #74 in 1965 in the U.S., one reached #66 in 1972 (but both are iconic songs today despite their anemic chart rankings), and the other two reached #1 in 1974.

They are: "My Generation" by the Who (the #74 song), "Changes" by David Bowie (the #66 song), "You Ain't Seen Nothing Yet" by Bachman Turner Overdrive and "Bennie and the Jets" by Elton John. The latter two songs both hit #1. "You Ain't Seen Nothing Yet" was a song composed by Randy Bachman especially for his brother Gary, the first manager of Bachman-Turner Overdrive, who had a stutter. It was never intended for public consumption. In fact, it was intended solely for Gary. "He'll have the only copy in the world of this song by BTO," said Bachman, in a spectacularly wrong prediction. The band typically used the song as a "work track" in the studio to get the amplifiers and microphones set properly.

BTO was in Seattle, Washington, recording their third album, *Not Fragile*, and had eight songs prepared. When the album was completed, Charlie Fach of Mercury Records flew to Seattle to hear the finished product. After listening to the eight songs BTO had recorded, Fach complained that he "didn't hear that magic thing," and asked if the band had anything else. Bachman said: "We have this one song, but it's a joke. I'm laughing at the end. I sang it on the first take. It's sharp, it's flat, I'm stuttering to do this thing for my brother." Fach asked Bachman to play the recording of the song, and Fach said "That's the track."

Bachman agreed to include it on the album, but only if he could re-record the vocal. He went into the studio the next day. "I tried to sing it, but I sounded like Frank Sinatra. It didn't fit." Fach told him to leave it the way it was, stuttering and all. When *Not Fragile* was released, radio stations jumped on "You Ain't Seen Nothing Yet" right away. "I started to hear it getting played and I was embarrassed. I'd turn the radio down. My wife would say to me, 'Look, at last, they're playing a song of yours like mad.'"[23]

Name two a cappella songs from the Decade. There were probably many but most are obscure. Not these two, at least to fans of music from the Decade. One was an original composition cowritten by the singer that was never released as a single and one was a traditional song that hit the top 20. (As hints, both were by female singers, one mostly associated with rock and blues, and the other with folk music. The title of the first is a brand name and the second was composed centuries ago.)

One is "Mercedes Benz" by Janis Joplin. The song title contains no hyphen although the automobile brand name is hyphenated. It was recorded in one take on October 1, 1970, 3 days before she died. It was also the last song she ever recorded. It was written by Joplin, Michael McClure and Bob Neuwirth.

The other is "Amazing Grace" by Judy Collins, which reached #15 in 1970. "Amazing Grace" is one of the oldest songs ever to appear in the *Billboard* Hot 100. The words were written by English poet and clergyman John Newton (1725–1807) and published in 1779. Newton wrote the words from personal experience. After leaving the Royal Navy, he became involved in the Atlantic slave trade. In 1748, a violent storm battered his vessel severely and he called out to God for mercy, a moment that marked his spiritual conversion. However, he continued his slave trading career until 1754 or 1755, when he ended his seafaring and began studying Christian theology. Ordained in the Church of England in 1764, "Amazing Grace" was written to illustrate a sermon on New Year's Day of 1773. It debuted in print in 1779 in *Olney Hymns*. In 1835 it was joined to a then-existing tune called "New Britain" to which it is most frequently sung today.

The 1968 song "Abraham, Martin and John," written by Dick Holler and first performed by Dion, is a tribute to four assassinated Americans. Three of them are obviously Abraham Lincoln, Martin Luther King and John Kennedy. Who is the fourth?

Robert Kennedy, who was killed shortly before the song was written (King and Kennedy were assassinated only two months apart). While the other three "freed people," as for Bobby, Dion saw him walking up a hill with the other three. Holler also cowrote the novelty song "Snoopy and the Red Baron" which was a #2 hit in 1966 for the Royal Guardsmen.

"Abraham, Martin and John" was a hit for other artists as well, including Smokey Robinson and the Miracles (#33 in 1969), Marvin Gaye (#9 in England in 1970, but never released as a single in the U.S.), Tom Clay (as part of his 1971 medley "What the World Needs Now Is Love/Abraham, Martin, and John"), and comedian Moms Mabley (#35 in 1969). The Louisiana Music Hall of Fame, in honoring Louisianian songwriter Dick Holler, states that this song is the only one in history to make the *Billboard* top 40 five times with five different artists, but it should be noted that Gaye's version would not technically be considered on that list because it was not released as a single.[24]

This man (1) cowrote the huge hit song "Build Me Up Buttercup," which was a #3 song for the Foundations in 1969, (2) wrote "Handbags and Gladrags," which was a modest hit for Rod Stewart, (3) was a lead singer for Manfred Mann for several years in the late 1960s, including on their top 10 cover of the Bob Dylan song "Quinn the Eskimo (The

Mighty Quinn),"and (4) appeared as King Herod on the original 1970 recording of *Jesus Christ Superstar.* **Who is he?**

Michael D'Abo. D'Abo actually sang some of the lyrics from "Quinn the Eskimo" differently than they were written by Bob Dylan. D'Abo explained: "I had to make up some of the words as I couldn't make out everything [Dylan] was saying. It was learning a song phonetically in a foreign language. I never had the first idea what the song was about except that it seems to be 'Hey gang, gather round, something exciting is about to happen because the big man's coming.' As to who the big man is and why he is an Eskimo, I don't know."

In listening to Dylan's original rendition of the song, one can sympathize with D'Abo. The only way to know for sure what the lyrics (supposedly) are (even assuming that Dylan is singing his actual lyrics, which he may well not be) is from the printed lyrics on his website.[25]

Johnny Cash had a string of top 10 hits and #1 hits on the U.S. country chart but only one top 10 song on the *Billboard* **Hot 100. It reached #2. As a hint, the song was released in 1969 and was recorded live. What song is it?**

"A Boy Named Sue" by Shel Silverstein. It was recorded at San Quentin Prison and appears on Cash's album *At San Quentin.*

There are five popular songs from the Decade which consist only of the name of a State. What are they are who are they by? For extra credit, name another one from 1973 by Linda Ronstadt.

"Alabama" by Neil Young (from *Harvest*)
"Arizona" by Mark Lindsay (formerly of Paul Revere and the Raiders)
"California" by Joni Mitchell (from *Blue*)
"Massachusetts" by the Bee Gees
"Ohio" by Crosby Stills Nash & Young (written by Neil Young)
The extra credit answer is "Colorado," which appears on Ronstadt's 1973 album *Don't Cry Now.*

Other state songs outside the Decade include "Iowa" by Slipknot, "Kansas" by the Devil Wears Prada, "Maryland" by Vonda Shepard, "Nebraska" by Bruce Springsteen, "New York" by U2, "Tennessee" by Johnny Cash and "Texas" by the String Cheese Incident.

Rock bands have notoriously short life spans in terms of keeping the exact same lineup. Even with respect to the most successful bands, additions and subtractions occur

constantly. That is not the case with one band however. They were formed in 1969 with three people. Two of those three (and a replacement for one of those two) were replaced by two other musicians within the year of formation. The original members and the two replacements have been the sole members of the band for the next 45+ years. Who is this three-member band? (As a hint, they were formed in Texas.)

ZZ Top, founded by guitarist Billy Gibbons. The other band members are bassist Dusty Hill and drummer Frank Beard. Naturally enough, Beard is the only one without a chest-length beard. Although most of their career has of course been post-Decade, their first four albums were released in the Decade.

ZZ Top's record of longevity without lineup changes is impressive but their career did not span the Decade since they started in 1969. The number of major bands who stayed together from the beginning of the Decade to the end is tiny indeed. However, there is a four-man English band that did it. Who is that band? There is also a five-man band, four of whom were from Canada, whose drummer left for about a year in 1966 but then returned to the lineup. What band is it? Both are very famous. (As a hint to the answers, read the questions carefully.)

I tried to give both answers in the questions themselves. The English group is the Who. The other is the Band. Levon Helm (the only American in the group) was the drummer who briefly left the group.

One would not think that the issue of why bands stay together or split apart would be prime fodder for a serious academic study, but that would be wrong. In 2014, Ronnie Phillips and Ian Strachan wrote a scholarly and fascinating article on exactly this topic, entitled "Breaking Up Is Hard to Do: The Resilience of the Rock Group As an Organizational Form For Creating Music."[26]

When we think of the Rolling Stones, we do not typically think of there being a pianist/organist in the band. However, on most of their studio albums released until 1985, there was one, and it was the same person. He was also briefly an actual member of the band during the first year of their existence from 1962–1963 (and in fact was a member of the group even before Mick Jagger and Keith Richards) but was dropped from the lineup because band manager Andrew Loog Oldham felt that his burly, square-jawed appearance did not fit the image for the band that Oldham was aiming for. However, he accepted the demotion and acted as the band's road manger. He played on one or more tracks on almost every one of their studio albums until his death in 1985, including songs such as "Time Is

On My Side," "Honky Tonk Women," "Let It Bleed," "Brown Sugar," and "It's Only Rock 'n Roll (But I Like It)." Who is he?

Ian Stewart. When the Stones were inducted into the Rock and Roll Hall of Fame in 1989, they asked that Stewart's name be included. "Stu was the one guy we tried to please," said Mick Jagger after he died. "We wanted his approval when we were writing or rehearsing a song." In Keith's autobiography, *Life*, he wrote: "Ian Stewart, I'm still working for him. To me, the Rolling Stones is his band."

Stewart was a bit older and much more strait-laced than the rest of the band. He also loved golf. As road manager (and given that the groupies were not of interest to him), he used this to his advantage. Said Richards: "We'd be playing in some town where there's all these chicks, and they want to get laid and we want to lay them. But Stu would have booked us into some hotel about ten miles out of town. You'd wake up in the morning and there's the Sugarloaf links. We're bored to death looking for some action and Stu's playing Gleneagles."[27]

This artist fronted a band (that contained his name) that had a top 10 hit in 1965 with "I Fought the Law" which was written by Sonny Curtis. He died in 1966 at age 24, found dead in a car parked outside his Hollywood apartment. It is unclear whether his death was due to suicide, accident or murder. Who is this singer?

Bobby Fuller of the Bobby Fuller Four. As for Curtis, he also wrote, performed and sang "Love Is All Around," the theme to *The Mary Tyler Moore Show*.[28]

The following is a list of dates. Name the songs which they come from. To get most of the songs without any hint is impressive. While all of the artists are well-known, some of the songs were big hits and others are more obscure.

1. May 1
2. May 10
3. May 21
4. June 3
5. June 6
6. July 4
7. July 4
8. September 3
9. November 5
10. December 1

Interestingly (and as a hint), with the exception of the May 10 reference which is "May the 10th"), all of all other dates are sung as "the [day] of [the month]." So for example, if there is a reference to June 1, that would be sung as the "first of June."

1. Bee Gees—"First of May"
2. The Band—"The Night They Drove Old Dixie Down"
3. Queen—"Great King Rat "
4. Bobbie Gentry—"Ode to Billie Joe"
5. C.W. McCall—"Convoy"
6. Creedence Clearwater Revival—"Born on the Bayou"
7. Chicago—"Saturday in the Park"
8. The Temptations—"Papa Was a Rollin' Stone"
9. John Lennon—"Remember"
10. James Taylor—"Sweet Baby James"

A Bruce Springsteen song has a date in the title but not in the song itself. What song?

"4th of July, Asbury Park (Sandy)"

This man is associated with the music industry, not as a singer, songwriter, or musician, but rather as a DJ. He is said to have influenced many artists and thus there are several songs from the Decade that either mention him by name (sometimes in the song title itself) or indirectly refer to him or use his distinctive voice, including by artists such as the Doors, the Grateful Dead ("Ramble on Rose"), the Guess Who, Todd Rundgren, the Stampeders ("Hit the Road Jack"), and Sugarloaf ("Don't Call Us, We'll Call You"). Who is this man?

Wolfman Jack. The songs referenced above are:

"Clap for the Wolfman" by the Canadian band the Guess Who.
"Wolfman Jack" by Todd Rundgren.
"Ramble on Rose" by the Grateful Dead.
"Hit the Road Jack" (featuring Wolfman Jack) by another Canadian band the Stampeders. The original version, written by Percy Mayfield and recorded by Ray Charles in 1961, has nothing to do with Wolfman Jack. However, the 1975 cover by the Stampeders begins with a man named Cornelius calling the Wolfman on the phone, telling him of how his girlfriend had thrown

him out of the house. At the end of the song, Cornelius tries to persuade the Wolfman to let him stay at his house. Wolfman checks with his friend Ray, tells Cornelius no, and hangs up the phone.

"Don't Call Us, We'll Call You" by Sugarloaf. The words "from stereo 92" are spoken by Wolfman Jack or someone imitating him.

"WASP (Texas Radio and the Big Beat)" by the Doors. According to song-facts, "Texas Radio" refers to high power Mexican radio stations that blasted into Texas in the 1950s. Not restricted by American regulations these stations, whose call letters started with X, and could have up to 150,000 watts. Morrison heard Wolfman Jack on Texas radio when he was a DJ on XERF-AM in Mexico. In the spoken intro, Morrison says that Texas radio "comes out of the Virginia swamps." Wolfman Jack started his career in Newport News, Virginia. In a 1975 song by ZZ Top, "Heard it on the X," while not mentioning the Wolfman by name, they reference that you could hear "the X" from anywhere.

Wolfman is also mentioned or can be heard on a number of songs from after the Decade, including "Radio Land" by Michael Martin Murphey, "The Haunted House of Rock" by Whodini, "Funk is Back" by Biz Markie, "The Beauty Way" by Lucy Kaplansky. The Wolfman died of a heart attack in 1995 at age 57.

The Rock and Roll Hall of Fame called this man "one of the most significant figures in the modern recording industry." Among his long list of accomplishments:

- **He wrote "Chains of Love," a hit for Pat Boone, the Ray Charles hit "Mess Around," and songs for the Clovers.**
- **He cowrote Steve Miller's huge hit "The Joker."**
- **He sang background vocals on Big Joe Turner's hit "Shake Rattle & Roll."**
- **He founded one of the most influential record labels in rock history. Although he sold his interest in the label in 1967, he continued to wield significant influence over the label thereafter. Among numerous other acts, his label signed or distributed (either solely or in partnership with others) Aretha Franklin, Otis Redding, Crosby, Stills & Nash (and later Young), Cream, Buffalo Springfield, Sonny & Cher, ABBA, Average White Band, Bad Company, Badfinger, Glen Campbell, Phil Collins, Emerson Lake & Palmer, Roberta Flack, Foreigner, Peter Frampton, Peter Gabriel, Hall & Oates, the J. Geils band, Jay-Z, Kid Rock, Dusty Springfield and the Temptations.**
- **He discovered the Rascals.**

- He discovered Led Zeppelin and signed them to their first contract. In 2007, Zeppelin reunited for a one-off show in tribute to him. This was the only live reunion of the band's three surviving members since their induction to the Rock and Roll Hall of Fame in 1995, and the only full concert the band ever did since breaking up in 1980.
- His label distributed the Rolling Stones after they established their own label, Rolling Stones Records, in 1971.
- He established the Rock and Roll Hall of Fame and the Museum's main gallery, the Exhibition Hall, is named after him.
- He cofounded the New York Cosmos soccer team of the North American Soccer League and was instrumental in bringing in legends like Pelé, Carlos Alberto and Franz Beckenbauer to the club.

Who was he?

Ahmet Ertegun, born in Turkey in 1923. He died in 2006 as the result of a brain injury suffered when he fell backstage at the Beacon Theater in Manhattan as the Rolling Stones prepared to play a concert that marked former President Bill Clinton's 60th birthday.

Considering the political turmoil during the Decade, there were relatively few songs which mentioned presidents by name in the lyrics. Below is a list of artists and bands that released during the Decade which do. Name the song.

1. Crosby, Stills, Nash & Young (Hint: Nixon)
2. The Rolling Stones (Hint: Kennedy)
3. David Bowie (Hint: Nixon)
4. Queen (Hint: Kennedy)
5. Chicago (Hint: Truman)
6. John Lennon (Hint: Kennedy)
7. Randy Newman (Hint: Coolidge)
8. Gil Scott-Heron (Hint: Nixon)
9. Dion (Hint: Kennedy)

1. "Ohio"
2. "Sympathy for the Devil"
3. "Young Americans"
4. "Killer Queen"

5. "Harry Truman"
6. "God"
7. "Louisiana 1927"
8. "The Revolution Will Not Be Televised"
9. "Abraham, Martin and John"

The "W" in the initials of this band (and they were often known just by their initials on their album covers) is formed by a sitting woman's naked derriere.

Average White Band (or AWB). The band name derived from a friend of the band who worked in the British Diplomatic Service who would describe places in his travels with remarks such as "Uganda is just too hot for the average white man." According to band member Alan Gorrie, "We couldn't think of a good name and that one struck us as a bit of a tongue-in-cheek joke, because we were anything but an average white band." That was especially true after African-American drummer Steve Ferrone joined the band in 1974.[29]

Other distinctive letters from band logos include the A of America, the backwards B on ABBA, the C of Chicago (kind of like the Coke C), the up arrow on the O from the Who, the elongated Q from Queen, the capital T of the Beatles, and the Y from Yes.

This singer-songwriter released two songs within a year that tell almost identical stories: in both a tough guy who everyone fears is beaten up by an even tougher guy, once for hustling the second guy and once for hitting on the second guy's wife. One song reached #8 and one reached #1. Who is the artist and what are the songs?

Jim Croce. The earlier release was "You Don't Mess Around with Jim" (#8 in 1972). Here Big Jim Walker hustled Willie McCoy from Alabama and wishes he hadn't after their fight. In "Bad Bad Leroy Brown," which reached the top spot a year later, the wife's husband who deals out a beating to Mr. Brown is unnamed.

Freddie Mercury of Queen was a fan of Croce's and paid tribute to him in a song title. What was the song?

"Bring Back That Leroy Brown," written by Mercury and released on Queen's third album, *Sheer Heart Attack*, that was released in 1974, about a year after Croce died.[30]

Speaking of covers, there are numerous polls that rate the best cover songs of all time. While obviously subjective, there are certain songs that appear on virtually every

list, often at or near the top. On the 2004 *Rolling Stone* list of the 500 Greatest Songs of all Time, there are two such covers in the top 50 where both the original and the cover were released during the decade. As discussed earlier, one of the songs, which came in at #47, was Jimi Hendrix's cover of "All Along the Watchtower," written by Bob Dylan. The other, coming in at #5, was written and originally performed by Otis Redding, a fact that few remember because of the much more famous cover version. What is the Redding song and who famously covered it?

"Respect," originally released by Redding in 1965, and obviously covered by Aretha Franklin. The only other covers in the top 50 are "Georgia on My Mind," a 1960 Ray Charles cover of a 1930 song by Hoagy Carmichael and Stuart Gorrell that was covered many times before Charles's version, and "Hound Dog," a 1957 Elvis Presley cover of a song written by Jerry Lieber and Mike Stoller and first recorded by Big Mama Thornton in 1953. Though few remember Thornton's version today, it spent 14 weeks on the R&B charts, including seven weeks at #1. There were actually at least ten covers of the song before Presley's recording in 1956. Given the bluesy nature of the song, it is hard to believe that it was written by two 19-year-old white teenagers.[31]

When most people think of the Irish singer-songwriter Gilbert O'Sullivan, they think of his depressing #1 U.S. song from 1972, "Alone Again (Naturally)." (In that song, he tells us that if he does not start feeling "less sour," he is going to "treat himself" by climbing to the top of a nearby tower and throwing himself off.) However he did have two other top 10 songs in the U.S. during the Decade, one reaching #7 and the other reaching #2. The #7 song still receives airplay today while the #2 song is virtually forgotten. What were the two songs?

"Get Down" from 1973 (#7) and "Clair" from 1972 (#2).

Paul Simon obviously had substantial success as a solo artist after the breakup of Simon and Garfunkel, including his 1986 album *Graceland*, which won the 1987 Grammy Award for Album of the Year. However, he had only one solo #1 on the *Billboard* Hot 100, which came during the Decade. What was it? (As a hint, it appears on *Still Crazy After All These Years*.)

"50 Ways to Leave Your Lover."

The song "Call Me" (not Blondie's version) was a top 30 hit in 1966 and #2 on the Easy Listening Chart. People hearing the song were not sure if it was a male or female singing, because the single was sung in a soft, very high tenor range that confused some disc jockeys, and in announcing the song, the DJs would often refer to the singer as a female. The confusion was also because the singer's first name was not distinctly male or female. Who was the singer?

Chris Montez. The song was first recorded by Petula Clark. Montez had a #4 hit in 1962 with "Let's Dance," in which his vocal is sung in a lower voice and has a more Latin feel than "Call Me." Indeed, in hearing the two songs together, one would not think that they were by the same singer. "Let's Dance" is featured in the movie *Animal House*, and indeed may be most remembered today based on being heard in that film. As for "Call Me," it too has a notable movie connection. Near the end of *When Harry Met Sally*, Harry (Billy Crystal) is trying to woo Sally (Meg Ryan) back into his life, and she is ignoring him. In one of his voice-mail messages, he sings the first verse of the song to her answering machine. [32]

This group consisted of all Native Americans who often performed in traditional Indian garb. A song of theirs from 1974 was the #4 song on the *Billboard* Hot 100 for the whole year. What is the name of the band and what was their one big hit?

Redbone and "Come and Get Your Love." They were headed by brothers Pat and Lolly Vegas.

This one is for Deadheads. For a long time, the band had a husband and wife as part of the lineup. The wife was primarily a vocalist who was with the group from 1972–1979. Her husband played keyboards with them from 1971–1979. In 1980, he died at age 32 of a car crash. In 1994, he was posthumously inducted into the Rock and Roll Hall of Fame as a member of the Dead. What is the name of the couple?

Keith and Donna Godchaux.

There was one song released during the Decade on which Art Garfunkel performs with Paul Simon after the two broke up. It was a top 10 hit. What was the song? For extra credit, name the two studio albums on which it appeared (one by each artist).

The song was "My Little Town," which reached #9 on the *Billboard* Hot 100. It appeared in 1975 on Simon's album *Still Crazy After All These Years* and Garfunkel's album of the same year called *Breakaway*.

In 1967, this album hit #1. Its title consists of three signs of the zodiac and the last name of the lead singer of the group. What is the album and the group?

Pisces, Aquarius, Capricorn & Jones, Ltd. by the Monkees.

Two original members of the Jefferson Airplane died on the same day, January 28, 2016. One was a vocalist, rhythm guitarist and the only person who appeared on every album by Jefferson Airplane and Jefferson Starship. He also cowrote "Wooden Ships" with David Crosby and Stephen Stills. The other member, much less famous, was a female who was the lead vocalist on the Airplane's first album, *Jefferson Airplane Takes Off*. Who are the two original members?

Paul Kantner and Signe Toly Anderson.

CHAPTER 12

We Write the Songs that Make the Whole World Sing (Songwriters)

I am always interested in songwriters who are relatively unknown to the public, yet who have an impressive list of well-known songs to their credit, especially when written for multiple artists and when the songs have a completely different vibe from one another. Therefore, the focus of this chapter is not on songwriters who are already world-famous and/or who composed music for themselves or their groups, such as John Lennon, Paul McCartney, Mick Jagger, Keith Richards, Elton John, Pete Townshend, Billy Joel and others. Rather the focus is on relatively (but undeservedly) anonymous songwriters who have an impressive list of well-known songs to their credit. To the extent that readers don't know the answers to any of the questions below, it is my hope that their reaction upon learning of the resumes of these songwriters will hopefully be (1) I know all of those songs and (2) I had no idea that they were written by the same person.

"Hang On Sloopy" was written by two men who each had an impressive list of hit songs they independently composed or produced. Besides "Hang On Sloopy," the first man cowrote the following:

- **"Boys," which was covered by the Beatles in 1963 for their debut album** *Please Please Me.*
- **"Come a Little Bit Closer," a #3 hit for Jay and the Americans in 1964.**
- **"Let's Lock the Door (And Throw Away the Key)," a #11 hit for Jay and the Americans in 1965).**
- **"Come on Down to My Boat," a #6 hit for Every Mother's Son in 1967.**
- **"C'mon On, Get Happy," the theme song to** *The Partridge Family* **TV show.**
- **"I'll Meet You Halfway," a #9 hit for the Partridge Family in 1971.**

He later got into publishing and the songs he published included "Candida" and "Knock Three Times" by Tony Orlando and Dawn, "Groovin'," "How Can I Be

Sure," "Lonely Too Long" and "People Got to Be Free" by the Young Rascals (later the Rascals), "I Like Dreaming" by Kenny Nolan and "The Night Chicago Died" by Paper Lace.

What was his name?

Wes Farrell.

Beside "Hang On Sloopy," the second man cowrote:

- "Twist and Shout," a hit for the Isley Brothers and the Beatles and further immortalized in *Ferris Bueller's Day Off*.
- "Tell Him," a #4 hit for the Exciters, later covered by numerous artists, including Linda Ronstadt.
- "Cry Baby," a #4 hit in 1963 for Garnet Mimms and the Enchanters, although the version most remembered today is Janis Joplin's great cover, recorded in 1970.
- "Everybody Needs Somebody to Love," recorded by Solomon Burke (1964), the Rolling Stones (1964) and Wilson Pickett (1967). Burke's version of the song was ranked at #429 on the 2004 *Rolling Stone* list of the 500 Greatest Songs of All Time.
- "I Want Candy," a #11 hit for the Strangeloves in 1965, which was famously covered by Bow Wow Wow.
- "Piece of My Heart." Today, almost no one remembers that it was originally recorded by Erma Franklin in 1967 (she was Aretha Franklin's older sister) but everyone remembers Janis Joplin's vocal on the 1968 cover by Big Brother and the Holding Company, which hit #12 on the *Billboard* Hot 100. (Franklin said when she heard "Piece of My Heart" on the radio by Joplin, she didn't recognize it because of the vocal arrangement.)

The man also wrote a number of hit songs on his own including "Nobody but Me" (The Isley Brothers, 1963), "Under the Boardwalk" (the Drifters, 1964), and "Brown Eyed Girl" (Van Morrison, 1967).
Who was this prolific songwriter?

Bert Berns, who wrote under the name of Bert Russell. With songwriting ability like Berns and Farrell, it's no wonder that they were able to come up with a hit like "Hang On Sloopy" when they combined their talents. Sadly, Berns died of a heart attack in December 1967, when he was only 38 years old. Farrell died of cancer at age 56 in 1996.

A few interesting tidbits about "Twist and Shout" (which Berns cowrote with Phil Medley): It is the only song covered by the Beatles that reached the top 10 for them. In fact, it hit #2 on April 2, 1964 and the only reason it did not hit #1 is because the Beatles had another song occupying the top spot, "Can't Buy Me Love." (They also had the third, fourth, and fifth spots at that time as well.) Another fact which is probably unknown to even diehard Beatles fans is that, other than "Hey Jude," it had the longest run of any Beatles song in the top 40 (23 weeks). It spent 16 weeks in the top 40 when originally released, and then another 7 weeks in 1986, propelled by Matthew Broderick's lip-synced performance in the parade scene in *Ferris Bueller's Day Off*. Although many people think that this song was originally recorded by the Isley Brothers, the original version was in fact first recorded by the Top Notes and the song was titled "Shake It Up, Baby."

This songwriting duo, one composing the music and the other writing the lyrics, was versatile and talented. As a team, they wrote the #1 song for Jim Croce, "I Got a Name," as well as "Killing Me Softly with His Song," a #1 hit for Roberta Flack in 1973. They also wrote the theme songs for *Happy Days, Laverne and Shirley, Angie, Lifestyles of the Rich and Famous, Wonder Woman* and the Emmy-winning theme for *The Paper Chase*. The lyricist also wrote the English lyrics to "The Girl from Ipanema." He also won an Academy Award in 1980 for Best Original Song, namely "It Goes Like It Goes" from the 1979 movie *Norma Rae,* sung by Jennifer Warnes. The music composer wrote the dramatic theme music to ABC's Wide World of Sports and the original Monday Night Football. It was a song called "Score," which is not so well-remembered today. (In the mid-1970s, it was replaced by the much more familiar theme, known as "Heavy Action," by Johnny Pearson. Who knew that the *MNF* themes had titles?) In any event, name the music writer and the lyricist of this duo.

Charles Fox (music) and Norman Gimbel (lyrics).

Although most of the hits by this man were released before the Decade, he did have two #1 hit songs during the Decade, and that ain't chopped liver. Most of the songs he wrote with his wife were for girl groups or female singers. Many of his songs are considered classics, even if one of his #1s is by the Archies. With his wife, he wrote the following:

"Da Doo Ron Ron" (The Crystals, #3)
"Then He Kissed Me" (The Crystals, #6)
"Be My Baby" (The Ronettes, #2)
"Chapel of Love" (The Dixie Cups, #1)

"Leader of the Pack" (The Shangri-Las, #1)
"River Deep-Mountain High" (Ike and Tina Turner)

With people besides his wife, he wrote the following:

"Tell Laura I Love Her" (Ray Peterson, #7)
"Sugar, Sugar" (The Archies, #1)
"Montego Bay" (Bobby Bloom, #8)
"I Honestly Love You" (Olivia Newton-John, #1)

His wife was Ellie Greenwich and their writing partner on virtually all of their songs together was Phil Spector. Who was this man?

Jeff Barry.

This songwriting duo might fairly be considered the most successful songwriting team in music history in terms of most chart success on both the *Billboard* Hot 100 and the R&B chart combined, performed by the widest variety of artists. The songwriting team of Holland-Dozier-Holland may have had equal success in terms of chart performance but a disproportionate number of their hits were written for the Supremes. This duo wrote or cowrote 16 songs that reached the top 10 on the *Billboard* Hot 100 (for *11* different acts), and three of those songs hit #1. Their record of diverse successes on the R&B chart is even more impressive: 19 #1 songs and 50 top 10 songs for *16* different acts. Most of their success was during the Decade. Who is the duo? (As a hint, they are known for creating the Philly soul sound.)

Kenny Gamble and Leon Huff. The performers who recorded their songs included the Soul Survivors, the Intruders, Jerry Butler, Archie Bell and the Drells, Wilson Pickett, Joe Simon, Harold Melvin and the Blue Notes, Billy Paul, the O'Jays, MFSB, the Three Degrees, Lou Rawls, the Jacksons, Sharon Paige, Teddy Pendergrass, and the Jones Girls. Their first top five hit was "Expressway to Your Heart" by the Soul Survivors in 1967. Their songs that hit #1 on both charts were "Me and Mrs. Jones" by Billy Paul, "Love Train" by the O'Jays and "TSOP (The Sound of Philadelphia)," a primarily instrumental piece by the Philadelphia International house band MFSB (with a few vocals by the Three Degrees). Other hits in their impressive repertoire include "If You Don't Know Me By Now" (#3 pop and #1 R&B for Harold Melvin and the Blue Notes), "I'm Gonna Make You Love Me" (#2 pop as a joint single performed by Diana Ross and the Supremes and the Temptations), "When Will I See You Again" (#3 pop and #4 R&B for the Three Degrees), "Enjoy Yourself" by the Jacksons (#6 pop and #2 R&B), "I Love Music" by the O'Jays (#5 pop and #1 R&B) and "Do It Any Way You Wanna" by People's Choice (#11 pop and #1 R&B).

Gamble and Huff each had one top 10 song on the *Billboard* Hot 100 that was *not* written with the other. As a hint, Gamble's song was by the Stylistics and Huff's was by the O'Jays. Both were top five songs that are often heard today. What are the two songs?

Gamble's was "Make Up or Break Up" (#5) and Huff's was "Back Stabbers" (#3).

This man worked with Gamble and Huff and was a double-threat as both a song-writer and producer. He is also considered one of the creators of the Philly soul sound. He certainly fits within the concept of this chapter, as he has a long list of records to his credit by different artists, yet remains fairly anonymous. The impressive list of huge hits on which he was a writer (or cowriter) or producer include the ones listed below (highest pop and R&B chart positions in parentheses). They were all released during the Decade except for "The Rubberband Man" which was released in 1976.

"La-La (Means I Love You)"—The Delfonics (writer and producer, #4 pop; #2 R&B)

"Ready or Not Here I Come (Can't Hide from Love)"—The Delfonics (writer and producer, #35 pop; #14 R&B)

"Didn't I (Blow Your Mind This Time)"—The Delfonics (writer and producer, #10 pop; #3 R&B)

"Stop, Look, Listen (To Your Heart)"—The Stylistics (writer and producer, #39 pop; #6 R&B)

"You Are Everything"—The Stylistics (writer and producer, #9 pop; #10 R&B)

"Betcha by Golly, Wow"—The Stylistics (writer and producer, #3 pop; #2 R&B)

"I'm Stone in Love with You"—The Stylistics (writer and producer, #10 pop; #4 R&B)

"I'll Be Around"—The Spinners (writer and producer, #3 pop; #1 R&B)

"Could It Be I'm Falling in Love"—The Spinners (producer, #4 pop; #1 R&B)

"I'm Doing Fine Now"—New York City (writer and producer, #17 pop; #14 R&B)

"One of a Kind (Love Affair)"—The Spinners (producer, #11 pop; #1 R&B)

"Break Up to Make Up"—The Stylistics (writer and producer, #5 pop; #5 R&B)
"I'm Coming Home"—originally by Johnny Mathis and then covered by the Spinners (writer and producer, #18 pop; #3 R&B)
"You Make Me Feel Brand New"—The Stylistics (writer and producer, #2 pop; #5 R&B)
"Mighty Love (Part I)"—The Spinners (producer, #20 pop; #1 R&B)
"Then Came You"—The Spinners (with Dionne Warwick) (producer, #1 pop; #2 R&B)
"They Just Can't Stop It (The Games People Play)"—The Spinners (producer, #5 pop; #1 R&B)
"The Rubberband Man"—The Spinners (writer and producer, #2 pop; #1 R&B)

Who was the writer/producer behind all of these songs?

Thom Bell. However, for the songs above where he is listed as a writer, he only wrote the music.

The lyrics for those songs were written by a fellow Philadelphian, a white female. The combination of an African-American male and white female songwriting team is highly unusual and they are likely the most successful such team ever. The songs for which she wrote the lyrics include:

"Stop, Look, Listen (To Your Heart)"—The Stylistics
"You Are Everything"—The Stylistics
"Betcha by Golly, Wow"—The Stylistics
"I'm Stone in Love with You"—The Stylistics
"Break Up to Make Up"—The Stylistics
"I'm Coming Home"—originally by Johnny Mathis and then covered by the Spinners
"You Make Me Feel Brand New"—The Stylistics
"The Rubberband Man"—The Spinners

Who was this woman?

Linda Creed, also known by her married name of Linda Creed Epstein. Ms. Creed passed away from breast cancer in 1986 and was inducted into the Songwriters Hall of Fame in 1992.

This duo wrote or cowrote numerous hits including "You've Got Your Troubles," a top 10 hit for the Fortunes in 1965, "My Baby Loves Lovin'," a top 20 hit for White Plains in 1970, "Here Comes That Rainy Day Feeling Again," a top 20 hit for the Fortunes in 1971, "I'd Like to Teach the World to Sing (in Perfect Harmony)," a top 20 hit for the Hillside Singers and a top 10 hit for the New Seekers in 1972, "Long Cool Woman in a Black Dress," a #2 hit for the Hollies in 1972, "Doctor's Orders," a top 10 hit in the U.K. for Sunny (of Sue and Sunny) in 1974, and a top 20 hit for Carol Douglas in the U.S., also in 1974. (As a hint, they are both British and have the first name: Roger.)

Roger Greenaway and Roger Cook.

Tandyn Almer, Terry Kirkman, Ruthann Friedman, and the team of Dick and Don Addrisi, all have something in common, namely that they each (independently) wrote top 10 songs for the same group. Two of the songs were #1, one was #2 and one was #7. All of them receive significant airplay on oldies stations today—i.e. none of them are obscure. They all came out in 1966 and 1967. Who is the group? For extra credit, name the songs that they each wrote.

The group is the Association. Tandyn Almer—"Along Comes Mary" (#7 in 1966), Terry Kirkman—"Cherish" (#1 in 1966), Ruthann Friedman—"Windy" (#1 in 1967), and Dick and Don Addrisi—"Never My Love" (#2 in 1967).

One of the great satiric songs about living the rock star life is "Life's Been Good" by Joe Walsh, which came out in 1978. Another is a song released in 1972 and written by Shel Silverstein. If ever there was a protean talent, Silverstein was it. He was a successful cartoonist, children's book author, playwright, screenwriter, and last but not least, song-writer. In this song, the singer rhapsodizes about how great it is to be a singer in a band, but repeatedly laments one thing that is absent for him and his band (both in the song and in real life). However, after the song, their wish came true in real life (sort of). What is the song and who was the band?

"The Cover of 'Rolling Stone'" by Dr. Hook and the Medicine Show. As a result of the song's success (it reached number six on the U.S. charts), the band was in fact on the March 29, 1973 cover of *Rolling Stone*; however, they were in caricature, rather than in a photograph, and with the caption, "What's-Their-Names Make the Cover." The lead singer on the song was Ray Sawyer, and he wore a patch following the loss of his right eye in a near-fatal car crash. People often assumed that he was the "Dr. Hook" in the band or that his name was inspired by Captain Hook of *Peter Pan* because of the eyepatch (even though Captain Hook never wore an eyepatch and of course was not a doctor either.) The band was actually named by guitarist George Cummings. While playing at a club in Union City, NJ, the owner asked Cummings what the name of his band was, and on the spur of the moment, he wrote down "Dr. Hook & the Medicine Show, straight from the South, serving up Soul Music." As for Sawyer, though he took the lead vocal on "The Cover of 'Rolling Stone,'" the band's usual lead singer was Dennis Michael Locorriere.[1]

Another wonderful song written by Shel Silverstein turned out to be one of the biggest hits for Johnny Cash. The first time Cash ever played it was in front of a live audience on February 24, 1969, where his performance was filmed. He had only received the song a few days before his first performance and since he was not sure of the lyrics, he can be seen reading from a piece of paper when he played the song. Cash was pleased and surprised at how well the song went over with the audience. It was the barely rehearsed live performance that was released as a single, and that went to #1 on the country charts and #2 on the *Billboard* Hot 100. What is the song? As a hint, the audience who Cash played for were all inmates at California's San Quentin State Prison (talk about a captive audience!).

"A Boy Named Sue." It was Johnny's wife June who suggested that he perform the song at the prison performance even though he hardly knew the song. There's a spontaneity and joy about the performance, with Cash obviously amused by Silverstein's clever lyrics which he seemed to be learning (and laughing about) as he read them. And the inmates loved it, whooping and laughing along.

There are two theories about the inspiration for the title. One is that Silverstein wrote it with his friend, humorist Jean Shepherd, who was often taunted as a child because of his feminine-sounding (and spelled) name. (Shepherd narrated and cowrote the 1983 classic film, *A Christmas Story*.) This is according to Shepherd biographer Eugene Bergmann. However, according to a 1970 article in the *New York Times* ("Johnny Cash is Indebted to a Judge named Sue"), the song was inspired by male attorney Sue K. Hicks, a friend of John Scopes, the defendant in the 1925 "Scopes Monkey Trial." Sue was named after his mother who died after giving birth to him. Hicks, who lived until 1980 and knew about the song, didn't consider it to be a source of derision. "It is an irony of fate that I have tried over 800 murder cases and thousands of others, but the most publicity has been from the name 'Sue' and from the evolution trial," he said.[2]

Silverstein also wrote many other hit songs including "One's on the Way" (a hit for Loretta Lynn), "25 Minutes to Go," sung by Johnny Cash, about a man on Death Row with each line counting down one minute closer to his execution, "The Unicorn," a semi-novelty huge hit for the Irish Rovers in 1968, "Sylvia's Mother," the first big hit for Dr. Hook and the Medicine Show, and a sequel to "A Boy Named Sue" called "Father of a Boy Named Sue."

Otis Redding wrote and recorded one of the most famous songs of the rock era. It is #5 on *Rolling Stone*'s list of the 500 Greatest Songs of All Time and #4 on the "Songs of the Century" list created in 2001 by the Recording Industry Association of America (RIAA) and the National Endowment for the Arts. When released, Otis's song reached the top five on *Billboard*'s Black Singles Chart, and then became a huge mainstream hit. What song is it? I know what you're thinking . . . "(Sittin' On) the Dock of the Bay," right? Wrong. That song reached "only" #161 on the *Rolling Stone* list and "only" #22 on the Songs of the Century list. As a hint, the song was made famous by a female.

The answer is "Respect," written and recorded by Redding and 1965 and sung and released by Aretha Franklin in 1967. Producer Jerry Wexler brought Redding's song to Franklin's attention. While Redding's version was popular among his core R&B audience, Wexler thought the song had potential to be a crossover hit and to demonstrate Franklin's vocal ability. "Respect" was recorded by Franklin on February 14, 1967. While still maintaining most of the original lyrics, Franklin made it her own anthem by adding a few key lines, as well as the repeated "sock it to me" line, sung by Franklin's sisters Erma and Carolyn. This was an idea that Carolyn and Aretha had worked out together. Spelling out "R-E-S-P-E-C-T" was (according to engineer Tom Dowd) Carolyn's idea. In the line "Take care . . . TCB," "TCB" stands for taking care of business.[3]

Lamont Dozier and brothers Brian Holland and Eddie Holland, known as Holland-Dozier-Holland, were a prolific songwriting team for Motown. During their tenure at Motown from 1962 to 1967, Dozier and Brian Holland were the composers and producers for each song, and Eddie Holland wrote the lyrics and arranged the vocals. As a team, they wrote 12 #1 hit songs, all of which were performed by only two Motown groups. Who were the two groups?

The Four Tops and the Supremes (or Diana Ross and the Supremes).

Of those 12 songs, how many were recorded by the Supremes?

Ten. One of them, "You Keep Me Hangin' On," was also a #1 song for Kim Wilde in 1987.

Which were the two #1 Four Tops songs written by Holland-Dozier-Holland?

"I Can't Help Myself (Sugar Pie Honey Bunch)" and "Reach Out, I'll Be There."

What were the only two #1 songs for the Supremes (or Diana Ross and the Supremes after they changed their name) which were not written by Holland-Dozier-Holland?

"Love Child," which reached #1 in 1968, was cowritten by R. Dean Taylor (who later had a hit of his own with "Indiana Wants Me"), Frank Wilson, Pam Sawyer and Deke Richards, and "Someday We'll Be Together," which reached #1 in 1969 and was cowritten by Johnny Bristol, Harvey Fuqua and Jackey Beavers. However, "Someday We'll Be Together" shouldn't even count. Although Berry Gordy decided to release this as the final Diana Ross and the Supremes song, the other Supremes at the time, Mary Wilson and Cindy Birdsong, do not sing on the recording. The female backing vocals were sung by well-known backup singers Merry Clayton, Maxine Waters and her sister Julia Waters.

On "Someday We'll Be Together," cowriter Johnny Bristol was at first unable to get the vocal performance he desired from Ross, and so he decided to harmonize with her and offer words of encouragement. However, the engineer accidentally recorded both Ross's vocal and Bristol's ad-libs. He liked the results and left his ad-libs and words of encouragement to Ross on the final version, which can be heard in the background throughout the song (such as "you tell 'em" and "sing it pretty").

This man, who was ABBA's manager, is often called the fifth member of ABBA. He cowrote the lyrics for most of the band's biggest hits through 1977 including "Ring Ring" (1973), "Waterloo" (1974), "Honey, Honey" (1974), "I Do, I Do, I Do, I Do, I Do" (1975), "Mamma Mia" (1975), "S.O.S." (1975), "Fernando" (1976), "Dancing Queen" (1976), "Knowing Me, Knowing You" (1977), and "The Name of the Game" (1977). However, three of the band members later sued him, alleging that he had underpaid royalties. The case settled out of court. Who was this man?

Stig Anderson. He died in 1997 of a heart attack at age 66.[4]

The 1970 song "Band of Gold" about a wedding night gone wrong, sung by Freda Payne, reached #3 on the *Billboard* chart. It was cowritten by Edythe Wayne, which was a pseudonym for one of the most successful songwriters (or songwriting teams) in history. Another #3 hit also cowritten by Edythe Wayne, was the 1970 song "Give Me Just a Little More Time" by Chairmen of the Board. Who was Edythe Wayne?

"Edythe Wayne" was Holland-Dozier-Holland, who, while with Motown from 1962–1967, wrote so many of the hit songs of the Supremes and the Four Tops. Due to a legal dispute with Motown, from 1969 through 1972 they did not write material under their own names, but instead used the collective pseudonym "Edythe Wayne." These were their two biggest hits writing under that name. The background vocalists for "Band of Gold" included Telma Hopkins and Joyce Vincent Wilson (better known later as the "Dawn" part of Tony Orlando and Dawn) and Scherrie Payne, Freda's younger sister, who was a member of the Supremes from 1973–1977. Ray Parker Jr., who wrote and performed the theme song to the movie *Ghostbusters*, played lead guitar on the track.

When people think of Motown songwriters, they often think first of the wonderful team of Holland-Dozier-Holland. However, there was another man who, as a writer or cowriter, had an equally impressive—if not even greater—record of success for Motown. He also wrote for a wider variety of artists than Holland-Dozier-Holland, who wrote primarily for the Supremes and the Four Tops. The artists who performed this person's songs include the Temptations, Marvin Gaye, Gladys Knight and the Pips, the Undisputed Truth, Edwin Starr, Rose Royce and others. Despite this man's success (and while he is well-known to be sure), it may fairly be said that he is not nearly as famous as the Holland-Dozier-Holland team. The list of great songs which he wrote or cowrote—almost all of which were during the Decade—is truly impressive.

Year	Song	Artist	Pop rank	R&B rank
1965	"Too Many Fish in the Sea"	The Marvelettes	25	5
1966	"Beauty is Only Skin Deep"	The Temptations	3	1
1966	"Ain't Too Proud to Beg"	The Temptations	13	1
1966	"(I Know) I'm Losing You"	The Temptations	8	1
1966	"You're My Everything"	The Temptations	6	3
1967	"I Heard It Through the Grapevine"	Gladys Knight and the Pips	2	1
1968	"I Wish It Would Rain"	The Temptations	4	1
1968	"Cloud Nine"	The Temptations	6	2
1968	"I Could Never Love Another"	The Temptations	13	1
1969	"Runaway Child, Running Wild"	The Temptations	13	1
1969	"Too Busy Thinking About My Baby"	Marvin Gaye	4	1
1969	"I Can't Get Next to You"	The Temptations	1	1
1969	"That's the Way Love Is"	Marvin Gaye	7	2

1970	"Psychedelic Shack"	The Temptations	7	2
1970	"Ball of Confusion"	The Temptations	3	2
1970	"War"	Edwin Starr	1	3
1971	"Just My Imagination"	The Temptations	1	1
1971	"Smiling Faces Sometimes"	The Undisputed Truth	3	2
1972	"Papa Was a Rolling Stone"	The Temptations	1	5[5]
1973	"Masterpiece"	The Temptations	7	1
1976	"Car Wash"	Rose Royce	1	1

Who is this man?

Norman Whitfield. Clearly, Whitfield was to the Temptations was Holland-Dozier Holland was to the Supremes.

Who is Barrett Strong?

He is a lyricist. However, unlike some other lyricists who have written primarily for one other artist or band and who are famous in their own right (Bernie Taupin for Elton John and Robert Hunter for the Grateful Dead come to mind), Barrett Strong is comparatively anonymous. Yet his body of work is extensive. The band with which he is most closely associated is the Temptations. The songs for which he wrote the lyrics (with music by Norman Whitfield) include the following:

Year	Song	Artist	U.S. Pop rank	U.S R&B rank
1967	"I Heard It Through the Grapevine"	Gladys Knight and the Pips	2	1
1968	"I Wish It Would Rain"	The Temptations	4	1
1968	"Cloud Nine"	The Temptations	6	2
1968	"I Could Never Love Another"	The Temptations	13	1
1969	"Runaway Child, Running Wild"	The Temptations	13	1
1969	"Too Busy Thinking About My Baby"	Marvin Gaye	4	1

Year	Song	Artist	U.S. Pop rank	U.S R&B rank
1969	"I Can't Get Next To You"	The Temptations	1	1
1969	"That's the Way Love Is"	Marvin Gaye	7	2
1970	"Psychedelic Shack"	The Temptations	7	2
1970	"Ball of Confusion"	The Temptations	3	2
1970	"War"	Edwin Starr	1	3
1971	"Just My Imagination"	The Temptations	1	1
1971	"Smiling Faces Sometimes"	The Undisputed Truth	3	2
1972	"Papa Was a Rolling Stone"	The Temptations	1	5
1973	"Masterpiece"	The Temptations	7	1

"Lady Marmalade" was cowritten by a man who is most closely associated with the Four Seasons, and Frankie Valli individually, for whom he wrote or cowrote four #1 songs ("Sherry," "Rag Doll," "Big Girls Don't Cry" and "Walk Like a Man") and ten top 10 songs collectively. He also cowrote the Rays' classic 1957 song "Silhouettes," and produced over 30 top 30 songs, including "Sherry" (#1 for the Four Seasons), "Navy Blue" (#6 for Diane Renay, which he also cowrote), "A Lover's Concerto" (#2 for the Toys), "Devil with A Blue Dress On" (#4 for Mitch Ryder and the Detroit Wheels), "Jean" (#2 for Oliver) and "Good Morning, Starshine" (#6 for Oliver). Who is this man?

Bob Crewe.

Crewe was also a member of one of the best-named groups ever, headed by Sir Monti Rock III. Their biggest hits were "Get Dancin'" from 1974 (#10 U.S.) and "I Wanna Dance Wit' Choo (Doo Dat Dance)" from 1975 (#23 U.S.). What was the name of the group?

Disco-Tex and the Sex-O-Lettes. The group was name-checked by Elvis Costello in the 1991 song "Invasion Hit Parade" and by the Pet Shop Boys in their 1996 song "Electricity."[6]

This man wrote or cowrote "Best of My Love," "New Kid in Town" and "Heartache Tonight" (all #1 songs for the Eagles although the latter two are not from the Decade), "Faithless Love," "Prisoner in Disguise," "Hasten Down the Wind," and "Simple Man, Simple Dream" (all recorded by Linda Ronstadt). Who is he?

J.D. (for John David) Souther

This man wrote, among many other songs (1) "For Your Love" and "Heart Full of Soul," both top 10 hits for the Yardbirds in 1965, (2) "Bus Stop," a top 10 hit for the Hollies in 1966, (3) "Look Through Any Window," a top 10 hit in the U.K for the Hollies in 1965, (4) "Listen People" a top 10 hit for Herman's Hermits in 1966, and (5) "No Milk Today," a top 10 hit in the U.K. for Herman's Hermits in 1966. He then became a founding member of the band 10cc (and has been with them ever since) and, while with the band, wrote or cowrote top 10 hits such as "I'm Not in Love" and "The Things We Do for Love." What is his name?

Graham Gouldman.

This man wrote an eclectic group of songs for a variety of artists in a variety of genres. He was also a musician and singer himself. In 1958, he wrote a recorded a novelty hit called "The Purple People Eater Meets the Witch Doctor." He wrote "Down in the Boondocks," a top 10 hit for Billy Joe Royal in 1965, "I Knew You When," a top 20 hit for Royal the following year, "Yo-yo," a #3 hit for the Osmonds in 1971, "Hush," a huge #4 hit for Deep Purple in 1968, and "Birds of Feather," a #23 hit for the Raiders in 1971. He also wrote and performed "Walk a Mile in My Shoes" (with the Believers), a #12 hit in 1971.

Despite these successes, there are two other songs he wrote for which he is probably more remembered than any of the others. One of them, "Games People Play," performed by him, won the Grammy Award for Song of the Year in 1970. "I Never Promised You a Rose Garden" was also written and performed by him, but his version was not a hit. However, Lynn Anderson's version became one of the biggest crossover hits in history (#1 country, #3 pop). Anderson won a Grammy Award for her vocals, and the writer earned two Grammy Nominations for the song, Best Country Song and Song of the Year. Who is this man?

Joe South. He also wrote more hits for Anderson, such as "How Can I Unlove You" (*Billboard* Country #1) and "Fool Me" (*Billboard* Country #4). He also played guitar on a number of songs and albums including Tommy Roe's "Sheila," Bob Dylan's classic *Blonde on Blonde* album, and Aretha Franklin's "Chain of Fools."

This husband and wife songwriting duo had a wonderful career, writing hits over a 35-year period from the early 1960s to the late 1990s. He generally wrote the music and she generally was the lyricist. As a team, before the Decade, they wrote "Blame It On the

Bossa Nova" (Eydie Gorme), "On Broadway" (The Drifters), "Walking in the Rain" (The Ronettes), and "Saturday Night at the Movies" (the Drifters). During the Decade, they wrote "We Gotta Get Out of this Place" (the Animals), "Kicks" (Paul Revere and the Raiders), "I Just Can't Help Believing" (B.J. Thomas). Working separately, he sang and cowrote (with Gerry Goffin) that tender ballad "Who Put the Bomp (in the Bomp, Bomp, Bomp)" and "Sometimes When We Touch" (performed by Dan Hill, who also wrote the lyrics). She wrote the lyrics for "He's So Shy" (The Pointer Sisters) and "Running with the Night" (Lionel Richie). As if these accomplishments were not impressive enough by themselves, they do not include their cowriting of two #1 songs during the Decade (by the same group), one of which is merely the most frequently played song on the radio and television in rock music history. Who is this songwriting duo?

Barry Mann and Cynthia Weil. Their two #1 songs are "You've Lost That Lovin' Feelin'" (the most played song, also cowritten by Phil Spector) and "(You're My) Soul and Inspiration," both performed by the Righteous Brothers. After the Decade, they wrote "Here You Come Again" (Dolly Parton), "Don't Know Much" (Linda Ronstadt and Aaron Neville) and "Somewhere Out There" (Linda Ronstadt and James Ingram).

CHAPTER 13

It's Not Just a Man's World (Female Groups, Composers and Singers)

It is often said that rock and roll is a man's world. Nevertheless, there certainly has been no shortage of successful female singers, songwriters, musicians ... and members of bands—*so long*, that is, as the bands are either "coed" (think ABBA and Fleetwood Mac) or have male members in the band even if the stars are female (think Blondie and Heart). There have been comparatively few all-female bands, and most of those were singers only as opposed to musicians as well (such as The Bangles, The Go-Gos, Destiny's Child, Expose, Bananarama, TLC, En Vogue, Spice Girls, The Pussycat Dolls, Salt-N-Pepa, Sister Sledge, Wilson Phillips, The Dixie Chicks [perhaps more country] and others).

Wikipedia defines "girl groups" as apopular music act featuring several female singers who generally harmonize together.

Of the *Billboard* list of top 10 "girl groups" of all time, how many were active at any point during the Decade?

Only one—The Supremes, who came in at #1.

Among girl groups, the rarest breed of all is one which writes all of its own songs (with no co-writers) and plays all of its own instruments. There is at least one such band however and according to the band's website, they are "the most successful all-female rock band of all time!" (This is undoubtedly a true statement, as it is difficult to think of others who were truly successful who meet these criteria.) Who is this band? (It was not in existence during the Decade.)

The Go-Gos. The band only released three albums (prior to a 2001 reunion album) and had no #1 hits, but their debut album *Beauty and the Beat* did reach #1 and a single off of that album, "We Got the Beat," reached #2. There were other all-female bands which played their own instruments but they generally did not compose their own songs, at least exclusively. Examples would be The Runaways and The Bangles (although lead singer Joan Jett was a co-writer of some Runaways songs and lead singer Susanna Hoffs was a cowriter of some Bangles songs.)

The heyday of girl groups was in the years just prior to the Decade, say from 1961–1964. Virtually all of these groups were African-American, including the Supremes, the Vandellas, the Toys, the Dixie Cups, the Shirelles, the Chiffons, the Crystals, the Ronettes, the Exciters, the Marvelettes and the Blossoms (who recorded the #1 song "He's a Rebel," even though producer Phil Spector credited it to the Crystals). One exception was the Angels, a 3-woman group whose 1963 song "My Boyfriend's Back" reached #1, but their career had ended by the time the Decade started. Another rare exception was this group, which consisted of two sets of sisters, one set of whom were identical twins. Although their biggest hit singles (including a #1 song and a #5 song) were released in 1964, those singles appeared on their initial album in 1965 and their only other studio album was released the same year. They released a number of other singles before disbanding in 1967. Who was this group consisting of four white girls (and given that none of the four had yet reached 18 in 1964, "girls" is probably appropriate)?

The Shangri-Las. The lineup at first consisted of lead singer Mary Weiss and twins Mary Ann and Marge Ganser. Then Mary's older sister Betty joined the group. Their #1 song was "Leader of the Pack" and their #5 song was "Remember (Walking in the Sand)." Mary Ann died of a seizure in 1970 when she was only 22 years old.

As shown above, there were some successful girl groups before the Decade and there have been some after as well. As a general matter however, the relative absence of girl groups over the history of rock and roll is astonishing, especially considering all of the talented solo female singers and songwriters who have had success over that era. During the Decade in particular, with the obvious exception of the Supremes and the Shangri-Las, all-female groups (at least who reached the charts) were almost completely nonexistent. There were four however:

One had a #1 hit in 1974 about a prostitute.
One was by a group of women who were related (who had most of their success after the Decade).
One was a trio of singers who were the backup singers for Barry White.
One had a #2 song on the *Billboard* Hot 100 in 1974 that was the epitome of Philly soul, written by Kenny Gamble and Leon Huff. Every line in the song is a question.

Who were the four groups?

Labelle, the Pointer Sisters, Love Unlimited and the Three Degrees respectively. Labelle's song was "Lady Marmalade." The Pointer Sisters had top 20 songs with "Yes We Can Can"(1973), "Fairytale"(1974), and "How Long (Betcha' Got a Chick On the Side)" (1975). Love Unlimited had a top 20 song with "Walkin' in the Rain with the One I Love"(1972) and their 1974 song "I Belong to You" was #1 on the R&B chart. The #2 hit by the Three Degrees was "When Will I See You Again." Oddly, despite the fact that every line in the song is a question (with question marks after each), the title itself, though also a question, does not have a question mark.

The wonderful Joni Mitchell had only one song in the top 20 in her career. What was it? As a hint, it appeared on *Court and Spark*.

"Help Me," which reached #7 in 1974. Prince liked this song so much, he mentions it as his favorite song (and even sings a line from it) in "The Ballad of Dorothy Parker."

When it comes to influential female singer songwriters from the Decade (or from any time for that matter) who are mentioned as being influential on other artists, three names are frequently heard: Joni Mitchell, Carole King and this artist who, unlike Mitchell and King, actually had no hits of her own as a singer. Yet, artists as diverse as Mitchell, Bette Midler, Rickie Lee Jones, Kate Bush, Elton John, Cyndi Lauper, Todd Rundgren, Elvis Costello, Alice Cooper, Steely Dan and Melissa Manchester have all spoken of her importance to their careers. Because she did not like the "business end" of the business, she essentially walked away from it at age 24. In 2012, she was inducted into the Rock and Roll Hall of Fame. Who is this woman?

Laura Nyro, who passed away in 1997 at age 49 from ovarian cancer, the same disease that claimed her mother. Ironically, the only song which Nyro performed herself which even broke into the top 100 (barely) was not her own. She recorded the Carole King-Gerry Goffin tune "Up on the Roof" for her 1970 album *Christmas and the Beads of Sweat*, which reached #92 on the *Billboard* Hot 100.

The following artists each had hits with songs written by Laura Nyro. Name the song or songs.
The 5th Dimension (three songs which reached numbers #13, #3 and #1 respectively on the *Billboard* chart).

"Sweet Blindness," Stoned Soul Picnic," and "Wedding Bell Blues" respectively. Nyro was only 18 when she wrote "Wedding Bell Blues." They also recorded "Blowing Away," "Save the Country," and "Black Patch," all by Nyro. In December 1968, Liza Minnelli did a bizarre version of "Sweet Blindness" on *The Ed Sullivan Show*, with two male dancers, as if doing a Vegas revue. It can be seen on YouTube.[1]

Barbra Streisand

"Stoney End." Producer Richard Perry chose this song and convinced Streisand to sing it, despite her not being comfortable with the reference to Jesus in the song (Streisand is Jewish.) The Nyro-penned tunes "Time and Love" and "Hands Off the Man (Flim Flam Man)" appear on the same album, which is in fact titled *Stoney End*.[2]

Three Dog Night

"Eli's Coming." This was a #10 hit for the group in 1969. It originally appeared on Laura's wonderful 1968 album *Eli and the 13th Confession*.

Blood Sweat and Tears

"And When I Die." This song was written when Nyro was only 17 years old. She sold it to Peter, Paul and Mary for $5,000 and they recorded it and released it but it was not a hit. Then it was covered by Blood, Sweat, and Tears and reached #2 on the *Billboard* charts in 1969, one of their three songs to reach #2 ("You Made Me So Very Happy" and "Spinning Wheel" being the others).

In 1972, which of the following artists became the first female ever to have three songs simultaneously on the *Billboard* Hot 100, one of which was #1?

   a. Melanie
   b. Carole King
   c. Joni Mitchell
   d. Judy Collins
   e. Joan Baez

The answer is Melanie and the songs were "Brand New Key" (#1), "Ring the Living Bell" (#31), and "The Nickel Song" (#35). If the lyrics to "Brand New Key" are read in a certain way, the song could easily be construed as a song about a young woman singing about her desire to have sex with a young man, obviously using metaphors. The song was in fact banned on certain radio stations.

Commenting on the song, Melanie said: "'Brand New Key' I wrote in about fifteen minutes one night. I thought it was cute; a kind of old thirties tune. I guess a key and a lock have always been Freudian symbols, and pretty obvious ones at that. There was no deep serious expression behind the song, but people read things into it. My idea about songs is that once you write them, you have very little say in their life afterward. It's a lot like having a baby. You conceive a song, deliver it, and then give it as good a start as you can. After that, it's on its own. People will take it any way they want to take it."

Sadly, Melanie doesn't receive any royalties for songs she wrote before 2004 because her husband, Peter Schekeryk, who was also her producer and manager, sold her publishing and performance rights without telling her. She found out only after he died in 2010.[3]

Who was the first woman inducted into the Rock and Roll Hall of Fame? As hints, she was inducted in the second year of admission (1987). Also, of the first 25 inductees in the first two years, she was one of only three (along with Marvin Gaye and arguably Smokey Robinson) who had the bulk of her success during the Decade in terms of chart performance.

Aretha Franklin.

This woman has had more *Billboard* Hot 100 songs than any female artist (57) except Aretha Franklin. This includes 12 top 10 songs, two of which reached #1 (although sung with other artists). Who is she?

Dionne Warwick. Her two #1 songs were "Then Came You" with the Spinners (1974) and "That's What Friends Are For," with Elton John, Gladys Knight and Stevie Wonder (1985).

In 2004, Christopher Loudon of *Jazz Times* wrote that this woman was "blessed with arguably the most sterling set of pipes of her generation. [She is that] rarest of rarities—a chameleon who can blend into any background yet remain boldly distinctive . . . It's an exceptional gift; one shared by few others." *Dirty Linen* magazine described her as the "first true woman rock 'n' roll superstar." In 1977, she graced the cover of *Time* magazine under the heading "Torchy Rock." Who are they referring to?

Linda Ronstadt.[4]

Here are a few questions about Bobbie Gentry's 1967 song "Ode to Billie Joe," which is ranked #412 on *Rolling Stone's* list of the 500 Greatest Songs of All Time.

Who wrote the song?

a. Bobbie Gentry
b. Glen Campbell
c. Jimmy Webb
d. Willie Nelson
e. Charlie Daniels

The answer is a. Gentry (a beautiful Southerner like Jeannie C. Riley who sang *Harper Valley P.T.A.*) was one of the first female country singers to write and produce her own material. She was born Roberta Streeter and chose her stage name from the 1952 film *Ruby Gentry*, a woman born into poverty but determined to make a success of her life. In the early '70s, she was headlining in Vegas and hosting her own TV series. Then around 1975, she simply checked out. She has not been heard from in over 40 years. All requests for interviews, recordings and performances have been denied.[5]

The first line of the song refers to a certain date. What is that date?

June 3.

In the song, Billie Joe McAllister jumped off the Tallahatchie Bridge. True or false: the bridge is fictional.

False (a fact undoubtedly known to Mississippians and Bobbie Gentry fans). The bridge collapsed however in 1972 after being set alight by vandals. It crossed the Tallahatchie River at Money, Mississippi, and has since been rebuilt. The November 10, 1967 issue of *Life* magazine contained a photo of Gentry crossing the original bridge. When the song became a hit, *Rolling Stone* magazine reported that it is only a 20-foot drop off the bridge and the water was deep enough that a person would not get hurt jumping off. Photos of the bridge and the river seem to confirm this.[6]

Finally, as with another enduring mystery question (who is the song "You're so Vain" about?), people always want to know: What did Billie Joe and "a girl who looked a lot like [the narrator]" throw off the Tallahatchie Bridge? Gentry herself has never revealed this, commenting only: "The real message revolves around the nonchalant way the family talks about the suicide," she said. "The song is sort of a study in unconscious cruelty. But everybody seems more concerned with what was thrown off the bridge than they are with the thoughtlessness of the people expressed in the song. What was thrown off the bridge really isn't that important."[7]

This person is the youngest singer-songwriter in history to have a top 20 song which he or she solely composed and performed. Who is the singer-songwriter and what is the song? As hints, the singer-songwriter is female. She wrote the song when she was 14 and it was released in 1967 when she was 16.

The singer-songwriter is Janis Ian and the song is "Society's Child." (The full title is "Society's Child (Baby I've Been Thinking)," even though she does not sing the parenthetical part in the song.) The song reached #14 on the *Billboard* Hot 100 in 1967. The song is about a young girl who witnesses the humiliation that her African-American boyfriend receives from the girl's mother and the taunts that she herself endures from classmates and teachers. It closes with her decision to end her relationship with the boyfriend because of her inability to deal with the social pressure. Ian said: "My parents were the complete opposite of the parents in the song. They wouldn't have cared if I married a Martian, as long as I was happy. I felt bad for my dad because everyone assumed he was a racist." Twenty-two record companies passed on the song before it was picked up by Verve Records. She performed the song live at age 16 on *The Smothers Brothers Show* and the performance can be seen on YouTube.[8]

Janis Ian has a special connection with *Saturday Night Live*. What is it?

She was the first musical guest on the original episode on October 11, 1975. She performed "At Seventeen" and "In the Winter." George Carlin was the host.

The list of female drummers in the rock era, and especially during the Decade, is small indeed. According to musicradar.com, this woman was the one of the best singing drummers in history. While this woman rarely played drums on studio recordings, she did often play them in concert (with her name on the drum head).

Karen Carpenter. According to her brother Richard, she considered herself a "drummer who sang."[9]

On the *Rolling Stone* list of the 100 Greatest Guitarists of All Time (created by David Fricke in 2011), there are only two women on the entire list. This suggests that (1) the list is poorly compiled, (2) Fricke is misogynistic, (3) women can't play guitar as well as men, or

(4) (and perhaps most likely) the number of male players is so much higher than the number of female players that the 50:1 ratio is about right. In any event, one of the two women was Joan Jett, coming in at #87. The only other woman on the list came in at #72—and thus is the highest ranking woman. The peak of her career was during the Decade. Who is it?

Joni Mitchell, who is famous for her "open" (non-standard) tuning.

This woman was that rare breed, a female session musician, in her case on percussion (and sometimes drums). She also played bongos, congas, tambourine, tom-toms, casaba, maracas, cowbell, bells, shaker and triangle. While she is certainly not a household name, the list of songs and albums on which she played percussion is impressive indeed. She played on 22 songs that reached the top 10 in the *Billboard* Hot 100, and six which reached #1. She played on "Me and Bobby McGee" by Janis Joplin, "Ain't No Sunshine" by Bill Withers, "Sweet Seasons" by Carole King, "Don't Let Me Be Lonely Tonight" by James Taylor, "Diamond Girl" (album and song) by Seals and Crofts, "Miracles" by Jefferson Starship, "Let's Get It On" by Marvin Gaye (album and song), "For the Roses" by Joni Mitchell (album), "Take Me in Your Arms (Rock Me a Little While)" by the Doobie Brothers, *Bob Dylan: Live at Budokan*, and *Bella Donna* by Stevie Nicks. Who is this woman?

Bobbye Porter, also known as Ms. Bobbye Porter or Ms. Bobbye Porter Hall after she got married.[10] She also played with Kim Carnes, Lynyrd Skynyrd, Randy Newman, Rod Stewart, Dolly Parton, Leo Sayer, Donovan, Freda Payne, Dwight Yoakam, Poco, the Temptations, Mary Wells, Boz Scaggs, Marc Bolan, Judy Mowatt, Hugo Montenegro, Aretha Franklin, Smokey Robinson, Diana Ross, the Doors, the Mamas and the Papas, Harry Chapin and Tracy Chapman.

Try to identify the woman described below in as few hints as possible:

1. She was born Mary Isobel (sometimes spelled Isabel) Catherine Bernadette O'Brien.
2. She was named a member of the Order of the British Empire (OBE).
3. She had six top 20 singles on the U.S. *Billboard* Hot 100 and 16 on the U.K. singles chart. Although not all released during the Decade, her prime years were during the Decade.
4. She has been described as "Britain's greatest pop diva [and was also] the finest white soul singer of her era."

5. She died in 1999 at age 60 just before she was about to be inducted into the Rock and Roll Hall of Fame. At her induction ceremony, Elton John said "I'm biased but I just think she was the greatest white singer there ever has been."

Who was this singer?

The great Dusty Springfield, "the white queen of soul." Her two biggest hits in the U.S. during the Decade were "You Don't Have to Say You Love Me" and "Son of a Preacher Man," the latter of which gained renewed popularity when it was featured in the 1994 film *Pulp Fiction*. Her most classic album—although it was not a success when released—was *Dusty in Memphis*, released in 1969. *Rolling Stone* ranked it #89 of the 500 greatest albums of all time, calling it "blazing soul and sexual honesty, that transcended both race and geography." Interestingly, despite the title of the album, Dusty actually recorded her final vocals in New York. (In fact, according to *Rolling Stone*, "she never sang a note [in Memphis].") She had extreme anxiety about performing with some of the great Memphis session musicians who were recruited for the recording sessions as well as being compared to the greats who recorded in the same studios. For the first and only time in her career, she sang with just the basic rhythm tracks to guide her.

As with so many songs, "You Don't Have to Say You Love Me" has an interesting story behind it. It was originally an Italian song released in 1965 called "Io che non vivo (senza te)"—"I, who can't live (without you)"—music by Pino Donaggio and lyrics by Vito Pallavicini. Springfield heard the song performed live at the 1965 Sanremo Festival, and despite having no awareness of the lyrics' meaning the song moved her to tears. Springfield obtained an acetate recording of the song, but allowed a year to go by before actively pursuing the idea of recording an English version. Then, in 1966, she had an instrumental track of the song recorded. She then asked her friend Vicki Wickham to write lyrics to the song, despite the fact that Wickham had no experience as a songwriter and did not speak Italian. Springfield recorded her vocal the next day but was not satisfied with her vocal until she had recorded 47 takes.

Wickham's friend Simon Napier-Bell picks up the story from there: "Vicki and I used to eat together, and she told me that Dusty wanted a lyric for this song. We went back to her flat and started working on it. We wanted to go to a trendy disco so we had about an hour to write it. We wrote the chorus and then we wrote the verse in a taxi to wherever we were going. It was the first pop lyric I'd written, although I've always been interested in poetry and good literature. We'd no idea what the Italian lyric said. That seemed to be irrelevant and besides, it is much easier to write a new lyric completely." So in short, the lyrics were written by two women who had never done so before and who had no idea what the original Italian lyrics were about. As it turns out, the two songs are not so dissimilar in subject matter: In both songs, the singer seems terrified at the thought of being apart of his/her partner for even a moment. The difference is that in the English version, the partner has already left the relationship while in the Italian version, that hasn't happened yet, but the singer is fearful that the partner may be contemplating it.[11]

Another interesting tidbit about Springfield: She was responsible for giving Led Zeppelin their big break. In November 1968, while recording *Dusty in Memphis*, she suggested to Jerry Wexler (one of the heads of Atlantic Records) that he should sign the newly formed U.K. band, Led Zeppelin. She knew their bass guitarist, John Paul Jones, from his session work on her earlier albums. Without ever having seen them and partly on her advice, Wexler signed Led Zeppelin to a $200,000 deal with Atlantic, which, at the time, was the biggest contract for a new band. It was a move he would not regret.[12]

This talented woman has had a varied career. She was born Sharon Lee Myers. She recorded "Needles and Pins" which went to #1 in Canada, supported the Beatles on their first American tour, wrote "Don't Doubt Yourself Babe" for the debut album of the Byrds, wrote "Come and Stay With Me," a top 10 U.K. hit for Marianne Faithful, cowrote songs with Randy Newman, cowrote the #1 Kim Carnes song, "Bette Davis Eyes," costarred with Bobby Vinton in "Surf Party," dated Elvis Presley and Jimmy Page, and, on top of all that, had two top 10 U.S. hits of her own, one of which she cowrote with her brother Randy Myers. Who is she?

Jackie DeShannon. In 1965, the Burt Bacharach/Hal David song "What the World Needs Now," reached #7 and in 1969, the song that she cowrote, "Put a Little Love in Your Heart," reached #4.

This woman was the first Canadian female solo singer to reach #1 on the *Billboard* adult contemporary chart, and also the first to earn a Gold record for one of her signature songs, released in 1970. Who is the artist and what is the song?

Some might think that the artist is Joni Mitchell, but it is Anne Murray, and the song is "Snowbird." Her other #1 hits on the U.S. adult contemporary chart during the Decade included "Danny's Song," "A Love Song," and "You Won't See Me." Her only #1 song on the *Billboard* Hot 100 was "You Needed Me," released in 1978.

When it comes to lead singers and their backup vocal groups, it is relatively uncommon to have a female lead singer and a male backup vocal group, and that was especially

the case during the Decade. The most successful of these during the Decade, and possibly ever, had six top five hit singles on the *Billboard* Hot 100, all during the Decade. Who was the group?

Gladys Knight and the Pips. They also had 18 top five hits on the R&B chart.

Another such group was a one-hit wonder, that hit being "The Boy from New York City," with lead singer Mary Ann Thomas. What was the name of the group?

The Ad-Libs. Examples from after the Decade include the Pretenders, Blondie, Joan Jett and the Blackhearts and Miami Sound Machine, although in each of those cases, the male group members actually played instruments as opposed to being merely backup singers.

CHAPTER 14

Commonality: Songs or Bands that have Something in Common

T his chapter is devoted to songs and bands that have something in common. I suspect that, with respect to many questions in this chapter, the answers may not be immediately apparent. For those who don't know the answers to any particular questions, it is my hope that the answers will bring a flash of recognition as in the moment where you slap the palm of your hand against your forehead and say to yourself: "That's right! I should've thought of that!"

What do these seemingly unrelated songs have in common? As a suggestion, if you listened to the songs one after the other, the answer would be fairly clear. The answer has to do with timing or length, but not necessarily of the whole song itself.

"Baba O'Riley" by the Who
"Colour My World" by Chicago
"Funeral for a Friend/Love Lies Bleeding" by Elton John
"Heart of the Sunrise" by Yes
"Jet Airliner" by Steve Miller (album version)
"Locomotive Breath" by Jethro Tull
"Papa Was a Rolling Stone" by the Temptations (album version)
"Roundabout" by Yes
"Shine On You Crazy Diamond" by Pink Floyd (original version)
"Smoke on the Water" by Deep Purple
"Stairway to Heaven" by Led Zeppelin
"The End" by the Doors
"Theme from *Shaft*" by Isaac Hayes

. . .and one from outside the decade: "I Need a Lover" by John Cougar Mellencamp. They all have unusually long intros. The length of each is set forth below.

"Baba O'Riley" by the Who (1:06)

"Colour My World" by Chicago (0:59)

"Funeral for a Friend/Love Lies Bleeding" by Elton John (5:35)

"Heart of the Sunrise" by Yes (3:41)

"Jet Airliner" by Steve Miller (album version) (2:07)

"Locomotive Breath" by Jethro Tull (1:28)

"Papa Was a Rolling Stone" by the Temptations (album version) (4:05)

"Roundabout" by Yes (0:59)

"Shine On You Crazy Diamond" by Pink Floyd (original version) (5:10)

"Smoke on the Water" by Deep Purple (0:51)

"Stairway to Heaven" by Led Zeppelin (0:54)

"The End" by the Doors (1:07)

"Theme from *Shaft*" by Isaac Hayes (2:40)

"I Need a Lover" by John Cougar Mellencamp (2:32)

Following is a list of 10 songs. The bands that recorded them all have something in common. What is it?

"Different Drum"

"Last Train to Clarksville"

"More Today Than Yesterday"

"Nobody but Me"

"Red Rubber Ball"

"Stairway to Heaven"

"Sweet Home Alabama"

"Ticket to Ride"

"Turn! Turn! Turn!"

"Walk Away Renee"

The bands that recorded them all have misspelled words in their names. Given the undoubtedly erudite audience for this book, I'm sure there is no need to provide the correct spellings!

"Different Drum"—Linda Ronstadt and the Stone Poneys

"Last Train to Clarksville"—The Monkees

"More Today Than Yesterday"—Spiral Starecase

"Nobody but Me"—The Human Beinz

"Red Rubber Ball"–The Cyrkle
"Stairway to Heaven"—Led Zeppelin
"Sweet Home Alabama"–Lynyrd Skynyrd
"Ticket to Ride"—The Beatles
"Turn! Turn! Turn!"—The Byrds
"Walk Away Renee"—The Left Banke

With respect to "Different Drum," although credited to "Linda Ronstadt and the Stone Poneys," Ronstadt was the only member of that trio who actually performed on the track, with the instruments being played by studio musicians.

What do the following bands, all of whom were active at some point in the Decade, have in common?

Fleetwood Mac
Paul Revere and the Raiders
Santana
The Dave Clark Five
The J. Geils Band
The Jeff Beck Group
The Spencer Davis Group
Manfred Mann (later the Manfred Mann Earth Band)

In each case, the band is named after someone (or in Fleetwood Mac's case, two people, namely Mick Fleetwood and John McVie) who are not the lead singers. The lead singers were usually as follows:

Fleetwood Mac: Christine McVie, Stevie Nicks or Lindsay Buckingham, typically depending on who wrote the song
Paul Revere and the Raiders: Mark Lindsay
Santana: Greg Rolie
The Dave Clark Five: Mike Smith
The J. Geils Band: Peter Wolf
The Jeff Beck Group: Rod Stewart
The Spencer Davis Group: Steve Winwood
Manfred Mann: Paul Jones and then Mike D'Abo and, after the band changed its name to the Manfred Mann Earth Band in 1971, Mick Rogers

The following 10 songs all share an attribute which is quite uncommon. What is it?

"It's Only Love"—The Beatles
"I Will"—The Beatles
"Sgt. Pepper's Lonely Hearts Club Band (Reprise)"—The Beatles
"Mercedes Benz"—Janis Joplin
"The 59th Street Bridge Song (Feelin' Groovy)"—Simon and Garfunkel
"The Letter"—The Box Tops
"New York Telephone Conversation"—Lou Reed
"Lazing On a Sunday Afternoon"—Queen
"Lily of the Valley"—Queen
"One More Try"—The Rolling Stones

They are all under two minutes in duration.

What do the following songs have in common? Hint. It has to do with the Beatles.

"American Pie" by Don McLean
"Friends of Mine" by the Guess Who
"Glass Onion" by the Beatles
"How Do You Sleep" by John Lennon
"Just Like Me" by Paul Revere and the Raiders
"Shooting Star" by Bad Company
"Summer Rain" by Johnny Rivers
"All You Need is Love" by the Beatles

They all mention Beatles songs in their lyrics:

"American Pie" by Don McLean ("Helter Skelter")
"Friends of Mine" by the Guess Who ("Magical Mystery Tour")
"Glass Onion" by the Beatles ("Strawberry Fields," "I Am the Walrus," and "The Fool on the Hill")
"How Do You Sleep" by John Lennon ("Yesterday")
"Just Like Me" by Paul Revere and the Raiders ("Love Me Do")
"Shooting Star" by Bad Company ("Love Me Do")
"Summer Rain" by Johnny Rivers ("Sgt. Pepper's Lonely Hearts Club Band")
"All You Need is Love" by the Beatles ("She Loves You")

In "Young Americans," David Bowie sings "I heard the news today oh boy" from Lennon's song "A Day in the Life"(changing "read" to "heard" but with the same notes).

What do the following songs have in common? (As a hint, all songs were written by George Harrison or Eric Clapton.)

"For You Blue" by the Beatles
"It's All Too Much" by the Beatles
"Something" by the Beatles
"Why Does Love Got to be So Sad" by Derek and the Dominos
"Layla" by Derek and the Dominos
"Bell Bottom Blues" by Derek and the Dominos
"She's Waiting" by Eric Clapton
"Wonderful Tonight" by Eric Clapton

They are all about Pattie Boyd Harrison, and more specifically their love or (especially in the case of Eric Clapton) yearning for her, although there is some question whether "Something" is about her or not. She married Harrison in 1966, separated from him in 1974 and they divorced in 1977. She married Clapton in 1979, left him in 1984, and divorced him in 1988. Ms. Boyd Harrison must have been something, to have not one but two of the most famous (and desirable) rock stars in the world not only competing with each other for their attention, but writing song after song about her loveliness and charms. For the most part, Harrison's songs about her (written while they were married) are simply love songs while Clapton's (mostly written while she was with Harrison or when their marriage was falling apart) are anguished songs of lament.

As for "Something," Boyd wrote in her autobiography that it was about her. However, when asked about this in 1996, Harrison said, "Well no, I didn't [write it about her]. I just wrote it, and then somebody put together a video. And what they did was they went out and got some footage of me and Pattie. So then, everybody presumed I wrote it about Pattie, but actually, when I wrote it, I was thinking of Ray Charles."[1]

With respect to each song listed below, the songwriter or someone from the band commented on the song and those comments share a common thread. What is the shared theme?

"A Horse with No Name" by America
"Are You Experienced?" by Jimi Hendrix

"Being for the Benefit of Mr. Kite!" by the Beatles
"Crystal Blue Persuasion" by Tommy James and the Shondells
"Eight Miles High" by the Byrds
"Lookin' Out My Back Door" by Creedence Clearwater Revival
"Lucy in the Sky with Diamonds" by the Beatles
"Mellow Yellow" by Donovan
"Mr. Tambourine Man" by Bob Dylan (and later the Byrds)

In each case, the songwriter or someone from the band denied that it was about drugs or written while on drugs (although in some cases, with the passage of time, they sometimes retracted those denials). The initial denials were sometimes necessitated when radio stations would not play the songs for that reason.

In the case of "A Horse with No Name," "horse" was a street name for heroin at the time.

Similarly, the BBC banned "Being For the Benefit of Mr. Kite!" because they believed that "Henry the horse" was also a reference to heroin, but John Lennon dismissed this as "rubbish."

"Eight Miles High" was also banned by some stations but publicist Derek Taylor strenuously denied that the song was drug-related, and issued an indignant press release claiming that the song was about the band's flight to England and not drug use.

In the case of "Lookin' Out My Back Door," according to the drug theory, the "flying spoon" in the song was a cocaine spoon, and the crazy animal images referenced in the song were an acid trip. However, songwriter John Fogerty said that the song was actually written for his then three-year old son, Josh, and that the reference to a parade passing by was inspired by the Dr. Seuss book, *And to Think That I Saw It on Mulberry Street*.

The supposed drug connection with "Mellow Yellow" was that there was a rumor started by *The Berkeley Barb* in 1967 that one could get high from smoked banana skins, though this was later debunked by *The Straight Dope*. Instead, Donovan said that it was a reference to vibrators: "[The song] is about being cool, laid-back, and also the electrical bananas that were appearing on the scene—which were ladies' vibrators."[2]

What do the following famous bands have in common?

The Animals
The Band
The Beach Boys
Buffalo Springfield
The Rolling Stones

The Temptations
The Yardbirds

They all had five members, at least during their prime years. I could have added the Dave Clark 5 and the Jackson 5 but that might have given it away.

What do the following songs have in common?

"Help Me Rhonda" by the Beach Boys
"Can't You See" by the Marshall Tucker Band
"'39" by Queen
"Happy" by the Rolling Stones
"December, 1963 (Oh, What a Night)" by the Four Seasons
"Bridge Over Troubled Water" by Simon and Garfunkel
"With a Little Help from My Friends" by the Beatles
"Strangers" by the Kinks
"Good Vibrations" by the Beach Boys
"We're an American Band" by Grand Funk Railroad
"Take it to the Limit" by the Eagles

In each case, the song is sung by someone who is not normally considered the lead singer in the band (even though, in some cases, the songs listed below are not the only ones where the singer mentioned handled lead vocals).

"Help Me Rhonda" is sung by Al Jardine instead of Mike Love or Brian Wilson
"Can't You See" is sung by Toy Caldwell instead of Doug Gray
"'39" is sung by Brian May instead of Freddie Mercury
"Happy" is sung by Keith Richards instead of Mick Jagger
"December, 1963 (Oh, What a Night)" is sung by drummer Gerry Polci instead of Franki Valli
"Bridge Over Troubled Water" is sung by Art Garfunkel. (He and Paul Simon did sing harmonies on many songs, but there were a few where Garfunkel sang the entire song himself, another being "For Emily, Wherever I May Find Her.")
"With a Little Help from My Friends" is sung by Ringo Starr
"Strangers" is sung by Dave Davies instead of his brother Ray

"Good Vibrations" is sung by Carl Wilson

"We're an American Band" is sung by drummer Don Brewer instead of Mark Farner

"Take it to the Limit" is sung by Randy Meisner instead of Glenn Frey or Don Henley

The previous question involved songs that were hits but that were not sung by the person (or persons) usually considered to be the lead singer of the band. However, at least they were *in* the band. The following questions involve instances where the lead singer was not even in the band when the song was recorded. It is not at all unusual of course for bands to recruit musicians from other bands to play instruments on their songs. What is unusual is for a band who already has a non-instrument-playing lead singer to use a lead singer who is not with the band for a song. The Beach Boys had a massive hit doing just that, with the usual lead singer, Mike Love, singing backup. As a hint, the lead singer on this song was Dean Torrence of Jan and Dean and the track appeared on the group's *Beach Boys' Party!* album. What is the song?

"Barbara Ann," written by Fred Fassert. This song reached #2 on the *Billboard* Hot 100 in 1965. Befitting its name, the album was packaged as if it had been recorded at an actual party. However, it was in fact recorded in the studio, with friends adding sounds and vocals to create an informal atmosphere. With the exception of a bass guitar, all the instruments were acoustic. Like the other songs on the album, "Barbara Ann," with Torrence handling lead vocals, sounds very informal, like a bunch of friends sitting around the campfire. (Brian Wilson would later recall that "half the people in the room were singing while the other half were munching on potato chips.") Although the single version is 2:05, the album version was 3:23, the difference being the boys goofing around both at the start and end of the song. Torrance is not credited on the album jacket, but Carl Wilson can be heard saying "Thanks, Dean" at the very end of the album version of the track.[3]

Members of the Beach Boys and Jan and Dean collaborated on other occasions. Brian Wilson cowrote "Surf City" and "Dead Man's Curve," both of which were big hits for Jan and Dean. Ironically, in 1966, Jan Berry was involved in a near-fatal car crash just a few blocks away from the actual "dead man's curve" referred to in the song located at Sunset and Vine in Los Angeles. He was in a coma for several months. He eventually recovered.

This #1 song has also an unusual history indeed in that, once again, the lead singer was never a member of the band that recorded it and the band did not even have the same name by which they were previously known after it became a hit. The original name of the

band was Thee Sixpence [*sic*]. When the song was ready to be recorded, the group members decided that none of their voices sounded right for the vocals. Therefore, they asked a 16-year-old named Greg Munford, who happened to be a guest visiting the studio that day, to sing lead vocal. They liked his voice on the song and decided to keep it. Even so, the song was considered a throwaway song and was relegated to the B-side to "The Birdman of Alkatrash" and was released in April 1967.

DJs started playing the B-side and it began to rise up the charts. Shortly afterwards, the 45 was re-released a month later with the A and B sides switched and the name of the group changed to the name it is now known. Munford never joined the band. As bassist George Bunnell said "He was in the band as long as it took him to sing the song." The song was on the *Billboard* charts for 16 weeks and hit #1 in November 1967. The song is heard on *Austin Powers: International Man of Mystery* (1997) and several episodes of *The Simpsons*. What is the song? As a hint, the new name of the band was Strawberry Alarm Clock.

"Incense and Peppermints." Two members of Thee Sixpence, Ed King and Mark Weitz, wrote the music to the song. The producer sent the music to John Carter and Tim Gilbert, two members of a group called the Rainy Daze, and they wrote the lyrics. According to Weitz, a dispute ensued between the group's producer and manager regarding songwriting credits which resulted in Weitz and King, the actual band members who wrote the music, being left off of the credits. According to Weitz, "I was determined to sue all parties concerned, but was talked out of this action by [our producer, who mentioned] the fact that it would destroy the future livelihood of the band, and we would lose the tour bookings that the band . . . I agreed to call off the dogs. After two years, I made a second attempt to initiate the lawsuit against [our manager]. Upon the untimely breakup of the [Strawberry Alarm Clock] in 1970, and due to the high cost of continuing on with the lawsuit, I was forced to drop the case. . . . To this day, [Carter and Gilbert] have received 100 percent of the royalties."

King went on to become a guitarist with Lynyrd Skynrd and cowrote their signature song "Sweet Home Alabama."[4]

What do the following bands have in common?

The Eagles
The Band
The Monkees
Kiss
The Carpenters
Queen
The Beatles

They are all bands in which the drummer was the singer, either always (The Carpenters—Karen Carpenter), frequently, (The Eagles—Don Henley, the Band—Levon Helm, the Monkees—Mickey Dolenz), or occasionally (Kiss—Peter Criss, Queen—Roger Taylor, the Beatles—Ringo Starr [11 songs]). Dolenz sang lead on most of the Monkees' biggest hits, including their "Last Train to Clarksville," "(I'm Not Your) Steppin Stone," "I'm a Believer," "Pleasant Valley Sunday," as well as their theme song. The same is true of Helm, who sang lead on songs such as "Up on Cripple Creek," "The Night They Drove Old Dixie Down," "Ophelia," and "The Weight."

Roger Taylor's talents as a vocalist are understandably overshadowed by being in the same band as Freddie Mercury. However, Taylor had a four-octave voice and his extremely high falsetto was frequently used to great effect. Notable Queen songs on which Taylor's vocals can be heard include "Keep Yourself Alive," "Loser in the End," "Tenement Funster," "In the Lap of the Gods" (falsetto screams), "I'm In Love With My Car," "'39" (high falsetto vocals during instrumental bridges) and "Bohemian Rhapsody" (high-falsetto vocals, such as the "let me go" lines andthe final "for me . . ." during midsection).

What do the following songs have in common?

"A Boy Named Sue" by Johnny Cash
"Bye-Bye Love" by Simon and Garfunkel
"Crossroads" by Cream
"Folsom Prison Blues" by Johnny Cash
"Give Peace a Chance" by John Lennon
"Memphis" by Johnny Rivers
"My Ding-a-Ling" by Chuck Berry
"No Woman No Cry" by Bob Marley
"Rock and Roll All Nite" by Kiss
"Thank God I'm a Country Boy" by John Denver

The best-known versions of each of these songs were all recorded live.

What do the songs "You Are So Beautiful" by Joe Cocker, "In-A-Gadda-Da-Vida" by Iron Butterfly, and "The End" by the Beatles have in common? As a kind of hint, the Israeli folk song sung at weddings everywhere, "Hava Nagila," would also fit within the answer to this question.

They all have less than 35 unique words. "You Are So Beautiful" has 31. "In-A-Gadda-Da-Vida" has only 30 if you count in-a-gadda-da-vida as one word. If not, it has 34 unique words even though they are slurred. Given that it is more than 17 minutes long, this song clearly wins the prize for fewest words of a song over five minutes long that is not an instrumental. "The End" is 21 unique words and "Hava Nagila" is only 10.

One would think that it would be harder to have a non-instrumental song with fewer than 10 words or that "In-A-Gadda-Da-Vida" might win the award for fewest words per minute. Both of these thoughts would be wrong. There is a song from the Decade which has only six unique words and it went to #1 no less and stayed there for three weeks in late 1975. Since this is probably not enough information to figure out the song, the reason there are so few words is that the group (consisting of three women) was German and spoke no English and apparently couldn't memorize a page of lyrics in a language unfamiliar to them. As another hint, the name of the group was Silver Convention.

The song is "Fly, Robin, Fly," the title containing one-third of the unique words of the whole song (the others being "up," "to," "the" and "sky.") According to songwriter Sylvester Levay, the song was going to be called "Run Rabbit Run," and the lyrics were changed just a few minutes before the song was recorded. One wonders what the second line of the song would have been in that case, unless it was going to be a song about flying rabbits.

What do the following songs have in common?

"Across the Universe"—The Beatles
"Before the Next Teardrop Falls"—Freddie Fender
"Lady Marmalade"—Labelle
"Michelle"—The Beatles
"Suite: Judy Blue Eyes"—Crosby Stills & Nash

They are all songs from the Decade with English titles and sung primarily in English but with one or more lines sung in a foreign language.

What do the following have in common?

Bad Company
Black Sabbath
Free
Ziggy Stardust

The Monkees
King Crimson

They are all instances in which a band (or in the case of Ziggy Stardust, an individual) released both an album during the Decade and a song on that album which are either exactly the same as the band name or in which the song and album contain the same words as in the group even if other words are included as well. The only ones where there is an exact match are Bad Company (song appears on 1974 self-titled album) and Black Sabbath (same, except album released in 1970). Free's 1969 album contained a song called "Free Me." The first song on the Monkees' 1966 self-titled debut album is "(Theme from) The Monkees." King Crimson's 1969 debut album was called *In the Court of the Crimson King*, which in turn contained a song called "The Court of the Crimson King." This is the only example where the words are reversed. While Ziggy Stardust is of course David Bowie's alter ego, his 1972 album is called *The Rise and Fall of Ziggy Stardust and the Spiders from Mars*, which in turn contains a song called "Ziggy Stardust." Mott the Hoople almost counts: their 1973 album *Mott* contains a song called "Ballad of Mott the Hoople."

Examples from after the decade, all of which are exact matches, include Iron Maiden, Motörhead, Electric Wizard, Pennywise, Children of Bodom, Damn Yankees, Bang Camaro, Deicide, Iced Earth and Living in a Box.

CHAPTER 15

"The Streak" and Other Classics (Novelty Songs)

There is sometimes an overlap between novelty songs and one-hit wonders. However, while the writers of novelty songs are usually one-hit wonders, the reverse is obviously not true. But what is a novelty song in the first place? It is typically a comical or nonsensical song. It is sometimes a parody of an existing song and can be written with respect to a current event such as a holiday or a fad such as a dance. Many use unusual lyrics, subjects, sounds, or instruments. They are virtually never intended by the composer to be taken seriously.

The Decade was not the prime time for novelty songs. For example, one list of the top 100 novelty songs of the '50s and '60s includes only 12 from the Decade and most of those are obscure.[1] Most of the "biggies" preceded the Decade, including "The Chipmunk Song" by the Chipmunks, "Monster Mash" by Bobby (Boris) Pickett, "Alley-Oop" by the Hollywood Argyles, "Itsy Bitsy Teenie Weenie Yellow Polka Dot Bikini" by Brian Hyland, "Hello Mudduh, Hello Fadduh!" by Allan Sherman, "Charlie Brown" by the Coasters, "Tie Me Kangaroo Down, Sport" by Rolf Harris, "Beep Beep" by the Playmates, "The Purple People Eater" by Sheb Wooley, and many others. There were some novelty songs released during the Decade however.

One of the great novelty songs of the 1970s was "The Streak." It was released in March 1974 as the lead single on the album *Boogity Boogity*. It was a #1 song on the *Billboard* Hot 100 for three weeks in May and June 1974. Who wrote and performed the song?

Ray Stevens (born Harold Ray Ragsdale). The song obviously capitalized on the then popular craze of streaking. One of the most high-profile streaks took place at the 46th Academy Awards on April 2, 1974 (just a few days after "The Streak" was released) in which advertising executive Robert Opel streaked past David Niven on live TV, which undoubtedly helped propel the popularity of the song. Niven, unfazed, cracked: "Isn't it fascinating to think that probably the only laugh that man will ever get in his life is by stripping off and showing his shortcomings?"

While most composers of successful novelty songs tend to be one-hit wonders, Stevens is an exception to this in two respects. First, he had an earlier novelty hit in 1962 with "Ahab the Arab" (pronounced ay-rab to rhyme with Ahab) which reached #5 on the *Billboard* Hot 100 that year. (He also wrote "Harry the Hairy Ape," "Santa Claus Is Watching You," and "Jeremiah Peabody's Polyunsaturated Quick-Dissolving, Fast-Acting, Pleasant-Tasting Green and Purple Pills" which reached #35 in 1961.) Second, he actually had a non-novelty, #1 hit song that he wrote and performed, "Everything is Beautiful," which held that spot for two weeks in the summer of 1970. It won the 1971 Grammy Award for Best Male Pop Vocal Performance. Stevens was also offered the song "Raindrops Keep Fallin' On My Head" by Burt Bacharach and Hal David, but he didn't like the song so he passed on it. Bacharach and David instead gave it to B. J. Thomas who had a #1 hit with it in 1970.[2]

One novelty song must be considered one of the most bizarre songs ever, even by the standards of novelty songs. It reached #3 on the *Billboard* Hot 100 in August 1966. Here are a few hints about it: (1) It is about a man seemingly going mad after a breakup. (2) It was written and performed by Jerry Samuels (albeit under a different name which had a roman numeral in it). (3) There is no singing in the song.

"They're Coming to take Me Away, Ha-Haaa!" by Napoleon XIV. Samuels was a recording engineer. Using a device called a variable-frequency oscillator (VFO), he was able to alter the pitch of a recording—i.e., making voices higher or lower—without changing the tempo.[3]

It is not clear whether Napoleon is addressing a woman who has left him, or a dog. When he was being taken away by men in their white coats, the addressee laughed, which dogs are not known to do. However, in the final verse, he calls the addressee a mutt and threatens to take it to the A.S.P.C.A.

In 1967, Bill Cosby had a #4 song on the *Billboard* Hot 100 (although he is talking more than singing). It's largely forgotten today, but #4 is #4. The title, the music and the chorus were closely based on the Stevie Wonder song "Uptight (Everything's Alright)," which is not *exactly* the name of Cosby's song.

"Little Ole Man (Uptight, Everything's Alright)."

Here is the only information for this one: A Sesame Street song that hit the top 20.

"Rubber Duckie." It was sung by Ernie (voiced by Jim Henson) on *Sesame Street* and reached #16 on the *Billboard* Hot 100 in September 1970.

The prime of Chuck Berry's career was obviously before the Decade. However, incredibly, he never had a #1 song before the Decade—classics such "Maybelline," "Roll Over Beethoven," "Sweet Little Sixteen," and "Johnny B. Goode" never quite made it to the top. However, he did have a #1 song during the Decade. The song was not written by Berry, it was released in 1972 and it is considered a novelty song. What is the song?

"My Ding-a-Ling." The song was written and recorded by Dave Bartholomew in 1952 under the title "Little Girl Sing Ting-a-Ling." Berry recorded a version called "My Tambourine" in 1968, but the version which topped the charts was recorded live during the Lanchester Arts Festival at the Locarno ballroom in Coventry, England, on February 3, 1972. In the live version, Berry makes the chorus a call-and-response, in which the women in the audience sing "my" and the men respond by shouting "ding-a-ling!" He calls the song his "alma mater."

Interestingly, Berry's version, as risque as it is, is actually toned down from Bartholomew's because Berry's version at least uses double entendre. At the start of the song, Berry tells us that when he was a boy, he received a gift from his grandmother which was bells on a string and she told him that it was a "ding-a-ling-a-ling." He plays with it in school, and holds on to it in dangerous situations like falling after climbing the garden wall, and swimming across a creek infested with snapping turtles. Bartholomew's original doesn't bother with the grandmother or the toy and gets right down to business. For example, "When you're young and you're on the go, your ding-a-ling won't ever get sore."

In season three of *The Simpsons*, in an episode called "Lisa's Pony," a Springfield Elementary School student attempted to sing the song during the school's talent show. He barely finished the first line of the refrain before an irate Principal Skinner rushed him off the stage, angrily decreeing, "This act is over!"

CHAPTER 16

Politicians Honoring the Music (State Songs—Rock, Official, Unofficial and Otherwise)

Certain states have songs associated with them. There is perhaps a certain hierarchy with these associations. The highest honor is undoubtedly to have a song designated as an "official state song." Then would come "official state *rock* song" and then "*un*official state rock song." Also, some songs are affiliated with universities for no apparent historical reason. This chapter will examine songs fitting in these categories.

Incredibly, one person is the cowriter of not one but two official state songs. (What are the odds of that?) An official state song is even more impressive than an official "rock" song like "Hang on Sloopy" because it is not a subcategory song (although in both cases, the states in question have cheated a bit by going with more than one official State song). Both songs were released during the Decade. Try to guess the artist, the two songs and the states.

John Denver. The songs are "Take Me Home, Country Roads" and "Rocky Mountain High." The former was primarily written by Bill Danoff and Taffy Nivert, although Denver received a cowriting credit. They played an early draft of the song to Denver in 1970. They were hoping to sell it to Johnny Cash but they agreed to let Denver hear it. They sang the song for Denver and as he recalled, "I flipped." The three stayed up until 6:00 a.m., changing words and moving lines around. Denver recorded the song and put it on his breakthrough album, *Poems, Prayers and Promises*. The song reached #2 on the *Billboard* Hot 100.

Ironically, Danoff had never been to West Virginia when he wrote the lyrics. Neither had Nivert or Denver. In fact, Danoff considered using his home state of Massachusetts rather than West Virginia, as both four-syllable state names would have fit the song's meter, but he decided that West Virginia sounded better. Danoff's lack of familiarity with West Virginia is apparent from the song's lyrics. The places mentioned prominently in the lyrics—the Shenandoah River and the Blue Ridge Mountains—have only marginal associations with the state of West Virginia, and would seem to be more appropriate to describe western Virginia. The river passes through only the very eastern tip of the Eastern Panhandle of West Virginia in Jefferson County. Similarly, the vast majority of the Blue Ridge also lies outside the state, only crossing into West Virginia in Jefferson County.

Notwithstanding the fact that none of the three songwriters wrote the song because of any love of (or even knowledge of) West Virginia, or the odd geographic references, on March 7, 2014, the West Virginia Legislature approved a resolution to make "Take Me Home, Country Roads" one of the official state songs of West Virginia and the resolution was signed into law the next day.

Danoff and Nivert later formed Starland Vocal Band which had a #1 song with "Afternoon Delight" in 1976.[1]

Obviously Denver has much more of a connection with Colorado, having moved there in 1971 (indeed he changed his last name from Deutschsendorf to Denver years earlier, although he lived in Aspen). In 2007, the Colorado State Senate voted 26-8 to adopt "Rocky Mountain High" as Colorado's second State song (along with "Where the Columbines Grow," adopted in 1915). In 2013, the song title became even more befitting of the State after Colorado legalized marijuana. In the House, the resolution passed 50-11 after the failure of a Republican-offered amendment that would have clarified that the song is about Colorado's elevation and "in no way reflects or encourages" drug use. Senator Bob Hagedorn, the Democrat who sponsored the measure in the Senate, accused his dissenting colleagues of making too much of the lyrics simply because it refers to friends sitting around the campfire and being high. The Senate "Joint" Resolution naming the song as the second state song was No. 07-023.[2]

This question may be as easy as they come to Ohio residents and especially to students or alumni or anyone associated with Ohio State University. To others, it may be impossible to answer. There is a song is played during every Ohio State home football game. It is also played at Cleveland Indians games and is their official song. In 1985, it was named the Official Rock Song of the State of Ohio. Fans chant the letters "O, H, I, O" during the pauses in the chorus while mimicking the shape of the letters with their arms, à la "YMCA" by the Village People. Yet, at least based on the lyrics to the song, it has no connection with the State of Ohio whatsoever. (So if you were thinking perhaps the Neil Young anti-Kent State protest song "Ohio," that would not be the song.) What is the song and who is it by?

"Hang On Sloopy" by the McCoys, released in 1965. This song, written by Wes Farrell and Bert Russell, was originally recorded in 1964 by the Vibrations, an African-American soul group, but their version of the song was called "My Girl Sloopy" (even though the lyrics are identical with the McCoys' version.) The official website of the OSU athletics department is hangonsloopy.com.

There are two explanations given for the Ohio connection. One is that it was written in honor of Dorothy Sloop. She was an American jazz musician born in Steubenville, Ohio who went by the nickname "Sloopy." However, there is no record of either of the songwriters corroborating this. The other (as per an OSU website on Ohio State traditions, no less) is that it was first played by the OSU band on October 9, 1965 after a band member, John Tatgenhorst, begged the director to try playing it. After the crowd reaction, the band began to play it at every game.

In 1985, the Ohio House of Representatives adopted Concurrent Resolution #16, that provides in part as follows:

> WHEREAS, The members of the 116th General Assembly of Ohio wish to recognize the rock song "Hang On Sloopy" as the official rock song of the great State of Ohio; and . . .
>
> WHEREAS, "Hang On Sloopy" is of particular relevance to members of the Baby Boom Generation, who were once dismissed as a bunch of long-haired, crazy kids, but who now are old enough and vote in sufficient numbers to be taken quite seriously; and
>
> WHEREAS, Adoption of this resolution will not take too long, cost the state anything, or affect the quality of life in this state to any appreciable degree, and if we in the legislature just go ahead and pass the darn thing, we can get on with more important stuff; and
>
> WHEREAS, Sloopy lives in a very bad part of town, and everybody, yeah, tries to put my Sloopy down; and . . .
>
> Therefore be it Resolved, that we, the members of the 116th General Assembly of Ohio, in adopting this Resolution, name "Hang On Sloopy" as the official rock song of the State of Ohio.

Ohio is currently the only state with a song that has an official rock song. From 2009 to 2011, "Do You Realize" by the Flaming Lips was the Official Rock Song of Oklahoma (which is the home state of the band). The original resolution actually fell three votes short of the 51 votes necessary for ratification—one Republican state legislator attacked the band for its use of offensive language, while another said he opposed the song because band member Michael Ivins had once worn a red T-shirt with a sickle and hammer—so Democratic Governor Brad Henry issued an executive order to make it the official state song. However, Henry's successor, Republican Governor Mary Fallin, effectively removed the song's designation as the Official

Rock Song of Oklahoma by not renewing the executive order when she took office in 2011, a fact that no one was apparently aware of until the AP reported on it in 2013.[3]

The lead singer of the McCoys was Rick Zehringer, who was only 17 years old when "Hang On Sloopy" was recorded. He changed his name and then composed and sang a hit song in 1974. What was his new name and what was his hit?

Rick Derringer. The song was "Rock and Roll Hoochie Koo," which hit #23 and still gets airplay today.

Another honored college football tradition, though of more recent vintage than Ohio State and "Hang On Sloopy," involves the University of Pittsburgh and the Neil Diamond song "Sweet Caroline." Pitt students have made it "Pitt-centric" by replacing the repeating phrase "So good" of the original song with "Go Pitt" and the "Ba ba ba" of the original with, "Let's Go Pitt."A great montage of Pitt fans enthusiastically rocking out to the song in various games, in both warm weather and cold, can be found on You Tube. However, there is no connection between the song and either Neil Diamond or Pennsylvania.[4]

Another connection between a song and a state is "Louie Louie" by the Kingsmen and the State of Washington. Of course, "Louie Louie" is a pre-Decade song but not all great songs came out of the Decade! As with the Pitt Panthers band playing "Sweet Caroline," the University of Washington Huskies band frequently plays "Louie Louie." As with "Sweet Caroline" and Pitt, there is no obvious connection between "Louie Louie" or its composer Richard Berry and Washington. In 1985, Seattle television personality Ross Shafer spearheaded an effort to have "Louie Louie" replace "Washington, My Home" by Helen Davis as Washington's official state song. Though intended as a joke, Whatcom County Councilman Craig Cole introduced a resolultion in the state legislature, citing the need for a "contemporary theme song that can be used to engender a sense of pride and community, and in the enhancement of tourism and economic development." His resolution also called for the creation of a new "Louie Louie County." While the House did not pass it, the Senate declared April 12, 1985 as "Louie Louie Day." Finally, April 11, Richard Berry's birthday, is celebrated as "International Louie Louie Day."[5]

Finally, some may wonder: What about Bruce Springsteen's "Born to Run"? How come that hasn't been mentioned yet and why has it never been designated as the New Jersey State song, whether "official," "unofficial," "rock" or otherwise? After all, many consider that song to be more associated with a State than any other (perhaps aside from the two John Denver songs). There have been some efforts made. In 1980, the State Assembly passed a resolution declaring "Bruce Springsteen to be the New Jersey Pop Music Ambassador to America and calling for the adoption of his song 'Born to Run' as the unofficial theme of our State's youth.'" However, the State Senate turned sour on the idea and the resolution was never put to a vote.

Whether or not Springsteen is New Jersey's favorite son (some might throw Jon Bon Jovi into the mix), the song itself is hardly a paean to the State, since it talks about wanting to get out of there as soon as possible. While no towns are specifically mentioned in the song (nor is New Jersey itself), it does mention Highway 9, which cuts right through the state, leaving no doubt that the town that the singer so desperately wants to escape from is located in Jersey. In this respect, the song is thematically similar to "Thunder Road," the opening track on the *Born to Run* album, which concludes with Springsteen again wanting to pull out from his home town.

Ironically, the one Springsteen song that might best be considered an homage of sorts to his home state is "Jersey Girl," but that post-decade song was written by Tom Waits. The song was never released on a studio album by Springsteen, but it has been a fan favorite at his concerts and is one of the best-known cover songs associated with Springsteen.[6]

CHAPTER 17

That's a Catchy Jingle!
(Television Commercials That Became
Music Hits—and Vice Versa)

Television commercials had a surprisingly symbiotic relationship with popular songs during the Decade. This chapter will examine that relationship.

Carly Simon wrote a song in 1971 about the emotions she was feeling while waiting for Cat Stevens to pick her up for their first date together. Portions of the song, including the title, were used as the centerpiece of a television advertising campaign of a major food corporation for many years. What is the song and what was the product?

"Anticipation" was used by the H. J. Heinz company to advertise their ketchup and to highlight the fact that, even though it sometimes takes a long time for the ketchup to come out of the bottle, and it makes Simon wait, the wait is worth it.

It is not uncommon for corporations to take well-known songs and use them as part of their commercial jingles. What is unusual is for the process to work in reverse, but it has occurred on several occasions. In 1971, an advertising executive with McCann-Erickson wrote down a line on a napkin, which gave him an idea for a song for a product made by a company his agency represented. He and some songwriters he knew took the line and made a song out of it which was then used as the basis for a television commercial. After the song became popular from the commercial, one of the songwriters decided to change the lyrics to the song by deleting all references to the product and to release it as a full-length song. This happened, and the song went on to sell 12 million copies, reaching #7 on the *Billboard* Hot 100 in 1972 and #1 in England.

First question: What is the original name of the song (which contains the name of the product being advertised in it)? (As a hint, the commercial first aired in July 1971

and featured a multicultural group of young people lip-syncing the song on a hill outside Rome, Italy.)

"I'd Like to Buy the World a Coke" (which was the original line written down by Bill Backer of the McCann-Erickson agency). Five hundred young people were hired for the chorus from embassies and schools in Rome. Close-ups of the young leads were actually filmed at a racetrack in Rome, separate from the larger chorus shots. Everyone held a Coke bottle in their right hand. Speaking of Coke, another one of their famous jingles (perhaps the most famous and one that can be heard in the hilltop spot) is "It's the real thing," which debuted in 1969. The best-known version of this jingle was sung by the Fortunes, best remembered for their 1965 top 10 hit "You've Got Your Troubles."[1]

Second question: What is the name of the song when it was rereleased without the reference to Coke?

"I'd Like to Teach the World to Sing (in Perfect Harmony)"

Third question: Which group (or groups) had a big hit with the song?

The New Seekers *and* the Hillside Singers. The commercial was sung by the New Seekers. After it eventually became successful, it was decided to make a full-length version of the song without reference to the product. Because the New Seekers were then unavailable, McCann-Erickson contacted producer Al Ham, who agreed to assemble a group of vocalists, including his wife and their daughter. They called themselves the Hillside Singers and their version of the song reached #13 on the *Billboard* Hot 100. At that point, the New Seekers decided to record a full-length version of the song after all and their version reached #7 on the chart.

Fourth question (for true experts): What is the name of the song from which the music is adapted?

"True Love and Apple Pie" (sometimes called "Mom, True Love and Apple Pie")[2]

"I'd Like to Buy the World a Coke/I'd Like to Teach the World to Sing" is not the only example of a song first being written for a television commercial and then being reworked into a non-commercial full-length song. In 1968, an ad agency commissioned a song to help its client, California-based Crocker National Bank, appeal to young people. The song

played over footage of a young couple getting married. The commercial was very popular and Crocker National's business flourished. A member of the group that later made it famous recognized the voice of the vocalist, Paul Williams, and since they were under contract to the same record label, asked Williams if he had a hand in writing the song, which he did. (He wrote the lyrics.) Williams was asked to write a full-length version of the song, which he and cowriter, Roger Nichols, did. What is the song and who made it famous? (As a hint, the song is very popular at weddings.)

"We've Only Just Begun," performed by the Carpenters. It was Richard Carpenter who heard the jingle and asked Williams to rework it. Unlike "I'd Like to Buy the World a Coke," the song did not make any reference to the product being advertised, so it was primarily a matter of adding an original verse and a bridge. As Williams later recounted: "The ad agency called us and said, 'Look, we're going to show a young couple getting married, driving off into the sunset, and it's going to say "You've got a long way to go, we'd like to help you get there with Crocker Bank." And I went, okay, what rhymes with Crocker? And they said very specifically, No, we don't want a jingle." What they asked for is what we would today call a music video." The song was ranked at #405 on *Rolling Stone* magazine's list of 500 Greatest Songs of All Time. The original one-minute commercial can be seen on YouTube.

A third example of a song being a television commercial hit before being a commercial hit is the instrumental *No Matter What Shape (Your Stomach's In)*. This was originally an ad for Alka-Seltzer. It was then recorded as a full-length song (though only lasting 2:13) by the short-lived American pop group the T-Bones which later became Hamilton, Joe Frank & Reynolds. It reached #3 on the *Billboard* Hot 100.[3]

Before he was famous, this singer-songwriter wrote a number of commercial jingles including "Like a good neighbor, State Farm is there," "I am stuck on Band-Aid brand 'cause Band-Aids stuck on me", the Stridex song ("Give your face something to smile about"), and one for a bathroom cleaner called Bowlene ("I've got the bathroom bowl blues"). He also sang, but didn't write, a number of others including the McDonald's commercial ("You deserve a break today"), the Pepsi song ("Join the Pepsi people"), and the Dr Pepper song ("It's the most original soft drink ever in the whole wide world"). In concert, he performs some of these songs as part of his "very strange medley." He has also said that he was asked to write a commercial for a douche product and refused, but possibly he was joking. Who is this man?

Barry Manilow. Incidentally, the Dr Pepper jingle above was written by Randy Newman although he has never seemed as eager as Manilow to perform it in concert.

Another musician was not nearly as well-known as Manilow but may have been an even more successful jingle writer. Tom Dawes was a guitarist for the group the Cyrkle (pronounced circle). He wrote or cowrote "Plop, Plop, Fizz, Fizz" for Alka-Seltzer," 7Up, the Uncola," "Our L'eggs Fit Your Legs," "We're American Airlines, Doing What We Do Best," "Something Special in the Air" (also for American Airlines), "Coke Is It," and "You, You're the One," for McDonald's.[4]

CHAPTER 18

Don't Judge an Album by its Cover
(Album Covers)

In the post-album world of CDs and the post-CD world of digital downloads, the notion that people would spend hours studying the packaging in which the music arrived seems about as dated as when families would sit around the fireside listening to the radio. But during the Decade, that is exactly what music fans would do when eagerly anticipated new albums would arrive. When the albums were double-LPs (do young people even know what LP even stands for anymore?), there was twice the excitement. Fans would study the front, the back, the liner notes, the lyrics (if any), all while listening to the music. If this book was about music from the 21st century, it is unlikely that there would be a chapter called famous CD covers.

What makes for a classic album cover? First, it certainly helps if the album is a mega-seller. Albums that quickly fade into obscurity are rarely considered to have memorable covers, no matter how imaginative or innovative the design. In addition, there has to be something eye-catching about it. One technique which often accomplishes this is the absence of words on the cover or any indication as to what band or artist is releasing the album. In other words, the mixture of a best-selling album combined with the band's apparent desire to not publicize its identity on the cover often seems to be a recipe for a memorable image. Here are some questions about iconic record covers released during the Decade.

This album, released in 1965, is called *Whipped Cream and Other Delights*. It features a sultry model who at first glance appears to be wearing a wedding dress, but on closer examination, it appears instead that the dress is all whipped cream (especially given the album title)—a lot of whipped cream. The album sold six million copies. Who is the artist?

Herb Alpert and the Tijuana Brass. The model is Dolores Erickson, who was three months pregnant when the photo was taken. She became known as the "whipped cream lady." In fact, except for the dollop on her head, the rest was all shaving cream, because whipped cream would melt under the hot lights. Many years later, a *New Yorker* article said that the photo "fogged the minds of many young men, as they gazed at the album cover and attempted to ascribe person-alized come-hitherhood to the woman staring back. In the picture, she sits holding the stem of a rose in her left hand, above which the inner portion of a bare breast protrudes from the foam. She is licking cream from the index finger of her right hand, and a dollop of the stuff rests atop her forehead, like a tiara. . . . In the virtually pornless atmosphere of the suburban mid-sixties it was—and we're relying on the testimony of our elders here—the pinnacle of allure." In keeping with the food theme of the album, the tracks include "A Taste of Honey," "Green Peppers," "Tangerine," "Lemon Tree," "El Garbanzo," "Ladyfingers," "Butterball," "Peanuts" and "Lollipops and Roses." Alpert is the "A" in A&M Records, the "M" being his partner Jerry Moss.[1]

Which album includes the words "Welcome the Rolling Stones—good guys"?

Perhaps the most famous album cover of all, *Sgt. Pepper's Lonely Hearts Club Band* by the Beatles. In the lower right-hand corner of the cover, a cloth Shirley Temple doll is wearing a striped sweater which says "Welcome the Rolling Stones" on the front of the sweater and "good guys" on the left sleeve. Among those who was under consideration for the cover was Adolf Hitler, desired by John Lennon. Did he make the final cut? It's difficult to say. There are photos on the Internet of the Hitler cutout which was going to be used as part of the shoot, but many sources say it was removed from the stage before the final shoot. However, Sir Peter Blake, the artist who created the cover, said in 2007 that Hitler did make the final line-up for the sleeve, but was simply obscured by the Fab Four. "Yes he is on there—you just can't see him." Given the extensive care and attention which went into creating the collage, it's hard to imagine that one of the faces—especially as polemic as Hitler's—would (accidentally) be placed so as not to be visible, but if Blake says so . . . Lennon also wanted Jesus on the cover, but it was decided that that would be a bad idea due to the controversy caused by Lennon's "we're more popular than Jesus" comment a year earlier.

Of the people who *are* on the cover, though virtually all of them are famous, they were also mostly either dead or past their prime at the time the shot was taken. Perhaps the most notable exception (besides the Beatles themselves) was Bob Dylan.[2]

This album contains no words on the cover and no indication of who it is by. It con-sists of a framed painting of a hunched-over old man with a very large bundle of sticks tied to his back. The framed picture is in turn affixed to the internal, papered wall of a partly demolished house. The front and back covers together then revealed that the house was set against the backdrop of a dowdy modern apartment building, thus creating an unexpected (and one might say depressing) juxtaposition of the rural and urban. In any event, one

looking at the cover would have absolutely no idea whose music was on the album inside. One of the band members stated that this was intentional. What is the album? As a hint, it is one of the biggest-selling albums of all time.

It is the album known as *Led Zeppelin IV*, which includes, among other classics, "Stairway to Heaven." In discussing the cover, Barney Hoskyns, who wrote an entire book about this one album called *Led Zeppelin IV-Rock of Ages*, stated that "releasing an album without 'Led Zeppelin' on the cover (or even on the spine) is a giant 'Fuck You' to anyone who ever accused them of being a 'Superhype'. Smarting from the negative press they'd suffered since the band formed in late 1968, Page wants to prove that their music can stand on its own merits." Page himself concurred: "The cover wasn't meant to antagonize the record company. It was designed as our response to the music critics who maintained that the success of our first three albums was driven by hype and not talent. So we stripped everything away, and let the music do the talking." In fact, the record executives (at Atlantic) were not happy with what seemed to be a suicidal marketing move. However, Zeppelin's commercial power at that time was strong enough that they got to call the shots, and history has proved their decision to be correct.[3]

Of the front covers of albums released by Led Zeppelin during the Decade besides *Led Zeppelin IV*, one had the name of the band on the cover but no photos of the band's members, one had no words at all (like *Led Zeppelin IV*) and one had a title and the name of the band but no photos of the band members. What are the three albums referred to?

The first is their debut album *Led Zeppelin* (1969), the second is *Houses of the Holy* (1973) and the third is *Physical Graffiti* (1975).

Another album—also, like *Led Zeppelin IV*, among the best-selling of all time—also includes no words on the cover and no indication of which artist or band was releasing the album. (Clearly, cover anonymity is not a bar to success.) This one features a ray of light hitting a prism on one side and coming out as a full spectrum of colors on the other side. What is the album?

Dark Side of the Moon. Designer Storm Thorgerson brought seven designs into the Abbey Road studio where they were still recording. "The band trooped in, swept their gaze across the designs, looked at each other, nodded, and said 'That one,' pointing at the prism. Took all of three minutes. No amount of cajoling would get them to consider any other contender, nor endure further explanation of the prism, or how exactly it might look. 'That's it,' they said in unison, 'we've got to get back to real work,' and returned forthwith to the studio upstairs."[4]

This album consists of a somewhat overripe banana against a white background. Early copies of the album had the banana as a sticker and invited the owner to "Peel slowly and see." Peeling back the banana skin as a sticker, revealed a flesh-colored banana underneath. What is the album and the band?

The Velvet Underground & Nico. The banana is an Andy Warhol print and his name appears on the cover. He also nominally produced the album. This may be the only album in history where the only name which appears on the cover is that of the producer—or in this case, credited producer.

Four Beatles album covers released during the Decade did not contain the name of the band, and one of those four did not contain any writing at all. Which were the albums?

The albums which did not mention the name of the band were *Rubber Soul, Revolver, Abbey Road* and *Let it Be.* Of those, the one that contained no writing at all was *Abbey Road.*

On which Beatles album cover do all of the band members appear, but unrecognizably?

Magical Mystery Tour. All four Beatles are dressed in animal costumes (including masks which obscure most or all of their faces). John is in front dressed as a black walrus (notwithstanding the line about Paul being the walrus in John Lennon's song *Glass Onion,* which appears on the White Album). Behind John are, from left to right, Paul dressed as a hippo, George dressed as a bunny and Ringo dressed as a chicken.[5]

Sometimes albums are famous or groundbreaking not only for what is on the front cover, but for what is on the back cover. What is the first rock album ever to have the lyrics printed on it?

Sgt. Pepper's Lonely Hearts Club Band.[6]

What do the following album covers have in common?

Music from Big Pink **by the Band**
Song to a Seagull, Clouds, Ladies of the Canyon, and Court and Spark **by Joni Mitchell**
Revolver **by the Beatles**
Tea for the Tillerman **by Cat Stevens**
So Far **by Crosby, Stills, Nash & Young**

The Who by Numbers **by the Who**
Self-Portrait **by Bob Dylan**

They all have hand-painted or hand-drawn covers. In the case of all of the Joni Mitchell albums, as well as *Self-Portrait* and *Tea for the Tillerman*, they were painted by the artists themselves. Mitchell also painted the *So Far* cover and Dylan also painted the cover of *Music from Big Pink*. *Revolver* was drawn and designed by Klaus Voormann *The Who by Numbers* was drawn by bassist John Entwistle as a connect-the-dots drawing.

This hit-filled second album by the Doors was ranked number 407 on *Rolling Stone*'s list of the 500 greatest albums of all time. Unlike all of the band's other studio albums made with Jim Morrison, this album cover does not feature a group shot of the band, due to Jim Morrison's refusal to appear on the cover. Instead, the front includes, in the foreground, a dwarf kneeling in front of a large bald man with a thick black mustache (picture G. Gordon Liddy or, for wrestling fans, the Iron Sheik). The man is wearing a weight belt and a zebra shirt. He is lifting a heavy barbell over his head. In the background is a man in whiteface juggling three red balls, a man playing a trumpet, and a man hoisting another man in the air. A group shot of the band does appear on a poster in the background of both the front and back covers, bearing captions of the band and album name. Because of the subtlety of the artist and album title, most record stores put stickers across the cover to help customers identify it more clearly. In 2003, VH1 named this cover one of the greatest album covers of all time. What is the name of the album?

Strange Days. Photographer Joel Brodsky drew inspiration from Federico Fellini's 1954 circus film, *La Strada*, and decided to photograph a group of acrobats and jugglers on the streets of New York. However, getting the shot was a nightmare. Even though the acrobats were supposedly actual circus performers, "they were terrible," says Brodsky. "The guy underneath could only hold up his partner for a few seconds—he kept on dropping him." The trumpet player was a passing cab driver who was paid $5 to appear in the shot. The dwarf—though represented by an agent—didn't want to be in the shot. They could not find a real juggler, so Brodsky's assistant, Frank Kollegy, stood in. "He couldn't juggle worth a damn," says Brodsky. "Every time he threw a ball up, we'd spend the next five minutes chasing it down the street. He ended up juggling with two balls. We added the third in later."[7]

The cover of this album by the Who shows a photograph of the band apparently having just urinated on a large concrete piling protruding from a slag heap (they are shown zipping up their zippers). However, according to photographer Ethan Russell, most of the

Female artists are not well represented in the Rock and Roll Hall of Fame and especially white females. The Hall opened in 1986 and there were 78 inductees before the first white female was inducted in 1995. It was this woman. As a hint, this is not the look with which she is normally associated. Who is she? (Answer on p. 241)

When we think of the Rolling Stones, we do not typically think of there being a pianist/organist in the band. However, there was one on most of their studio albums released until 1985, and it was the man on the left in the photo below. He was also briefly an actual member of the band (and, in fact, was a member of the group even before Mick Jagger and Keith Richards). However, he was dropped from the lineup because band manager Andrew Loog Oldham felt that his burly, square-jawed appearance did not fit the image for the band that Oldham was aiming for. However, he accepted the demotion and acted as the band's road manager. Nevertheless, he played on one or more tracks on almost every one of their studio albums until his death in 1985, including songs such as "Time Is On My Side," "Honky Tonk Women," "Let It Bleed," "Brown Sugar," and "It's Only Rock 'n Roll (But I Like It)." Who is he? (Answer on p. 167)

Above is one of the more impressive gatherings of songwriting and behind-the-scenes musical talent ever assembled for one photo, although they were all relatively unknown when this photo was taken. They all worked in the famous Brill Building in New York City. The husband and wife songwriting duo kneeling at the front left wrote numerous hits, together or separately, including "On Broadway" (The Drifters), "We Gotta Get Out of this Place" (The Animals), "Kicks" (Paul Revere and the Raiders), "Who Put the Bomp (in the Bomp, Bomp, Bomp)," "He's So Shy" (The Pointer Sisters), and, as if these accomplishments were not impressive, they cowrote two #1 songs by the Righteous Brothers, namely "(You're My) Soul and Inspiration" and "You've Lost That Lovin' Feelin'," the latter of which is one of the most frequently played songs in rock music history.

The husband and wife songwriting duo immediately next to them wrote or cowrote, together or separately "Will You Love Me Tomorrow" (The Shirelles), "The Loco-Motion" (Little Eva), "Up on the Roof (The Drifters), "One Fine Day" (The Chiffons), "I'm Into Something Good" (Herman's Hermits), and "Pleasant Valley Sunday" (The Monkees). The woman also released her own album that is one of the biggest-selling albums in music history.

The man kneeling at the far right has had a hugely successful career as a singer and songwriter. There has been only one time in history when an artist has reached #1 with a song and then reached the top 10 again with a completely reworked version of the same song. The first version, released in 1962, was an up-tempo pop song. The second version, released in 1975, was a slow ballad with a very different arrangement. This man wrote and performed for both songs.

The man fourth from the right was responsible for the Monkees and the Archies, starred in his own musical variety show from 1973–1981, and has been called "the man with the golden ear." Finally, the man standing third from left was a Grammy-winning record producer, talent manager, songwriter, film director, and film producer. He produced albums for a number of highly successful artists including The Mamas and the Papas, Grass Roots, Carole King, and Cheech and Chong. He was also executive producer of *The Rocky Horror Picture Show*, the longest-running theatrical film in history. (Answers on pp. 190, 15, 17, 106, 34)

A greatest hits album was released with the songs of the man in the center of this photo. It spent over four hundred weeks on the *Billboard* 200, a period of longevity on the charts surpassed by very few albums. It has sold over 25 million copies, making it one of the biggest sellers of all time. Yet this artist and his band, also pictured, never had any top 40 singles. What is the album and who was the man pictured in the center? As a hint, this is not the look with which he was normally associated. (Answer on p. 27)

This internationally famous group was banned from touring in the United States from 1965–1969, during the height of their career. Though no specific reason was given, it was widely attributed to their rowdy onstage behavior, including fights with one another. Who is the band? (Answer on p. 158)

The group pictured here is the only one in history who had #1 songs on the *Billboard* Hot 100 before, during, and after the "Beatles era" of 1963–1970. It is an American group, whose #1 songs were in 1962, 1963, 1964 and 1975. Who is the group? (Answer on p. 18)

This band appeared on *The Ed Sullivan Show* more times than the Beatles or Rolling Stones *combined*. Andrew Loog Oldham, former manager of the Rolling Stones, once said: "During that first 18 months of the British invasion, every time [the Beatles] looked over their shoulders, it was not the Stones, or the Kinks or Who. It was [this band.]" The band was unusual for its day in that it was named for its drummer and leader, who is third from left in the photo. When Tom Hanks inducted them into the Rock and Roll Hall of Fame in 2008, he joked that they were "one of the few British bands of the day that never replaced their drummer. What would they have been called?" Who was this band? (Answer on p. 121)

There were only two groups in the 1960s, both pictured above, whose first seven singles were all top 10. They were both American. The leader of the group at the top was their drummer, and the leader and songwriter of the group in the bottom photo was the man on the right. Who were the two bands? (Answers on p. 23)

Top photo by Michael Ochs Archives/Getty Images
Bottom photo by Michael Ochs Archives/Getty Images

As America's involvement with the Vietnam War expanded, the early- to mid-1960s were rife with anti-war protest songs, including "Blowin' in the Wind" and "The Times They Are A-Changin'" by Bob Dylan, "Turn! Turn! Turn!" by the Byrds, "Universal Soldier" by Donovan, and "Eve of Destruction" by Barry McGuire. However, as if in "answer" to all of these songs, came one which, while not pro-war per se, certainly cast the army in a positive light. It was cowritten and performed by the soldier pictured above. The song was a huge success, holding the #1 spot for five weeks and becoming the #1 hit on the *Billboard* Hot 100 chart for the entire year of 1966. It is ironic today to think that one of the biggest-selling song of the 1960s specifically relating to the military or war was a *pro*-military song. What is the song and who is the singer who cowrote it, pictured above? (Answer on p. 245)

These three men are easily among the most successful songwriting teams in history, having written 13 #1 songs, mostly performed by the Supremes and the Four Tops. They also had 22 other top 10 songs. Who are they? (Answer on p. 184)

The man in the center of this photo is the third highest-selling singles artist in British history, behind only Elvis and the Beatles. He is the only act in British history to have had #1 songs in five consecutive decades, from the '50s through the '90s. He had more top 40 hits and top 10 hits than the Beatles. Yet for all that success, he was comparatively invisible in the United States. The woman on the right sang the only song in history by a British artist to reach #1 on

the *Billboard* Hot 100 (and in fact stayed there for five weeks) and yet not chart at all in the United Kingdom. It was released in 1967 and is the title of a film of the same name. What is the song and who was the artist? (Answers on pp. 16 and 23)

This person is the youngest singer-songwriter in history to have a top 20 song which he or she solely composed and performed. She wrote the song when she was 14 and it was released in 1967 when she was 16. She was also the first musical guest ever on *Saturday Night Live*. Who is the singer-songwriter and what is the song? (Answer on p. 197.)

The primary causes of early death of musical artists from 1965–1975 are plane crashes, drug or alcohol abuse, and shootings. However, the woman in this photo died at age 24 from brain cancer. She had four top 10 songs on the *Billboard* Hot 100 and five top five songs on the R&B chart. All of the songs were duets with the man pictured with her. Who are these two talented artists? (Answer on p. 78)

The woman in the photo below was born Mary Catherine Bernadette O'Brien. She was named a member of the Order of the British Empire (OBE). She had six top 20 singles on the U.S. *Billboard* Hot 100. She has been described as "Britain's greatest pop diva and the finest white soul singer of her era." She died in 1999 at age 60 just before she was about to be inducted into the Rock and Roll Hall of Fame. At her induction ceremony, Elton John said "I'm biased but I just think she was the greatest white singer there ever has been." She is pictured here with Paul McCartney, Tom Jones, and Ringo Starr. Who is she? (Answer on p. 199)

This band released a song that is one of the few that has sold over 10 million copies. It was released in 1967 and in 1977, it was named joint winner (along with Queen's "Bohemian Rhapsody") of the Best British Pop Single 1952–1977 at

the Brit Awards. The song was not by such obvious candidates as the Beatles, the Stones, or the Who. In fact, it was more or less by a one-hit wonder—but what a hit! First question: What is the song? For extra credit, spell correctly, the name of the group that released it. (Answer on p. 234)

The man on the right (pictured with John Lennon, Paul McCartney, George Harrison and McCartney's girlfriend, Jane Asher) likely spent more time in the physical presence of the Beatles than any person in history, including George Martin (i.e., it's not George Martin!). He was not a professional singer or musician. Among many other connections with the group, (1) he sang in the chorus of "Yellow Submarine," (2) he played harmonica on "Being for the Benefit of Mr. Kite!," (3) on "A Day in the Life," he was one of the five piano players simultaneously hitting the last chord of the song, (4) he played tambourine on "Dear Prudence" and trumpet on "Helter Skelter," (5) according to his diary, he helped Paul McCartney write the lyrics for "Fixing a Hole," (6) he appeared in four (out of five) Beatles films, namely *A Hard Day's Night*, *Help!*, *Magical Mystery Tour*, and *Let It Be*, (7) he was present at their 1969 rooftop concert, and (8) he was the only member of the Beatles entourage who attended the marriage of Paul McCartney and Linda Eastman in 1969. Who was he? (Answer on p. 61)

These two lovely Southern women (with era-appropriate bouffant hairdos), were both one-hit wonders in the late 1960s, but what iconic hits they were. The first was written and performed by the woman on the left. It is ranked #412 on *Rolling Stone*'s list of the 500 Greatest Songs of All Time. The singer-songwriter's real name is Roberta Streeter. Commenting about the song, she said: "The real message revolves around the nonchalant way the family talks about the suicide. The song is sort of a study in unconscious cruelty. But everybody seems more concerned with what was thrown off the bridge than they are with the thoughtlessness of the people expressed in the song. What was thrown off the bridge really isn't that important."

The other hit song, performed by the woman pictured on the right, was written by Tom T. Hall, who said it was based on a true story: "I was about nine years old [and] got to know this lady. I was fascinated by her grit. To see this very insignificant, socially disenfranchised lady—a single mother—who was willing to march down to the local aristocracy and read them the riot act so to speak, was fascinating." It was first song ever sung by a woman that rose to #1 on both the *Billboard* Hot 100 and country charts, a feat that would not occur again until Dolly Parton's "9 to 5" in 1981. The song was later the basis of a television series. What are the two songs and who are these women? (Answers on pp. 39 and 196)

Photos from Associated Press

This band had two top 10 hits, "Let's Live for Today" in 1967 and "Midnight Confessions" in 1968. Their lead guitarist on both of those songs was a regular on the television show *The Office* throughout its nine-year run. His name on the show is the same as his name in real life, and he is the man pictured at left above. Who is he and who is the band? (Answer on p. 156)

There has been only one group in history whose only album went to #1 in the United States. The group is pictured above. They are one of the first "supergroups." Who is the band (Answer on p. 30)

When it comes to influential female singer-songwriters, three names are frequently mentioned: Joni Mitchell, Carole King, and this artist, who, unlike Mitchell and King, actually had no hits of her own as a singer. Yet, artists as diverse as Mitchell, Bette Midler, Rickie Lee Jones, Kate Bush, Elton John, Cyndi Lauper, Todd Rundgren, Elvis Costello, Alice Cooper, Steely Dan, and Melissa Manchester have all spoken of her influence on their careers. Because she did not like the "business end" of the business, she essentially walked away from it at age 24. In 2012, she was inducted into the Rock and Roll Hall of Fame. Who is this woman? (Answer on p. 193)

The man pictured here is the only person in history inducted into the Rock and Roll Hall of Fame with a band even though he was not a member of the band. The reason is that he wrote the lyrics to many of their best-known songs. The band was the Grateful Dead. Who is this man? (Answer on p. 238)

This is a photo of Derek and the Dominoes. They released one of the most famous songs in rock history in 1971. That song was cowritten the man on the far right, a renowned guitarist, and by the man on the far left. That man played drums on hundreds of albums and hit singles including "Rikki Don't Lose That Number" by Steely Dan, "Wichita Lineman" by Glen Campbell, "Sundown" by Gordon Lightfoot, "A Kind of Hush" by the Carpenters, "All Things Must Pass," by George Harrison, "Classical Gas" by Mason Williams, and "It Never Rains in Southern California" by Albert Hammond. He has also been in prison since 1984 serving a sentence of 16 years to life for murdering his mother with a hammer after he developed paranoid schizophrenia. What is the name of the song and who are the two band members referenced above? (Answer on p. 278)

The man pictured at left was the leader and songwriter for a band that had a short-lived existence, but for two years—1969 and 1970—they may fairly be considered to have been the most successful band in the world. In describing the breakup of the band, he stated: "I was alone when I made that music. I was alone when I made the arrangements.... I was alone when I produced and mixed the albums. The other guys showed up only for rehearsals and the days we made the actual recordings.... [However] they insisted on writing songs [and] were obsessed with the idea of more control and more influence. So finally the bomb exploded and we never worked together again." Who is the band and who is the songwriter who made that statement? (Answer on p. 122)

There has likely been only one time that *two* members of the same band have committed suicide. In both cases, they felt that they were being taken advantage of by their business manager and record label. One of them is Pete Ham (top right), who was the main songwriter for the band and who penned two top 10 songs, "Day After Day" and "No Matter What." He died in 1975 at age 27. His bandmate Tom Evans (bottom right), who never got over Ham's suicide, also committed suicide in 1983 at age 36. The two co-wrote "Without You," made famous by Harry Nilsson. Who is the band? (Answer at p. 76)

The man pictured here, is routinely considered as among the best singing drummers in history. Who is he and what band was he with? (Answer on p. 167)

This songwriting duo (pictured with Patti LaBelle) might fairly be considered the most successful songwriting team in music history in terms of chart success on both the *Billboard* Hot 100 and the R&B charts combined, performed by the widest variety of artists. They wrote or cowrote 16 songs that reached the top 10 on the *Billboard* Hot 100 (for *11* different acts), and three of those songs hit #1. Their record of diverse successes on the R&B chart is even more impressive: 19 #1 songs and 50 top 10 songs for *16* different acts. Who is the duo, known for creating the Philly soul sound? (Answer on. p. 179)

This is a photo of the largest rock festival held between 1965 and 1975. Woodstock, right? Wrong. Rather, it was a one-day event that is almost completely forgotten today because, notwithstanding the huge attendance, the event was considered a dud. It took place on July 28, 1973 and there were only three bands performing: the Grateful Dead, the Band, and the Allman Brothers. An estimated 600,000 people attended. What was the name of the event? As a hint, the name of the event makes reference to the location where it was held, which is usually thought of a a race car site. (Answer on p. 93)

These men are three of the most successful singer-songwriters in Canadian history. The songs that were written or cowritten by the man on the left and the right (separately or together) include "American Woman," "No Sugar Tonight/New Mother Nature," "You Ain't Seen Nothin' Yet," "Undun," "Laughing," and "These Eyes." Who are these men, and which bands were they associated with, together or apart? The man in the center has been called Canada's "greatest songwriter" and his songs include "Sundown," "Carefree Highway," "If You Could Read My Mind," "Rainy Day People," and "The Wreck of the Edmund Fitzgerald." Who is he? (Answers on p. 31 and p. 261)

The Eurovision Song Contest is an annual song competition that has been held among the member countries of the European Broadcasting Union since 1956. It is one of the most watched non-sporting events in the world. In 1974, a then- unknown band, who went on to become one of the most successful acts in music history, performed a song at this competition. In 2005, at the 50th anniversary of the contest, their song was chosen as the best one in the competition's history. The two female members of the band are shown here. What is the name of the band and what was the song? (Answer on p. 237)

band members were unable to pee, so rainwater was tipped from an empty film canister to achieve the desired effect. This cover was also on the VH1 list of the greatest album covers of all time. What is the name of the album?

Who's Next.[8]

Speaking of zippers, the original cover of this album contained an actual working zipper. What album was it?

Sticky Fingers by the Rolling Stones. The zipper could be pulled down to reveal an inner card showing a pair of white cotton briefs and a male torso. The briefs contained the name of American pop artist Andy Warhol, below which read "THIS PHOTOGRAPH MAY NOT BE—ETC." Designer Craig Braun said "if we put jeans and a working zipper, [then] people were going to want to see what was back there." However, even with a piece of protective cardboard separating each album, the first shipment of records arrived at retailers with some damage. Because of the weight of the stacked albums during transport, the zipper pull from one record was denting the vinyl on top of it, right on the grooves for "Sister Morphine," the third track on the B-side. Braun finagled a solution: "I got this idea that maybe, if the glue was dry enough, we could have the little old ladies at the end of the assembly line pull the zipper down far enough so that the round part would hit the center disc label," he said. "It worked, and it was even better to see the zipper pulled halfway down." Eventually the real zipper was removed altogether.[9]

In 1965, the Beach Boys were one of the biggest bands in the world. In July of that year, they released an album with only four of the five band members on the cover. They were on a boat, looking not particularly nautical. The missing member was Al Jardine and that was because he was ill on the day of the scheduled photo shoot. Bizarrely, given the fame of the band, rather than simply rescheduling the shoot, it went ahead as scheduled and the album was released with only Mike Love and Dennis, Carl and Brian Wilson on the cover. This would be like releasing a Beatles album or a Monkees album with only three members on the cover. The album contained two of the band's greatest hits, "California Girls" and "Help Me Rhonda." What was the name of the album?

Summer Days (and Summer Nights!!) (Be sure to include the two exclamation points!!) Jardine commented on his non-appearance on the back of the album cover:

Sorry I missed the boat on this album cover. That very day the pictures were taken I had to spend in bed with a flu bug instead of on a yacht with the photographer. You know, recording sessions are a lot of fun. A lot of fun, that is, unless you've just come in off the road from a three-week tour of 10 states into the arms of our leader Brian. He sets up camp for us in Studio B and we have at it. Now, I'm not saying it's hard work or anything, but it is. I was once told a musician expends as much energy in half an hour as a lumberjack does in eight hours.[10]

In describing the creation of this album cover, music journalist David Hepworth wrote: "Twenty-eight years old, snub-nosed, freckly and frizzy-haired, she had prepared herself for [A&M Records house photographer Jim] McCrary's lens by putting on a sensible pullover and jeans, much as she would have done had she been weeding the garden ... They tried various shots until McCrary asked if he could move the cat Telemachus into the frame. The cat was placed on a cushion on the window seat in from of [the artist.] McCrary ... was unaware that he had shot a cover that would prove more famous, more popular and more ubiquitous than everything else he had photographed put together." What was the album?

Carole King's 1971 landmark album *Tapestry*.[11]

Lastly, what is the title of the album bearing the famous (or perhaps more accurately infamous) "butcher cover"? As a hint, it has to do with the Beatles.

Yesterday and Today, the ninth Capitol album by the Beatles. Photographer Robert Whitaker wanted to make a statement as to what he considered to be the band's absurd fame at the time. "I had toured quite a lot of the world with them by then, and I was continually amused by the public adulation of four people. I was trying to show that the Beatles were flesh and blood." To accomplish this, he posed them in butcher smocks. John, Paul and Ringo are seated, each with big slabs of raw meat on their laps. On Paul's lap is the decapitated head of a baby doll. There are also two headless baby dolls resting on each of his shoulders. George, standing behind, is holding another baby's head. Whitaker called the piece "A Somnambulant Adventure," "somnambulant" meaning sleepwalking.

The photo was not intended to be used as an album cover. However, Lennon thought it would be a good idea to use it for the cover of their upcoming album because of the band's "boredom and resentment at having to do *another* photo session and *another* Beatles thing." McCartney supported the idea as well. Harrison on the other hand later thought the whole idea "was gross, and I also thought it was stupid. Sometimes we all did stupid things thinking it was cool and hip when it was naïve and dumb; and that was one of them."

Reaction to the butcher cover was immediate and negative. Capitol received complaints from some dealers. (Sears sold the original album cover for one day.) The record was immediately recalled and all copies were ordered shipped back to the record label. Capitol decided instead to go with a much more conventional (read: dull) cover, namely the band posed around an open steamer trunk, with Paul sitting inside. They are all wearing jackets or ties. Perhaps proving John's point about the band's initial pleasure with the butcher cover versus the much more boring "steamer trunk" cover, all four band members look totally pleased to be posing in the former and totally bored in the latter.

Faced with so many jackets already printed, Capitol decided to paste the "steamer trunk cover" over the butcher cover. As word of this maneuver became known, owners of the altered cover attempted, usually unsuccessfully, to peel off the pasted-over cover, hoping to reveal the original image hidden beneath. Copies that have never had the steamer cover pasted onto them, known as "first state" covers, are very rare and command the highest prices. Copies with the pasted-on cover intact above the butcher image are known as "second state" or "pasteovers." Covers that have had the Trunk cover removed to reveal the underlying butcher image are known as "third state" covers; these are now the most common (and least valuable, although their value varies depending on how well the cover is removed).

Today, other than items signed or created by the band members themselves, the butcher covers may be the most valuable Beatles memorabilia, especially depending on their "state." First state butcher covers are those that were never opened and remain still sealed in their original shrink wrap. The rate of appreciation of these rarities has also been astonishing. The first documented collector's sale of a mono butcher cover LP in 1974 was for $457.00. In 2006, they were valued at $20,000. However, in 2016, an original mint condition stereo copy of the album, still in shrink wrap, sold at auction by Heritage Auctions for a record $125,000.[12]

CHAPTER 19

Winner Winner! (Awards and Honors)

As we saw in chapter 1, one way for musicians to be recognized is through success on the *Billboard* charts. Another is for them to win awards (especially at the Grammys or at the Academy Awards), or to be inducted into the Rock and Roll Hall of Fame. This chapter will focus on these artists as well as the honored songs they have released.

The song is one of only 40 singles ever released that has sold at least 10 million copies worldwide. In 1977, the song was named joint winner (along with Queen's "Bohemian Rhapsody") of the Best British Pop Single 1952–1977 at the Brit Awards. The song was not by such obvious candidates as the Beatles, the Stones or the Who. In fact, it was more or less by a one-hit wonder, at least in the U.S. First question: What is the song? (It was released in 1967.)

"Whiter Shade of Pale." As of 2009, it was the most played song in the last 75 years in the United Kingdom.[1]

Spell correctly the name of the group that released it.

Procol Harum. This song was the subject of a major royalty battle among band members Matthew Fisher and Gary Brooker. Originally, the writing credits went to Brooker for the music and Keith Reid for the lyrics and it stayed that way until 2005, when Fisher brought a claim in the British High Court against Brooker, claiming that he cowrote the music for the song. Fisher won the case in 2006 and was awarded 40 percent of the composers' share of the music copyright, but only for royalties after 2005. In 2007, that decision was reversed by the Court of Appeal, which upheld Fisher's coauthorship, but ruled that he should receive no royalties as he had taken too long (38 years) to bring his claim to litigation. Full royalty rights were returned to Brooker. Then in 2009, that decision was reversed again, as the Law Lords unanimously ruled in Fisher's favor. They noted that the delay in bringing the case had not caused any harm to Brooker and in fact he benefitted from it. Again however, Fisher was only awarded future royalties.[2]

One woman sang two songs during the Decade that won an Academy Award for Best Original Song. Who is the woman and what were the songs? (The movies in which the songs were heard were *The Poseidon Adventure* and *The Towering Inferno* (reminding us that the '70s were the era of disaster movies.)

The singer was Maureen McGovern and the songs were "The Morning After" (winner in 1972) and "We May Never Love This Way Again" (winner in 1974). In *The Poseidon Adventure*, the song "The Morning After" was performed by the character of Nonnie, played by Carol Lynley but is actually sung by a vocal double, Renee Armand. In *The Towering Inferno*, McGovern performs the song herself. Other women have won two Oscars for best songs (including Barbra Streisand and Jennifer Warnes), but not twice in the Decade. In terms of songwriting, only one woman was a two-time winner during the Decade. Marilyn Bergman cowrote the lyrics for "The Windmills of Your Mind" (music by Michel Legrand) from *The Thomas Crown Affair* in 1968 and also cowrote the 1973 winner, "The Way We Were" (music by Marvin Hamlisch) from the film of the same name.

In 2004, the American Film Institute released a list of the top 100 songs in American film, called "100 years . . . 100 songs." (Notwithstanding the title of the list, the earliest song is from 1932 and the last is from 2002, so it is really 72 years . . . 100 songs.) Eight of the movies on the list were released during the Decade, although not all of the songs from those movies charted on the *Billboard* Hot 100. Five of the songs below also won the Academy Award for Best Song. Only one of those songs was by what would be considered a traditional rock band. The list below provides the movie and sometimes the song. In each case, give the other. The year of the movie is omitted. (By the way, the #1 song was "Over the Rainbow" from *The Wizard of Oz*, released in 1939.) For extra credit, name the only one of the films referenced in the list below that won the Academy Award for Best Picture.

Barbra Streisand (name the film)
Butch Cassidy and the Sundance Kid (name the song)
Easy Rider (name the song)
Isaac Hayes (name the film)
Midnight Cowboy (name the song)
Nashville (name the song)
Simon & Garfunkel (name the film)
The Thomas Crown Affair (name the song)

Barbra Streisand—"The Way We Were" (#8 ranking in the poll, #1 peak position on *Billboard* Hot 100) from the movie of the same name. Academy Award winner for 1973. She had three other songs on the list, "People" and "Don't Rain on My Parade," both from *Funny Girl*, and "Evergreen (Love Theme from *A Star is Born*)" from the movie of the same name. "People" charted before the Decade started and "Evergreen" reached #1, but not until after the Decade.

Butch Cassidy and the Sundance Kid—"Raindrops Keep Fallin' on My Head" by B.J. Thomas (#23, #1). Academy Award winner for 1969.

Easy Rider—"Born to Be Wild" by Steppenwolf (#29, #2). The only rock band on the list.

Isaac Hayes—"Theme from *Shaft*" from the movie of the same name (#38, #1). Academy Award winner for 1971.

Midnight Cowboy—"Everybody's Talking" by Nilsson (#22, #6). This is the only movie in this list that won the Academy Award for Best Picture.

Nashville—"I'm Easy" by Keith Carradine (#81, #17). This was his only top 40 hit. Although it did not hit the charts until 1976, the movie was released in 1975. It won the Academy Award for Best Song in 1975.

Simon & Garfunkel—"Mrs. Robinson" from *The Graduate* (#6, #1).

The Thomas Crown Affair—"The Windmills of Your Mind." The song in the film is sung by Noel Harrison and did not chart. However, Dusty Springfield's cover version reached #31. Academy Award winner for Best Song in 1968.[3]

The only song from the Decade that won the Academy Award for Best Song and reached #1 on the *Billboard* Hot 100 but yet is not on the list is "The Morning After," which is heard in *the Poseidon Adventure*.

Only one woman won a Grammy for Best Album during the Decade. Who was it and what was the album? (It is one of the best-selling albums of all time.)

Carole King—*Tapestry*.

Only one woman won the Grammy Award for Record of the Year twice during the Decade and it was in consecutive years, 1973 and 1974. Who was the woman and what were the songs? (The woman is African American.)

Roberta Flack—"The First Time Ever I Saw Your Face" (1973) and "Killing Me Softly With His Song"(1974).

A separate award from Record of the Year is Song of the Year. Many people are not aware of the distinction between the two because they sound like they are referring to

the same thing (and we know that Record of the Year is different from Album of the Year because that is a separate category). Do you know the distinction?

Record of the Year goes to the performing artist, the producer, recording engineer, and/or mixer for that song. In this sense, "record" means a particular song as recorded, not its composition. Song of the Year goes to the songwriter who actually wrote the lyrics and/or melody to the song. Thus, "song" in this context means the song as composed, not its recording.

There were two occasions during the Decade when one artist won Album of the Year, Song of the Year and Record of the Year at the Grammys in the same year. This occurred in 1971 and 1972 (for albums released in 1970 and 1971 respectively.) In one of these cases, the song that won both Record of the Year and Song of the Year had the same title as the album. In the other, the album had one title, the Song of the Year had a second and Record of the Year had a third (but both were on the album). What are the various albums and songs referred to?

Bridge Over Troubled Water by Simon and Garfunkel is the first. The second is *Tapestry* by Carole King (the album title), "It's Too Late" (Record of the Year) and "You've Got a Friend" (Song of the Year). The only times that an artist won "the big four" awards (the above three plus Best New Artist) in a single year were in 1981 and 2003, when Christopher Cross and Norah Jones respectively accomplished the feat.

The Eurovision Song Contest is an annual song competition held among the member countries of the European Broadcasting Union (EBU) since 1956. Each member country submits a song to be performed onlive television and radio and then casts votes for the other countrys' songs to determine the most popular song in the competition. The contest has been broadcast every year since its inauguration and is one of the longest-running television programs in the world. It is also one of the most watched non-sporting events in the world.

There have been a number of previously unknown Eurovision artists and groups whose careers were directly launched into the spotlight following their win, while others had previously established themselves with at least one hit. The most famous example of the former from outside the Decade was Celine Dion's win in 1988 for "Ne partez pas sans moi (Don't leave without me)." Although Canadian, she represented Switzerland in the contest. Three examples of the latter, all from the U.K., include Lulu, who won in 1969 for "Boom Bang-a-Bang," when her song "To Sir With Love" was a worldwide hit two years earlier, the Brotherhood of Man, who won in 1976 for

"Save Your Kisses for Me" when their song United We Stand Was a hit in 1970, and Katrina and the Waves who also won for the U.K. in 1997 for "Love Shine a Light" when their song "Walking on Sunshine" was a worldwide hit 12 years earlier. However, there was only one instance from the Decade of a previously unknown artist or group becoming an international success after winning this contest. Who was it and what was the song? (As a hint, the year was 1974, and the winner went to become one of the most successful acts in human history.)

The group was ABBA and the song was "Waterloo." The group was honored at the 50th anniversary celebration of the contest in 2005, when "Waterloo" was chosen as the best song in the competition's history.[4]

The song "Waterloo" appeared on ABBA's second album, of the same name. The title of their first album was also the name of their first single to chart in Europe, reaching top five in a number of countries. It was submitted by the group for the 1973 Eurovision Song Contest but another Swedish song was chosen instead. After the success of "Waterloo," the song was released in the U.S. along with a video, and the song became popular in the U.S. as well (ABBA was one of the first groups to consistently release videos with many of their singles.) The English lyrics were written by Neil Sedaka and Phil Cody. What is the same of that first album and the lead single of the same name?

Ring Ring.

There has been only one person in history inducted into the Rock and Roll Hall of Fame with a band even though he was not a member of the band. The reason is that he wrote the lyrics to many of their best-known songs. Who is this man?

Robert Hunter, who was inducted with the Grateful Dead in 1994. Hunter wrote the lyrics to songs such as "Uncle John's Band," "Friend of the Devil," "Truckin'," "Casey Jones," "Sugar Magnolia," "Greatest Story Ever Told," "Dark Star," "China Cat Sunflower," "St. Stephen," and "Touch of Grey." It was Hunter who wrote the classic line which perhaps best sums up the band's career, "what a long strange trip it's been," which is from the song "Truckin'." Elton John's lyricist Bernie Taupin is not in the Hall of Fame. However, at John's own induction ceremony, Elton said "without Bernie the journey would not have been possible. I kind of feel cheating standing up here accepting this because without Bernie, there wouldn't have been any Elton John at all." He then proceeded to call Taupin up to the stage and gave him the award.

The following were nominated for a Grammy for best vocal performance of 1965. Who won?

   a.   The Anita Kerr Quartet—"We Dig Mancini"
   b.   The Statler Brothers—"Flowers on the Wall"
   c.   The Beatles—"Help!"
   d.   Herman's Hermits—"Mrs. Brown, You've Got a Lovely Daughter"
   e.   We Five—"You Were on My Mind"

The Anita Kerr Quartet—"We Dig Mancini." Some songs fall into the category of not being recognizable by title but being recognizable once heard. This is not one of those songs. Nevertheless, it beat out the other four songs, each of which are classics today.

There is only one person (a male) who is a three-time inductee into the Rock and Roll Hall of Fame. Twice it was for his work with bands and once as a solo artist. While his career started slightly before the Decade and continued well after, the prime of his work was during the Decade. Who is this person?

Eric Clapton. He was inducted with the Yardbirds, with Cream, and on his own.

Paul Simon wrote a song which appears on his solo album *There Goes Rhymin' Simon*. One of the tracks had wonderful background vocals by a Southern gospel group. A year later, that group recorded the song on their own (a virtually identical version of Simon's song) and a Grammy for Best Soul Gospel Performance of 1974 for their performance. What is the song and who is the group?

The song is "Loves Me Like a Rock" and the group is the Dixie Hummingbirds.

Simon won a Grammy Award for Best Album in 1976 (for *Still Crazy After All These Years*, which was released in 1975). In his acceptance speech, he thanked Phoebe Snow and Art Garfunkel, who performed with him on the album, and he concluded by saying "most of all, I'd like to thank [X], who didn't make an album this year." He was referring to an artist who won the Grammy for Best Album in both of the two previous years and would win it again the following year. What artist was he referring to? For extra credit, name the 3 albums released by that artist that won the Grammy for Best Album.

The artist is Stevie Wonder, and the three albums were "Innervisions" (1974), "Fulfillingness' First Finale" (1975) and "Songs in the Key of Life" (1977).

There is no exact consensus as to the most recorded song of all time. However, there is consensus as to which song takes this honor among songs released during the Decade. What song is it?

"Yesterday" by the Beatles.[5]

Only one band was inducted into the Rock and Rock Hall of Fame on its own and has had each of its members inducted with members of other bands. Name the band itself and the other bands with whom they each were members that were also inducted. (Virtually every song for which they are remembered today is on their debut album, the only one they released during the Decade.)

Crosby, Stills & Nash. David Crosby was inducted with the Byrds in 1991, Stephen Stills with Buffalo Springfield in 1997, and Graham Nash with the Hollies in 2010. What about Crosby Stills Nash & Young? Neil Young was a bandmate of Stephen Stills in Buffalo Springfield and so he was inducted with that group in 1997. The problem is that Crosby, Stills, Nash & Young was never inducted as a band. This is puzzling in some respects. On one hand, they only released three studio albums, and the last two of them, *American Dream* from 1988 and *Looking Forward* from 1999 are mostly forgotten today, with no memorable singles. Only their debut effort, *Déjà Vu*, was a huge success. However, if the argument for excluding them is that they released only one great album, then why did CSN get in? While their 1977 self-titled album was successful, it is clear that they were inducted on the basis of their own debut album and not any others.

Only one inducted band has had each of its members also inducted individually. Which band?

The Beatles. Ringo was not inducted until 2015 in the Award for Musical Excellence category, which "honors those musicians, producers and others who have spent their careers out of the spotlight working with major artists on various parts of their recording and live careers." Until 2010, this was the "sidemen" category.

One Rolling Stones member is in the Rock and Rock Hall of Fame twice. Who and why?

Ron Wood. He also got in as a member of Small Faces/Faces in 2010.

Female artists are not well represented in the Rock and Roll Hall of Fame. Who was the first woman inducted?

Aretha Franklin.

White female artists are even rarer in the Rock and Roll Hall of Fame. There were 78 inductees before the first one was inducted in 1995. Who was it?

Janis Joplin.

Who was the first white female inducted into the Rock and Roll Hall of Fame as a member of a group? What was the group? (As a hint, the other members of the rock band were all male.)

Grace Slick and Jefferson Airplane respectively.

As of 2016, there are three bands inducted that have more than one white female. None of them were all female. One of these groups released all of their albums during the Decade, while the other two started during the Decade but had most of their success after. Who were the three groups?

The Mamas and the Papas, Fleetwood Mac and ABBA.

There are only two solo female artists in the Hall of Fame as performers who wrote, without collaboration, virtually all of their own songs. Both achieved their greatest success during the Decade. One was inducted in 1997 and the other (posthumously) in 2012. Who are they?

The first was Joni Mitchell and the second was Laura Nyro. The reason for the "performers" qualification is because Carole King was inducted in 1990 as a non-performer (in her case, as a songwriter). The reason for the "without collaboration" qualification is because Madonna wrote much of her material with others.

CHAPTER 20

One is Better than None
(One-Hit Wonders)

What is a one-hit wonder in the first place? There is no hard and fast definition. Wikipedia refers to it as "the combination of artist and song that scores huge in the music industry with one single, but is unable to repeat the achievement." Generally, "scores huge" refers to a top 40 hit, and usually well within the top 20. The site also refers to Wayne Jancik's book, *The Billboard Book of One Hit Wonders*, which defines a one-hit wonder as "an act that has won a position on *Billboard*'s national top 40 just once." Wikipedia called this definition "conservative" because it distinguishes between a solo performer and any group he or she may have performed with. So by this definition, influential and famous artists such as Janis Joplin and Jimi Hendrix would be considered one-hit wonders because they each had only one top 40 hit on their own. In the case of Joplin, her lone solo hit was "Me and Bobby McGee," which reached #1. "Piece of My Heart" reached #12, but that wouldn't count because it was recorded with her band Big Brother and the Holding Company. In the case of Hendrix, his lone solo top 40 hit in the U.S. was the Bob Dylan song "All Along the Watchtower," which reached #20 in 1968.

The above definitions of one-hit wonders can be overinclusive not only because they include influential artists, but also because they can include artists who are not primarily thought of his musicians at all. For example, though released outside the Decade, Steve Martin's "King Tut" and Rick Dees' "Disco Duck" would make them one-hit wonders, even though no one thinks of them in that way. Nevertheless, even if an exact definition may be difficult to create, the concept is well understood.

In my view, one-hit wonder songs tend to be good songs. When an established group or artist releases a single, it has the benefit of its built-in reputation not only to get the song considered by DJs in the first place but also to help get it boosted up the charts, even though it may not be as good as prior hits that put the act on the map in the first place. By contrast, a one-hit wonder song has to succeed completely on its own merits, without the benefit of rocket propulsion based on past performance.

Often, successful novelty songs are recorded by one-hit wonders. However, those are generally comedic-type songs and are dealt with in their own chapter in this book. Also, not all writers of novelty songs are one-hit wonders, Ray Stevens being an example.

This Dutch group had a #1 song on the U.S. charts in 1970. However, the lead singer of the band, Mariska Veres, did not speak any English when the song was recorded and so she sang the words phonetically. Who is the band and what is the song?

The song is "Venus" and the band is Shocking Blue. This is one of the few instances where a song has reached #1 on the *Billboard* Hot 100 twice through two different artists. The British female band Bananarama also had a #1 hit with it in 1986.[1]

This song reached #1 on the *Billboard* Hot 100 in 1973. It was written by Bobby Russell. However, Russell didn't want to record it himself because he didn't think much of the song. The song was turned down by a number of artists, including Sonny Bono, who rejected it for Cher because it might offend listeners in the Southern United States, because part of the story involves a judge in a Southern state finding an innocent man guilty in a "make-believe trial." Russell's wife liked the song however and offered to record it herself. She was the one who had the hit with the song. (The artist who performed the song says Cher did not know Sonny turned the song down until years later, although the song does seem perfect for Cher.) Who is the performer and what is the song? (She is far better known for her career in television than as a singer.)

The artist is Vicki Lawrence and the song is "The Night the Lights Went Out in Georgia." Lawrence is of course well known for her role as one of the ensemble members of *The Carol Burnett Show*. Bobby Russell also penned the hits "Honey" for Bobby Goldsboro and "Little Green Apples" for O.C. Smith. He and Lawrence got divorced in 1974.

For a three-and-a-half-minute pop song, the "plot" is rather involved, one writer calling it "possibly the most complicated narrative ever recorded." Essentially, it's about a woman whose brother is hanged for a murder. It turns out that her sister-in-law had been cheating on her brother. She found out about this from her supposed friend Andy, who also confessed to sleeping with her sister-in-law himself. The sheriff who arrested Andy at the scene of the crime and the trial judge both believed that it was the brother who had killed Andy. However, at the end of the song, the singer/narrator reveals that she was the one who killed both Andy and the sister-in-law as well. Suffice it to say that, as between (1) the narrator and singer of the song, who is a double murderer, (2) her sister-in-law, who is a serial adulterer, (3) Andy, who not only slept with the singer's sister-in-law, but then tells her about it, even though he calls himself her "best friend," (4) the sheriff who wrongly arrests the brother, and (5) the judge who wrongly sentences the brother to death by hanging (and then casually tells the sheriff: "supper's waiting at home and I got to get to it"), there is not a lot of honor to go around in this song.

There is also a bizarre video of this song (introduced by Dick Clark) in which Ms. Lawrence is on the beach surrounded by surfboards and a crowd of people watching her "sing" (read: lip sync)—at least at first. Shortly after however, most of the crowd seems to become totally oblivious to her "performance" and instead starts tossing footballs and frisbees and wresting with each other. Maybe they got bored after too many takes. Nevertheless, why anyone thought that this was a good setting and atmosphere for this particular song is a mystery.[2]

The following is a series of related questions. Bo Donaldson and the Heywoods were a one-hit wonder. What was their song which reached #1 in 1974?

"Billy Don't Be a Hero." That song was written by two British songwriters named Mitch Murray and Peter Callendar. They first gave the song to another band (which we'll call the "other band") who also had a #1 hit with it in the UK. However, before they could release it in the U.S., it was snatched up and re-recorded by Donaldson's group. While the other band also released "Billy Don't be a Hero" in the U.S., it never reached higher than number 96 on the *Billboard* Hot 100. **However, Murray and Callendar then wrote another song and offered it to the other band. This time, they did have a huge #1 hit with the song, also in 1974. Who is the "other band" and what is the song? (As a hint, it makes reference to a shootout between Al Capone and the police which never occurred.)**

The band was Paper Lace and the song is "The Night Chicago Died." The song starts with a reference to "the East side of Chicago," which basically means Lake Michigan. Murray later explained the reason: [Peter Callendar and I had] never been to Chicago at the time we wrote that song—many other parts of the USA, but not Chicago. Having been brought up on a tasty diet of American gangster movies, the term 'East Side' usually meant the seamy side of a city."

The song also refers to a shootout between Al Capone's gang and the police. This never happened. The songwriters may have been inspired by the real-life Saint Valentine's Day Massacre, which involved Capone's men killing seven of Bugsy Moran's gang members, but that had nothing to do with the police.

Since Paper Lace also had a #1 hit in England with "Billy Don't Be a Hero," they might be called two-hit wonders. Paper Lace was not allowed to perform "The Night Chicago Died" in the U.S. due to contractual issues, but their label assured them that they could make a hit of the song anyway.

Finally, there is a connection between Mitch Murray and the Beatles. After the Beatles had a modest hit with "Love Me Do," producer George Martin was looking for a follow-up song. He suggested "How Do You Do It?," which had been written by Murray. The band was decidedly unenthusiastic about this idea, preferring to release one of their own songs. They did however record an uninspired version of the song which can be heard on *Beatles Anthology 1*. Martin then gave the song to another one of his acts, Gerry & the Pacemakers, who did have a #1 hit with it in England in 1963. The Beatles instead released "Please Please Me" which went straight to #1 in the U.S. and the rest, as they say, is history.[3]

Manfred Albrecht Freiherr von Richtofen is mentioned by (last) name in a song that reached #2 on the *Billboard* Hot 100 in December 1966. What is the song? For extra credit, name the group that recorded it.

"Snoopy and the Red Baron" by the Royal Guardsmen. Richtofen was a fighter pilot with the Imperial German Army Air during World War I. He is considered the top ace of the war, being officially credited with 80 air combat victories. He was shot down and killed near Amienson April 21, 1918 at age 26.

Long before "We Didn't Start the Fire" by Billy Joel (1989) and "It's the End of the World as We Know It" by R.E.M. (1987) was another lyric-heavy, rapid fire, semi-stream of consciousness, catchy ditty, that was released in 1974. It reached #8 on the *Billboard* Hot 100 and is still heard on the radio today. What was the song and who recorded it? As a hint, it was created by an ad hoc group of studio musicians, with Joey Levine (who wrote "Chewy Chewy" and "Yummy Yummy Yummy") as the lead singer.

"Life is a Rock (But the Radio Rolled Me)" by Reunion.

As America's involvement with the Vietnam War expanded, the early to mid–1960s were obviously rife with anti-war protest songs, including "Blowin' in the Wind" (1962), "Masters of War" (1963), "Talking World War III Blues" (1963), and "The Times They Are A-Changin'" (1964), all by Bob Dylan, "Where Have All the Flowers Gone" (by Pete Seeger and Joe Hickerson) and "Turn! Turn! Turn!" by Pete Seeger (or by "the Bible" if you will), "Universal Soldier" (1964), written and recorded by Buffy Sainte Marie (but mostly associated with Donovan today, whose version appeared in 1965), and "Eve of Destruction" (1965) by Barry McGuire. However, as if in "answer" to all of these songs, came one which, while not pro-war per se, certainly cast the Army in a positive light. It was cowritten and performed by a soldier. The song was a huge success, holding the #1 spot for 5 weeks, becoming the #1 hit on the *Billboard* Hot 100 chart for the entire 1966 year. The single and the album of the same name sold over ten million copies. It is ironic today to

think that one of the biggest-selling songs of the 1960s specifically relating to the military or war was a pro-military song. What is the song and who is the singer who cowrote it?

"Ballad of the Green Berets" by Staff Sgt. Barry Sadler, himself a Green Beret. The song was written (along with Robin Moore) while Sadler was recuperating from a leg wound suffered as a medic in the Vietnam War. The tune itself is borrowed from the traditional folk song "The Butcher Boy." He performed the song on Ed Sullivan in full Green Beret military regalia. In the film *Caddyshack,* greenskeeper Carl Spackler, played by Bill Murray, mumbles the song under his breath while he is connecting the wires to the plunger as he prepares for his final battle with his gopher nemesis.

In 1978, Sadler shot and killed the estranged boyfriend of a woman he was seeing. Sadler pleaded guilty to voluntary manslaughter and was sentenced to up to five years in the Tennessee State Penitentiary. The judge later reduced the sentence to 30 days with two years' probation. On September 7, 1988 in Guatemala City, Sadler was shot in the head at night in a taxicab. He was training Nicaraguan rebels in Guatemala at the time. The motive of the shooting has never been clearly established. He was airlifted back to the United States where he was hospitalized and remained in a coma for several months. He was released eventually, but with significant brain damage. He died at age 49 on November 5, 1989 of complications from his gunshot injury.[4]

Becoming a one-hit wonder is not easy. Having that song reach #1 is even more difficult and highly unusual because it means that the artist was unable to ever reach the top 40 again, despite having a #1 hit. The following songs by one-hit wonders reached #1 during the Decade. In each case, I will name either the song or the artist. Name the other. (This is a partial list.)

Song	Artist	Year
_____	The New Vaudeville Band	1966
"Judy in Disguise"	_____	1968
_____	The Lemon Pipers	1968
"Love is Blue"	_____	1968
"Grazing in the Grass"	_____	1968
_____	Steam	1969
_____	Stories	1973
"I Can Help"	_____	1974
"The Hustle"	_____	1975

Answers (in bold):

Song	Artist	Year
"Winchester Cathedral"	The New Vaudeville Band	1966
"Judy in Disguise"	**John Fred and his Playboy Band**	1968
"Green Tambourine"	The Lemon Pipers	1968
"Love is Blue"	**Paul Mauriat and His Orchestra**	1968
"Grazing in the Grass"	**Hugh Masekela**	1968
"Na Na Hey Hey Kiss Him Goodbye"	Steam	1969
"Brother Louie"	Stories	1973
"I Can Help"	**Billy Swan**	1974
"The Hustle"	**Van McCoy**	1975

There is one song that was left off of the above list. Excluding manufactured bands like Steam and The New Vaudeville Band (i.e. typically bands like these that were created for the sole purpose of giving a name to a group of otherwise unaffiliated musicians who recorded a hit song and then who "broke up," possibly after one album), the other artists listed above at least had other songs that reached the top 100, if not the top 40. However, there was only time in the Decade (and possibly only one time ever) that an act (1) released a #1 song in the U.S. (also in the U.K.) and (2) never cracked the *Billboard* Hot 100 again (or any other chart) anywhere in the world, thus making the band the ultimate one-hit wonder. Moreover, it wasn't just "any" #1 song: it held that position for six consecutive weeks. As a hint, it is about what life may be like in the future—the very distant future. What song was it and who recorded it?

"In the Year 2525 (Exordium et Terminus)" by Zager and Evans. Their next most successful song, "Mr. Turnkey," only hit #106. It's about a rapist who nails his own wrists to the wall as self-punishment for his crime, and kills himself in the process. Given its pleasant and uplifting subject matter, one wonders why it didn't chart higher.

The song by this one-hit wonder came out in 1975. It was cowritten and performed by a female artist. She is the mother of a major television and movie star, and at the end of live performances of the song, she can be heard singing her daughter's name. It opens with birds singing. Who is the artist and what is the song?

The artist is Minnie Riperton and the song is "Lovin' You." Her daughter is Maya Rudolph. While the version of the song which appears on her album *Perfect Angel* (and the one which was released as a single) ends with the familiar "La la la la la la la . . . do do do do do," on live performances, she sometimes sang "Maya, Maya, Maya" instead. An example of such a version can be seen and heard when she sings the song on Burt Sugarman's *Midnight Special* which can be seen on YouTube. Riperton died tragically of breast cancer in 1979 at age 31. (The only other #1 love songs by one-hit wonders in the 1970s were "You Light Up My Life" by Debby Boone and "Don't Give Up on Us" by David Soul.)

The group that released this song was Every Mother's Son. Their hit rose to #6 in 1967. What is the song?

"Come on Down to My Boat." The song was cowritten by Jerry Goldstein (who cowrote "My Boyfriend's Back," a 1963 hit for the Angels). The band was signed to MGM because of their clean-cut image, something that was becoming a rarity by 1967. (A look at their debut album cover, and a YouTube clip of them playing their hit, makes "clean-cut" seem like an understatement.) Oddly, the name of the track on the eponymous debut album is "Come and Take a Ride in My Boat." The song was originally recorded in 1966 by the Rare Breed and their version is not too different from the hit version.[5]

This 1970 song by a one-hit wonder (at least in the U.S.) is about a man on the run from the law. It opens with the sound of a wailing police siren—a very realistic sound. So realistic in fact that the sound was removed from some copies supplied to radio stations, after complaints that drivers hearing the song on the radio had mistakenly pulled over, thinking that it was real. What was the song and who was the artist?

"Indiana Wants Me" by R. Dean Taylor. The siren is also heard during the instrumental section in the middle of the song. At the climax of the song, the voice of a cop on the bullhorn is heard, commanding the singer to give himself up. The song was released on the Rare Earth label, formed by Motown in an attempt to establish itself in the rock music market, and was one of the few hits for Motown by a white artist.

In 1970, then Vice President Spiro Agnew gave a speech at the Sahara Hotel in Las Vegas in which he called rock music "blatant drug-culture propaganda" and warned that it "threatens to sap our national strength unless we move hard and fast to bring it under control." In that speech, he mentioned this song by name. At about the same time, the Lawrence Welk Show was trying to broaden its appeal by including current pop songs, country music, and religious music. In early 1971, accordionist Myron Floren introduced this song as "one of the newer songs" as Welk singers Gail Farrell & Dick Dale launched

into a wholesome rendition. Dale wears an all-white suit, pink shirt and red tie, while Gale is wearing what looks like a German dirndl dress. At the close of the song Lawrence Welk looked on approvingly and said "And there you heard a modern spiritual by Gail & Dale." It may have been the most inappropriate song ever played on that show given its intended audience and one can only assume that Welk or his producers heard the word "Jesus" and immediately assumed that it must be, as Welk called it, "a spiritual." (After all, how could a song that mentions Jesus not be a spiritual?) What is the song and who is it by?

"One Toke Over the Line" by Brewer and Shipley. The band had heard about the recording but didn't believe it and, in those pre-Internet, pre-YouTube days, it was obviously not so easy to find. Accordingly, for many decades, they questioned whether evidence of the performance actually existed. However, a clip of the performance was finally located in 2007 and was immediately put on YouTube. Brewer later commented: "That was on at exactly the same time the Nixon administration was coming down on us because of the song and Lawrence Welk referred to it as a 'modern day spiritual.'"[6]

CHAPTER 21

The Wizards Behind the Glass (Producers and Engineers)

What do producers and engineers do anyway, and what is the difference? Phil Ek, who does both, has explained the difference this way: "A producer is the person who creatively guides or directs the process of making a record, like a director would a movie. Engineering is the technical aspect of recording—the placing of microphones, the turning of pre-amp knobs, the setting of levels. The physical recording of any project is done by an engineer. The engineer would be more the cameraman of the movie. Engineering is the bread and butter/nuts and bolts recording of the project, and the producer is the guy who directs that."[1] While one person can fulfill both roles, the person often seen hunched over the sound board is usually the engineer.

What makes a great music producer? Almost every producer will answer this question differently, just as every film director likely would. However, commonly heard themes include having a great chemistry with the artist, understanding what the artist is trying to accomplish and translating their sometimes vague ideas into a tangible melody on the best instruments. While many of the best are not well-known to the general public, virtually every artist for whom they worked their behind-the-scenes magic has acknowledged their invaluable contributions to the music on which they worked, the same way that actors and actresses that win awards almost invariably save their most profuse thanks for their directors. This chapter focuses primarily on producers and engineers who have had success with a wide variety of acts. Here are some questions about some of the most prolific and successful producers and engineers of the Decade.

This man, in addition to being a record executive, produced songs and albums for artists such as, most notably, Aretha Franklin, Ray Charles and Bob Dylan, in addition to the Allman Brothers, Chris Connor, Aretha Franklin, Led Zeppelin, Wilson Pickett, Buffalo Springfield, Dire Straits, and Dusty Springfield. Songs he produced include "(You Make Me Feel Like) a Natural Woman" by Aretha Franklin, "Respect" by Aretha Franklin, "Son of a Preacher Man" by Dusty Springfield and "For What It's Worth" by Buffalo Springfield

(the Stephen Stills-penned song that begins "There's something happening here"). He also signed Led Zeppelin. As a measure of his success and influence, he was the first producer inducted into the Rock and Roll Hall of Fame and in only its second year of existence (1987). Who was this man?

Jerry Wexler.[2] According to his obituary in *Rolling Stone*: "Because of him, we use the term 'rhythm and blues' and we hail Ray Charles as 'Genius' and Aretha Franklin as 'Queen.' We came to know of a record label called Stax and a small town called Muscle Shoals, Alabama. We witnessed the rise of Led Zeppelin and the Allman Brothers, and we care about a thing called soul." His obituary in the *New York Times* also credits him with coining the term "rhythm and blues."

This man produced every one of five consecutive Rolling Stones albums which many consider to be their five best albums ever, released in the prime of their career, namely: *Beggars Banquet* (1968), *Let It Bleed* (1969), *Sticky Fingers* (1971), *Exile on Main Street* (1972) and *Goats Head Soup* (1973). Despite the huge success of the Rolling Stones albums he had produced, he was fired by the band due to his heroin addiction. Who was this man?

Jimmy Miller.[3] He also produced "Gimme Some Lovin'" and "I'm a Man" by the Spencer Davis Group, albums for Traffic, and the only album by the supergroup Blind Faith (the only group in history whose sole album went to #1 in the U.S.) which was eponymously titled.

This man was both a producer and engineer, and to call him prolific would be an understatement. He is credited with inventing the concept of multitracking and was one of the first people to use faders. As an engineer he recorded numerous albums by Ray Charles, the Drifters, the Coasters, Aretha Franklin (including her song "Respect"), Ben E. King, Ruth Brown, the Rascals, the Young Rascals and Bobby Darin (including Darin's rendition of the Kurt Weill/Bertolt Brecht tune "Mack the Knife"), and all Cream albums. He produced or coproduced many albums by the Allman Brothers (including the classic *Eat a Peach*), Eric Clapton (including *461 Ocean Boulevard*), Dusty Springfield (including the classic *Dusty in Memphis*), Black Oak Arkansas, Lynyrd Skynyrd, Aretha Franklin, and Rod Stewart, as well as *Layla and Other Assorted Love Songs* by Derek and the Dominos (including "Layla" itself), *The Sound of Wilson Pickett*, *Miami* by the James Gang, and numerous others. He also produced singles such as "Good Lovin'" by the Young Rascals, "Son of a Preacher Man" by Dusty Springfield and "Mr. Bojangles" by Jerry Jeff Walker. He also produced many hit movie soundtracks including *The Color of Money* (1986), *Goodfellas* (1990) and *Pulp Fiction* (1994). Finally, in his 20s he worked on part of the Manhattan Project that led to the production of the first atomic bomb. Who was this man?

Tom Dowd. During Aretha Franklin's induction speech at the Rock and Roll Hall of Fame in 1987, she specifically thanked him for his important contribution in the creation of the classic "Aretha" sound. There is a YouTube clip showing Aretha and Dowd working out an arrangement of the song "Ain't No Way," written by Aretha's sister Carolyn. In 2003, a documentary was released about his life, called *Tom Dowd and the Language of Music* He was posthumously inducted into the Rock and Roll Hall of Fame in 2012 (he passed away in 2002) and Robbie Robertson gave the induction speech.[4]

Just during the Decade, this man produced the following songs (chart rankings in the U.S.):

"Ferry Cross the Mersey," by "Gerry & the Pacemakers (1965, #6)
"Goldfinger," by Shirley Bassey (1965, #8)
"You'll Never Walk Alone," Gerry & the Pacemakers (1965, #48)
"Trains and Boats and Planes," Billy J. Kramer and the Dakotas (1965, #47)
(sometimes called Billy J. Kramer "with" the Dakotas)
"Girl on a Swing," Gerry & the Pacemakers (1966, #28)
"Live and Let Die," Paul McCartney and Wings (1973, #2)
"Tin Man,"America (1974, #4)
"Lonely People," America (1975, #5)
"Sister Golden Hair," America (1975, #1)

He produced the 1975 album *Blow by Blow* by Jeff Beck. He also produced some hit songs and albums by another well-known group.

George Martin. Of course, I could have mentioned that he produced every one of the Beatles albums, but that would have been a giveaway. Hence his Beatles work is referenced obliquely, through the wildly understated last sentence. The point is that he did have a very successful career as a producer even outside of his Beatles work. Top 10 songs which he produced outside of the Decade include:

"Little Children" Billy J. Kramer and the Dakotas (1964, #7)
"Bad to Me" by Billy J. Kramer with the Dakotas (1963, #9)
"Don't Let the Sun Catch You Crying" by Gerry and the Pacemakers (1964, #4)

"Ebony and Ivory" by Paul McCartney & Stevie Wonder (1982, #1)

"Say, Say, Say" by Paul McCartney & Michael Jackson (1983, #1)

"No More Lonely Nights" by Paul McCartney (1984, #6)

"Morning Desire" by Kenny Rogers (1985, #1 on country chart)

"Candle in the Wind 1997" by Elton John (1997, #1) (re-recording of this 1973 song after death of Princess Diana). According to the Recording Industry Association of America, this is the best-selling single of all time besides "White Christmas."

Martin passed away at age 90 in 2016.[5]

It can be argued that this producer, who was originally a staff producer for Columbia Records, was more responsible for the stardom of Simon and Garfunkel than any other person. He took their song "The Sound of Silence" (that originally appeared on their debut album *Wednesday Morning, 3 AM)*, and *without the duo's knowledge or consent*, added electric overdubs (such as electric guitar) onto the song more than a year after it first came out. The song hit #1 in December 1965 and the rest is history. This is probably the only time in history that a producer took an existing song on an album that he produced and then altered the arrangement long afterwards, without his artists' knowledge, and in the process turned an ordinary song into a worldwide success and launched the careers of one of the most famous duos in rock history. "Launched" is no understatement. Due to the failure of *Wednesday Morning, 3 AM*, the group had broken up and Simon had moved to England. It was the success of the souped-up single that caused Paul and Art to get back together, and the new album, *Sounds of Silence*, was mostly recorded after the single began climbing the charts.

Who was he?

Tom Wilson. His accomplishments were certainly not limited to his role in "The Sounds of Silence." He also produced three of Bob Dylan's most famous and hit-laden albums, namely *The Times They Are a-Changin'*, *Another Side of Bob Dylan*, and *Bringing It All Back Home*, as well as the final four tracks Dylan recorded for *The Freewheelin' Bob Dylan*. In addition, although he did not produce most of *Highway 61 Revisited*, he did produce its opening track, "Like a Rolling Stone," which was voted the #1 song of all time by *Rolling Stone* magazine in 2011 and which Dylan himself has described as the best song he wrote. (Interestingly, the producer's electric overdubs onto "The Sound of Silence" were done at the close of the recording session for "Like a Rolling Stone" on June 15, 1965, using many of the same musicians who had just finished working on the classic Dylan track.)

Continuing, in 1966, he signed the Mothers of Invention to Verve Records and was the producer on the group's seminal debut album *Freak Out!* He also produced another classic debut album, *The Velvet Underground and Nico* (with the Andy Warhol banana on the cover). Finally, he was Harvard-educated and was one of the very few African-American producers who worked primarily with white artists. At various times, Dylan and Frank Zappa and John Cale of the Velvet Underground all acknowledged Wilson's talents as a producer. He died of a heart attack in 1978 when he was only 47 years old.[6]

The British publication *NME (New Musical Express)* prepared a list of the 50 greatest producers ever. The top spot did not go to well-known giants in the industry such as Phil Spector, Quincy Jones, George Martin, Dr. Dre, Max Martin, Rick Rubin, or any of the other producers mentioned above, but rather to a British man who is virtually unheard of in this country (and not much better known in the U.K.). His string of successes was rather modest compared to most of the other producers on the list (although unlike most other producers, he did have a #1 hit of his own in 1962). Nevertheless, he was a fascinating, brilliant and tortured man who committed suicide in 1967 when he was only 37 years old. While he was producing music through 1966, most his success was before the Decade. He is considered a pioneer of the modern recording studio. Who is this man?

His name was Joe Meek. His #1 song was an instrumental called "Telstar" that he wrote and produced by his group the Tornados (you would recognize it if you heard it). The song was named after the Telstar communications satellite, which was launched into orbit in July 1962. It was written and produced by Meek despite the fact that he could not play any instruments and could not read music. It was recorded in Meek's studio in a small flat above a shop in North London. It was the first #1 song ever by a British group in the U.S. Since World War II, there had only been three British names that topped the U.S. chart, all individuals: Clarinetist Acker Bilk with the instrumental "Stranger on the Sure" (1962); Laurie London (a 14-year old boy, despite the name) with "He's Got the Whole World in His Hands"(1958), and Vera Lynn's "Auf Wiederseh'n Sweetheart."

Sadly, Meek never got to receive any royalties from his #1 hit. A French composer, Jean Ledrut, filed a lawsuit accusing Meek of plagiarism, claiming that the tune of "Telstar" had been copied from "La Marche d'Austerlitz", a piece from a score that Ledrut had written for the 1960 film *Austerlitz*. The movie was not released in the U.K. until 1965, and Meek was not even aware of the movie or the song. Nevertheless, as per British custom, the royalties were frozen while the litigation dragged on. Although the suit was eventually resolved in Meek's favor, that did not occur until three weeks after his suicide.

So what did he produce? While he produced songs for many British artists, the only song he produced besides "Telstar" which would be recognizable to American audiences is "Have I the Right" by the Honeycombs, which reached #5 in the U.S. in 1964. (The Honeycombs were unusual in that they consisted of four men plus a female drummer, Honey Lantree.)

Given Meek's relatively modest list of hit songs, it is clear that his placement atop the NME chart is based primarily on his influence and innovation, which are well summed up as follows:

> He pioneered studio tools such as multiple over-dubbing on one- and two-track machines, close miking, direct input of bass guitars, the compressor, and effects like echo and reverb, as well as sampling. Unlike other producers, his search was for the 'right' sound rather than for a catchy musical tune. [Meek produced] everything on the three floors of his 'home' studio and was never afraid to distort or manipulate the sound if it created the effect he was seeking. Meek was one of the first producers to grasp and fully exploit the possibilities of the modern recording studio. His innovative techniques—physically separating instruments . . . processing the sound through his fabled home-made electronic devices, the combining of separately-recorded performances and segments into a painstakingly constructed composite recording—comprised a major breakthrough in sound production. Up to that time, the standard technique for pop recording was to record all the performers in one studio, playing together in real time.

Meek suffered from extreme paranoia and depression and, in February 1967, he killed his landlady and then himself with a single-barreled shotgun. He was only 37.[7]

This man is likely the only person in history who has had success as a producer, an engineer, a musician and who has released a solo top five hit. He produced Pink Floyd's first, second and fourth studio albums, *The Piper at the Gates of Dawn*, *A Saucerful of Secrets*, and *Ummagumma*. He was the engineer on all of the EMI studio recordings by the Beatles until 1965, when he was promoted from engineer to producer. The last Beatles album he worked on was *Rubber Soul*. He engineered the sound for almost 100 Beatles songs in total. (Because of his easygoing and unflappable nature, John Lennon gave him the nickname "normal" and he later wrote a memoir called *John Lennon Called Me Normal*.) Prior to embarking on his solo career, he gave himself the nickname "Hurricane." Who is he?

Norman (which is where Lennon's nickname came from) "Hurricane" Smith.[8] He also played drums. During the sessions for the Pink Floyd song "Remember a Day," drummer

Nick Mason became agitated that he could not come up with the right drum part for the song. This man, however, knew what Mason wanted with the drums, so he played the part himself. He also wrote and sang a song which reached #3 on the *Billboard* Hot 100 called "Oh, Babe, What Would You Say?"

Besides Norman (Normal) Smith, the Beatles had one other primary sound engineer. He started working as an assistant engineer at EMI when he was only 15. He was present for the first-ever EMI recording session by the finalized line-up of the Beatles in 1962 (i.e. with Ringo Starr on drums), during which the group recorded their first hit single "Love Me Do." He was promoted to main engineer in 1966 when he was only 20 years old. His first engineered album was *Revolver* and his first song was "Tomorrow Never Knows." He received Grammy Awards for the engineering of *Sgt. Pepper's Lonely Hearts Club Band* and *Abbey Road*. Who is he?

Geoff Emerick.[9] After the Beatles, he worked with numerous artists including Paul McCartney, Elvis Costello, Badfinger, Art Garfunkel, America, Supertramp, Cheap Trick, Nazareth, Kate Bush and Jeff Beck. In 2006, Emerick released his memoir, *Here, There, and Everywhere: My Life Recording the Music of the Beatles.*

This man had his hand in an impressive number of hit songs and albums, as a producer, musician and songwriter. He also founded his own music studio in Memphis, Tennessee. He produced Elvis Presley's 1969 album *From Elvis in Memphis* and the hit songs "In the Ghetto," "Suspicious Minds," and "Kentucky Rain." He produced the original version of "Always on My Mind" by Mark James (later a huge hit for Elvis Presley), Neil Diamond's hits "Sweet Caroline" and "Brother Love's Travelling Salvation Show," and Willie Nelson's cover of "City of New Orleans" (which earned songwriter Steve Goodman a posthumous Grammy Award for Best Country Song at the 27th Grammy Awards in 1985).

As a writer, he cowrote "Do Right Woman, Do Right Man" (recorded by Aretha Franklin) with fellow Memphis producer and songwriter Dan Penn, and "The Dark End of the Street," which became the best-known song of the soul singer James Carr (and which was covered by many artists, notably Linda Ronstadt on *Heart Like a Wheel*). He produced *and* cowrote BJ Thomas's 1975 #1 hit song "(Hey Won't You Play) Another Somebody Done Somebody Wrong Song," which earned him a Grammy Award for Best Country Song and also cowrote and produced "Luckenbach, Texas (Back to the Basics of Love)," a #1 post-Decade country hit for Waylon Jennings.

Who is this accomplished man?

Lincoln Wayne Moman better known as Chips Moman. The studio he started in Memphis, American Sound Studio, produced over 120 *Billboard* Hot 100 songs, including, in addition to all the songs noted above, "Keep on Dancing" by the Gentrys, "Son of a Preacher Man" by Dusty Springfield, "The Letter" and "Cry Like a Baby" by the Box Tops, "Angel of the Morning" by Merrilee Rush, "Hooked on a Feeling" by BJ Thomas, "I'm in Love" by Wilson Pickett, and "Skinny Legs and All" by Joe Tex.[10]

This man worked as a producer or engineer on some of the most iconic albums of the rock era. He was an engineer on Bob Dylan's 1965 album *Highway 61 Revisited*, which includes the classic "Like a Rolling Stone." He was also an engineer on a number of songs by the Lovin' Spoonful including "Summer in the City" and recorded numerous other artists including the Dave Clark Five, the Yardbirds, the Byrds, Journey (on their first album *Journey*), Willie Nile, Laura Nyro, and Blood, Sweat & Tears. However, he is easily most famous not for any of those associations, but for his work with Simon and Garfunkel, and, after their breakup, Paul Simon individually. Who is this man?

Roy Halee. He produced *Bookends* and *Bridge over Troubled Water*. He coproduced and/or engineered Simon's eponymous first solo album, as well as *There Goes Rhymin' Simon*, *Graceland* and *Rhythm of the Saints*. He is mentioned by his full name in the Paul Simon song "A Simple Desultory Philippic (or How I Was Robert McNamara'd into Submission)" which appear on S&G's third album *Parsley Sage Rosemary and Thyme*. He was entered in the TEC (Technical Excellence and Creativity) Awards Hall of Fame in 2001. (In "A Simple Desultory Philippic," Simon sings that he has been "Roy Halee'd and Art Garfunkel'd").[11]

In the Decade, this man produced a slew of successful albums, working with a wide variety of the biggest stars in the music business. These include a number of albums considered to be the best work of the artists that released them, including *No Secrets* by Carly Simon, *Nilsson Schmilsson* by Harry Nilsson, *Ringo* by Ringo Starr, and *Breakaway* by Art Garfunkel. He also produced one or more albums for artists as diverse as Tiny Tim, Ella Fitzgerald and Barbra Streisand and Johnny Mathis. After the Decade, continuing to show his range, he produced albums for Donna Summer, the Pointer Sisters, Art Garfunkel, Diana Ross, Leo Sayer and El DeBarge.

When the critics summarize his career, one word that always pops up is "success." Bruce Eder of AllMusic.com called him "the most renowned producer in the field of popular music during the 1970s" and wrote that "his mere involvement with a recording project was enough to engender a mention in the music trade papers and even the popular music press, and the array of gold- and platinum-selling albums with which he was associated

made his name synonymous with success."As early as 1973, when he was still at a relatively early stage of his career, *Village Voice* said that "the rungs on the ladder of success seem so much closer together when [he] is your guide." In 1989, the *New York Times* called him "one of the successful independent producers in the history of pop." Who is this clearly "successful" producer?

Richard Perry.[12]

This British engineer turned producer has a resume that is as dazzling as anyone's in terms of number or artists he has worked with and number of hit albums and songs he has been instrumental (no pun intended) in creating. It has been commented that he was present for so many important moments in rock history that he is "the Forrest Gump of Rock." He started working in 1959 and was still going strong in 2017.

In the Decade alone, he produced albums for the Steve Miller Band (four albums), Led Zeppelin, the Eagles (three albums including their debut album, and *Desperado* and their *Greatest Hits (1971–1975)* album which for a time was the biggest selling album of all-time until Michael Jackson's *Thriller* came along), the Rolling Stones (their 1970 live album, *Get Yer Ya-Yas Out!*), the Who (four albums including their 1971 and 1978 masterpieces *Who's Next* and *Who Are You?*), Faces (*A Nod Is As Good as a Wink . . . to a Blind Horse*), Boz Scaggs, Humble Pie, and the Ozark Mountain Daredevils (two albums).

He also engineered the Beatles' 1969 rooftop concert and engineered and mixed the initial version of their album *Let It Be*.

Before becoming a producer, he worked as an engineer, especially with the Rolling Stones. He engineered *Beggar's Banquet* and *Let It Bleed*, two of the Rolling Stones' best albums (and in fact worked on every one of their albums until *Black and Blue*).

He also worked on albums and singles such as *Mad Dogs and Englishmen* by Joe Cocker, *Quadrophenia* by the Who, *Stage Fright* by the Band, *Harvest* by Neil Young, *My Generation* by the Who, and *You Really Got Me* by the Kinks.

After the Decade, he produced for Joan Armatrading (four albums, including her great debut album), Eric Clapton (three albums including *Slowhand* from 1977—Clapton called him "one of the greatest record producers of all time"), the Clash, Bob Dylan, John Hiatt, Stevie Nicks, Linda Ronstadt and on and on. Who is this talented man?

Glyn Johns. He was inducted into the Rock and Roll Hall of Fame in 2012 by Robbie Robertson. His contributions to *Let It Be* were largely erased by Phil Spector, who remixed all of the tracks, adding orchestra and choir to three tracks. More than 45 years later, in promoting his autobiography *Sound Man*, he told the New York times that he was still horrified by what Spector did to the album: "I was disappointed that Lennon got away with giving it to Spector, and even more disappointed with what Spector did to it. It has nothing to do with the Beatles at all. *Let It Be* is a bunch of garbage. As I say in the book, he puked all over it. I've never listened to the whole thing, I've only listened to the first few bars of some things and said, 'Oh, forget it.' It was ridiculously, disgustingly syrupy." Paul McCartney obviously agreed with Johns' criticism of Spector's overdubs, because in 2003, he initiated the release of *Let It Be . . . Naked*, which was essentially the album that he and Johns envisioned, which is to say with all of Spector's orchestral flourishes removed.[13]

CHAPTER 22

I Read the News Today, Oh Boy (Songs about Historical Events)

To say that the Decade was a time of political and social upheaval, while clichéd, is also true. The America of 1965 could scarcely imagine what the country would look like a mere ten years later and the cataclysmic changes the country would go through in that time (although the always prescient Bob Dylan did release "The Times They Are a-Changin'" in 1964.) The Decade almost perfectly spans the country's involvement in the Vietnam War. Of the 58,220 deaths of American combat troops in that conflict, all but about 400 of them occurred during the Decade. Perhaps because the Vietnam War likely had a more direct impact on the songwriters of the era than any other issue, it is not surprising that there was no shortage of anti-war protest songs. A few of many examples include "I-Feel-Like-I'm-Fixin'-To-Die Rag" by Country Joe and the Fish, "Eve of Destruction" by Barry McGuire, "Alice's Restaurant Massacree" by Arlo Guthrie, "Fortunate Son" by Creedence Clearwater Revival, "One Tin Soldier" by the Original Caste, "Give Peace a Chance" by John Lennon and "War" by Edwin Starr. For the most part however, other events of the Decade were not frequently represented in the music of the Decade. Rock songwriters tend not to be historians. There were, however, a few songs that really were about specific historical events.

Below are references to six well-known songs that reference events from the Decade. Three list the event and three list the artist. In each case, name the song title(s).

1. Event—Kent State shootings on May 4, 1970
2. Artists—Joni Mitchell and Melanie (Same event, two different songs)
3. Event—Assassinations of Martin Luther King and Robert Kennedy in 1968
4. Artist—Gordon Lightfoot (1975 event)
5. Event—"Bloody Sunday" in Northern Ireland on January 30, 1972 (three songs)
6. Artist—Deep Purple (one of their biggest hits)

1. "Ohio" written by Neil Young and performed by Crosby, Stills, Nash & Young. This was of course about the killing of four Kent State students by the Ohio National Guard on May 4, 1970. Students had been protesting the Cambodian Campaign, which President Nixon announced during a television address on April 30. Two of the four students killed were not even involved in the protest but were simply walking from one class to the next at the time of their deaths. The song was both written by Young and recorded by the group within 17 days of the shootings.

2. "Woodstock" by Joni Mitchell. This was written by Mitchell shortly after the August 1969 festival that she did not attend. Melanie Kakfa did perform at Woodstock and her hit song about her experience there, "Lay Down (Candles in the Rain)," was also written within a few months of the event.

3. "Abraham, Martin and John," written by Dick Holler and first performed by Dion is a tribute to four assassinated Americans, Abraham Lincoln, Martin Luther King, John Kennedy and Robert Kennedy. This was written by Holler only a few weeks after Robert Kennedy's assassination on June 5, 1968 and King's assassination was only two months prior to that. Laura Nyro's song "Save the Country" was also inspired by the same two 1968 assassinations and also urges listeners to "save the dream of the two young brothers.") Finally, the Rolling Stones' song "Sympathy for the Devil" was written (primarily by Mick Jagger) just before the Robert Kennedy assassination. After that occurred, the reference to killing Kennedy was changed to "the Kennedys."

4. "The Wreck of the Edmund Fitzgerald" by Gordon Lightfoot. The wreck occurred on November 10, 1975 and the song was recorded in Toronto the following month. A less well-known Lightfoot song also about an actual event was "Black Day in July" about a 1967 Detroit riot, known as the 12th Street Riot. That song appeared on Lightfoot's 1968 album *Did She Mention My Name?*
    On November 10th, 1975, the SS *Edmund Fitzgerald* sank in Canadian waters approximately 17 miles from the entrance to Whitefish Bay, at the mouth of Lake Superior. Although the *Fitzgerald* had reported being in difficulty earlier in the evening, no distress signals were sent before she sank. Her crew of 29 perished in the 535-foot-deep water, with no bodies ever recovered.
    There were a few instances of artistic license in the song. For example, although Lightfoot sings that the freighter was bound for Cleveland, she was in fact heading for Detroit to discharge her cargo of iron ore pellets. The Maritime Sailors Cathedral is actually the Mariners' Church of Detroit, which apparently is not "musty" as Lightfoot sang. On the 10th anniversary of the sinking, he went to the

church for the first time and told a parishioner: "I made a mistake referring to this as a musty old hall, but I had never been here before. There's nothing musty about this place. It's beautiful. From now on in concert, I'm going to sing rustic old hall instead." And now he does.

Another change in the way Lightfoot sings the song in live performances involves the cause of the wreck. Lightfoot wrote that at 7:00 p.m., the hatchway gave in, but he always felt guilty that this might have implied error by the crew. In 2010, a Canadian documentary concluded that there was little evidence that failure to secure the hatches caused the sinking. Upon learning this, Lightfoot changed the lyric to simply reference the fact that it became dark at 7:00, rather than making any reference to the hatchway. Lightfoot was happy to make the change: "The whole verse was really conjecture right from start to finish anyway. It's the only verse in the whole song where I gave myself complete poetic license." He can be seen performing the revised version on YouTube.[1]

5. "Give Ireland Back to the Irish" by Paul McCartney. This song was written in immediate response to Bloody Sunday, an incident that occurred in Northern Ireland on January 30, 1972. British soldiers shot 26 unarmed civilians during a protest march against internment. Fourteen people died. Many of the victims were shot while fleeing from the soldiers and some were shot while trying to help the wounded. In the same year, John Lennon and Yoko Ono released a song about the same incident, "Sunday Bloody Sunday." A more well-known song about both that incident and another incident in Northern Ireland in 1920—also called Bloody Sunday—is the U2 song of the same title, but which is a completely different song from Lennon's. Lennon also wrote a song in 1972 called "The Luck of the Irish," an ironic reference to how *unlucky* the Irish have been over the centuries, especially in relation to the English.

6. "Smoke on the Water" by Deep Purple. This song references a fire that occurred in 1971 at a casino complex in Switzerland when an audience member at a Frank Zappa concert fired a flare gun into the rattan-covered ceiling. The band watched the fire from their adjacent hotel, thus making this song an extremely rare instance of the songwriters actually being eyewitnesses to the (newsworthy) event in question. The song is credited to the whole band.

There were other songs written during the decade, sometimes referencing other events of the decade and sometimes referencing event that preceded the decade. Perhaps the most well-known song of the latter category is "American Pie" by Don McLean about the plane crash near Clear Lake, Iowa on February 3, 1959 that killed Ritchie Valens, Buddy Holly and

J.P. Richardson, better known as The Big Bopper. Other songs from the decade referencing actual events include the following:

1. Song title: "Sniper"
    Songwriter and performer: Harry Chapin
    Event: In the early morning hours of August 1, 1966, Charles Whitman murdered his wife and his mother in their homes. Later that day, he brought a number of guns to the campus of the University of Texas at Austin where, shooting down from the Main Building known as The Tower, he killed 14 people and wounded 32 others, firing at random from the 28th-floor observation deck. Justin Peters of Slate.com sharply criticized this "bizarre tribute" and "creepily sentimental" song, calling it "one of the most disturbing songs of the 1970s," because he thought that the song was far too sympathetic to Whitman and even makes him out to be a kind of hero. The song was the title track of Chapin's second album, *Sniper and Other Love Songs*, released in 1970.[2]

2. Song title: "Louisiana, 1927"
    Songwriter and performer: Randy Newman
    Event: The Great Mississippi River Flood of 1927, the most destructive river flood in the history of the United States. While Newman's 1974 song focuses on the flood's effect on Louisiana, it devastated many other States as well, especially Mississippi and Arkansas. Over 600,000 people were left homeless. Led Zeppelin released a song about the same event in 1971 called "When the Levee Breaks," but their song was a cover of a song written by Kansas Joe McCoy and Memphis Minnie in 1929, only two years after the flood.

3. Song title: "The Night They Drove Old Dixie Down"
    Songwriter: Robbie Robertson; Performer: The Band
    Event: For those who may be both rock fans (obviously anyone reading this book) *and* Civil War fans: What happened on May 10, 1865, the date referenced in the song? Some may immediately assume that it was the date of General Robert E. Lee's surrender to Ulysses Grant at Appomattox, but that would not be the case. That event occurred about a month earlier, on April 9. Rather, it is the date that Union troops captured Confederate President Jefferson Davis near Irwinville, Georgia. Davis's plan had been to escape by sea from Florida and to sail to Texas where he hoped to establish a new Confederacy.

CHAPTER 23

Talented Malcontents Joining Together (Supergroups)

Peeople may think of supergroups as, well, super groups, as in groups that are great together and/or had tremendous success. In fact, they are neither. Rather, a supergroup is simply a band formed by musicians who were either members of successful bands previously, or were stars in their own right. *Guitar World* defines a supergroup as follows: 1. There have to be at least three members. 2. They have to have released at least one album—no all-star jams. 3. A majority of their band members have to have been in well-known bands *before* the supergroup formed. 4. A supergroup cannot be formed by a well-known musician joining a pre-existing band—no Van Hagar.[1]

I would suggest that a supergroup is better defined as one where the members were leaders of their prior bands and thus famous in their own right (e.g. singers, songwriters named after, etc.) as opposed to those who were not. A good example of this from after the decade was The Traveling Wilburys, formed in 1988 and consisting of Bob Dylan, George Harrison, Jeff Lynne, Roy Orbison and Tom Petty even though Dylan and Orbison were previously solo acts.

As early as 1974, *Time* magazine was already wondering whether supergroups were on their way out, referring to them in the past tense: "A potent but short-lived rock phenomenon was the supergroup—an amalgam formed by the talented malcontents of other bands. While they lasted, [they] played enormous arenas and made megabucks, and sometimes megamusic. Their performances were fueled by dueling egos. Musical infighting built up the excitement they generated, but it also made breakups inevitable."[2] Perhaps for this reason, there are relatively few supergroups that last. So supergroups may not produce quality music and may not be successful either. Nevertheless, they always attract our interest, whether they are successful or whether they crash and burn.

Which band is generally considered to be the first (and many say greatest) supergroup?

Cream, consisting of guitarist Eric Clapton, bassist Jack Bruce and drummer Ginger Baker. Bruce and Baker had both been members of the Graham Bond Organisation. Bruce was also with John Mayall and the Bluesbreakers (as was Clapton) and Manfred Mann. Clapton was also of course a member of the Yardbirds. One of the reasons that the band broke up was because Baker and Bruce were constantly fighting, as had been the case when they were with the Graham Bond Organisation. They were known to sabotage each other's equipment and to fight onstage. In an interview about the formation of the band, Clapton said: "When Ginger invited me to join, I asked him who else was in the band. He said, 'I don't know yet.' So I suggested Jack. He said, "No, what did you have to go and mention him for?" I said, "Because I just played with him and he's a great bass player and you guys played together with Graham Bond and Alexis, so I thought you'd be pleased." And he said, "No, we don't get on very well at all." So I withdrew at that point. Then I said I would only go in with Ginger if he would go in with Jack. So he had to say OK."[3]

There were comparatively few supergroups during the Decade. Certainly Crosby, Stills & Nash was one, as was Crosby, Stills, Nash & Young. However, in addition to Cream, Clapton was a member of two other supergroups after Cream, both of which released only one album (albeit classic ones in both cases). Who were the groups? Both of them had four members. For extra credit, can you name at least two of the other members in each besides Clapton?

First was Blind Faith, consisting of Clapton, Baker, Steve Winwood, and Ric Grech. Winwood had been with the Spencer Davis Band and Traffic. Their only album was self-titled. Second was Derek and the Dominos, which also included Bobby Whitlock, Jim Gordon and Carl Radle. Their only album was *Layla and Other Assorted Love Songs*. Gordon cowrote "Layla" with Clapton. Whitlock was a keyboardist with Sam and Dave and Booker T and the MG's, Gordon was a very well-known session drummer and Radle played bass guitar with Delaney & Bonnie, an American musical duo composed of husband-and-wife singer/songwriters Delaney and Bonnie Bramlett.[4]

This early supergroup originally consisted of vocalist and guitarist Steve Marriott from Small Faces, vocalist and guitarist Peter Frampton from the Herd, former Spooky Tooth bassist Greg Ridley and seventeen-year-old drummer Jerry Shirley. Although they had no top 50 songs in the U.S., their initial single, "Natural Born Boogie," hit #4 in the U.K. What is the name of the band?

Humble Pie. Marriott died on April 20, 1991 at age 44 when a fire swept through his home in Essex, England. Many believe Marriott was jet-lagged after returning from a trip to America and fell asleep in bed with a lit cigarette. At the inquest, a verdict of accidental death by smoke inhalation was recorded. Marriott's blood was found to contain Valium, alcohol and cocaine.

This band is one of the rare supergroups who achieved more success as a supergroup than did any of its members or their prior or subsequent groups. They sold over 40 million albums worldwide.[5] Their first four studio albums, all released during the Decade, reached top 10 in the U.K and top 20 in the U.S. However, they were not a singles band, having no hits to speak of during the Decade, either in the U.S. or U.K. (although they did have a #2 song in the U.K in 1977). The keyboardist was previously with the Nice, the guitarist and bass guitarist (same person) was previously with the Gods and King Crimson and the drummer was with Atomic Rooster and the Crazy World of Arthur Brown. Although the band claimed to be one of the most successful live bands in the world in 1973 and 1974, it was widely disliked by music critics due to their bombastic style and their frequent incorporation of classical music into their own. Who was the band?

Emerson Lake and Palmer, or ELP for short. Their best-known song is "Lucky Man," which appeared on their self-titled debut album in 1970. As for their apparent sense of self-importance, one critic recalled a joke from the 1970s: "How do you spell pretentious? E-L-P."[6] Robert Christgau said of the band, "these guys are as stupid as their most pretentious fans" and called ELP the "world's most overweening 'progressive' group."[7]

The band acknowledged and even seemed to embrace the criticism: Carl Palmer said "Rock critics and rock musicians think of Emerson, Lake & Palmer as pompous and pretentious. Which we are!" In the liner notes for the DVD version of their 1973 album, *Brain Salad Surgery*, Jerry McCulley wrote, "If you're looking for safe, critic-approved, politically correct pop music enlightenment, boy did you get the wrong catalog number. Emerson, Lake & Palmer—ELP to you—were perennial contenders for Most Critically Reviled Rock Band on the Planet. But in 1973 and '74, only the Rolling Stones, the Who, and Led Zeppelin were bigger concert draws—and none of them were playing Copland, Mussorgsky, Ginastera, or Brubeck. Or anything remotely resembling ELP's own complex, manic—and yes—bombastic, largely Hammond- and Moog-driven compositions, for that matter."[8] A 2007 review of a retrospective album released by the group echoed its own self-assessment as "the world's most reviled proggers [progressive band]."[9]

Emerson and Lake both died in 2016, Emerson by apparent suicide and Lake from cancer.

Of the first five albums released by this supergroup (two in the Decade and four after), four of them hit the top 10 in both the U.S. and the U.K. Their self-titled debut

album, released in 1974, hit #1 in the U.S. They were formed in London in 1973 by two former Free band members—singer Paul Rodgers and drummer Simon Kirke—as well as Mott the Hoople guitarist Mick Ralphs and King Crimson bassist Boz Burrell. What is the name of the band?

Bad Company.

CHAPTER 24

I'm Not Just a Pop Star! (Crossover Songs)

Reaching the top of the pop and country charts with one song is not an easy feat. Since 1961, it has happened only 17 times and only once since 1999. Ten of those 17 times were during the Decade. Oddly, six of those times were in one year, 1975, when it seemingly was easy as could be, and there were four other instances in the rest of the Decade. While any crossover hit would obviously have to appeal to both pop and country audiences, the majority of crossover hits started out as country songs and then bled over onto the *Billboard* Hot 100. Rarely does the chart success go in the opposite direction. Incidentally, the country equivalent of the Hot 100 is the *Billboard* Hot Country Singles chart.

Only one artist songs that topped both charts twice in the Decade, both times in 1975. In each instance, the song was #1 for one week only. Who was he and what were the songs? (As a hint, one of the songs was the live version of a song.)

The artist is John Denver. The first song (where the live version hit #1) was "Thank God I'm a County Boy" and the second song is "I'm Sorry."

Another song to top both charts in 1975 holds the honor of being the longest song title (including the parenthetical) to top the *Billboard* Hot 100 during the Decade. What was the song?

"(Hey Won't You Play) Another Somebody Done Somebody Wrong Song" by B.J. Thomas, which topped both charts for 1 week.

Another 1975 dual chart-topper had the first verse sung in English and then that verse repeated in Spanish. What was the song?

"Before the Next Teardrop Falls" by Freddie Fender.

The other dual #1 songs from 1975 are "Rhinestone Cowboy" by Glen Campbell and "Convoy" by C.W. McCall (which was released in 1975 and topped the country chart in 1975 but did not top the *Billboard* Hot 100 until January 1976). The other three songs from the Decade not released in 1975 were "Honey" by Bobby Goldsboro (1968), "The Most Beautiful Girl" by Charlie Rich (1973) and "I Can Help" by Billy Swan (1974).

Only one song in this category released during the Decade was recorded by a woman (though written by a man), and it happened in September 1968. The song was later turned into a television series in 1981 and 1982. What is the song?

"Harper Valley PTA" recorded by Jeannie C. Riley and written by Tom T. Hall.

As we saw, there were no songs in the Decade which topped both the pop and country charts which were not recorded by solo artists. In fact, since 1960, the only "group" which released a song which hit #1 on both the pop and country charts is Lonestar. Their song "Amazed" turned the trick in 1999 (country) and 2000 (pop). Aside from that, every such song from 1960 to the present has been by a solo artist, except for "Islands in the Stream," the 1983 duet by Kenny Rogers and Dolly Parton.

Let's consider some other country/pop crossover hits that may not have hit #1 on both charts, but are well-remembered classics anyway.

Released in 1968, this song was #1 on the country chart and #19 on the *Billboard* Hot 100. It was cowritten by the female singer and by her producer Billy Sherrill. The song was controversial. Commenting on it, she said: "The song took me 20 minutes to write and 20 years to defend." The song was selected by the Library of Congress as a 2010 addition to the National Recording Registry, which selects recordings annually that are "culturally, historically, or aesthetically significant." What is the song and who is the artist?

"Stand by Your Man." At first, Wynette didn't like the melody and hated having to hit the high note in the song. However, once it became a hit, she always defended it. The song was in the news in 1992 when soon-to-be First Lady Hillary Clinton told CBS's *60 Minutes* during the Gennifer Flowers interview that she "wasn't some little woman 'standing by my man' like Tammy Wynette." The condemnation from the public was immediate, even coming from Wynette herself. Ironically, Wynette, while recording the song, was preparing to divorce her second husband, Lloyd Amburgey, for her third, George Jones. In all, she was married five times, and left each of her first four husbands.[1]

This song was written and first recorded by Joe South. Several other male vocalists then covered it, including Freddy Weller and Dobie Gray. A certain female country singer wanted to record this song but her husband and producer thought it was inappropriate

for her because he thought the song was designed to be sung by a man to a woman. Given that it was written and first recorded by man who sings in the first person (including a reference to purchasing diamond rings for his woman), her husband probably was right. Nevertheless, the October 1970 release topped the U.S. *Billboard* country chart for five weeks and reached #3 on the U.S. *Billboard* Hot 100 pop chart. It remains one of the most successful country crossover recordings of all time. What was the song?

"I Never Promised You a Rose Garden," performed by Lynn Anderson.[2]

Between 1973 and 1975, this female artist had an impressive streak of five consecutive singles which hit the top 10 on both the pop and country charts and of those ten rankings (five for each), seven of them were top five (including two #1s on the *Billboard* Hot 100). She is one of the best-selling artists of all time. Who is it?

Olivia Newtown-John. The five songs were "Let Me Be There" (#6 pop, #7 country), "If You Love Me (Let Me Know)" (#5 and #2), "I Honestly Love You"(#1 and #6), "Have You Never Been Mellow" (#1 and #3) and "Please Mr. Please"(#3 and #5).

This song was unusual in that it was a #1 hit for Ray Price on the country chart in 1973, #1 for Gladys Knight and the Pips on the soul single chart and #3 for the same group on the *Billboard* Hot 100 in 1974. It was written by Jim Weatherly, who commented about the song: "I thought it was really strange that nobody'd written a song with that title—possibly somebody had, but I'd never heard it—so I just sat down and let this stream of consciousness happen. I basically wrote it in a very short period of time, probably 30 minutes or an hour." What is the song?

"You're the Best Thing That Ever Happened to Me." Notwithstanding Weatherly's love of the title, Gladys Knight changed it—slightly. Their cover of the song was called "Best Thing That Ever Happened to Me."[3]

Although many Eagles songs had a country feel, there was only one single that reached the top 10 on both the pop chart and country chart. What song was it?

"Lyin' Eyes," which reached #2 on the *Billboard* Hot 100 and #8 on the country chart in 1975.

CHAPTER 25

Wash Your Mouth with Soap! (Censorship and Swear Words)

Musicians and censors have been at war since the dawn of rock and roll. For example, Elvis Presley's first two appearances on *The Ed Sullivan Show* in 1956—which included his swinging hips and bodily gyrations on full display—caused a massive outrage among certain segments of the populace and it was therefore agreed that for his third live appearance on January 6, 1957, all of the TV images would be kept above the belt, thus shielding the public from the sight of his wiggling hips.

During the Decade, there were also frequent performances of songs by bands on live television. As was the case a decade earlier, the show hosts and censors of the time often remained very sensitive about any songs whose lyrics which may be too suggestive of sex or drugs (and there was no shortage of them in the latter half of the 1960s). By present day standards, the notion of what was considered "obscene" or would not pass muster with television censors during the Decade seems almost comical. In any event, sometimes the performers gave in to the demands and sometimes they did not.

This chapter will look at a few of the famous instances where musicians and censors butted heads as well as the occasional use of swear words in songs during the Decade.

CENSORSHIP

On January 15, 1967, the Rolling Stones performed a set on the *Ed Sullivan Show* that included new tracks from their soon-to-be-released album, *Between the Buttons*. One of the songs that they intended to perform was "Let's Spend the Night Together." However, CBS and Sullivan demanded that they change the title lyric (contained repeatedly in the song itself) when they performed the song live because it was thought to be too overtly sexual. When the band balked, Ed issued an ultimatum, "Either the song goes or you go." The band was repeatedly reminded about the line change during dress rehearsal.

On September 17, 1967, the Doors were to play two songs on the Sullivan show, one of which was "Light My Fire." Shortly before their performance, a producer came into their dressing room and told them they needed to change a line in the song. According to the Ed Sullivan website, "though Jim Morrison was furious and adamant about not changing the song, the group relented and told the executive they would alter the lyrics as requested." Their performance (which followed a comedian they did not know named Rodney Dangerfield) was against a backdrop composed of an assortment of actual doors. After playing "People Are Strange," they played "Light My Fire," which was the last performance of the evening.

a. **Which band gave in to the demand that the lyrics be changed and which did not?**
b. **In the case of the band that did give in, what lyric were they forced to sing instead?**
c. **In the case of the band that didn't give in, what line was meant to be changed and what were they supposed to sing instead?**

Answers: The Stones gave in and the Doors did not. While performing their song, Mick did as he was told, which was to sing "Let's Spend Some Time Together" but rolled his eyes and sarcastically exaggerated the altered line. As for the Doors, instead of singing about getting higher (perceived as an obvious reference to drug use), the band was instructed to sing "girl we couldn't get much better." When it came time for the line, Morrison sang it exactly as written. As per the Ed Sullivan website:

> As he finished the now infamous lyric, the camera caught guitarist Robby Krieger with a quick but telling smirk. But Sullivan's producer and CBS executives were not smiling. Following the Doors' performance, the ever gracious yet stoic Sullivan can be seen clapping his hands and mouthing the words, "That was wonderful. Just great!" But instead of shaking hands with the group, he went straight to a commercial for Purina Dog Chow. Backstage, the show's producer was furious and told the band, "Mr. Sullivan wanted you for six more shows, but you'll never work with *The Ed Sullivan Show* again." Morrison, seemingly unperturbed, replied, "Hey man. We just *did* the Sullivan Show."

They never appeared again. Both performances on the Sullivan show can be seen on YouTube.[1]

The British Broadcasting Corporation (BBC) has a special history of censoring rock songs for all kind of reasons, especially by the Beatles for some reason. The songs include "Cover of *Rolling Stone*" by Dr. Hook and the Medicine Show (for product placement), "Eve of Destruction" by Barry McGuire (controversial subject matter), "Give Ireland Back to the Irish" by Paul and Linda McCartney (controversial subject matter), "Hi Hi, Hi," also by Paul and Linda McCartney (supposed drug reference). **Following is a list of songs banned at one** time or another by the BBC as well as the reason. Identify the offending phrase from the song.

"Come Together" by the Beatles (product placement)

Coca-Cola.

"I Am the Walrus" by the Beatles (sexual reference)

The phrases "pornographic priestess" and "let your knickers down" were deemed inappropriate and the record was banned by the BBC.

"A Day in the Life"(drug reference)

Turning on.[2]

"Lucy in the Sky with Diamonds" (no hint)

This one is probably about as easy as they come. It was first believed that the John Lennon-penned song was a reference to LSD because of the first letters of "Lucy" and "sky" and "diamonds." However, Lennon explained (on the Dick Cavett show and elsewhere) that his son Julian had drawn a picture that *he* called *Lucy in the Sky with Diamonds* and that Lennon had never even realized the LSD connection until after *Sgt. Pepper's* had already been released. He said: "After that, I was checking all the songs to see what the letters spelled out. They didn't spell out anything."[3] Julian's classmate, Lucy O'Donnell (later Lucy Vodden) died of lupus in 2009 at age 46.

"Lola" by the Kinks (product placement)

It wasn't the fact that this song was about a drag queen that offended the BBC. Rather, it was product placement, namely Coca-Cola. Ray Davies was forced to change the reference to "cherry cola" to avert the ban.[4]

SWEAR WORDS

Swear words in rock music were rather uncommon during the Decade. After all, rap music was still many decades away (although swear words gradually became more common in rock music after the Decade anyway). Also, with the advent of satellite radio, there were fewer FCC concerns. Swear words were used during the Decade however, even though such comparatively tame words such as "damn" and "bitch," were sometimes controversial enough to be censored.

According to Wikipedia, this song is the first #1 song ever to use the word "damn." It won the Academy Award for Best Song. More famously, it is remembered for its unusual use of self-censorship: The singer was about to say "motherfucker," but his background singers cut him off after "mother" ("shut your mouth!"). Who is the singer-songwriter and what is the song?

The song is "Theme from *Shaft*" and the singer-songwriter is Isaac Hayes. The song came out in 1971. Hayes told NPR that wanted to play Shaft himself, the private detective chick magnet. He was promsied by director Gordon Parks that he could audition for the lead role so long as he wrote the music for the film. However, even though he was never given the chance to audition, he kept his end of the bargain anyway. The backup singer who shuts Hayes down with the signature line "shut your mouth!" is Tony Orlando and Dawn's Telma Hopkins. (Since Hopkins also sang on "Knock Three Times," which came out a few months earlier, one writer commented that she "featured prominently on the most white-bread hit of the year as well as one that was, ostensibly at least, the sound of the street.") Hayes was the first African-American composer to win an Academy Award and in fact the first African-American winner for any award other than in the acting categories.[5]

This Pink Floyd song has the word "bullshit" loud and clear. It charted at #13, is frequently heard on oldies stations and appears on *Dark Side of the Moon*.

"Money."

As we saw above, Isaac Hayes censored himself in the "Theme from *Shaft*," so that he merely implied motherfucker without actually saying it. However, Jefferson Airplane had no such reservation, not only on the recorded version of the song, but also on live TV no less. According to Songfacts, "the uncensored performance of this song for *The Dick Cavett Show* episode broadcast on August 19, 1969 marked the first time that the f-word [and for that matter, the m-f word as well] was ever said/sung on television." (The performance of the song can be seen on YouTube.) The song was We Can Be Together by Jefferson Airplane. **What was the line that uses the motherfucker word? As a hint, songwriter Paul Kantner was inspired by a line often used by The Black Panther Party at the time.**

Up against the wall motherfucker.[6]

A song by an ex-Beatle contains the working "fucking" (twice). As a hint, to no surprise, it's not by Paul, George or Ringo. What is the song?

"Working Class Hero" by John Lennon. It includes the phrases "fucking crazy" and "fucking peasants." West Virginia Congressman Harley Staggers, driving in his car, heard the song uncensored on WGTB. He sent an angry letter to the FCC, demanding action. General Manager Ken Sleeman, under threat of a $10,000 fine and a year in prison, replied: "The people of Washington are sophisticated enough to accept the occasional four-letter word in context and not become sexually aroused, offended, or upset." No charges were filed.[7]

Joni Mitchell is of course an artist whose stature and influence cannot be measured by chart performance. Therefore, to answer specific questions about her work, generally requires knowledge of more than just her "hits." Perhaps surprisingly to some, she uses the work "fuck" in a song. What song? The song originally appeared on *For the Roses* and she also performs it live on *Miles of Aisles*. Name the song.

"Woman of Heart and Mind."

Which part from the Johnny Cash song "A Boy Named Sue" was censored in the radio version when it first came out?

The words "son of a bitch" referring to his dad who named him Sue.[8]

When censorship occurs, it is usually words that are censored and not visual images. However, in 1968, John Lennon and Yoko Ono released an album on which the front cover showed them completely frontally nude while the rear cover showed them nude from behind. Not surprisingly, the album was sold in a plain brown bag where all that could be seen were their face and the album title. For half credit, what is the second half of the title? For full credit, what is the whole title?

The full title is "Unfinished Music #1: Two Virgins."[9]

CHAPTER 26

Hear Me but Don't See Me (Studio Musicians—and Singers)

This chapter looks primarily at the unsung (no pun intended) heroes of the music industry, namely the fabulous studio musicians who actually played the instruments on a huge number of hit songs and albums during the Decade. In many cases, these musicians formed loosely affiliated "groups." While the names of many of these groups—and certainly their individual members—may be unknown to the general public, the number of recordings on which they have performed is astonishing.

Who was the Wrecking Crew?

The Wrecking Crew was a nickname coined by drummer Hal Blaine for a very talented group of studio musicians that played anonymously (i.e. not generally credited on the songs and albums on which they played) on many records before, during and (to a lesser extent) after the Decade. The name derived from the impression that he and the younger studio musicians made on the business's older generation, who felt that they were going to wreck the music industry.

The Crew backed dozens of popular singers. There are a number of ways to contribute to a song. One can write it, sing it, produce it, arrange it, engineer it, or play an instrument on it. If each of those means of contribution are to be weighted equally, then the Wrecking Crew is by far the most successful "group" in music history. No one else even comes close. As their biographer noted, "if a rock-and-roll song came out of an LA recording studio between 1962 and 1972, the odds are good that some combination of the Wrecking Crew played the instruments."

While there were about 40 musicians who were considered members of the Wrecking Crew at one time or another, the core group was 10–15 musicians and some of the most prolific members included Larry Knechtel on keyboards (he played the opening solo on "Bridge Over Troubled Water" for which he earned a Grammy award, amazingly the only Wrecking Crew member to win one), Joe Osborne on bass, Carol Kaye on guitar and bass,

Glen Campbell on guitar, and Hal Blaine on drums. Blaine alone played on over 50 #1 hits and over 150 top 10 hits.

A tiny sampling of the songs on which the instruments heard are mostly theirs include most songs or most hits by: the Fifth Dimension (including "Let the Sunshine In/Aquarius," "Stoned Soul Picnic"), the Association (including "Windy" and "Never My Love"), the Beach Boys (including "California Girls," "Fun, Fun, Fun," "Good Vibrations," "I Get Around,") the Byrds (including "Mr. Tambourine Man"), Glen Campbell (who was a Wrecking Crew member himself), the Captain and Tenille ("Love Will Keep Us Together"), the Carpenters ("Close to You"), Cher ("Gypsies, Tramps and Thieves," "Half-Breed"), Sam Cooke ("Twistin' the Night Away"), the Crystals ("Da Doo Ron Ron" and "He's a Rebel"), Jan & Dean ("Dead Man's Curve," "Surf City," and "Little Old Lady (From Pasadena),") Gary Lewis and the Playboys ("This Diamond Ring"), Barry McGuire ("Eve of Destruction"), the Mamas and the Papas ("California Dreamin'," "Dedicated to the One I Love," and "Monday Monday"), Henry Mancini ("The Pink Panther Theme"), Scott McKenzie ("San Francisco (Be Sure to Wear Flowers in Your Hair)"), Harry Nilsson ("Everybody's Talkin'"), the Monkees (most of their songs), the Partridge Family ("Come On Get Happy"),—Paul Revere and the Raiders ("Indian Reservation"), the Righteous Brothers ("Unchained Melody" and "You've Lost That Lovin' Feelin'"), Simon and Garfunkel (most of their songs), Nancy Sinatra ("These Boots are Made for Walkin'"), Sonny and Cher ("I Got You Babe" and "The Beat Goes On"), Herb Alpert and the Tijuana Brass (they essentially were the Tijuana Brass), Ike and Tina Turner ("River Deep-Mountain High"), the Ventures ("Hawaii 5-0"), and Mason Williams ("Classical Gas").

And that is just a *tiny sampling* of their work. Of course, with certain acts such as Simon and Garfunkel, since they were only two people, one of whom did not play an instrument, or the Mamas and the Papas, who also had only one instrument-playing member (John Phillips), there is nothing surprising about the fact that session musicians would be employed to assist in the recording of most of their songs. However, in other instances, it is more surprising since there was an actual band whose members played instruments, including when they performed live. For example, on most Beach Boys recordings, the band only sang vocals and often the only member present in the studio during the recording sessions was Brian Wilson. On a number of Byrds songs, including the classic Bob Dylan-penned "Mr. Tambourine Man," the only Byrd to play on the recording is Roger McGuinn. On the Turtles' hit "Happy Together," it was again the Wrecking Crew playing the instruments.

Hal Blaine played drums on six consecutive Grammy Record of the Year winners: Herb Alpert & the Tijuana Brass in 1966 for "A Taste of Honey"; Frank Sinatra in 1967 for "Strangers in the Night"; The 5th Dimension in 1968 for "Up, Up and Away"; Simon and Garfunkel in 1969 for "Mrs. Robinson"; The 5th Dimension in 1970 for "Aquarius/Let the Sunshine In"; and Simon & Garfunkel in 1971 for "Bridge Over Troubled Water."

This woman was the only female member of the Wrecking Crew and was one of the most prolific and widely heard bass guitarists in history, playing on an estimated 10,000 recording sessions in a 55-year career. Her electric bass credits include "Homeward Bound" and "Scarborough Fair/Canticle" (Simon and Garfunkel), "California Girls," "Sloop John B" and "Help Me Rhonda" (The Beach Boys), "Going Out Of My Head" (The Lettermen), "I'm a Believer" (The Monkees), "Indian Reservation" (Paul Revere & the Raiders), "Little Green Apples" (O.C. Smith), "Midnight Confessions" (The Grass Roots), "Wichita Lineman," "Galveston," "Rhinestone Cowboy" (Glen Campbell), "Somethin' Stupid" (Frank and Nancy Sinatra), "These Boots Are Made for Walkin'" (Nancy Sinatra), "This Diamond Ring" (Gary Lewis and the Playboys), "The Way We Were" (Barbra Streisand) and "Soul and Inspiration" (the Righteous Brothers).

She went on to write a series of successful books about how to play the bass. Who is she?

Carol Kaye. She also played guitar, and her many guitar credits include "Then He Kissed Me" (the Crystals), "Danke Schoen" (Wayne Newton), "Johnny Angel" (Shelley Fabares), "La Bamba" (Ritchie Valenz), "The Beat Goes On" (Sonny and Cher), and "You Lost That Lovin' Feelin'" (the Righteous Brothers).

This member of the Wrecking Crew:

- was a member of Derek and the Dominos
- cowrote "Layla" along with Eric Clapton for which he won a Grammy Award
- played drums on dozens (if not hundreds) of hit singles including "Rikki Don't Lose That Number" by Steely Dan, "Wichita Lineman" by Glen Campbell, "Sundown" by Gordon Lightfoot, "A Kind of Hush" by the Carpenters, "All Things Must Pass," by George Harrison, "Classical Gas" by Mason Williams and "It Never Rains in Southern California" by Albert Hammond.
- played drums on dozens (if not hundreds) of successful albums including *Diamonds and Rust* by Joan Baez, *Pet Sounds* by the Beach Boys, *The Pretender* by Jackson Browne, *Mad Dogs and Englishmen* by Joe Cocker, *Beautiful Noise* by Neil Diamond, *Bigger Than Both of Us* by Hall and Oates, *Imagine* by John Lennon, *Nilsson Schmilsson* by Harry Nilsson and *No Secrets* by Carly Simon.
- has been in prison since 1984 serving a sentence of 16 years to life for the murder of his mother.

Who is he?

Answer: Jim Gordon. Although primarily a drummer, Gordon wrote and played the piano parts on "Layla" and also played drums on the track. As a teenager, he began to hear voices in his head. Through most of the 70s, he was able to keep the problem under control. By the late 1970s however, perhaps compounded by years of heroin and cocaine addiction, the voices began to get louder and take control of him. He developed full-blown schizophrenia and, in a manner reminiscent of the mathematician John Nash, whose struggles with paranoid schizophrenia were described in the book and movie *A Beautiful Mind*, the voices became louder. He went to the local psychiatric hospital more than a dozen times, but to little effect.

One of the voices he heard was that of his 72-year-old mother, Osa. In 1983, he attacked her in her apartment with a hammer and fatally stabbed her. In his crazed mind, he believed that it was a matter of self-defense. Although at the trial the court accepted that Gordon had acute schizophrenia, he was not allowed to use an insanity defense because of changes to California law due to the Insanity Defense Perform Act. On July 10, 1984 he was sentenced to 16 years to life in prison. As of 2017, he was still serving his sentence at the California Medical Facility, a medical and psychiatric prison in Vacaville, California. He was most recently denied parole in 2015 and is next eligible in 2018.[1]

While the Wrecking Crew members were primarily session musicians, there certainly were exceptions, in addition to Glen Campbell, keyboardist Mac Rebennack—better known as Dr. John—had a long career as a performer after his Wrecking Crew days, including two hit songs ("Right Place, Wrong Time" and "Such a Night") and was a 2011 Hall of Fame inductee. Finally, fellow keyboardist Leon Russell also had a long career as a performer after his Wrecking Crew days, cowriting three top five songs (though for others, namely "Everybody Loves a Clown" and "She's Just My Style" for Gary Lewis and the Playboys and, perhaps most famously, "Superstar," a #2 hit for the Carpenters). He was was also a 2011 Hall of Fame inductee. Russell died in 2016 at age 74 after suffering a heart attack.[2]

Who Were the Funk Brothers?

This group of musicians was essentially the Motown equivalent of the Wrecking Crew, at least while Motown was based in Detroit from 1959–1972. The Funk Brothers played on Motown hits such as "My Girl," "I Heard It Through the Grapevine," "Baby Love," "Signed, Sealed, Delivered I'm Yours," "Papa Was a Rollin' Stone," "The Tears of a Clown," "Ain't No Mountain High Enough," "(Love Is Like a) Heat Wave," "Please Mr. Postman" as well as most songs by the Motown stable of stars including the Supremes, the Temptations, the Four Tops, Stevie Wonder, the Miracles, Marvin Gaye, Martha and the Vandellas, and the Isley Brothers.

The role of the Funk Brothers is described in Paul Justman's 2002 documentary film, *Standing in the Shadows of Motown*, based on Allan Stutsky's book of the same name. The opening titles claim that the Funk Brothers have "played on more #1 hits than the Beatles, Elvis Presley, the Rolling Stones and the Beach Boys combined." However, that claim only holds up if one includes members of the Wrecking Crew who were also considered occasional members of the Funk Brothers after Motown relocated to Los Angeles in 1972.

Although the name "The Funk Brothers" was a loosely-applied designation, the National Academy of Recording Arts and Sciences recognized 13 official Funk Brothers, as follows: Keyboards: Joe Hunter (1959–1964), Earl Van Dyke (1964–1972), and Johnny Griffith (1963–1972). Guitarists: Robert White (1959–1972), Eddie "Chank" Willis (1959–1972), and Joe Messina (1959–1972). Bass: James Jamerson (1959–1972) and Bob Babbitt (1967–1972). Drums: William "Denny" Benjamin (1959–1969), Richard "Pistol" Alan (1959–1972) and Uriel Jones (1963–1972). Percussion: Jack Ashford (1959–1972) and Eddie "Bongo" Brown (1959–1972).

Who is MFSB, what does it stand for, what label is it most closely associated with, and what songwriters is it most closely associated with?

MFSB was a pool of the studio musicians who supplied the music for many songs by Kenny Gamble and Leon Huff for Philadelphia International Records in the 1970s. As for their name, the "clean" version means "Mother, Father, Sister, Brother," because they were connected musically, while the "other" version was "Mother-Fucking Sons of Bitches," referring to their musical prowess. They played for groups such as Harold Melvin and the Blue Notes, the O'Jays, the Stylistics, the Spinners, Wilson Pickett and Billy Paul. They also released songs under their own name, with their biggest hit unquestionably being "TSOP (The Sound of Philadelphia)," a primarily instrumental piece (with a few vocals by the Three Degrees), that reached #1 on both the *Billboard* Hot 100 and the R&B chart in 1974.[3]

According to the seventiesmusic website, this man is credited with providing the lead vocals for on hit singles for more groups than any other recording artist in history. Yet, he is relatively unknown. How did that happen? While session musicians are of course common, this British man was something much more unusual—a session lead singer. As stated on the seventiesmusic website: "The bubble gum bands tended to be manufactured bands. First a song was written. It was recorded by session musicians and, if it was a hit, a band would be formed to travel around and perform it." This man was repeatedly chosen to

be the lead singer for several of these "manufactured bands." Although these bands would sometimes stay together to record and tour afterwards (often in very different form from the lineup that had the hit), this man left each band after each hit.

In 1970 alone, this session singer sang lead vocal on "Love Grows (Where My Rosemary Goes)" by Edison Lighthouse, which reached #5 in the U.S. in 1970 and #1 in the U.K., he sang lead vocal on "My Baby Loves Lovin'" for another studio group, White Plains, that reached #13, he sang lead vocal on "United We Stand" by Brotherhood of Man, a #13 song in the U.S., and he sang on the popular novelty song "Gimme Dat Ding" by another studio band, the Pipkins (in which the singer sounds a lot like Wolfman Jack). As if all that were not enough, he sang lead vocal on "Beach Baby" in 1974 by yet another studio creation, First Class, which climbed to #4 that year. Therefore, he was a one-hit wonder five times over! Who is this man?

Tony Burrows. "Love Grows (Where My Rosemary Goes)" was written by Tony Macaulay and Barry Mason. When the song became a hit, a group needed to be assembled rapidly to feature the song on the television show *Top of the Pops*. Mason and Macaulay established a group called Greenfields and brought them to the auditions a week before their appearance on *Top of the Pops*. Once chosen and rehearsed, they appeared on the show as "Edison Lighthouse." Thus, prior to that appearance, there was no Edison Lighthouse. The other groups similarly did not exist before the above songs had been written and a group had to be put together to record them.

It has been written that three of the above songs were released so closely together in early 1970 that Burrows performed them with each different "band" on the same *Top of the Pops* show. While this is not accurate, he did appear as a member of Edison Lighthouse and Brotherhood of Man on both the January 29, 1970 and February 19, 1970 shows and as a member of Edison Lighthouse and White Plains on the February 12, 1970 and February 26, 1970 shows. A YouTube clip analyzes his career as a repeat one-hit wonder.[4]

Some or all of this group of Southern session musicians played on a number of top 10 songs, including "When a Man Loves a Woman" (#1 for Percy Sledge in 1966), "Mustang Sally" (#9 for Wilson Pickett in 1966), "Respect" (#1 for Aretha Franklin in 1967), "I Never Loved a Man (The Way I Love You)" (#9 for Aretha Franklin in 1967), "Take a Letter, Maria" (#2 for R.B Greaves in 1969), "I'll Take You There" (#1 for the Staples Singers in 1971) and "Kodachrome" (#2 for Paul Simon in 1973), "Still Crazy After All These Years" and "Take Me to the Mardi Gras," also both by Simon. Although many of the singers with whom they performed were soul or R&B stars (such as everyone on the above list other than Simon), the four main members were all white. What is the name of this group of session musicians? (As a hint, they also went by the name of The Swampers and are name-checked as such in the Lynryd Skynryd mega-hit "Sweet Home Alabama.")

The Muscle Shoals Rhythm Section. The four founding members were Barry Beckett (keyboards), Roger Hawkins (drums), David Hood (bass), and Jimmy Johnson (guitar). They worked with numerous other artists including Bob Seger ("Main Street," "We've Got Tonight," "Old Time Rock and Roll"), Willie Nelson ("Bloody Mary Morning"), Luther Ingram ("If Loving You is Wrong, I Don't Want to Be Right"), Mary MacGregor ("Torn Between Two Lovers"), Rod Stewart ("Sailing"), Leon Russell ("Tightrope"), Joe Cocker ("High Time We Went"), Dr. Hook ("Sharing the Night Together"), Jimmy Cliff ("Sitting in Limbo," featured in the film *The Harder They Come*), Sanford-Townsend Band ("Smoke From a Distant Fire") and Tony Joe White ("The Train I'm On").[5]

American Sound Studio was a recording studio located at 827 Thomas Street in Memphis, Tennessee headed by Chips Moman. It was an unassuming windowless one-story building. Unlike its more well-known Memphis counterparts, such as Sun, Stax and Hi, this one is obscure today. The studio was not in operation for very long, lasting only from 1967 to 1972. Unlike Stax, Moman's studio wasn't connected to a record label; anyone was free to use it. Despite its short life, an impressive list of hit songs was recorded there, most of which were played by American's house band, composed of drummer Gene Chrisman, bassists Tommy Cogbill and Mike Leech, guitarist Reggie Young and keyboardists Bobby Emmons and Bobby Wood.

According to some sources, nearly 120 *Billboard* Hot 100 songs were recorded at American Sounds Studios. What was the name of the studio band?

The Memphis Boys, sometimes also known as the Memphis Cats or the 827 Thomas Street Band. In 2011, Roben Jones wrote a book called *Memphis Boys: The Story of American Studios* and in 2012, NPR's *Fresh Air* ran a piece called *The Forgotten Story of American Studios*.[6]

The Academy Award for Best Documentary Feature of 2013 went to a film called *20 Feet from Stardom*. It focuses on the lives of female backup singers, who had contributed to hundreds of rock and roll songs, but whose identities (like those of the Wrecking Crew and the Funk Brothers) are largely unknown to the public. Sometimes what they added to the songs was subtle and sometimes obvious. One of those singers portrayed was Merry Clayton. What song is she most closely associated with, at least as a backup singer? (As a hint, it's a Rolling Stones song.)

"Gimme Shelter." She's the one singing about rape and murder being just a shot away. In an interview with Terry Gross on NPR's *Fresh Air*, she explained how the gig came about. "Well, I'm at home at about 12—I'd say about 11:30, almost 12 o'clock at night. And I'm hunkered down in my bed with my husband, very pregnant, and we got a call from a dear friend of mine and producer named Jack Nitzsche. Jack Nitzsche called and said you know, 'Merry, are you busy?' I said 'No, I'm in bed.' He says, 'Well, you know, there are some guys in town from England. And they need someone to come and sing a duet with them, but I can't get anybody to do it. Could you come?' He said 'I really think this would be something good for you.'"

At that point, Clayton recalled, her husband took the phone out of her hand and said to Nitzsche, "Man, what is going on? This time of night you're calling Merry to do a session? You know she's pregnant." Nitzsche explained the situation, and just as Clayton was drifting back to sleep her husband nudged her and said, "Honey, you know, you really should go and do this date." Clayton said that she had no idea who the Rolling Stones were.

Clayton arrived at the studio in pajamas, a fur coat and curlers in her hair. Keith Richards was there and explained what he wanted her to do.

> I said, 'Well, play the track. It's late. I'd love to get back home.' So they play the track and tell me that I'm going to sing—this is what you're going to sing: 'Oh, children, it's just a shot away.' They had the lyrics for me. I said, 'Well, that's cool.' So I did the first part . . . and we got down to the rape, murder part. And I said, 'Why am I singing rape, murder?' . . . So they told me the gist of what the lyrics were, and I said 'Oh, okay, that's cool.' So then I had to sit on a stool because I was a little heavy in my belly. I mean, it was a sight to behold. And we got through it. And then we went in the booth to listen, and I saw them hooting and hollering while I was singing, but I didn't know what they were hooting and hollering about. And when I got back in the booth and listened, I said, 'Ooh, that's really nice.' They said, 'Well, you want to do another?' I said, 'Well, I'll do one more,' I said, 'and then I'm going to have to say thank you and good night.' I did one more, and then I did one more. So it was three times I did it, and then I was gone. The next thing I know, that's history.

Clayton sang with such emotional force that her voice cracked on the third time she sang "Rape! Murder! It's just a shot away," at which point, Jagger can be heard shouting "Woo!" in the background in amazement at her vocal. ("I was just grateful that the crack was in tune," she told Gross.) In the isolated vocal track which can be heard on the documentary (and can be seen on You Tube), both the voice crack and Jagger's "Woo!" can be heard much more clearly. Despite giving what would become the most famous performance of her career, it turned out to be a tragic night for Clayton. Shortly after leaving the studio, she lost her baby in a miscarriage. It has frequently been written that the stress from the emotional intensity of her performance caused the miscarriage.

Clayton also sang the song "Yes" in the 1987 film *Dirty Dancing*, which was also on the soundtrack album. The song peaked at #45 in 1988.[7]

CHAPTER 27

Glory Be to God (Gospel Music and Religion-Themed Songs)

Not surprisingly, gospel songs released during the Decade that climbed the *Billboard* Hot 100 chart (and there weren't many) had more of a gospel-rock feel than straightforward gospel. This chapter examines hot songs released during the Decade that had biblical overtones.

This song is the second highest charting such song on the *Billboard* Hot 100 during the Decade. It was composed by Canadian singer-songwriter Gene MacLellan and first recorded by fellow Canadian Anne Murray in 1970. However, the most popular version of the track is the cover by then unknown Canadian band Ocean. It peaked at #2 on the U.S. *Billboard* Hot 100 in 1971. What is the song?

"Put Your Hand in the Hand." MacLellan also wrote "Snowbird," which was a #2 hit for Murray on Canada's pop chart, #1 on both the Canadian adult contemporary and country charts and #8 on the *Billboard* Hot 100. MacLellan was stricken with childhood polio and had to wear an eyepatch (and suffered facial disfigurement) as the result of a car crash that killed his father. He was extremely shy. He stopped performing in 1972 and started performing missionary work. He committed suicide by hanging in 1995 at age 46, and was posthumously inducted into theCanadian Country Music Hall of Fame later that year.[1]

This classic song sold two million copies in 1969–70 and reached #3 on the *Billboard* Hot 100 in 1970, and it where it lasted for 15 weeks on the Top 100. *Billboard* ranked the record as the #22 song of 1970. The singer-songwriter is generally regarded as a one-hit wonder. Notwithstanding the song lyrics and its references to Jesus, the songwriter is an observant Jew. Who is the artist and what is the song?

"Spirit in the Sky" by Norman Greenbaum. *Rolling Stone* ranked the song #341 on the list of top 500 Greatest Songs of All Time. Greenbaum stated that he was inspired to write the song after watching Porter Wagoner on TV singing a gospel song. Greenbaum later said: "I thought, 'Yeah, I could do that,' knowing nothing about gospel music, so I sat down and wrote my own gospel song. It came easy. I wrote the words in 15 minutes." In the same interview, he also said the inspiration for the song was western movies: "What did we grow up watching? Westerns! These mean and nasty varmints get shot and they wanted to die with their boots on. So to me that was spiritual, they wanted to die with their boots on." Though never hitting #1 in the U.S., it did so on three separate occasions in the U.K., namely Greenbaum's original version, as well as covers by Doctor and the Medics (1986) and Gareth Gates and the Kumars (2003).

The song is often used to introduce the starting lineup of the Los Angeles Angels of Anaheim for home games at Angel Stadium. It has also been used in many movies. In the Ron Howard movie *Apollo 13*, the Fred Haise character opened the TV broadcast to earth from the Odyssey Command Module with "Spirit in the Sky."

Of the legacy of the song, Greenbaum observed: "It sounds as fresh today as when it was recorded. I've gotten letters from funeral directors telling me that it's their second-most-requested song to play at memorial services, next to 'Danny Boy.'"[2]

This song by the Edwin Hawkins Singers reached #4 on the *Billboard* Hot 100 in 1969. It is much more in the nature of a traditional gospel song than "Spirit in the Sky" or "Put Your Hand in the Hand." What is the song?

"Oh Happy Day." Hawkins' arrangement of the song was based on an 18th-century hymn.

In 1966, Art Reynolds wrote a gospel-rock song that was recorded by his own group, the Art Reynolds Singers, on their 1966 album, "Tellin' It Like It Is." It was covered by a number of artists and groups including the Byrds. Then the song was covered by, of all groups, the Doobie Brothers, who heard the Byrds' version. The Doobies' version was a hit. What was the song?

"Jesus is Just Alright." While the group put their own stamp on the song, it is still an unusual marriage of a rock band with lyrics that are so unambiguously and specifically in praise of Jesus. (None of the other gospel or religiously-themed songs released during the Decade were by rock bands.) When Tom Johnston, cofounder of the Doobie Brothers, was asked by Songfacts about the overtly religious nature of the song, he said:

That's the silly part about the whole thing, because nobody was [religious]. And the funny thing about that, we weren't anti-religious. We weren't anything.

We were just musicians out playing a gig. We didn't think about that kind of stuff very often. We would be out playing that song when that came out as a single, and all these One Wayers, which was a big movement at that time, would be at the show, and they would run up to the stage with their fingers pointed straight up. At first we didn't get it, and we finally said, 'Oh, I know what's going on.' So when we would play that song, they would go nuts. They would throw scriptures on the stage, that sort of thing. Little did they know they were trying to enlist the support of the wrong guys."[3]

This song was a #1 hit for the Staples Singers in 1972 and was the only gospel or religiously-themed song released during the Decade that hit #1. Although it had a gospel feel, it might be considered more in the nature of inspirational soul. What was the song?

"I'll Take You There." It was released on the Stax label and was written by Stax Vice President Al Bell (born Alertis Isabell and credited as such on the 45) after attending the funeral of his little brother, who was shot to death. At first, lead singer Mavis Staples didn't care for the song. Said Bell: "Mavis couldn't get into it, she couldn't feel it, so I stood there on the floor and tried to sing it to the guys, and as they got the music, they got into it . . . After a while, Mavis started feeling it and giving into that rhythm. Of course, she took it to heights that only a Mavis Staples can take it."

The entire song contains only two chords, C and F. All of the music was recorded by the Muscle Shoals Rhythm Section and *Rolling Stone* editor David Fricke described the song as the "epitome of the Muscle Shoals Sound." *Billboard* ranked it as the #19 song for 1972 and it ranked #276 on the *Rolling Stone* list of the 500 Greatest Songs of All Time.[4]

This song was a Christian hymn first published in 1931, with words by English author Eleanor Farjeon, set to a traditional Scottish Gaelic tune known as "Bunessan." The famous piano intro and arrangement was not actually played or written by the artist with whom the song is associated but by Rick Wakeman of Yes. The song reached #6 on the *Billboard* Hot 100 in 1972. What is the song and who is the artist?

"Morning Has Broken" by Cat Stevens. Because the hymn was only 45 seconds long in its original form, Stevens was told it had to be lengthened, and it was, partly through Wakeman's piano parts.[5]

This is the only song that is taken almost entirely and almost verbatim from scripture that reached #1 on the *Billboard* Hot 100 (although some of the Biblical verses are

rearranged and it was a cover version that did the trick, the original having been written before the Decade). What is the song and whose version was #1? (As a hint, the lyrics are taken from Ecclesiastes 3:1-8.)

"Turn! Turn! Turn! (To Everything There Is a Season)" by the Byrds. Their cover of this song hit #1 in 1965. The song was written by Pete Seeger. The only parts of the song that do not come from Ecclesiastes (as spoken by King Solomon) are the title lyrics and the closing line, refencing that it is not too late for peace. For many years, Seeger has donated a portion of the royalties to the Israeli Committee Against House Demolitions. In explaining why (and in joking about his minimal contribution to the lyrics), he said: "All around the world, songs are being written that use old public domain material, and I think it's only fair that some of the money from the songs go to the country or place of origin, even though the composer may be long dead or unknown. With 'Turn, Turn, Turn' I wanted to send 45 percent, because [in addition to the music] I did write six words and one more word repeated three times, so I figured I'd keep five percent of the royalties for the words."[6]

Another well-known song from the Decade quoting the Bible is "Rivers of Babylon," a song released by the Jamaican reggae group the Melodians in 1970. The lyrics are adapted from the texts of Psalms 19 and 137 in the Bible. The Melodians' original version of the song appeared on the soundtrack album of the 1972 movie *The Harder They Come*.

In 1974, a practicing nun had a song that reached #4 on the *Billboard* Hot 100. Like "Turn! Turn! Turn!," the lyrics to this song were taken entirely from the Bible. Who was the woman who performed the song and what is the title of the song?

The woman was Janet Mead. The lyrics were a verbatim recital of the Lord's Prayer and thus it was imaginatively titled "The Lord's Prayer." She earned a Grammy Award nomination for Best Inspirational Performance. Because Pete Seeger added a few words of his own to "Turn! Turn! Turn!," this is the only top 10 song where all of the lyrical content comes from the Bible (bearing in mind that there are of course different translations of the Lord's Prayer) and the only one based on the words of Jesus. Mead, who was Australian, was the second woman to have a top 10 single on the *Billboard* Hot 100 chart while serving as a nun. Sister Luc-Gabrielle (Jeanine Deckers), also known as Sœur Sourire and as The Singing Nun, had a #1 hit in 1963 with "Dominique," sung in French. Mead donated all of her royalties to charity and resisted calls to continue her pop career. In fact, she said that the record's success created a "horrible time" in her life—the worldwide success brought a pressure that led her to question her faith.[7]

This song from *Jesus Christ Superstar* had an unusual chart history, entering the *Billboard* Hot 100 on three separate occasions. It peaked at #74 in February 1970, then left the chart, then climbed again to #60 in March of 1971, then left again and then entered a third time, reaching #14 in June 1971. What song?

The title track, "Superstar."

Finally, on the subject of gospel songs, the only Grammys Elvis Presley ever won were for his gospel music and he won three: Best Sacred Performance 1967 for his *How Great Thou Art* album, Best Inspirational Performance in 1972 for the *He Touched Me* album and Best Inspirational Performance Song in 1974 for "'*How Great Thou Art' Recorded Live in Memphis*."

CHAPTER 28

We Should Be More Famous! (Influential but Unknown)

To many music purists, an ongoing source of frustration is what they consider to be the disconnect between the artists and bands that have actually made it big in the music business versus those that didn't, but *deserved* to. This chapter is intended to spotlight a few of those underappreciated bands.

In its initial incarnation, this band released three studio albums, one in 1972 (called *#1 Record*), one in 1974 (*Radio City*) and one that was completed in 1975 but not released until 1978 (*Third/Sister Lovers*). They never had anything close to either a hit single or hit album and none of their songs would be considered widely recognizable today. Yet, *Rolling Stone* magazine wrote that the band acquired "near mythic status" and that, "in less than four years, [they] created a seminal body of work that never stopped inspiring succeeding generations of rockers, from the power-pop revivalists of the late 1970s to alternative rockers at the end of the century to the indie rock nation in the new millennium." Jason Ankeny of AllMusic.com agrees: "The quintessential American power pop band, [they] remain one of the most mythic and influential cult acts in all of rock & roll. [The] group's three studio albums nevertheless remain unqualified classics, and their impact on subsequent generations of indie bands on both sides of the Atlantic is surpassed only by that of the Velvet Underground." Who is this influential yet largely unknown band? (As a hint, their lead singer was Alex Chilton, formerly the lead singer of The Box Tops, whose song "The Letter" reached #1 in 1967 when Chilton was only 16 years old.)

Big Star. Interestingly, while some artists complain that they never got the recognition they deserved, lead singer Alex Chilton went in the opposite direction. In a 1992 interview, he said, "I'm constantly surprised that people fall for Big Star the way they do. . . People say Big Star made some of the best rock 'n' roll albums ever. And I say they're wrong." Chilton died of a heart attack in 2010 at age 59.[1]

The bio of this band is similar to that of Big Star in certain respects. They released three albums, released in 1969, 1970 and 1971 respectively (the first of which was—unusually for a debut album—live). Although their debut album did reach #30 on the *Billboard* 200 chart, beyond that, they never came close to having a hit album or single. Yet, as with Big Star, they are considered highly influential. The original band line-up consisted of vocalist Rob Tyner, guitarists Wayne Kramer and Fred "Sonic" Smith, bassist Michael Davis, and drummer Dennis Thompson. They were mentioned on the cover of *Rolling Stone* in 1969 even before their first album was released (although the review of the album was actually not favorable).

Again, the critics often swooned (and sometimes swoon today). Jason Ankeny of AllMusic.com wrote: "Alongside their Detroit-area brethren the Stooges, [the band] essentially laid the foundations for the emergence of punk; deafeningly loud and uncompromisingly intense . . . [B]oth their sound and their sensibility remain seminal influences on successive generations of artists." VH1 ranked them #38 on its list the 100 Greatest Hard Rock Artists. Their debut album was ranked #294 on *Rolling Stone*'s 2004 list of the 500 Greatest Albums of All Time list. Who was this band? For extra credit, name their debut live album.

MC5. Their debut album was *Kick Out the Jams.* Tyner died of a heart attack in late 1991 at age 46. Smith also died of a heart attack, in 1994 at age 45. He was married to Patti Smith.[2] Some may argue that this band was too famous or too successful to be grouped in with bands such as Big Star. But when considering their lackluster album sales and lack of hit singles—together with their outsized influence among critics and future musicians—they are indeed comparable. In what may be the greatest disconnect ever between (eventual) critical reaction to an album and actual sales, in 2003, *Rolling Stone* named the band's debut album as the 13th greatest album of all time, and yet it never reached higher than 129 on the *Billboard* Hot 200. Somehow their three studio albums led to nine compilation albums.

Richie Unterberger wrote in AllMusic.com: "By the 1980s, they were acknowledged not just as one of the most important rock bands of the '60s, but one of the best of all time, and one whose immense significance cannot be measured by their relatively modest sales." Modest sales indeed. They never had a charting single. The highest chart ranking of their three albums after the first one was #197. Yet, in 2004, *Rolling Stone* ranked the band #19 on its list of the 100 Greatest Artists of All Time. The band was inducted into the Rock and Roll Hall of Fame in 1996, by Patti Smith. Who is the band?

The Velvet Underground, fronted by Lou Reed, who wrote or cowrote all of their songs while he was with the band. Their first album was entitled *Velvet Underground and Nico*. In a

1982 interview, Brian Eno said that, while that album may have sold only 30,000 copies in its early years, "everyone who bought one of those 30,000 copies started a band." Although Andy Warhol (who designed the iconic over of their first album, with the banana) was the credited producer, he had very little direct influence or authority over the album beyond paying for the recording sessions. Most of the actual production was done by Tom Wilson who also worked with Bob Dylan, the Mothers of Invention, Simon and Garfunkel, and Eric Burdon and the Animals. Nico (born Christa Päffgen) was a German-born vocal collaborator on the first album.

Some Velvet Underground songs, such as "Sweet Jane," "Heroin," and "White Light/White Heat" became more well-known after they appeared on Reed's 1974 live album *Rock 'n' Roll Animal* and on his compilation albums thereafter.[3]

It is not just bands that can fall into the influential but unknown category. This musician released 13 albums (9 during the Decade) with a rotating ensemble of musicians called the Magic Band. His masterpiece was a 1969 double album called *Trout Mask Replica*. He worked frequently with Frank Zappa, who also gave him his stage name. He had numerous admirers in the business, both contemporary and those who came along after, including Tom Waits, R.E.M., New Order, and Mark Mothersbaugh of Devo. According to *Rolling Stone*, both John Lennon and Paul McCartney were fans of his, but the feeling was not mutual. His real name was Don Vliet. What was the name of his musical persona?

Captain Beefheart. Jason Ankeny of AllMusic.com called him "one of modern music's true innovators. . . . While he never came even remotely close to mainstream success, [his] impact was incalculable, and his fingerprints were all over punk, new wave, and post-rock." Music critic Lester Bangs called him ". . . one of the four or five unqualified geniuses to rise from the hothouses of American music in the Sixties." (Perhaps in a bit of overstatement, Bangs also wrote that he was "far more significant and far-reaching than the Beatles.") Similarly, John Peel, in a 1997 BBC TV documentary about him, said: "If there has ever been such a thing as a genius in the history of popular music, it's [him] . . . He's a psychedelic shaman who frequently bullied his musicians and sometimes alarmed his fans, yet he remained one of rock's greatest innocents."

Interestingly, his greatest success in life—at least financially—came not from his music but from his art. His large expressionist paintings and drawings have commanded high prices, and have been exhibited in art galleries and museums across the world. He died in 2010 at age 69 after suffering for many years from multiple sclerosis.[4]

CHAPTER 29

While My Guitar Gently Weeps (Instrumental and Unusual Instruments)

The opposite of an a cappella song is an instrumental. In 2013, Baauer had a #1 instrumental song, "Harlen Shake." The last one before that was in 1985, almost 30 years prior ("Miami Vice Theme" by Jan Hammer). However, during the Decade, instrumental hit songs were not so uncommon. The first part of this chapter will look at some of those instrumentals.

INSTRUMENTALS

The following artists all released instrumental songs that all reached #1 on the *Billboard* Hot 100. What are the song titles?

Paul Mariat
Hugh Maskela
Henry Mancini
The Edgar Winter Group
Love Unlimited Orchestra
MFSB featuring the Three Degrees (almost entirely instrumental)
Average White Band
Van McCoy
Silver Convention

Answers:

"Love is Blue"—Paul Mariat (February 10, 1968 for five weeks)
"Grazing in the Grass"—Hugh Maskela (July 20, 1968 for two weeks)
"Love Theme from Romeo and Juliet"—Henry Mancini (July 28, 1969 for two weeks)

"Frankenstein"—The Edgar Winter Group (May 26, 1973 for one week)
"Love's Theme"—Love Unlimited Orchestra (February 9, 1974 for one week)
"TSOP (The Sound of Philadelphia)"—MFSB featuring the Three Degrees (April 20, 1974 for two weeks). Note that there are many "doo doos" in the song.
"Pick Up the Pieces"—Average White Band (February 22, 1975 for one week)
"The Hustle"—Van McCoy and the Soul City Symphony (July 26, 1975 for one week)
"Fly, Robin, Fly"—Silver Convention (November 29, 1975 for three weeks)

When "Grazing in the Grass" was a #1 instrumental song in 1968, there was another instrumental in the top five. In fact, just before that, it held the #2 spot for 3 weeks while Herb Alpert's "This Guy's in Love with You" held down the top spot. It was obviously a huge hit and the tune would be very recognizable to anyone hearing it today who is a fan of music from the Decade. Yet, it is probably the only time in music history that the artist to whom it was attributed, Cliff Nobles, had nothing whatsoever to do with the song. He didn't sing on it (obviously, because it was an instrumental), he didn't write it, he didn't play any instruments on it, he didn't produce it and he didn't arrange it. He wasn't even present in the studio when the tune was created.

So how is that possible? Because he did sing on the A-side of the 45, a now long-forgotten song called "Love Is All Right," written by Jesse James, who also wrote the music. They did not know what to do with the B-side, so they simply released the backing track from "Love Is All Right." That track had already been laid down before Nobles put on his vocal, so it was not created to be an instrumental. Radio DJs were of course supposed to play the A-side but they liked the B-side better, and the song began its surprising run up the charts. What is the name of this "accidental" instrumental that sold a million copies within three months of its release?

"The Horse." Nearly 50 years after its release, the song continues to be a staple of American marching bands and pep bands and is often heard at sporting events. (If the title doesn't ring a bell, you would recognize it if you heard it.) The prominent horn section in the song featured members of what eventually became the group MFSB. Despite being the writer and producer of the song, James, like Nobles, was also not present when the backing track was created that became "The Horse." The song also hit #2 on the *Billboard* R&B chart in the summer of 1968, at a time when Hugh Maskela's "Grazin' in the Grass" held down the top spot, resulting in the rare occurrence of instrumentals occupying both the #1 and #2 slots of the R&B chart in the same week.

True or flase: *Dueling Banjos,* made famous in the 1972 movie *Deliverance,* consists solely of dueling banjos. What are they?

There are only two instruments, but one of them is a guitar. However, that was not the case with respect to the original version of the song. In 1955, Arthur "Guitar Boogie" Smith composed an instrumental composition called *Feudin' Banjos.* That song did consist of two banjos. Smith's song was used in *Deliverance* without permission and without attribution, which, not surprisingly, led to a lawsuit by him. He won the suit, thereby receiving songwriting credit and royalties. The film version of the song, arranged and recorded by Eric Weissberg and Steve Mandell and subsequently issued as a single, went to #2 for four weeks on the *Billboard* Hot 100 in 1973. In the movie, the guitar part is played by Ronny Cox, who was hired for the role specifically because he could play the guitar. The banjo part appears to be played by actor Billy Redden, who plays "Lonnie," a mentally challenged but extremely gifted banjo player. However, Redden could not actually play the banjo and a local musician, disguised using careful camera angles, reached around from behind him to play the banjo.[1]

UNUSUAL INSTRUMENTS

Most songs contain a typical array of instruments: guitars, bass, drums, keyboards, etc. However, some songs have instruments that are not run of the mill and whose distinctive sound can add a refreshing element to the song. Perhaps not surprisingly, many of the songs are by the ever-innovative Beatles or by ex-Beatles. For many of the songs below, I have included cites to YouTube clips of the various instruments being played, but of course to view those clips first would be cheating. Instead, listen to the songs *without* the video clips and see if you can match the songs to the instruments. Although there are a total of 22 different instruments, I have divided them into five separate sections, to give you a better chance. **In each section below, match the instrument to the song in which it appears. The instrument can easily be heard at least once, if not throughout the song, and is not "buried" in the mix.**

Group 1 songs

1. "Maggie May"—Rod Stewart
2. "Lady Jane"—The Rolling Stones
3. "You're Sixteen"—Ringo Starr
4. "Good Vibrations"—The Beach Boys

Group 1 instruments

a. **Appalachian Dulcimer.** This is an instrument with three or four strings and is typically played on one's lap, plucking or strumming the strings. The fingerboard is as long as the body.

b. Not a kazoo, but actually a voice imitating a kazoo.

c. **Tannerin or Electro-Theremin.** Let's start with the theremin itself. You don't touch a theremin to play it, but instead move your hand across the electronic field. According to songfacts, this instrument, which produces an unusual, high-pitched sound, was very hard to play and was used mostly as a sound effects device. The writer of this song was familiar with the instrument as it was used to create eerie sounds in horror movies like *The Day the Earth Stood Still* and *It Came from Outer Space*, and he wanted its sound for this song. However, he could not find an actual one so he found an inventor named Paul Tanner who had been a trombonist with the Glenn Miller Orchestra. Tanner developed a similar device called an Electro-Theremin or, naturally enough, a Tannerin), and actually played the device on this recording and it can be heard during the choruses.

d. **Mandolin.**

Group 1 answers

1.d. Every so often there is an unusual instrument heard on a song which gives it a distinctive feel. George Harrison's sitar work on "Norwegian Wood" would be such an example. Another one is the use of the mandolin that is heard throughout Rod Stewart's signature song "Maggie May." The instrument was played by Ray Jackson from a group called Laindisfarne. He played the instantly recognizable intro and improvised his song-ending solo on the spot in the studio.

However, Jackson's contribution was dissed in several ways. First, in giving credits on the album cover, Stewart ungraciously wrote: "The mandolin was played by the mandolin player in Lindisfarne. The name slips my mind." Second, despite not only playing the great mandolin part, but also coming up with it on the spot, Jackson was paid a grand total of 15 pounds. Third, when the song was played in concert, Stewart asked a friend of his to mime the mandolin part while Jackson's recorded version was actually playing. Years later, Jackson threatened to bring suit to be compensated for his contributions to the song, saying "I am convinced that my contribution to 'Maggie May,' which occurred in the early stages of my career when

I was just becoming famous for my work with Lindisfarne, was essential to the success of the record." Stewart's camp dismissed the claim as "ridiculous," and "any musical contributions he may have made were fully paid for at the time as 'work-for-hire.'" It was a well-spent 15 pounds for Stewart. Not surprisingly, Jackson also played the mandolin on the ballad "Mandolin Wind" that appears on the same album as "Maggie May," *Every Picture Tells a Story*.[2]

2.a. Brian Jones had only recently learned to play the dulcimer in 1966 when the Stones recorded "Lady Jane." He can be seen on YouTube playing the instrument on the group's fourth appearance on The Ed Sullivan Show that year. Joni Mitchell also played this instrument on her 1971 album *Blue* and can be seen playing the instrument in a solo performance of "California."

3.b. Paul McCartney is credited on the liner notes of the album *Ringo* as having played the solo on a kazoo. But reviewer Michael Verity has quoted the song's producer, Richard Perry, saying it wasn't actually a kazoo. "In fact, the solo on 'You're Sixteen,' which sounds like a kazoo or something, was Paul singing very spontaneously as we played that track back, so he's singing the solo on that." In McCartney's autobiography, *In His Own Words*, he confirms that he is "voicing" the kazoo (or, as some call it, a "mouth sax"): "It's not a kazoo. It sounds like a kazoo, but it's me doing an imitation. It was put through a fuzz thing. It's a bit daft, really, because it winds up sounding like a kazoo. I could have just done it on a kazoo."

4.c. The songwriter referred to is Brian Wilson. Jimmy Page plays a theremin on "Whole Lotta Love" and can be seen playing it during live performances of the song on various YouTube clips.

Group 2 songs

5.   "For Your Love"—The Yardbirds
6.   "Uncle Albert/Admiral Halsey"—Paul and Linda McCartney
7.   "Strawberry Fields" (including intro)—The Beatles
8.   "Getting Better" and "Lucy in the Sky with Diamonds"—The Beatles

Group 2 instruments

a.   **Flugelhorn**
b.   **Harpsichord**
c.   **Tanpura (also spelled in other ways, including tambura)—a long-necked string instrument often heard in Indian music. It produces a droning sound.**

d. **Mellotron. The mellotron is an electro-mechanical polyphonic tape replay keyboard. It has a behavior similar to a sampler, but generates its sound via audio tape. In a YouTube clip, Mike Pinder of The Moody Blues demonstrates how the instrument works. Pinder actually worked for the company that developed the instrument.**

Group 2 answers

5.b. Organist Brian Auger was asked by the Yardbirds to come in and play keyboards on "For Your Love." When he arrived at the recording studio, he discovered that there was no organ, or even a piano, on site. All that was available was a two-tiered harpsichord. Auger had never played one before, but he crafted the intro and recorded the track. Upon leaving, he wondered, "Who, in their right mind, is going to buy a pop single with harpsichord on it?" The song (written by 19-year-old Graham Gouldman) was of course a big hit for the Yardbirds (their first one), peaking at #6 on the *Billboard* Hot 100. John Meszar also plays a harpsichord on "Scarborough Fair/Canticle" by Simon and Garfunkel.

6.a. Most jazz flugelhorn players use the instrument as an auxiliary to the trumpet, but in the 1970s, Chuck Mangione gave up playing the trumpet and concentrated on the flugelhorn alone, notably on "Feels So Good."

7d. Some bands fell in love with the mellotron during the Decade and used it extensively, the Moody Blues being one. It was played by keyboardist Mike Pinder. It was also used frequently by Genesis, Yes and King Crimson. Pinder was the one who introduced the instrument to John Lennon, who was inspired to use it on "Strawberry Fields Forever," although it is Paul McCartney who plays the instrument on the track.

8.c. The tanpura/tambura also appears notably on "Hurdy Gurdy Man" by Donovan.

Group 3 songs

9. **"Paint It Black"—The Rolling Stones**
10. **"Do You Believe in Magic"—The Lovin' Spoonful**
11. **"Penny Lane"—The Beatles**
12. **"4th of July, Asbury Park"—Bruce Springsteen**

Group 3 instruments

a. **Accordion**
b. **Autoharp**

c.   Sitar

d.   Piccolo trumpet

Group 3 answers

9.c   Although the sitar is frequently associated with George Harrison (who first used the instrument in "Norwegian Wood") "Paint It Black" was the first #1 song to feature it, played by the master of all instruments, Brian Jones. Even though the original title of the Jagger-Richards composition had no punctuation, on both the Decca and London versions of the 45, the song was called "Paint It, Black," leading some to wonder whether the band was trying to make a racial statement.

10.b   John Sebastian also plays autoharp on "You Didn't Have to Be So Nice" and Judith Durham, the golden-voiced singer of the Seekers, plays it on "A World of Our Own." Others playing autoharp include Brian Jones of the Rolling Stones on "Ride On, Baby" from *Flowers* and "You Got the Silver" from *Let It Bleed*) and Robbie Robertson of the Band (on "Daniel and the Sacred Harp" from the album *Stage Fright*).

11.d   Trumpet player David Mason (not to be confused with Dave Mason who cofounded the band Traffic) recorded the piccolo trumpet solo. The solo was inspired by a performance of Johann Sebastian Bach's second Brandenburg Concerto, which songwriter Paul McCartney had seen on television. It plays about one octave higher than the standard instrument and, according to producer George Martin, is "a devilishly difficult instrument to play well in tune." According to lead sound engineer Geoff Emerick, prior to this recording, the high "E" was considered unobtainable by trumpet musicians but it has been expected of them since the performance on the record. Mason was paid 27 pounds and 10 shillings for his performance on the recording.

Interestingly, "Penny Lane" is one of only five Beatles songs not owned by Sony/ATV, the others being the A- and B-sides of their first two U.K. singles, "Love Me Do/P.S. I Love You" (owned by McCartney); "Please Please Me/Ask Me Why" (owned by Universal Music) The first four were released before the formation of Northern Songs. That company was acquired by Sir Lew Grade's ATV, controlled by Australian businessman Robert Holmes A'Court. In 1985, Northern Songs was sold by A'Court to Michael Jackson. But A'Court insisted on two strings. One was that Jackson had to play at a telethon in Perth, which he did. The other was that A'Court wanted a keepsake from the deal, which was one Beatles song. Some sources say that he chose "Penny Lane" himself, while others say that he gave his 16-year-old daughter Catherine the option, and that she chose

"Penny Lane" instead of his recommended song "Yesterday." In any event, he died at age 53 in 1990 and Catherine owns the copyright today.

12.a The accordion is played by Danny Federici in this song. Another song which includes an accordion is (obviously) "Squeeze Box" by the Who. Of the obvious sexual innuendo and the surprising success of the song, Pete Townshend wrote: "Intended as a poorly aimed dirty joke. I had bought myself an accordion and learned to play it one afternoon. The polka-esque rhythm I managed to produce from it brought forth this song. Amazingly recorded by the Who to my disbelief. Further incredulity was caused when it became a hit for us in the USA." Townshend also plays banjo on this song.

Group 4 songs

13. "Tears of a Clown"—Smokey Robinson
14. "Nights in White Satin"—The Moody Blues
15. "(Don't Fear) the Reaper"—Blue Öyster Cult
16. "Under My Thumb"—Rolling Stones
17. "Only a Northern Song"—The Beatles

Group 4 instruments

a. Cowbell
b. Glockenspiel. This is similar to the xylophone, except that the xylophone's bars are made of wood, while the glockenspiel's are metal plates. The glockenspiel is also usually smaller and higher in pitch.
c. Marimba. The marimba is a percussion instrument consisting of a set of wooden bars struck with mallets. It produces a more resonant and lower-pitched sound than the xylophone.
d. Bassoon
e. Flute—And no, it is not as easy as picking a Jethro Tull song.

Group 4 answers

13.d "Winchester Cathedral" also features a bassoon.
14.e. Ray Thomas plays a flute solo in the middle of this song. Another flute solo is at the beginning of "Can't You See" by the Marshall Tucker Band.

15.a. Yes, I know that is a bit of a cheat because this song did not come out until 1976. Nevertheless, this fantabulous song has a "Decade feel" to it. Besides, for anyone who is a fan of *Saturday Night Live*, the connection between this song and cowbell will instantly ring a (cow)bell. In a 2000 sketch, Will Ferrell, as band member Gene Frenkle, plays the cowbell while the band is recording the song in the studio. The session is being produced by legendary producer Bruce Dickinson, played by Christopher Walken. After hearing the first take, Dickinson decides that the song needs "more cowbell" and tells Frenkle to "really explore the studio space this time" and up the ante on his cowbell playing, which he does. The other band members are visibly annoyed by Frenkle's overzealous cowbelling, but Dickinson tells everyone, "I got a fever, and the only prescription—is more cowbell!"

Guitarist Buck Dharma, who wrote the song, thought the sketch was fantastic and said he never gets tired of it. The cowbell is certainly identifiable, especially at the start of the song, and the instrument is admittedly unusual in a rock song. Still, it takes a clever writer to come up with the idea of making the use of the cowbell in the song the centerpiece of the sketch, and Ferrell did so hilariously. When the cable entertainment channel E! named its 101 Most Unforgettable SNL Moments in 2004, "Cowbell" ranked number five. Interestingly, the instrument was an afterthought. The song was recorded without it, and it was added as an overdub at the last minute.[3]

16.c. Any time there is an unusual instrument being played on a Stones song released in the 1960s, it is safe to assume that Brian Jones was playing it, and this is such an example. He also plays it on "Out of Time." It is also heard on "Island Girl" by Elton John and at the start of "Mamma Mia" by ABBA.

17.b Played by John Lennon on this George Harrison composition. George Martin, the Beatles' producer, plays one on "Being for the Benefit of Mr. Kite!" to help create the atmosphere of a circus performance. Danny Federici of the E Street band plays a keyboard-operated glockenspiel on certain Springsteen songs, including, most notably, "Born To Run."

Group 5 songs

18. **"Superstar"—The Carpenters**
19. **"Baby You're A Rich Man"—The Beatles**
20. **"Wild Thing"—The Troggs**
21. **"The Fool On the Hill"—The Beatles**
22. **"It's a Long Way to the Top (If You Wanna Rock 'n' Roll)"—AC/DC**

Group 5 instruments

a.   Oboe.
b.   Ocarina. An ocarina is a wind instrument typically having an oval body with four to 12 finger holes and a projecting mouthpiece. It can be made of various materials including ceramic, plastic, wood, glass, metal, or bone.
c.   Recorder, Jew's harp and penny whistle. A Jew's harp consists of a flexible metal or bamboo tongue or reed attached to a frame. The tongue/reed is placed in the performer's mouth and plucked with the finger to produce a note. A penny whistle is a six-holed woodwind instrument.
d.   Bagpipes
e.   Clavioline—an oboe-like sound from an amplified keyboard that was a forerunner to the analog synthesizer.

Group 5 answers

18.a The well-known introduction to the song is played on the oboe.
19.e. Played by John Lennon. Other songs that used a clavioline include "Telstar" by the Tornados and *Runaway* by Del Shannon. It can be heard at the beginning of the song and throughout the track.
20.b. The ocarina can easily be heard on the middle eight.
21.c. Paul McCartney plays the recorder and penny whistle, while John Lennon plays the Jew's harp.
22.d. Bon Scott performed the bagpipes solo, despite having never previously played them.[4]

All Kinds of Names (Band Names, Brand Names, Girls' Names, Singers' Names, Etc.)

This chapter focuses on all aspects of the names of solo artists and bands.

BAND NAMES

Which of the following bands is named after a real person who was a member of the band?

Jethro Tull
Lynyrd Skynryd
Manfred Mann
Marshall Tucker
Procol Harum
Uriah Heep

None of them. Jethro Tull was a real person but not a band member; rather, but was an English agricultural pioneer (1674–1741). Lynyrd Skynryd, was a mock tribute to Leonard Skinner, the high school gym teacher of some of the band members. He disapproved of male students with long hair, and who frequently hassled them.)

Marshall Tucker was a real person but not a band member. When the band first got together in 1972, they were rehearsing in an old warehouse. Someone looked at the tag on the warehouse door key and it said "Marshall Tucker" and it was suggested they call themselves the Marshall Tucker Band. It turns out that Marshall Tucker was the name of the person who rented the building before them. His name was still on the key tag because the warehouse owner hadn't changed it yet. He was a blind piano tuner, who, along with his partner, used the building for their piano business.

As for Procol Harum, lyricist Keith Reid explained: "It's the name of a cat, a Siamese cat. It's the pedigree name, and it belonged to a friend of ours, just somebody that we used to hang out with when we were forming the band. One day, somebody pulled out the cat's birth certificate and said 'Have a look at this,' and the name of the cat was Procol Harum. And somebody else, in fact a chap called Guy Stevens who was quite instrumental in Gary [Brooker, the singer and pianist] and myself getting together in the first place, said, 'Oh, you must call the group Procol Harum.' And we just accepted that. We never even questioned it, never even thought if it was a good name, we just went ahead with that suggestion."

Uriah Heep is of course a character from Charles Dickens's novel *David Copperfield*. Heep is Copperfield's obsequious clerk who pretends to be "humble" and to want to serve Copperfield well, but in reality cheats him. His name is sometimes used for a person who pretends to show great respect but is not sincere. The band's first album, released in 1970, was called . . . *Very 'Eavy . . . Very 'Umble*, referring to Heep's phrase in the novel, "Ever so 'umble."

As for Mann, he was born Manfred Sepse Lubowitz, in South Africa. In 1961, he began to write for *Jazz News* under the pseudonym Manfred Manne (after jazz drummer Shelly Manne), which was soon shortened to Manfred Mann.[1]

Some bands give themselves a name which is itself the first and last name of a person. Examples would be Jethro Tull, Uriah Heep and Amy Meredith (an Australian band). In one instance however, the lead singer legally gave himself the same name as the band. Since they broke up, since the band as a whole holds the copyright to the name, the lead singer has to pay his former bandmates royalties every year for the use of the name commercially, even though it is his "own name." Who is the band/singer?

Alice Cooper. The former Vincent Furnier changed his legal name to Alice Cooper after the band broke up. Meanwhile the remaining members of the group changed their name to *Billion Dollar Babies*, which was the title of the band's very successful 1973 album. However, they released only one album, *Battle Axe*, which was a flop, before disbanding. As for the songs released by the Alice Cooper band, most of them (including "I'm Eighteen" and "School's Out") were credited to all five band members (besides Cooper, Michael Bruce, Glen Buxton, Dennis Dunaway, and Neal Smith).

In 2013, music writer Michael Walker wrote a book with the lengthy title *What You Want Is In the Limo: On the Road with Led Zeppelin, Alice Cooper and the Who in 1973, the Year the Sixties Died and the Modern Rock Star Was Born*. Not surprisingly, much of the book is about the Bacchanalian experiences of those bands during their tours that year. He points out that, until just a few years earlier, backstage accoutrements were just an afterthought. For example, the Beatles required a TV set and some Coke (not the drug!). Elvis (in his earlier years) required ten soft drinks and four cups of water. By 1973 however, the entitlement that came to define rock stardom had taken root, and the Alice Cooper tour is one of the prime exemplars of the decadence, especially when it came to the specificity of the liquid refreshments. Walker cites their backstage hospitality rider as being "typical":

> Purchaser shall provide three (3) cases of Budweiser, three (3) cases of Michelob, one (1) gallon of apple juice, one (1) gallon of orange juice, two (2) cases of Coca-Cola, one (1) case of ginger ale and assorted fruit. This is to be placed in a cooler with ice in Alice Cooper's dressing room. Additional food appropriate to the occasion is encouraged. The Michelob beer must be in bottles and the cases of Budweiser must be in cans. In states where the sale of beer must have an alcoholic content of less than 6 percent (i.e. 3.2 beer), the beer must be imported from another state.[2]

True or false: In the band Paul Revere and the Raiders, there actually is a Paul Revere.

True, more or less: His real name was Paul Revere Dick. He died on October 4, 2014.

Usually when a group is called "X and the Y's" (such as Martha and the Vandellas, Jay and the Americans, Tommy James and the Shondells, etc.) the "Y's" are all of the same gender as each other and usually the same gender as the lead singer. In one instance however, there was a major band in the Decade which did not fit this pattern. The "X" was male, as were *most* of the "Y's." However, there was a female among them. She eventually married the lead singer. Who is the "X" and what is the name of the woman who sang with Y's? (As a hint, the band was a Motown act.)

Smokey Robinson and the Miracles is the group and singer Claudette Rogers Robinson was the woman who married Smokey. Robinson co-wrote the song "My Girl" with Miracles member Ronald White in dedication to Claudette. Even though the song was intended to be recorded by The Miracles, it instead became a smash #1 hit for the Temptations. Smokey and Claudette were divorced in 1986, after 27 years of marriage. Motown founder Berry Gordy gave Claudette the official title of the "First Lady of Motown" because, as a member of the Miracles (Motown's first group and first recording act), she was the first female artist ever signed to a Motown-affiliated record label (Tamla).

There has been only one time when a palindromic song by a palindromic band has reached the *Billboard* top 20 (a palindrome being a word that is spelled the same in both

directions). Who is the band and what is the song? (As a hint, it is by one of the biggest-selling bands in history.)

The band is ABBA and the song is "S.O.S." This was the band's second worldwide hit after "Waterloo." Both John Lennon and Pete Townshend have said that it is one their favorite pop songs.

True or false: Despite the name, Sly Stone had no family members in Sly and the Family Stone.

False: The band included his brother Freddie, who was a guitarist, as well as Rose, who played piano and sang vocals, and Vaetta (Vet) Stone, on background vocals. Their family name was actually Stewart, but when he changed his last name to Stone, the others did as well.

DERIVATIONS OF BAND NAMES

This band was named after a giant steam-powered dildo mentioned in the William S. Burroughs 1959 novel *Naked Lunch*. Which band is it?

Steely Dan. The actual name of the dildo is Steely Dan III from Yokahama.

This band was named after two of its members, the drummer and bassist. The band released nine albums in the Decade, starting in 1968. Yet, they remained relatively unknown, especially in America. After some lineup changes, the three British members of the band added two American members (one male, one female) who "orchestrated one of the most dramatic yet peaceful takeovers in rock history . . . From the moment [they] walked in the door, they handled the lion's share of songwriting." They became one of the most successful bands in the world in the mid to late 1970s. Who is the band and who were the new members?

Fleetwood Mac, named after drummer Mick Fleetwood and bassist John McVie. The new songwriters referred to were Stevie Nicks and Lindsey Buckingham, who joined in 1974. Interestingly, though named after Fleetwood and McVie, the band was not started by them. Rather, it was started by Peter Green, formerly of John Mayall & the Bluesbreakers, who left the band in 1970. The other primary songwriter for the group was McVie's then-wife Christine, who joined the group in 1970. On their classic breakout 1975 album *Fleetwood Mac* (featuring only Mick Fleetwood and John McVie on the cover) every song but one was written by Christine McVie or Buckingam or Nicks. The hits on that album include "Rhiannon" and "Landslide" by Nicks and "Over My Head" and "Say You Love Me" by McVie.[3]

Which band is named after the first letters of the first names of each member?

ABBA (Agnetha Fältskog, Björn Ulvaeus, Benny Anderson and Anni-Frid Lyngstad).

How did the E Street Band get its name?

From E Street, which runs through the New Jersey shore town of Belmar. 1105 E Street was the childhood home of original keyboard player David Sancious. His mother still lived there and allowed the band to rehearse in the garage. There is also a Tenth Avenue in Belmar which may have been an inspiration for "Tenth Avenue Freezeout," which appears on his *Born to Run* album. However, when asked in 2005 what the title means, Springsteen said "I still have no idea."[4]

BRAND NAMES

There are three well-known songs from the Decade that have titles consisting solely of a brand name. One was a major hit (#2 on the charts) by Paul Simon, one was a #5 hit for the Five Americans and the third is by Janis Joplin. What are the songs?

The first is "Kodachrome" by Simon, the second is "Western Union" and the third is "Mercedes Benz" by Joplin (with no hyphen in the title). ("Kodachrome" also makes reference to a Nikon camera.) The Five Americans were a one-hit wonder. However, keyboardist Johnny Durrill wrote "Dark Lady" for Cher.

Many other songs also mention brand names in their lyrics. Below are some songs from the Decade that mention brand names. What are the brand names? To keep it fair, I have limited the list only to major hits by major artists.

"Ramblin Man" by the Allman Brothers

Greyhound

"Young Americans" by David Bowie (two brand names)

Ford Mustang and Barbie Doll

"Taxi" by Harry Chapin

Dodge

"Bad, Bad Leroy Brown" by Jim Croce

[Lincoln] Continental and [Cadillac] El Dorado

"Crocodile Rock" by Elton John

Chevy

"Come Together" by the Beatles

Coca-Cola

"Levon" by Elton John

New York Times

"Lola" by the Kinks

Coca-Cola

"Blinded by the Light" by Bruce Springsteen

Curly Wurly [Curly Wurly is a brand of chocolate bar.]

"All the Young Dudes" by Mott the Hoople

Marks and Sparks [Marks and Sparks is a British retailer.]

"Money" by Pink Floyd

Lear Jet

"Killer Queen" by Queen

Moët et Chandon

"Devil with the Blue Dress" by Mitch Ryder

Chanel #5

"Walk on the Wild Side" by Lou Reed

Valium

"You're So Vain" by Carly Simon

Lear Jet

"America" by Simon and Garfunkel

Greyhound and Mrs. Wagner pies

GIRLS' NAMES IN SONG TITLES

The following songs, all released during the Decade, have titles consisting of solely of a girl's name. None of the songs are obscure. In some cases, there is a parenthetical after the girl's name and in some cases there may be more than one word. I'll name the artist or group and you name the song title.

America

"Daisy Jane"

Barry Manilow

"Mandy"

Crosby, Stills & Nash

"Guinnevere"

Derek & the Dominos

"Layla"

Dolly Parton

"Jolene"

Kenny Rogers

"Lucille"

Leonard Cohen

"Suzanne"

Looking Glass

"Brandy (You're a Fine Girl)"

Neil Diamond

"Cherry, Cherry"

Simon & Garfunkel

"Cecilia"

The Beach Boys

"Barbara Ann"

The Beatles (three songs)

"Julia," "Michelle," and "Eleanor Rigby"

The Hollies

"Carrie Ann"

The Kinks

"Lola"

The Rolling Stones

"Angie"

The Turtles

"Elenore"

Them

"Gloria"

Tommy James & the Shondells

"Mony Mony"

Tony Orlando & Dawn

"Candida"

NAME-CHECKS: ARTISTS, GROUPS, AND SONGS MENTIONED IN OTHER SONGS

Here are a few questions about artists, bands or songs being name-checked in other songs.

"Hair" by the Cowsills references this iconic San Francisco band. Who is it?

The Grateful Dead.

It is unusual for an artist or group to be mentioned in a derogatory way in the song of another. However, in one well-known song, there was not one but three artists arguably so criticized. The song takes shots at the Beatles no less, as well as the Mamas and the Papas and Donovan. What is the song?

"I Dig Rock and Roll Music" by Peter, Paul and Mary. The Beatles are accused of being interested primarily in money while singing about love, ("when the Beatles tell you they've got a word 'love' to sell you, they mean exactly what they say"), the Mamas and the Papas are accused of lyrical shortcomings ("they got a good thing goin' when the words don't get in the way") and Donovan for his garbled and sometimes incomprehensible lyrics.

Whether or not their barbs were more in the nature of good-natured teasing (or even tributes) is hard to know. However, it is worth noting that the song was written in 1967 when the popularity of the group was on the wane and folk music generally had been eclipsed by rock music. This may have explained why Mary Travers told the *Chicago Daily News* in 1966 that rock music "is so badly written. . . . When the fad changed from folk to rock, they didn't take along any good writers." This was one of their few songs in which one of them had a hand in writing (Paul Stookey wrote the lyrics).[5]

What 1973 song by George Harrison mentions the other three Beatles by name in the lyrics (although Ringo is referred to as Richie)?

"Living in the Material World." In the spoken outro to the reprise of "Just Because" on the *Rock n Roll* album, John says "Hi to Ringo, Paul & George & everyone back home in England."

Which Who song mentions Bob Dylan and the Beatles?

"The Seeker."

"Shooting Star" by Bad Company opens with a reference to a song. Which one?

"Love Me Do."

The Dutch band Golden Earring was a one-hit wonder in the U.S. and that hit was "Radar Love." In that song, they name-mention a woman who had more songs in the *Billboard* Hot 100 in the 1960s than anyone except Elvis, the Beatles and Ray Charles (most of which were before the Decade). She was 4'9" tall and sometimes known as Little Miss Dynamite. Who is she?

Brenda Lee.

The well-known song "Up on Cripple Creek" by the Band mentions this American musician and bandleader who specialized in performing satirical arrangements of popular songs. Who is he?

Spike Jones.

There is a song released in 1974 that, except for the chorus, is nothing but name-checks. There are about 120 artists, bands and songs referenced directly or indirectly, even though the song is only about 3:30 long. In fact, most of the 120 names are delivered in three separate verses of only 20 seconds each. What is the song and who is it by?

"Life is a Rock (But the Radio Rolled Me)" by Reunion.

In 1970 and 1972 respectively, Neil Young wrote two songs which alluded to racism in the South although they did not mention any people or bands by name. In 1974, Lynyrd Skynyrd "responded" to the two songs with a song of their own, which does repeatedly mention Young by name. What are the three songs? For extra credit, Young then responded back to Skynyrd with yet another song. What was that one?

The 1970 song is "Southern Man" from Young's album *After the Gold Rush*. The 1972 song is "Alabama" from *Harvest*. Skynyrd's well-known response is of course "Sweet Home Alabama."

The lyrics to "Southern Man" are vivid, describing the racism towards blacks in the American South. In the song, Young tells the story of a Southern white man (symbolically the entire white South) and how he mistreated his slaves. Young pleadingly asks when the South will make amends for the fortunes built through slavery. The song also mentions cross-burning. The lyrics to "Alabama" are somewhat more elliptical but nevertheless Young appears to chastise the state for past sins. Despite the more opaque nature of the song, it has been described as "an unblushing rehash of 'Southern Man.'"

Lynyrd Skynyrd responded in 1974 with "Sweet Home Alabama" (which, given its iconic status today, surprisingly never reached higher than #8 on the *Billboard* charts), telling Neil that Southern man doesn't need him around.

A few notes about "Sweet Home Alabama": First, it was cowritten by guitarist Ed King and it is his countdown you hear at the start of the song before launching in to his famous Stratocaster riff. Second, the famous "Turn it up" line uttered by cowriter and lead vocalist Ronnie Van Zant at the beginning was actually not intended to be in the song. He was simply asking producer Al Kooper and engineer Rodney Mills to increase the volume in his headphones so that he could hear the track better. Finally, there is a semi-hidden vocal line in the second verse after the line "Well, I heard Mr. Young sing about her." In the left channel, you can just hear the phrase "Southern Man" being sung lightly, at approximately at 0:55.

Most people have generally assumed that this was in response to "Southern Man," not surprisingly given its direct reference to the title of that song. While this is accurate, Young himself wrote in his autobiography *Waging Heavy Peace* that he thought the song was also in response to "Alabama": "My own song 'Alabama' richly deserved the shot Lynyrd Skynyrd gave me with their great record. I don't like my words when I listen to it today. They are accusatory and condescending, not fully thought out, too easy to misconstrue." (It is interesting that if that is his reaction to "Alabama," he would not have had a similar, and indeed more intense, reaction to "Southern Man.")

After "Southern Man" came out, both Young and Ronnie Van Zant, who was one of the writers of "Sweet Home Alabama," often made it clear that they are fans of the other. Young has been known to play "Sweet Home Alabama" in concert. Van Zant is pictured on the cover of *Street Survivors*, wearing a T-shirt of Young's album *Tonight's the Night*.

Although "Sweet Home Alabama" is Skynyrd's signature tune, the band was actually formed in Jacksonville, Florida.

On October 20, 1977, the band's chartered plane ran out of fuel and crashed into a densely wooded thicket in a swamp near Gillsburg, Mississippi. At the time of the crash, there were seven band members (Van Zant, guitarists Allen Collins, Steve Gaines and Gary Rossington, bassist Leon Wilkeson, drummer Artimus Pyle and keyboardist Billy Powell) and three backup singers, known as the Honkettes (Cassie Gaines, the older sister of Steve Gaines, Leslie Hawkins and JoJo Billingsley). Van Zant, Steve and Cassie Gaines and three others were killed instantly. The other band members and Hawkins suffered serious injuries. Billingsley was not on the flight.[6]

NAMES IN BRUCE SPRINGSTEEN SONGS FROM THE DECADE

Bruce Springsteen included many names of people in his albums released during the Decade, including *Greetings from Asbury Park*, *The Wild, the Innocent & the E Street Shuffle* and *Born to Run*. First, there are two actual people on those albums who are mentioned by both first name and last name. One is on *Greetings* and one is on *Born to Run*. What are the songs and who are the people? One is easier than the other because the song is more iconic and the person mentioned in that song is probably more famous than the other.

The easier one is the mention of Roy Orbison in "Thunder Road," the opening track to *Born to Run*. Orbison's song "Only the Lonely" is indirectly mentioned as well. The other song is "Does This Bus Stop at 82nd Street?" which mentions Joan Fontaine. The song is on Springsteen's debut album *Greetings from Asbury Park*. Fontaine was a British actress who died at age 96 in 2013. She is the only actor or actress to ever win an Academy Award in a film directed by Alfred Hitchcock (*Suspicion*, 1941) and she and her elder sister Olivia de Havilland are the only set of siblings to have both won leading acting Academy Awards (the latter for *To Each His Own* [1946] and *The Heiress* [1949]).

Which other characters are mentioned in the following songs (the number in parentheses is the number of people mentioned):

Greetings from Asbury Park
"Blinded by the Light" (three)
"Spirit in the Night" (five)
"Does This Bus Stop at 82nd Street?" (two)

The Wild, the Innocent & the E Street Shuffle
"New York City Serenade" (four)
"Fourth of July, Asbury Park (Sandy)" (two)
"Wild Billy's Circus Story" (two)
"Rosalita" (seven)
"The E Street Shuffle" (two)

Born to Run
"Jungleland" (two)
"Tenth Avenue Freezeout" (two)
"Thunder Road" (one)
"Backstreets" (one)
"Born to Run" (one)

Answers:

Greetings from Asbury Park
"Blinded by the Light"—Young Scott, Go Cart Mozart, Little Early Pearly
"Spirit in the Night"—Crazy Janey, Killer Joe, Wild Billy, G Man, Hazy Davy

"Does This Bus Stop at 82nd Street?"—Broadway Mary, Joan Fontaine

The Wild, the Innocent &the E Street Shuffle
"Sandy"—Sandy, Madame Marie
"Wild Billy's Circus Story"—Missy Bimbo, Marguerita
"Rosalita"—Rosalita, Sloppy Sue, Big Bones Billy, Little Dynamite, Little Gun, Jack the Rabbit, Weak Knees Willie
"The E Street Shuffle"—Power Thirteen, Little Angel
"New York City Serenade"—Billy, Diamond Jackie, Fish Lady, Jazz Man

Born to Run
"Jungleland"—Magic Rat, Barefoot Girl
"Tenth Avenue Freezeout"—Bad Scooter, Big Man
"Thunder Road"—Mary and Roy Orbison
"Backstreets"—Terry
"Born to Run"—Wendy

ONE-NAMED SINGERS

There have been plenty of one-named singers, some of who use their actual names (Prince, Madonna, Beyonce, Jewel, Enya, Usher, and Adele) and some who use nicknames (Sting, Lorde, Rihanna, Sade). There are relatively few however who were famous during the Decade. Can you name four? A bit about each:

The real name of one is Roland Kent LaVoie. He had three top 10 hits in 1971 and 1972.

Another is Scottish (only hint).

The third is a female who performed at Woodstock and is well-known.

The real name of the fourth is William Oliver Swofford and he had two top 10 hits in 1969.

The first is Lobo (spanish for wolf). His top 10 songs were "Me and You and a Dog Named Boo" (#5 in 1971), "I'd Love You to Want Me" (#2 in 1972) and "Don't Expect Me to be Your Friend" (#8 in 1972).

The second is Donovan. The third is Melanie. The fourth is Oliver. His top 10 songs were "Good Morning Starshine" (from the musical *Hair*), which reached #3. The other song was "Jean," which reached even higher (#2) although, unlike "Good Morning Starshine," it is virtually forgotten today.

STAGE NAMES OF ARTISTS FROM THE DECADE

The following are the real names of 15 people who had more famous stage names and made their mark primarily in the 1960s. What were those stage names?

1. Martyn Buchwald
2. Ellen Naomi Cohen
3. Thomas Jackson
4. Marie McDonald McLaughlin Lawrie
5. John Ramistella
6. Mary Isobel Catherine O'Brien
7. Steven Georgiou
8. Steveland Morris
9. Virginia Pugh
10. Perry Miller
11. Roberta Lee Streeter
12. Rudy Martinez
13. Anna Mae Bullock
14. Philip Blondheim
15. Sharon Lee Myers

1. Martyn Buchwald—Marty Balin
2. Ellen Naomi Cohen—Cass Elliott
3. Thomas Jackson—Tommy James
4. Marie McDonald McLaughlin Lawrie—Lulu
5. John Ramistella—Johnny Rivers
6. Mary Isobel Catherine O'Brien—Dusty Springfield
7. Steven Georgiou—Cat Stevens
8. Steveland Morris—Stevie Wonder
9. Virginia Pugh—Tammy Wynette
10. Perry Miller—Jesse Colin Young
11. Roberta Lee Streeter—Bobbie Gentry
12. Rudy Martinez—Question Mark (of ? and the Mysterians)
13. Anna Mae Bullock—Tina Turner
14. Philip Blondheim—Scott McKenzie
15. Sharon Lee Myers—Jackie DeShannon

The following are the real names of 15 people who had more famous stage names and made their mark primarily in the 1970s. What were those stage names?

1.   Roberta Anderson
2.   Farrokh Bulsara
3.   John Deutschendorf
4.   David Robert Jones
5.   Arnold George Dorsey
6.   Janis Fink
7.   Malcolm John Rebennack
8.   Harry Wayne Casey
9.   Carole Klein
10. Vincent Furnier
11. Richard Starkey
12. Claude Bridges
13. Steven Tallarico
14. Barry Carter
15. William Perks

1.   Roberta Anderson—Joni Mitchell
2.   Farrokh Bulsara—Freddie Mercury
3.   John Deutschendorf—John Denver
4.   David Robert Jones—David Bowie
5.   Arnold George Dorsey—Englebert Humperdinck
6.   Janis Fink—Janis Ian
7.   Malcolm John Rebennack—Dr. John
8.   Harry Wayne Casey—KC (of KC and the Sunshine Band)
9.   Carole Klein—Carole King
10. Vincent Furnier—Alice Cooper
11. Richard Starkey—Ringo Starr
12. Claude Bridges—Leon Russell
13. Steven Tallarico—Steven Tyler
14. Barry Carter—Barry White
15. William Perks—Bill Wyman

"COMPANY," "CORPORATION," AND "INC." IN BAND NAMES

Lawyers know that when a company wants to incorporate, in most states it is required that their title contains a word such as "company," "incorporated," "corporation," or some abbreviation thereof, to let the world know that it has been legally formed as a company. Some rock bands have names in their title that would allow them to be legal corporations just based on their names—i.e. they include one of these words. How many groups from the Decade can you name that contain those words?

1910 Fruitgum Company. They had three top five hits in 1967 and 1968 "Simon Says," "1,2,3 Red Light" and "Indian Giver."

Bad Company. Their self-titled debut album reached #1 in 1974 and they had two top 10 singles in the Decade, "Can't Get Enough" and "Feel Like Makin' Love."

Big Brother and the Holding Company. Although this band was formed in 1965 and has been in existence (on and off) since then, it is indelibly associated with Janis Joplin, even though she was only with the band from 1966–1968. Their 1968 album *Cheap Thrills* topped the *Billboard* 200 chart.

Shirley & Company. This group, named after lead singer Shirley Goodman, had a hit in 1974 with "Shame Shame Shame" which reached #12 on the *Billboard* Hot 100 and topped the U.S. dance chart.

Hues Corporation. Their 1974 song "Rock the Boat" was a #1 song in the U.S. and the U.K.

As for "Inc.," I am not aware from any bands from the Decade containing this abbreviated word, but a shout-out must be given to the excellently named Lipps Inc. (pronounced "lip sync"), whose 1980 song "Funkytown" hit #1 in 28 different countries around the world.

CHAPTER 31

Imitation Is the Sincerest Form of Flattery (Not by Who You Think)

Certain songs sound like they are being sung by someone other than the actual artist. See if you can figure out the people with whom the following singers were often misidentified. If you don't know right away, listen to the track before answering, with your eyes closed, and think about whether the voice sounds like someone other than who is actually singing.

"A Horse with No Name" by America. Songwriter Dewey Bunnell acknowledged the similarity with this other singer, saying "I know that virtually everyone, on first hearing, assumed it was [him]. I never fully shied away from the fact that I was inspired by him. I think it's in the structure of the song as much as in the tone of my voice. It did hurt a little, because we got some pretty bad backlash. I've always attributed it more to people protecting their own heroes more than attacking me." Coincidentally, this song bumped a song by the other artist off the top spot on the *Billboard* Hot 100. Who is the artist and, for extra credit, name the #1 song it bumped off?

The artist is Neil Young and Young's #1 song (his only one) "Heart of Gold." In this song, the singer is alone in the desert with his horse that has no name. Commenting on the lyrics, comedian Rich Jeni said: "You're in the desert. You got nothing else to do. NAME THE FREAKIN' HORSE!"[1]

"I'm Easy" by Keith Carradine. The song is often mistakenly associated with this singer due to the similarity of Carradine's voice and vocal style to those of the singer, as well as the guitar playing in the song, which greatly resembles many of the singer's ballads. Who does Carradine sound like?

Jim Croce.[2]

"Stuck in the Middle with You" by Stealer's Wheel. Sung and cowritten by Gerry Rafferty, he has said that the song was sung as a parody of another artist. To Rafferty's surprise, his parody was a big hit, reaching #6 on the *Billboard* Hot 100 in 1973. Who is the artist he was trying to parody?

Bob Dylan.[3]

The lead vocal for "Still the One," a #5 hit for Orleans in 1976, sounds a lot like this famous singing drummer.

Don Henley of the Eagles.

"Long Cool Woman in a Black Dress" by the Hollies. Allan Clarke's vocal sounds a lot like the distinctive-voiced lead singer of another band from the Decade. Apparently this was intentional on Clarke's part. Who is the singer?

John Fogerty from Credence Clearwater Revival. Clarke consciously imitated Fogerty's vocal style.[4]

Of this song, AllMusic.com wrote: "[It is] the best and most accurate early Beatle imitation ever recorded; the lead vocals were a dead ringer for John Lennon and the whole production could have fit in snugly on the second side of *A Hard Day's Night*." Wikipedia concurs: "Somewhat ironically, the song is most famous today for being blatantly derivative of contemporary songs by the Beatles, due to [Buddy] Randell's lead vocal sounding uncannily similar to John Lennon, as well as the vocal whoops before the guitar solo and later in the song, which were very reminiscent of Paul McCartney especially for the ad-lib's in the final chorus. . . . Some listeners, unaware of its true source, mistake it for being a 'lost' Beatles track."

Band member Beau Charles made no bones about the group's goal: "We desperately tried to write something that sounded like the British Invasion." The band hails from Bergenfeld, NJ and an article about them is entitled "The Liverpool sound by way of Bergenfield, NJ, the home of [these] one-hit wonders." The song spent 13 weeks on the *Billboard* Hot 100 in early 1966. What is the song? As a hint, the name of the group was the Knickerbockers.)

"Lies." The words "somewhat ironically" in the above Wikipedia description are clearly a reference to the song title.[5]

In 1970, George Jackson wrote a song for the Jackson 5, but they decided to record "ABC" instead. Therefore, another group recorded it and the result was a song that reached #1 on the *Billboard* chart in 1971 and stayed there for five weeks. However, because the song sounded so much like a Jackson 5 song (including the vocals), many people assumed that it *was* a Jackson 5 song, especialy because they were on fire at the time. What was the song and who was the group who recorded it?

The song is "One Bad Apple" and the group is the Osmonds. Donny sounded a lot like Michael in this song, at least as Michael sounded in his Jackson 5 days.

The 1965 song "Rescue Me" by Fontella Bass reached #1 on the R&B charts and #4 on the *Billboard* pop singles chart. When she passed away in 2012, the *Huffington Post* wrote: "Bass's powerful voice bore a striking resemblance to that of [X], who is often mis-identified as the singer of that chart-topping hit." Who is X, who happens to be one of the most successful singers in history?

Aretha Franklin. Minnie Riperton provided background vocals, and Maurice White and Louis Satterfield, later of Earth, Wind & Fire, were on drums and bass respectively. According to Bass, the call-and-response moans heard in the song were unintentional. In an interview with the *New York Times* in 1989, she said, "When we were recording that, I forgot some of the words . . . Back then, you didn't stop while the tape was running, and I remembered from the church what to do if you forget the words. I sang, 'Ummm, ummm, ummm,' and it worked out just fine."

There was some question as to whether Bass had a hand in writing the song. The original 45 of the record (released on Chess Records) gave songwriting credit to Raymond Miner and Carl Smith only, as does BMI. However, when she passed away in 2012, virtually every obituary (including the *Washington Post*, the BBC, CBS News, the *Chicago Sun-Times* and the *Huffington Post*) credited her with being a cowriter of the song. She also sued to collect royalties from the song, claiming that she had cowritten some of the lyrics, and that she was assured by Smith and Miner that her contribution to the lyrics would be acknowledged. According to Bass: "I had the first million-seller for Chess since Chuck Berry about 10 years before. Things were riding high for them, but when it came time to collect my first royalty check, I looked at it, saw how little it was, tore it up and threw it back across the desk." Eventually, the case settled and she was credited with being a cowriter of the song.[6]

Just because "Son of a Preacher Man" is performed by a soulful white female, does not mean that the singer was this woman, as some people often thought. Who did sing it?

Janis Joplin. It is of course performed by Dusty Springfield.

Some people thought that Harry Chapin's song "Cat's in the Cradle" was by another artist, not only because of some similarity in the voices but also because the other artist also wrote and recorded a song about a dysfunctional relationship between a dad and his son. Who is the other artist and what is the other song?

The other artist is Cat Stevens and his song is "Father and Son."

Steven Tyler's vocal in "Dream On" sounds a lot like that of another famous singer, especially at the 3:30 mark when he starts wailing "dream on" in a higher voice. Which singer?

Robert Plant of Led Zeppelin.

"Lightning Strikes" by Lou Christie (a #1 song in 1966) sounds like it might have been recorded by this group and the chorus sounds particularly like it is being sung that group's lead singer. What group and what singer?

The Four Seasons and Frankie Valli.

CHAPTER 32

Fun with Numeracy (Numbers in Song Titles or Band Names)

All of the songs or artists examined in this chapterinvolve numbers in one way or another.See how well you can remember them.

Following is a list of 21 songs from the Decade and one song from after. Each contains a number from 0 to 20. Sometimes the numbers are cardinal and sometimes ordinal (e.g. third, eighth, etc.). Try to match the artist with the song title. To keep it fair, the song by each artist corresponds with the number across from which the artist is listed (e.g. the Bob Dylan song contains the number zero, etc.). Dylan appears twice (which is why there are only 20 artists listed), and the Gordon Lightfoot song was recorded after the Decade. In each instance, I tried to select well-known songs by well-known artists but some songs are nevertheless certainly not as well-known as others.

	Artist
0.	Bob Dylan
1.	The Fifth Dimension
2.	The Beatles
3.	Tony Orlando and Dawn
4.	Bruce Springsteen
5.	The Vogues
6.	Chicago
7.	Simon and Garfunkel
8.	The Byrds
9.	The Searchers
10.	Led Zeppelin

11.	The Grateful Dead
12.	Bob Dylan
13.	Big Star
14.	Gordon Lightfoot
15.	The Who
16.	Ringo Starr
17.	Janis Ian
18.	Alice Cooper
19.	The Rolling Stones
20.	The Doors

0.	Bob Dylan—"Love Minus Zero/No Limit"
1.	The Fifth Dimension—"One Less Bell to Answer"
2.	Beatles—"Two of Us"
3.	Tony Orlando and Dawn—"Knock Three Times"
4.	Bruce Springsteen—"4th of July Asbury Park (Sandy)"
5.	The Vogues—"Five O'Clock World"
6.	Chicago—"25 or 6 to 4"
7.	Simon and Garfunkel—"7 O'Clock News/Silent Night"
8.	The Byrds—"Eight Miles High"
9.	The Searchers—"Love Potion Number 9"
10.	Led Zeppelin—"Ten Years Gone"
11.	The Grateful Dead—"The Eleven"
12.	Bob Dylan—"Rainy Day Women #12 and 35"
13.	Big Star—"Thirteen"
14.	Gordon Lightfoot—"14 Carat Gold"(released after the Decade)
15.	The Who—"5:15"
16.	Ringo Starr—"You're Sixteen (You're Beautiful and You're Mine)"
17.	Janis Ian—"At Seventeen"
18.	Alice Cooper—"I'm Eighteen"
19.	The Rolling Stones—"19th Nervous Breakdown"
20.	The Doors—"20th Century Fox"

Here are some other questions about songs released during the Decade containing numbers in the titles, sometimes written out as a word (e.g. zero instead of 0) and sometimes not.

Songs with nothing but numbers:

Three Dog Night

"One"

Songs with only punctuation and numbers:
Queen
Len Barry

Queen—"39"
Len Barry—"1-2-3"

Songs with numbers and words in the title:
1910 Fruitgum Company
? and the Mysterians
The Four Seasons
The Beatles (four songs)
Paul Simon
Brewer & Shipley

1910 Fruitgum Company—"1,2,3 Red Light"
? and the Mysterians—"96 Tears"
The Four Seasons—"December, 1963 (Oh What a Night)"
The Beatles—("Eight Days a Week,""One After 909,""Revolution 9,""When I'm 64")
Paul Simon—"50 Ways to Leave Your Lover"
Brewer & Shipley—"One Toke Over the Line"

There was a #1 song with a number in the title which was in roman numerals. The song was released in 1965.

"I'm Henry VIII, I Am" by Herman's Hermits.

What is the largest number in a song from the Decade that was in the top 100? As a hint, the song itself only reached #57, but the album on which it appeared, which had the name name as the song, hit #1 in 1973.

"Billion Dollar Babies" by Alice Cooper.

Perhaps the most well-known song with a telephone number in the title is "867-5309/Jenny" by Tommy Tutone, released in 1981. However, in 1967, Wilson Pickett also had a hit song with a telephone number in the title. It reached #13 on the *Billboard* Hot 100 and hit #1 on the R&B chart. What was the song?

"634-5789 (Soulsville, USA)." Some may also remember "Beechwood 4-5789", a 1962 hit for the Marvelettes by the formidable (but atypical) songwriting combination of Marvin Gaye and Smokey Robinson (along with George Gordy). Interestingly, not only do both songs end with 5789, but the last 6 numbers are identical (since a 3 equates to the "e" of "Beechwood.") If the "6" in the Wilson Pickett song had been a "2", the phone numbers would have been completely identical. This appears to be a coincidence, as the songs have no other similarities, musically or lyrically. Maybe there is something catchy about "45789."

Besides the song "In the Year 2525," there were two songs from the Decade that reached the top 20 that had years in the title. One was the first charting single in the U.S. for the Bee Gees. The other has both a month and year in the title and was released in 1975 by a group who had most of its success before the Decade. What were the two songs?

The songs were "New York Mining Disaster 1941" and "December, 1963 (Oh, What a Night)" respectively.

There was one song released during the Decade (1967) that was a top 10 song and had a decimal point in the title. What was the song and who recorded it? (As a hint, the artist who recorded it went by one name and he sings the word "point" to reference the decimal point in the lyrics.)

The song was "98.6" and the artist went by Keith.

Name a band that had roman numerals in its name that released 3 songs during the Decade that reached #5 or higher. Also, name the songs.

The Classics IV. Their three top five songs were "Spooky" (#3), "Stormy" (#5) and "Traces" (#2)

CHAPTER 33

Who Needs Bandmates? (One-Man Bands)

"One-man band" is an oft-used term, and sometimes a cliché. In the musical sense, it refers to a musician (often a street performer) who plays a number of instruments simultaneously, using their hands, feet, limbs, and various mechanical or electronic contraptions. However, it can also be used figuratively to refer to a person who fulfills several different roles simultaneously. In this chapter, the focus is on musicians who play all of the instruments on particular songs or albums, but obviously not simultaneously—and of course there must be more than one instrument to count.

The songwriter and lead singer of one of the most successful bands of the late 1960s and early 1970s created a band called the Blue Ridge Rangers, and released an album of the same name in 1973, consisting mostly of covers of country songs. The anonymity was because he was trying to distance himself from his band. Yet, the band was fictional because he was the only member: He sang all the vocals (including the layered backings) and played all the instruments: guitar, drums, bass, pedal steel, banjo, organ and fiddle. The man's name does not appear anywhere on the album, but he posed on the cover as all five silhouetted members of the fictional band. Who is the one-man band who was the Blue Ridge Rangers?

John Fogerty, formerly of Creedence Clearwater Revival. Though not a huge seller, the album was well received by critics and the public alike. Jon Landau of *Rolling Stone* wrote: "If he seemed immodest in the Creedence Clearwater Revival, he has justified himself and proven that he can make a fine, fine record without anyone's help at all. *The Blue Ridge Rangers* may be the most successful one-man rock album yet, and if the general concept still doesn't make sense, at least Fogerty has made it work."[1]

This artist was a one-man band for three sides of a classic double album released in 1972, which yielded two top 20 hits. He played guitars, keyboards, drums and everything else. In 2003, the album was ranked #173 on *Rolling Stone* magazine's list of the 500 greatest albums of all time. While not having any "hits" other than these two, this artist (and producer) has been rightfully called an "immensely gifted musical visionary and icon." He

grew up in Upper Darby, just outside of Philadelphia. **Who was the artist, what is the double album being referred to, and what are his two top 20 hits on that album?**

The artist is Todd Rundgren, the album is *Something/Anything?* and the two songs are "I Saw the Light," which reached #16 and "Hello It's Me," which reached #5. (The latter song appeared on side four of the album which is the one where he was not working solo.) Rundgren was only 23 years old when he created the album. Rundgren wrote and recorded the material for the album at a prolific rate. He attributed his productivity to Ritalin. "It caused me to crank out songs at an incredible pace. 'I Saw the Light' took me all of 20 minutes. You can see why, too, the rhymes are just moon/June/spoon kind of stuff."

Rundgren had planned for the entire double album to be a solo effort, but after an earthquake struck Los Angeles where he was recording, he decided to relocate to New York City for a live recording session at the Record Plant, where he created side four. Rundgren simply rounded up whatever session musicians were available at the moment, none of whom were familiar with the material. The performers and Rundgren only rehearsed the songs a few times before committing the performance to tape, in order to sound spontaneous, and some of the banter between takes appears on the finished album. "Hello It's Me" was rehearsed and recorded in under two hours, and the horn lines and backing vocals at the end of the track were completely improvised.

Commenting on the album for AllMusic.com, Steven Erlewine wrote: "It's an amazing journey that's remarkably unpretentious. . . . *Something/Anything?* has a ton of loose ends throughout: plenty of studio tricks, slight songs (but no filler), snippets of dialogue, and purposely botched beginnings, but all these throwaways simply add context—they're what makes the album into a kaleidoscopic odyssey through the mind of an insanely gifted pop music obsessive. Rundgren occasionally touched on the sheer brilliance of *Something/Anything?* in his later work, but this extraordinary double album is the one time where his classicist songcraft and messy genius converged to create an utterly unique, glorious record."[2]

In addition to being a singer, songwriter and versatile musician, Todd Rundgren was also was a successful record producer. In fact, he produced one of the best-selling albums in history (though released in 1977). What is the album?

Bat Out of Hell by Meat Loaf. Rundgren also sang backing vocals and played guitar, keyboards, and percussion on a number of the tracks.

Another one–man band effort from the Decade was by a British artist. He wrote and released it just after the breakup of his famous band. It was released in 1970. Who is the artist and what is the name of the album? As a hint, they are the same.

The artist is Paul McCartney and the album is *McCartney*. McCartney played acoustic and electric guitars, bass, drums, piano, organ, percussion, Mellotron, toy xylophone and background vocals. The only other contributions to the album were harmonies and backing vocals added by his new wife Linda. Today, many of the songs on the album are highly regarded, with songs such as "That Would Be Something," "Every Night," "Junk," "Man We Was Lonely," "Teddy Boy," and especially "Maybe I'm Amazed."However, the album was not well-received by the critics or by the other Beatles. Many fans bore ill-will towards McCartney since he was perceived as the partial, if not the sole, instigator behind the breakup of the Beatles, which had occurred just a few months previously.

Perhaps the critics were predisposed to be out for blood as well. Chip Madinger and Mark Easter, who wrote about the post-breakup careers of the band members, said that the album receiving a "critical lambasting" and that the "general sentiment" among reviewers was "something to the effect of 'He broke up the Beatles for *this*?!?'" Richard Williams of *Melody Maker* suggested that "with this record, [McCartney's] debt to George Martin becomes increasingly clear . . ." Williams found "sheer banality" in all the tracks save for "Maybe I'm Amazed"and described "Man We Was Lonely" as "the worst example of his music hall side." Reviewing the album for *Rolling Stone*, Langdon Winner found the songs "distinctly second rate."

Critics who reviewed the album decades later had more mixed views. For example, Stephen Erlewine of AllMusic wrote that *McCartney* possesses "an endearingly ragged, homemade quality," with "That Would Be Something," Every Night," "Teddy Boy," and "Maybe I'm Amazed" all "full-fledged McCartney classics." However, he concluded, "Unfortunately, in retrospect it also appears as a harbinger of the nagging mediocrity that would plague McCartney's entire solo career."

McCartney's former bandmates were not impressed either. George Harrison said that with the exception of "Maybe I'm Amazed" and "That Would Be Something," the rest of the songs "just don't do much for me" and that "the only person he's got to tell him if the song's good or bad is Linda." As for John Lennon, in a December 1970 interview with *Rolling Stone*, Lennon dismissed *McCartney* as "rubbish" (although, to be sure, the year immediately following the breakup of the band was clearly a frosty one between Lennon and McCartney).[3]

This 1973 album is not strictly considered a one-man band effort because the artist does use other musicians for string bass, flute and percussion, but he does play an impressive array of instruments himself, including acoustic guitar, bass guitar, electric guitar, Farfisa, Hammond B3, Lowrey organs, flagolet, fuzz guitars, glockenspiel, "honky tonk" piano, mandolin, piano, percussion, "taped motor drive amplifier organ chord," and timpani. Since this is likely not enough to answer the question, here is some more information. Try to answer with as few clues as possible.

(1) The musician was only 19 when he composed the album.

(2) It is mostly instrumental, but not entirely.

(3) The entire first side is Part One of the title track and the entire second side is Part Two of the title track (i.e. the album consists essentially of one 48-minute number).

(4) The album reached #1 in the U.K. and stayed on the British charts for 279 weeks.

(5) The single (essentially taking the first four minutes of Part One) reached #7 on the *Billboard* Hot 100 in 1974.

(6) The album was the first release ever on Richard Branson's Virgin Records.

(7) The beginning of the song is famously-and repeatedly—heard in *The Exorcist*.

(8) Finally, there is one additional instrument played by the man who composed the music besides those listed above, but I can't name it because it is also the name of the album and the single!

What is the name of the album and the composer?

"Tubular Bells" by Mike Oldfield.

On this 1972 album, the artist played every instrument except for electric guitar on one track and trombone on another. He played drums, Moog bass, piano, Fender Rhodes, TONTO synthesizer, harmonica, Hohner clavinet, percussion and talk box. In 2003, the album was ranked #284 on *Rolling Stone's* list of the 500 greatest albums of all time. Even though the artist was only 21 when he released the album, it was his 14th studio album! What is the name of the artist and, more impressively, the album?

The artist is Stevie Wonder and the album is *Music of My Mind*.

CHAPTER 34

Being Concise (One-Word #1s)

The following songs all had one-word titles and all hit #1. In each case, based on the clue given, name the title and the artist.

1. **A product you can eat, although in this case this 1968 song refers to a woman's name.**
   "Honey" by Bobby Goldsboro

2. **This 1967 song also (apparently) refers to a woman's name and not to the weather.**
   "Windy" by the Association. Based on the song lyrics, it is almost difficult to tell whether the song is about a person or actually a tribute to wind itself. However, one line in the song is "smiling at everybody she sees." When Ruthann Freidman wrote the song, the word "she" was instead "he" and it was changed by the Association.[1]

3. **Tommy Roe had two one-word #1s and one of them (released before the Decade) is yet again a woman's name (being an Australian slang for "woman"). What are the two songs?**
   The first song is "Sheila," released in 1961, and the second is "Dizzy," released in 1969, both by Tommy Roe.

4. **The song, released in 1970 during the height of the Vietnam War, is one of the most popular protest songs ever. It was one of 161 songs on the Clear Channel no-play list after September 11, 2001. It is also tied for the fewest numbers of letters in a #1 song: three).**
   "War" by Edwin Starr, written by the great songwriting team of Norman Whitfield and Barrett Strong.[2]

5. **The first solo #1 by one of the most successful artists ever. It came out in 1972.**
   "Ben" by Michael Jackson. Many people forget that he had a solo #1 during the Decade because most of his solo success is thought to have started with his 1979 release, *Off The Wall*.

6. **This song appears on the album *Talking Book* and guitarist Jeff Beck had a hand in its creation—by providing a drum riff of all things.**

"Superstition" by Stevie Wonder. This song actually led to hard feelings between Beck and Wonder. Beck said, "the original agreement was that he'd write me a song, and in return, I'd play on his album." Beck went into the story in further detail in Annette Carson's book *Jeff Beck: Crazy Fingers*: "One day I was sitting at the drum kit, which I love to play when nobody's around, doing this beat. Stevie came kinda boogieing into the studio. 'Don't stop.' 'Ah, c'mon, Stevie, I can't play the drums.' Then [Wonder's] lick came out: 'Superstition.' That was my song, in return for *Talking Book*. I thought, 'He's given me the riff of the century.'"

Unfortunately for Beck, it didn't work out that way. It was going to be released by his group, Beck, Bogert and Appice, but even though Beck recorded his version of the song in July 1972, issues with his band delayed the release of his version of the song until the spring of 1973 long after Wonder's release of the song in October 1972. Although Beck would score a minor hit with his recording, there was no competing with Wonder's definitive take on the song.

Wonder agreed that the song was intended for Beck and that Beck's version was supposed to be released first. However, Motown intervened: "Motown decided they wanted to release 'Superstition.' I said Jeff wanted it, and they told me I needed a strong single in order for the album to be successful. My understanding was that Jeff would be releasing 'Superstition' long before I was going to finish my album. I was late giving them *Talking Book*. Jeff recorded *Superstition* in July, so I thought it would be out [first]."

Carmine Appice, Beck's drummer, added: "He was not supposed to release his version until our version was released but he did—so our version, which was going to be the original version, looked like a cover version."

A 2014 article about the creation and release of the song in ultimateclassicrock.com is provocatively (but not really fairly) titled "41 years ago: Stevie Wonder Steals a #1 song from Jeff Beck." However, if there were any hard feelings between the two, they have dissipated. They played the song together in concert at the 2009 Rock and Roll Hall of Fame 25th Anniversary Concert and the performance can be seen on YouTube.[3]

7. **Highly successful Canadian male singer-songwriter**
    "Sundown" by Gordon Lightfoot.

8. **The Rolling Stones released very few singles that had one word titles, but this was one, and their only one to reach #1.**
    "Angie."

9. **The only Beatles #1 song with an exclamation point in the title.**
    "Help!"

10. There has been only one time when there were three consecutive one-word #1 songs. They occupied that spot for a total of 10 weeks in May, June and July of 1967. The three artists who released the songs were the Young Rascals, Aretha Franklin and the Association.

    The songs were "Groovin'," "Respect," and "Windy" respectively.

11. One of the claims to fame of this band was the naked or nearly naked African-American women who graced a number of their album covers. They had two #1 songs. One of them had one word and hit the top spot in 1974. Name the song and the band.

    "Fire" by the Ohio Players.

CHAPTER 35

Let's Be Specific (Words, Phrases, and Titles)

INTERESTING WORDS AND PHRASES

In this section, we will consider certain words or phrases that come from particular songs from the Decade. Name the song.

hogshead

Of real fire! "Being for the Benefit of Mr. Kite!" A hogshead is a large wooden cask.

Captain Kangaroo

"Flowers on the Wall" by the Statler Brothers. While the group had a number of charting songs on the country chart, this was their only hit on the *Billboard* Hot 100, reaching #4 in 1966. At one point in the 1994 film *Pulp Fiction*, Bruce Willis's character sings along with the song, about smoking and watching the show.

On a more macabre note, in a publicly released video, Dylan Klebold, one of the two teens who committed the Columbine High School Massacre in April 1999, was filmed by a friend while driving in his car at some point prior to the shooting. They were both listening to "Flowers on the Wall" playing on the radio, with Klebold calling it "nice jamming tunage."[1]

Pompatus of love

This comes from "The Joker" by the Steve Miller Band, which reached #1 in 1973. This one is a puzzler on several levels. There is no such word as "pompatus," whether spelled that way or any other way (e.g. "pompitous" or "pompetus"). In fact, that may not even be the word Miller was singing, although that sounds like the closest pronunciation. There is good reason for that: Miller's apparent inspiration for the word was taken from a 1954 song by the Medallions called "The Letter" which itself used a "nonce word" (a made-up word), and no one appears to be sure what that word was either. However, since it is made up and difficult to hear on the actual recording, it is very likely not "pompitous", under that spelling or any other.

In "The Letter" (which can be heard on YouTube), lead singer Vernon Green is essentially reading a letter to his love. In the letter he makes reference to what may be "the puppetutes of love" or possibly "the pulpitudes of love." This follows another nonce word, "pizmotality," because the singer wants to whisper such words to his love.

Actor Jon Cryer tracked down Green in 1996 to ask him about the lyrics. While they were never written down, Green told Cryer that "pizmotality described words of such secrecy that they could only be spoken to the one you loved." And puppetutes? "A term I coined to mean a secret paper-doll fantasy figure [thus puppet], who would be my everything and bear my children."

surry down

"Surry" is another neologism, this time from Laura Nyro's song "Stoned Soul Picnic." The verb *surry* is spelled differently from the noun *surrey* (an old-time carriage). When asked what the word meant, Nyro said "Oh, it's just a nice word."

"Stoned" in this case refers not to drugs but to drinking alcohol—Nyro mentions wine and moonshine in the lyrics as the beverages of choice. Two years earlier, Ray Charles released "Let's Go Get Stoned," which was also about alcohol.[2]

rubber duck (or, from the same song, chartreuse microbus)

"Convoy," a #1 hit for Bill Fries, who went under the pseudonym of C. W. McCall. (The song didn't reach #1 until 1976, but was released in 1975.) Fries was 47 when the song came out. The song deals in part with the struggles truckers were facing at the time regarding restrictive speed limits (the 55 mph speed limit had been recently introduced in response to the first gas crisis of the '70s), bureaucracy (the line about tearing up swindle sheets references the practice of falsifying log sheets to show that drivers were getting proper sleep), and toll and fuel costs.

The conversation is between "Rubber Duck," "Pig Pen" and "Sodbuster," primarily through Rubber Duck's side of the conversation. The narration and CB chatter are by Fries. The convoy begins toward "Flagtown" (Flagstaff, Arizona) at night on June 6 on "I-one-oh" (I–10) just outside "Shakytown" (Los Angeles, California, due to its earth tremors). The convoy passes through Tulsa and "Chi-town" (Chicago), by which time there are police ("bears" or "smokies") in pursuit. The convoy includes a "suicide jockey" (truck hauling explosives), and

"11 long-haired friends of Jesus" (a reference to the then-current Jesus movement subset of Christianity) in "a chartreuse microbus" (a Volkswagen).

The song's running gag has Rubber Duck complaining about the smell of the hogs that Pig Pen is hauling. He repeatedly asks the offending driver to "back off" (slow down). By the end, Pig Pen has fallen so far back, when Rubber Duck is in New Jersey, Pig Pen has only gotten as far as Omaha (a reference to the headquarters of American Gramaphone, which released the song, and also a reference to the slaughterhouses for which Omaha is famous).

Mr. Mojo Risin'

"L.A. Woman" by the Doors, "Mr. Mojo Risin'" being an anagram for Jim Morrison. This was the title track to the last Doors album before Morrison died.

truthin'

"These Boots Are Made for Walking" by Nancy Sinatra, a #1 hit for her in 1966. There was a music video recorded for this song (one of the earliest music videos) that can be seen online. Also, fans of the movie *Austin Powers: International Man of Mystery* may recall that this was the song playing when Frau Farbissina introduced the Fembots, beautiful blonde humanoid creatures who wore white knee-high leather boots (hence the song).[3]

joo-joo eyeball

"Come Together" by the Beatles (written by John Lennon)

Gliddy gloop gloopy

"Good Morning Starshine" by Oliver.

queen of Corona

"Me and Julio Down by the Schoolyard" by Paul Simon. In an interview, Paul Simon was asked about one of the lines in the song about the "mama pajama" seeing something that was against the law:

Q: "What is it that the mama saw? The whole world wants to know."
A: "I have no idea what it is."

Simon speculated that perhaps it was "something sexual" but he really never thought about it. There is also a reference in the same song to a "radical priest" who wound up on the cover of *Newsweek*. The reference to the priest was to Father Daniel Berrigan, a very well-known anti-Vietnam activist and pacifist. He and his brother Philip were repeatedly arrested and imprisoned for actions they took in protest to the war. While Berrigan was never on the cover of *Newsweek*, he and Philip did appear on the January 25, 1971 cover of *Time* magazine under the caption: "The Curious Case of the Berrigans." Daniel died at age 94 on April 30, 2016.[4]

Jock-a-mo

"Iko Iko" which was a top 20 hit for the Dixie Cups in 1965. This song has an interesting history. The song, under the original title "Jock-A-Mo," was written in 1953 by James "Sugar Boy" Crawford in New Orleans and recorded by Crawford's group Sugar Boy and the Cane Cutters. He wrote down various Indian chants as he thought he had heard them. In fact, in his version, he said he was actually singing "chock-a-mo" and the title was misheard by Leonard Chess, President of Chess Records, who misspelled it as "Jock-a-mo" for the record's release. There is much disagreement as to what the rest of the chorus means (even putting aside the fact that Crawford appears not to have written down the lyrics at all and has stated that he did not know the actual words anyway). Suffice it to say that language experts seem to agree that it is some form of French Creole.

As for the recording of the song, it came about basically by accident. Group member Barbara Hawkins explained: "Well, we thought we were alone [in the studio] so we start playing around with the song. And there was an aluminum chair, a couple of drumsticks, an ashtray, and that's the instrumentation that you hear. We didn't realize [that producers] Jerry [Leiber] and Mike [Stoller] had the tapes running." Leiber and Stoller overdubbed a bass and percussion, and released the song.

Because the three Dixie Cup members—Barbara Ann Hawkins, her sister Rosa Lee Hawkins and their cousin Joan Johnson—did not know the origins of the song (except having heard it from their grandmother), they simply claimed authorship of the song for themselves. Not surprisingly, Crawford sued them. The Dixie Cups ludicrously denied that the two compositions were similar (given that they are almost identical), but the lawsuit resulted in a settlement in 1967 with Crawford making no claim to authorship or ownership of the song, but receiving a percentage of royalties for public performances.[5]

Et cetera. **(This may not be apparent to readers by itself, but the song is definitely recognizable. It was released in 1968.)**

"Elenore" by the Turtles. This song reached #6 on the *Billboard* Hot 100. It was intended to be a parody of the band's own previous hit, "Happy Together," which reached #1. Howard Kaylan, a band member and one of the cowriters of the song stated: "It was never intended to be a straightforward song. It was meant as an anti-love letter to [our record label] who were constantly on our backs to bring them another "Happy Together." So I gave them a very skewed version. Not only with the chords changed, but with all these bizarre words. It was my feeling that they would listen to how strange and stupid the song was and leave us alone. But they didn't get the joke. They thought it sounded good."[6]

Plasticine. (Hint: The word which follows is porters.)

"Lucy in the Sky with Diamonds" by the Beatles. Plasticine is a brand of modelling clay. The name is a registered trademark of Flair Leisure Products plc.

Gitche Gumee. (Hint: This is another word for one of the Great Lakes.)

"The Wreck of the Edmond Fitzgerald" by Gordon Lightfoot. This one is a bit of a cheat since the song was released in 1976 (where it reached #2 on the *Billboard* Hot 100), but the event on which the song was based took place in 1975 and the prime years for the Canadian singer-songwriter were during the Decade. Also, it's an excellent song. The Chippewa Native American tribe called the Lake Superior *gichigami*, meaning "be a great sea." Henry Wadsworth Longfellow wrote the name as "Gitche Gumee" in his 1855 poem "The Song of Hiawatha."

In the opening verse of the song, Lightfoot sings that the lake Gitche Gumee "never gives up her dead." This is taken directly from the lead of the article which appeared in *Newsweek* in 1975 two weeks after the event: "According to a legend of the Chippewa tribe, the lake they once called Gitche Gumee never gives up her dead."

This one sounds like gitchee gumme, but is a little different: gitchi gitchi. (As a hint, the woman who a had a big hit with this song swore that she did not know it was about prostitution.)

"Lady Marmalade" by LaBelle, which reached #1 in 1974. Lead singer Patti LaBelle said "I didn't know what it was about. Nobody, I swear this is God's truth, nobody told me what I'd just sung a song about." However, even if one doesn't speak French, it's hard to misinterpret the rest of the lyrics.[7]

Not many rock songs make reference to operas but this one does. The song was a #1 hit and the opera is Pagliacci. What is the song and who is the artist (who also wrote the

lyrics)? (As a hint, it was released on the Tamla label, a subsidiary of Motown, and came out in 1970.)

The song is "Tears of a Clown," by Smokey Robinson and the Miracles. In the song, his character is sad because his girlfriend left him, and compares himself to the characters in *Pagliacci* (Italian for "clowns"), who hide their hurt and anger behind empty smiles. Robinson had used this line before in the song "My Smile Is Just a Frown (Turned Upside Down)," which he had written in 1964 for Motown artist Carolyn Crawford. Surprisingly, this was the group's only #1 song (with Robinson—in 1975, after Billy Griffin had replaced Robinson as lead singer, they had a #1 hit with "Love Machine"). "Tears ofa Clown" was originally released on the 1967 album *Make It Happen*, but did not become a success until it was re-released in September 1970. It also hit #1 in the U.K. and on the R&B chart.

As mentioned above, Smokey Robinson wrote the lyrics to "Tears of a Clown." What is less well known is that the music was written by Henry Cosby and a famous fellow Tamla/Motown artist. Who is it?

Stevie Wonder.

Ooga-chaka. **For extra credit, name (1) the singer who first had a hit with the song in 1959, (2) the otherwise obscure band that had a #1 hit with the song in 1974.**

The song is "Hooked on a Feeling," written by Mark James. B.J. Thomas's version hit #5 in 1969 and the 1974 cover by Blue Swede hit #1. They based their rendition of the song on a 1971 version released by British singer Jonathan King, which created the ooga-chaka intro-duction (although in his version it sounds more like ooka-chaka).

The 1959 song "Running Bear" was a hit sung by Johnny Preston and written by J.P. Richardson, (better known as the Big Bopper), begins with repeated chants (by Richardson) sounding something like "oomba ooga" or "oomba ooba." However, when King was asked about this, he said, "Nope, not inspired by any other record. Just wanted different instruments to make a reggae rhythm and decided on male voices." However, in his 2009 autobiography *65: My Life So Far,* he characterized it as "six guys grunting like gorillas."[8]

Falletinme. (As a hint, this word is part of the title of a #1 song.)

"Thank You (Falletinme Be Mice Elf Agin)" which reached #1 for Sly and the Family Stone in 1969.

Hober reeber

This is from the first verse of the Monkees' song "No Time," a release off their first album where they largely played their own instruments and wrote a number of their own songs, *Headquarters*. The nonsensical lyrics that begin the song (by drummer Mickey Dolenz) are based on part of Bill Cosby's "A Nut In Every Car" routine from his 1963 album *Bill Cosby is a Very Funny Fellow Right!*

Although *No Time* was written by The Monkees, they gave songwriting credit to their recording engineer Hank Cicalo as a thank you for his help on the *Headquarters* album on which it appeared. Cicalo engineered many albums over the years, most notably Carole King's *Tapestry*. Headquarters was the group's third album overall and the first after their acrimonious split with manager Don Kirshner. Although it yielded no hit singles, it reached #1 on the *Billboard* 200 album chart and was certified double platinum in the U.S. with sales of more than two million copies within the first two months of release. (The album was knocked off the #1 perch after one week by *Sgt. Pepper's*.) Of course, The Monkees were so hot in 1967 after their first two albums (on which they played almost no instruments and wrote only one of the songs) that any album they released as a follow-up was likely to go instant platinum. Nevertheless, among Monkees fans, it is considered a very good album and it is included in the book *1001 Albums You Must Hear Before You Die*.⁹

REPETITION OF WORDS

Each of the following artists or groups recorded a song during the Decade consisting solely of the same word repeated two or more times. Some of the following are easy and some much less so. Name the song.

Gary Puckett and the Union Gap

"Woman, Woman"

Neil Diamond

"Cherry, Cherry"

The Beau Brummels

"Laugh, Laugh"

The Dixie Cups

"Iko-Iko"

Shirley and Company

"Shame Shame Shame"

The Mamas and the Papas

"Monday Monday"

The Hollies

"Stop Stop Stop"

Cher

"Bang Bang"

Sopwith Camel

"Hello Hello"

Tommy James and the Shondells

"Mony Mony"

The Castaways

"Liar Liar"

If there was one group that loved to repeat words in song titles, it was ABBA. At least 14 of their songs (some released during the Decade and some after) contained such repetition, including seven of their biggest hits (although others would be known only to hard-core ABBA fans). How many can you think of?

"Andante, Andante"
"Another Town, Another Train"
"Dum Dum Diddle"
"Gimme! Gimme! Gimme!"
"Hey Hey Helen"
"Honey Honey"
"I Do, I Do, I Do, I Do, I Do"
"Knowing Me, Knowing You"
"Money, Money, Money"
"My Love, My Life"
"On and On and On"
"One Man, One Woman"
"Ring, Ring"
"SOS"

This artist's first hit song reached #3 on the *Billboard* chart in 1971. It repeats the phrase "I know" 26 times in succession. This was meant to be a placeholder until he could think of lyrics, but the other musicians present during the recording said to leave it like that. Who is the artist and what is the song?

The artist is Bill Withers and the song is "Ain't No Sunshine." When the song was recorded, Withers was 31 years old, working in a factory making toilet seats for 747s. In discussing the famous third verse, he said:

I wasn't going to [leave all of the "I know's" in there, but] then Booker T. [Jones] said, "No, leave it like that." I was going to write something there, but there was a general consensus in the studio. It was an interesting thing because I've got all these guys that were already established, and I was working in the [airplane] factory at the time. Graham Nash was sitting right in front of me, just offering his support. Stephen Stills was playing [guitar] and there was Booker T and Al Jackson and Donald Dunn—all of the MGs except Steve Cropper. They were all these people with all this experience in all these reputations and I was this factory worker in here just sort of puttering around, so when their general feeling was, 'leave it like that,' I left it like that.

The song is 285th on *Rolling Stone*'s list of the 500 Greatest Songs of All Time and won the Grammy for Best R&B Song in 1972. In 1972, Withers had a #1 song with "Lean On Me" and a #2 song with "Use Me."[10]

This song reached #3 for Helen Reddy in 1973. However, she disliked it because she found the repetition of the song title in the chorus to be monotonous. In fact, the song was the subject of a nationwide contest in America in which listeners would submit to their local radio station their estimation of how many times the song title was heard. What is the song? (There is a parenthetical phrase in the title.)

The song is "Leave Me Alone (Ruby Red Dress)." So how many times does she sing "leave me alone?" The title phrase is heard 12 times in the chorus and the chorus is heard 3 times. It is heard once more (and possibly twice) in the fadeout. So the answer is 37 or 38 by Reddy herself. This does not include the phrase "leave me" (i.e. without the "alone") that she sings 12 times, or the 6 times per chorus it is sung by her backup singers. So, all told, including the backup singers, the title words "leave me" heard about 68 or 69 times.

When Reddy came out of retirement in 2013, she cited this song as "one song I will never ever sing again. That sort of songwriting doesn't do much for me, but it was a hit. However, I don't have to sing it anymore if I don't want to, and I don't want to."[11]

SPOKEN WORD HITS

There have been plenty of odd songs which have charted on the *Billboard* Hot 100, both in the Decade and in the rock era generally, but of all the head-scratchers that would make one ask "what was America thinking?", the ones which are the subject of the next three questions may take the cake. Admittedly, the answers to these questions are difficult but, in defense of the questions, they all involve top 10 "hits," as difficult as that may be to believe, upon hearing them, or hearing about them.

The first number climbed all the way to #8 in 1971. While there is singing and music, the person who the song is "by" Les Crane, does nothing more than read a 1927 poem by Max Ehrmann in a normal voice. The song won a Best Spoken Word Grammy in 1972. What is the name of the poem/song?

"Desiderata." Crane had an interesting life, to say the least. After spending four years in the Air Force as a jet pilot and helicopter flight instructor, he became a radio broadcaster. Casey Kasem credited him with being responsible for creating the Top 40 list of the most requested pop songs. Then he hosted a talk show in New York and the first appearance of the Rolling Stones on American television was on Crane's show. His confrontational interview technique, along with a "shotgun" microphone he aimed at audiences, earned him the name "the bad boy of late-night television." However, he was unable to successfully compete against Johnny Carson.

In 1966, Crane married one of the most desirable women in America at the time, Tina Louise, better known as Ginger from *Gilligan's Island*. She was the third of his five wives and they were married until 1974. Ironically, his fifth and final wife was actually named Ginger.

In the 1980s, he transitioned to the software industry and became chairman of the Software Toolworks, creators of the three-dimensional color chess series, *Chessmaster* and the educational series *Mavis Beacon Teaches Typing*.

Of his "hit song," he told the *Los Angeles Times* in 1987 that "I can't listen to it now without gagging."[12]

Four years prior to "Desiderata" was another spoken word song whose mere appearance on the charts, not to mention its ascendancy all the way to the #10 spot, would be just as astonishing to today's ears as *Desiderata*. It was written Victor Lundberg (who was a newscaster at a Grand Rapids radio station) and spoken by him over *Battle Hymn of the Republic*. In this case, the most famous line is the last one, where Lundberg tells his son that, if he burns his draft card, then he should also burn his birth certificate as he would disown him. After the song reached the top 10, it appears that America suddenly and collectively said to itself: "What the heck were we thinking?" On December 16, 1967, it dropped to #22, and the following week it fell off the chart entirely, a virtually unprecedented decline. The song was nominated for a Grammy for Best Spoken Word Recording but did not win. What was the title of the "song"?

"An Open Letter to My Teenage Son." There were numerous "response" records from the imaginary "sons" to whom the letter was written back to "Dad," including "A Teenager's Answer" by Keith Gordon, "A Teenager's Open Letter To His Father" by Robert Tamlin, "Letter From A Teenage Son" by Brandon Wade, "A Letter To Dad" by Every Father's Teenage Son (apparently a group named for the sole purpose of responding to this song), "Hi, Dad (An Open Letter To Dad)" by Dick Clair, and "An Open Letter To My Dad" by Marceline. Most of these imaginary sons were not too pleased with Dad's letter, especially his justification of war and the last line.

On June 5, 1973, Canadian broadcaster Gordon Sinclair offered a commentary opining that America's role in the world was underappreciated and that when many countries faced economic crises or natural disasters, Americans were among the most generous people and the first to offer assistance, but whenever America faced a crisis, it often faced that crisis alone. The editorial became a phenomenon in America after Byron MacGregor, a Detroit radio station news director, read Sinclair's commentary on the air. A record of MacGregor's recording was released by Westbound Records, against the background of

"America the Beautiful," played by the Detroit Symphony Orchestra. By January 1974, the record became one of the fastest-selling records in United States, reaching sales of two million within a month of its release. It eventually sold three and a half million copies in the United States, and hit #1 in *Cash Box*, as well as #4 on the *Billboard* Hot 100 chart in February 1974. All proceeds from the record were donated by MacGregor to the American Red Cross. What was the title of the song?

"The Americans." Sinclair referenced floods on the Yellow River, the Yangtze, the Nile, the Amazon, the Ganges and the Niger and earthquakes in Managua and Nicaragua as examples of Americans offering assistance, along with war and humanitarian aid. By contrast, in 1973, no other nations were offering to assist America in 1973 when its dollar was falling and the Mississippi River was flooding.[13]

In 1981, when Ronald Reagan made his first state visit to Canada, he praised both Sinclair and MacGregor as figures who had given the United States an inspiring tribute in one of its darkest hours. MacGregor was also posthumously honored with the National Americanism Award. The performance was widely heard again after the World Trade Center attack on September 11, 2001 and in 2005, after Hurricane Katrina.

CHAPTER 36

Subjects You Hated in School (Punctuation, Grammar and Spelling)

PARENTHESES

Some great songs have parentheses in the title. All of the following songs were released during the Decade. I will list the title and all you have to do is identify the parenthetical which is also part of the title. In some cases, the rest of the song is before the parenthetical and in some cases after.

"How Sweet It Is"—Marvin Gaye and James Taylor

"(To Be Loved by You)." This song, written by the Motown songwriting team of Holland-Dozier-Holland, was first recorded by Marvin Gaye in 1964 and his version reached #6 on the *Billboard* Hot 100. However, the most successful version is James Taylor's in 1975, which reached #5.

"Break on Through"—The Doors

"(To the Other Side)." This was the first single released by the Doors and was unsuccessful compared with later hits, reaching only #126 in the United States. Despite this, it became a concert staple and remains one of the band's signature and most popular songs.

"It's Only Rock 'n Roll"—The Rolling Stones

"(But I Like It)." This is the lead single from the Stones' 1974 album, *It's Only Rock 'n Roll.* The parenthetical is in the song title only, not the album title.

"I Didn't Get to Sleep at All"—The Fifth Dimension

"(Last Night)." This 1972 hit is one of the relatively few songs in which the parenthetical precedes the rest of the title rather than follows it.

"The Shoop Shoop Song"—Betty Everett

"(It's in His Kiss)." Although the most well-known versions of this song were recorded outside the Decade (Betty Everett's original in 1964 and Cher's remake in 1990), it was also covered several times during the Decade.

"4th of July, Asbury Park"—Bruce Springsteen

"(Sandy)." The Springsteen classic, with Danny Federici on accordion. This appears on the Boss's second album, *The Wild, the Innocent & the E Street Shuffle*.

"Mama Told Me"—Three Dog Night

"(Not to Come)." It is little known or little remembered that this #1 song for Three Dog Night in 1970 was written by none other than Randy Newman. It was actually written for Eric Burdon's first solo album, *Eric is Here*, that was released in 1967. Tom Jones also had a hit with it in 2000. It was also the #1 song in the U.S. on the inaugural American Top 40 broadcast in 1970. Newman's estimable talents as a songwriter were not reflected on the *Billboard* charts. Other than this song, his only other song in the top 50 was "Short People" from 1977 (#2). Of course, he has had phenomenal success in his "second career" writing music for movies, having earned a total of 20 Academy Award nominations for Best Original Score and Best Original Song.

"Since You've Been Gone"—Aretha Franklin

"(Sweet Sweet Baby)." The parenthetical is the start of the title of this 1968 song.

"Satisfaction"—The Rolling Stones

"(I Can't Get No)." Again, the parenthetical is the start of the song title for the 1965 song that made the Stones worldwide stars. Keith Richards wrote the music for this song, including the famous opening riff, and then Jagger wrote the lyrics. The riff came to Richards in a dream. He woke up and grabbed a guitar and a cassette machine, played the run of notes once, then fell back to sleep. "On the tape," he said later, "you can hear me drop the pick, and the rest is snoring." It has been written that this happened in a motel room in Clearwater, Florida, on the Stones' third U.S. tour, but in his 2010 autobiography, Richards said that it happened in his flat in St. John's Wood. It has also been written that the Stones have played this song on nearly every tour since its release, which would seem logical given its worldwide success and the fact that it is probably their signature song. However, despite the fact that it is not too difficult to find clips of the "early Stones" playing the song in concert, Richards denies in his autobiography that they played it often: "It's a hell of a song to play on stage. For years and years we never played it, or very rarely, until maybe the past ten or fifteen years. Couldn't get the sound right, it just sounded weedy. It took the band a long time to figure out how to play 'Satisfaction' on stage."[1]

"December 1963"—The Four Seasons

"(Oh, What A Night)." This song was released in 1975 and went to #1 in February 1976. According to the cowriter and longtime band member Bob Gaudio, the song was originally set in 1933 with the title "December 5th, 1933," and celebrated the repeal of Prohibition. Neither lead singer Frankie Valli nor cowriter (and Gaudio's wife) Judy Parker were thrilled about the lyrics—and Valli objected to parts of the melody—so Gaudio redid the words and Parker redid the melody until all were content with the finished product. It ended up being a nostalgic love song. Unusually for the group, the lead singer on the first verse was drummer Gerri Polci; Valli sings the bridge sections and backing vocals.

"The Dock of the Bay"—Otis Redding

"(Sittin' On)." The classic, recorded only days before Redding died in 1967 at just 26 years of age.

"Rocket Man"—Elton John. Here's my own parenthetical: (Who knew that this was not the full title of the song?)

"(I Think It's Going to Be A Long Long Time)"

"Turn! Turn! Turn!"—The Byrds

"(to Everything There Is a Season)." This song reached #1 in December 1965. The lyrics are taken almost verbatim from the Book of Ecclesiastes as found in the King James Version (1611) of the Bible (Ecclesiastes 3:1-8), though the sequence of the words was rearranged for the song. The music was written by Pete Seeger.

"Try"—Janis Joplin

"(Just a Little Bit Harder)." Like "Satisfaction" by the Rolling Stones, this is one of the few parenthetical songs in which the non-parenthetical part of the song is only one word.

"Rosalita"—Bruce Springsteen

"(Come Out Tonight)." This appears on the Boss's second album, *The Wild, the Innocent & the E Street Shuffle*.

"I'm Just a Singer"—Moody Blues

"(In a Rock and Roll Band)"

"A Natural Woman"—Carole King

"(You Make Me Feel Like)"

"Norwegian Wood"—The Beatles

"(This Bird Has Flown)"

"Brandy"—Looking Glass

"(You're a Fine Girl)." This song reached #1 on the *Billboard* Hot 100 in 1972. The band released only two albums and then "disbanded."

"Instant Karma"—John Lennon

"(We All Shine On)." This song has been described as one of the fastest songs in history to be released relative to when it was written. According to Lennon "[I] wrote it for breakfast, recorded it for lunch, and we're putting it out for dinner." While that is a slight exaggeration, it was written and recorded the same day (January 27, 1970) and released in Britain only 10 days later.[2]

"It's Alright, Ma"—Bob Dylan

"(I'm Only Bleeding)"

"Gimme! Gimme! Gimme!"—ABBA

"(A Man After Midnight)"

"Bang A Gong"—T Rex

"(Get It On)"

"The 59th Street Bridge Song"—Simon and Garfunkel

"(Feelin' Groovy)"

"Lay Down"—Melanie

"(Candles in the Rain)"

"I Can't Help Myself"—The Four Tops

"(Sugar Pie Honey Bunch)"

Here's a hard one: "Aquarius/Let the Sunshine In"—The Fifth Dimension

"(The Flesh Failures)"

Another hard one: "Opus 17"—The Four Seasons

"(Don't You Worry About Me)"

For the last song, I will give the parenthetical rather than the song and not the name of the artist. It's "(Hey Won't You Play)." As a hint, this song is often described as having the longest title of any song which reached #1 on the *Billboard* Hot 100. While that is not accurate, it does have the longest title of any such song which reached #1 during the Decade.

"Another Somebody Done the Somebody Wrong Song" by BJ Thomas. It reached #1 in April 1975. The longest title of a #1 song was a song issued in January 1981 by the studio group Stars on 45. Its official title in the US is "Medley: Intro Venus / Sugar, Sugar / No Reply / I'll Be Back / Drive My Car / Do You Want to Know a Secret / We Can Work It Out / I

Should Have Known Better / Nowhere Man / You're Going to Lose That Girl / Stars on 45."
It is sometimes shortened to "Stars on 45."

EXCLAMATION POINTS

There was one (and only one) Beatles song that has an exclamation point, but not at the end of the title. What is it? (As a hint, it appears on *Abbey Road*.)

"Oh! Darling"

Each of the following artists or groups released at least one song during the Decade with one or more exclamation points in the title. Name the song.

1. The Supremes (Hint: Like "Oh! Darling," one of the few songs where the exclamation point does not appear at the end of the title.)
2. The Beatles (two songs, besides "Oh! Darling") (The songs appear on two different albums, both released during the Decade.)
3. The Byrds (Hint: One of the few titles which has more than one exclamation point and they are not next to each other.)
4. Mitch Ryder and the Detroit Wheels
5. The Doors (Hint: Not one of their big hits, it appears on *Morrison Hotel*)

1. Supremes—"Stop! In the Name of Love"
2. The Beatles—"Help!" and "Being For the Benefit of Mr. Kite!"
3. The Byrds—"Turn! Turn! Turn!"
4. Mitch Ryder and the Detroit Wheels—"Sock It To Me Baby!"
5. The Doors—"Land Ho!"

QUESTION MARKS

Continuing in the punctuation vein, each of the following artists of groups released at least one well-known song during the Decade with a question mark in the title. Name the song.

1. The Bee Gees
2. The Lovin' Spoonful

3. **The Rolling Stones**
4. **Dionne Warwick**
5. **Billy Preston**
6. **Creedence Clearwater Revival**
7. **The Beach Boys**
8 **Chicago**

1. The Bee Gees—"How Can You Mend a Broken Heart?"
2. The Lovin' Spoonful—"Did you Ever Have to Make Up Your Mind?"
3. The Rolling Stones—"Have You Seen Your Mother, Baby, Standing in the Shadow?"
4. Dionne Warwick—"Do You Know the Way to San Jose?"
5. Billy Preston—"Will It Go Round in Circles?"
6. Credence Clearwater Revival—"Who'll Stop the Rain?"
7. The Beach Boys—"Wouldn't It Be Nice?"
8. Chicago—"Does Anyone Really Know What Time It Is?"

BAD GRAMMAR: "AIN'T"

Sometimes songwriters are not grammarians. Name the song by each of the following artists or groups with the word "ain't" in the title. Once again, they are all well-known titles.

1. **The Temptations**
2. **Helen Reddy**
3. **The Walker Brothers**
4. **Marvin Gaye and Tammi Terrell**
5. **The Four Tops**
6. **The Hollies**
7. **Bachman Turner Overdrive**
8. **Diana Ross**

1. The Temptations—"Ain't Too Proud to Beg"
2. Helen Reddy—"Ain't No Way to Treat a Lady"
3. The Walker Brothers—"The Sun Ain't Gonna Shine Anymore"
4. Marvin Gaye and Tammi Terrell—"Ain't Nothing Like the Real Thing"
5. The Four Tops—"Ain't No Woman Like the One I Got"
6. The Hollies—"He Ain't Heavy, He's My Brother"

7. Bachman Turner Overdrive—"You Ain't Seen Nothing Yet"
8. Diana Ross—"Ain't No Mountain High Enough"

SPELLED TITLES

Can you think of any songs from the Decade in which a word is spelled out? If not, below is a list of artists that released such songs, contained either in the title or in the song itself.

1. **Aretha Franklin**
   R-E-S-P-E-C-T

2. **The Shadows of Knight**
   G-L-O-R-I-A. Although this Van Morrison-penned song was first released by his band Them in 1964, the cover by the Shadows of Knight in 1966 was more successful, reaching #10 on the *Billboard* Hot 100.

3. **The Kinks**
   L-O-L-A

4. **Herman's Hermits**
   H-E-N-R-Y (from "I'm Henry VIII, I Am," although the name is pronounced Hen-e-ry in the song).

5. **Tammy Wynette**
   D-I-V-O-R-C-E

6. **Al Green**
   L-O-V-E

7. **The Guess Who (long version of song only)**
   A-M-E-R-I-C-A

CHAPTER 37

Thou Shalt Not Steal (Theft or "Borrowing" from Other Songs)

L ed Zeppelin has been frequently accused of stealing chord progressions, riffs, melodies or words from other artists to create their songs (including, most famously, "Stairway to Heaven"). As Bill Janovitz wrote in AllMusic.com: "There is quite an extensive list of . . . instances where it can be argued that Led Zeppelin went far beyond merely incorporating their blues and folk influences. American blues songwriter and bassist Willie Dixon in particular is one their "inspriations."

They have been repeatedly sued for, as one article put it, a "whole lotta borrowing," a play on Zeppelin's song "Whole Lotta Love." Many of the songs follow a familiar script: the band releases the song with no songwriting credit (and thus no royalties) to the person whose song they "sampled" as to the music, words or both. They are sued. A settlement then follows in which they add the songwriter's name to the writing credit and that person also receives royalties. **Below is a partial list of songs, some by Zeppelin and some being the songs allegedly "borrowed" by the group. Some of the songs below are Zeppelin hits that will be familiar to everyone and others will be familiar only to hardcore fans of the band. In each case, name either the other artist or band or the Zeppelin song. (For those who want to hear the similarities, there are various YouTube clips such as "Led Zeppelin steals songs" and "Led Zeppelin examples of plagiarism" in which the originals and the Zeppelin version of most of these songs can be heard back to back.)**

"Stairway to Heaven" (Led Zeppelin)

"Taurus" by Spirit, an instrumental originally released on their self-titled debut album in 1968. The track, composed by guitarist/singer Randy Craig Wolfe, better known as Randy California, was recorded in November 1967. The plucked guitar line that can be heard starting at 0:45 of "Taurus" is startingly similar to the opening measures of "Stairway to Heaven." As written in *Guitar World* magazine: "California's most enduring legacy may well be the fingerpicked acoustic theme of the song 'Taurus,' which Jimmy Page lifted virtually note for note for the introduction to 'Stairway to Heaven.'" Led Zeppelin opened for Spirit in an early American tour, leaving little doubt that Led Zeppelin had heard the song before.

In 2014, Randy California's estate filed a copyright infringement suit seeking a cowriting credit for California on "Stairway to Heaven." In 2016, after a week-long trial and a day of deliberation, a jury found that there was no plagiarism by Led Zeppelin. After the verdict, Page and Robert Plant issued a joint statement: "We are grateful for the jury's conscientious service and pleased that it has ruled in our favor, putting to rest questions about the origins of 'Stairway to Heaven' and confirming what we have known for 45 years. We appreciate our fans' support, and look forward to putting this legal matter behind us."[1]

Many were surprised that the jury found against the plaintiff. However, there is one possible explanation that is very logical and yet shocking at the same time. The jury never heard the original recordings of the two songs! That is because the court granted a motion filed by Zeppelin's attorney that prevented the jury from hearing (or hearing about) all kinds of evidence that they felt would be prejudicial and the judge granted most of their requests, thus excluding from the jury (1) recordings of the two songs at issue (even though one might think that would go the very heart of the case), (2) newspaper articles and book excerpts, (3) evidence of other claims of theft against Led Zeppelin (of which there are many), (4) evidence regarding the wealth of the band, and (5) evidence regarding the band's drug and alcohol use. Therefore, the only plagiarism at issue was the sheet music on file with the U.S. Copyright Office. (The two songs were played live in the courtroom by a guitarist.) Counsel for California's Estate commented that as a result of this evidentiary ruling, "it was like trying the case with two hands tied behind our back."

While "Stairway to Heaven" often appears at or near the top of many "best rock songs ever" lists, it does have its detractors, perhaps some tongue-in-cheek. Dave Barry says it would be a much better song "if they cut maybe 45 minutes out of it," and wondering if they really needed the part about "if there's a bustle in your hedgerow." He also quotes from musician Tim Rooney who came up with a list of "top 10 request songs that Top Forty bands hate most." This song was nos. 1, 4, 7, 9 and 10 on the list.

Another person who doesn't care for the song is Robert Plant himself. "I'd break out in hives if I had to sing "Stairway to Heaven" in every show. I wrote those lyrics and found that song to be of some importance and consequence in 1971, but [all these] years later, I don't know. It's just not for me." In 2002, Plant made a donation to an Oregon radio station that refused to play what he calls "that bloody wedding song." At a one-off concert in London, Plant reluctantly agreed to play the song with Led Zeppelin, but insisted that it appear in the middle of the set, and that Jimmy Page "restrain himself from turning the song into an even more epic solo-filled noodle." Plant no doubt appreciates the money made from the song however: In 2008, Conde Nast's Portfolio estimated that the song had generated $562 million in publishing royalties and record sales since its release.[2]

"You Need Love"—1953 by Willie Dixon recorded by Muddy Waters in 1962.

This provided "inspiration" for "Whole Lotta Love," the opening track on *Led Zeppelin II*, the band's highest-charting single on the *Billboard* Hot 100 at #4 (in fact the band's only top 10 single in the U.S.). The melody and some of the lyrics are similar to Waters' song, which was released in 1962 and was written by Willie Dixon. Once again, this led to another suit against Zeppelin, and a settlement. In 2014, listeners to BBC Radio 2 voted "Whole Lotta Love" as the greatest guitar riff of all time.[3]

"Dazed and Confused" (Led Zeppelin)

In 1967, Jake Holmes wrote and released a song of the same title on his album, *The Above Ground Sound of Jake Holmes*. In August 1967, Holmes opened for the Yardbirds when Jimmy Page was a member of that band. According to Holmes, "that was the infamous moment of my life when 'Dazed and Confused' fell into the loving arms and hands of Jimmy Page." When 'Dazed and Confused' appeared on Led Zeppelin's album in 1969, Holmes was aware of it but didn't follow up. In the early 1980s, however, he sent a letter to Page asking for "some credit at least and some remuneration," but no reply was received. In 2010, Holmes sued Page for copyright infringement. The parties settled out of court.

Holmes has had an interesting career in his own right, aside from his writing of "Dazed and Confused." He was an extremely successful jingle writer, most notably the U.S. Army recruitment jingle "Be All That You Can Be" and the "Be a Pepper" jingle for Dr Pepper (which he wrote with Randy Newman). He also wrote or cowrote a slew of others including "Building a better way . . . to see the U.S.A." for Chevrolet, "We fly the world" for Pan American, "Raise your hand if you're Sure" for Sure deodorant, "Aren't You Hungry for Burger King Now?" for Burger King, "Best a Man Can Get" for Gillette, and "Come see the softer side of Sears, Roebuck and Company."

"Babe, I'm Gonna Leave You" (Led Zeppelin)

Anne Bredon (then known as Anne Johannsen) wrote a song of the same title in the late 1950s. It was recorded by Joan Baez (credited and becoming widely popular as "traditional") and released on her 1962 album *Joan Baez in Concert*. (Baez's cover did not have a writing credit.) Despite using the same title and melody and many of the same words as

Bredon's version, Zeppelin bizarrely credited the song as "trad. arr. Page" on their self-titled debut album.

Bredon had no idea about the Zeppelin version until 1981, when the son of Janet Smith, a college friend of Bredon's, heard his mom strumming the tune at home and said "Gee, Mom, I didn't know you did Led Zeppelin songs." This led to a threatened lawsuit. The parties settled the matter so that the Zeppelin song is now credited as "Anne Bredon/Jimmy Page & Robert Plant" and she was to receive a share of all past and future royalties from the song.

"Killing Floor" by Chester Burnett aka Howlin' Wolf

Many hear Wolf's tune in the 1969 Zeppelin song "The Lemon Song" from *Led Zeppelin II*. The melody, guitar riff and many lyrics (including the words "killing floor") are similar between the two songs. Once again, Burnett was not credited on the original version of the song, once again there was a lawsuit and once again Zeppelin was forced to settle. As part of the settlement, Burnett's name was added to the writing credits.

"Since I've Been Loving You" (Led Zeppelin)

This is a slow blues number on *Led Zeppelin III* released in 1970. In this case, the band "borrows" from Moby Grape's song "Never," and some of the lyrics, including the entire first verse, are identical.

"Down by Backwaterside" by Bert Jansch

There are similarities with this and the Zeppelin song "Black Mountain Side." Jansch recorded and arranged a traditional Irish folk song called "Down by Backwaterside" on his 1966 album *Jack Orion*. This arrangement was learned by Al Stewart, who followed Jansch's gigs closely, and who, in turn, taught it to Page, who was a session musician for Stewart's debut album.

"Bring it On Home" by Willie Dixon

A song of the same title appears on *Led Zeppelin II*. It was written by Willie Dixon and the first known recording of the song was by Sonny Boy Williamson in 1963. This song was a little different than some of the others because here Page specifically acknowledges that he was paying tribute to Williamson, though, as with the other songs, that didn't mean that Williamson was credited as a writer or given royalties. The intro and outro were deliberate homages to Williamson's song, whereas the rest of the track was an original Jimmy Page/Robert Plant composition. In 1972, Arc Music, the publishing arm of Chess Records, brought a lawsuit against Led Zeppelin for copyright infringement over "Bring It On Home." The case was settled out-of-court for an undisclosed sum.

The accusations (and in some cases admissions) of plagiarism don't stop there. Their song "Boogie with Stu" on the album *Physical Graffiti* borrowed heavily from the Ritchie Valens song "Ooh! My Head." The listed writers of the song were all four band members, occasional Rolling Stone pianist Ian Stewart and a "Mrs. Valens," Ritchie's mother. Jimmy Page acknowledged the use of Valens' song but claimed that the band was trying to do the right thing: "What we tried to do was give Ritchie's mother credit, because we heard she never received any royalties from any of her son's hits, and Robert did lean on that lyric a bit. So what happens? They tried to sue us for all of the song!" An out of court settlement was reached. Ironically, Valens' 1959 song is itself a thinly veiled cover of Little Richard's song from the year before called "Ooh! My Soul." However, Richard was never credited in the Valens song and it was not an issue in the Led Zeppelin litigation.[4]

As a final tidbit on Zeppelin, one song that they were never accused of plagiarizing was "The Rain Song," which appears on their 1973 album *Houses of the Holy*. This song came about in part because George Harrison once commented to drummer John Bonham that the band never does any ballads. While this was not really accurate ("Tangerine," "Going to California," and "Thank You" are all ballads that pre-date *Houses of the Holy*), Jimmy Page took Harrison's comment as a spur to write this ballad, one that lasts over seven minutes. (Robert Plant wrote the lyrics and has described this as his best vocal performance.) In addition, as a "subtle but unmissable" tribute to Harrison, the first two notes of the song are recognizably borrowed from Harrison's own ballad *Something*. Listen closely and you'll hear them—they come at the eight-second mark.[5]

Not all accusations of plagiarism are levelled at Led Zeppelin of course; it only seems that way. The most highly publicized plagiarism case of all involved the George Harrison song "My Sweet Lord," which was the first #1 single by an ex-Beatle (1971). What song was he accused of plagiarizing and who was performed it?

"He's So Fine" by the Chiffons. **Some have suggested that the coproducer of the song was partly to blame for the similarity between the songs. Who was it?**

Phil Spector. *Record Collector* editor Peter Doggett wrote in 2001 that, despite Harrison's inspiration for "My Sweet Lord" having come from "Oh Happy Day," "in the hands of producer and arranger Phil Spector, it came out as a carbon copy of the Chiffons' [song]." The authors of a Beatles book commented on the "sad" fact that Spector, as "master of all that was 'girl-group' during the early '60s," failed to recognize the similarities.[6]

The lawsuit was filed by the owner of the rights to "He's So Fine," Bright Tunes Music, in February 1971, only a few months after the song was released. However, by that time, the song was already a huge worldwide success, and not surprisingly, copyright infringement lawsuits do not tend to be filed when the allegedly offending song is a failure. Instead, would-be plaintiffs naturally wait until the cash has piled up. As the saying goes "where there's a hit, there's a writ." Harrison ultimately lost the case. In 1976, Judge Richard Owen concluded that Harrison had "subconsciously" copied "He's So Fine" and concluded: "Did Harrison deliberately use the music of 'He's So Fine'? I do not believe he did so deliberately. Nevertheless, it is clear that 'My Sweet Lord' is the very same song as 'He's So Fine' with different words, and Harrison had access to 'He's So Fine.' This is, under the law, infringement of copyright, and is no less so even though subconsciously accomplished."

Harrison had to pay the plaintiff approximately $1.6 million in damages for this song. As it turned out, the "plaintiff" was none other than the Beatles' own former business manager Allen Klein. While the lawsuit against Harrison was pending, and knowing the true value of "My Sweet Lord," Klein shrewdly (some might may incredibly disloyally as well) purchased Bright Tunes for $587,000.[7]

The John Lennon song "Come Together" opens with a line about "ol' flattop." Lennon was sued by Chuck Berry's publisher Big Seven Music Corp. for stealing the guitar riff from Berry's song "You Can't Catch Me" as well as the opening line from that song, also referencing "flat top." In 1973, a settlement was reached whereby Lennon agreed to record three of Big Seven's songs on his next album. However, when that 1974 album, *Walls and Bridges*, failed to contain all three of the songs, the court awarded the company $6,795.

Finally, in one of the odder copyright infringement cases, John Fogerty was sued for plagiarizing one of his own songs! In fact, the case went all the way to the United States Supreme Court. While with Creedence Clearwater Revival, Fogerty wrote "Run Through the Jungle," a song that reached #4 on the *Billboard* Hot 100. He sold the exclusive publishing rights to the song and those rights eventually wound up with Fantasy, Inc. In 1985, long after CCR had disbanded, Fogerty published and registered a copyright to his new song "The Old Man Down the Road," that was released on an album distributed by Warner Brothers. Fantasy sued Fogerty and Warner Brothers, alleging that "The Old Man Down the Road" was merely "Run Through the Jungle" with new words. In other words, Fogerty was accused of copying his own composition. The copyright infringement claim went to trial and a jury returned a verdict in favor of Fogerty. The reason the case went to the Supreme Court was not over that issue but rather over an issue about whether successful defendants in copyright infringement cases are entitled to seek reimbursement of legal fees.[8]

CHAPTER 38

No Truth in Advertising (Title of Song not Appearing in the Song Itself)

S ome famous songs do not contain the song title in the lyrics. See if you can identify the songs based on the bands and descriptions provided.

Bob Dylan. Notwithstanding repeatedly advising his listeners to "get stoned," Bob Dylan has always insisted that the song is not about drugs.

"Rainy Day Women #12 and 35." During his May 27, 1966, performance at the Royal Albert Hall, London, when talking about whether or not this song was about drugs, Dylan said: "I have never have and never will write a drug song."

As to the meaning of the title, while there have been numerous theories about it, none seem to have emanated from Dylan himself. He did however comment on the song itself: "'Rainy Day Women #12 & 35' happens to deal with a minority of, you know, cripples and Orientals and, uh, you know, and the world in which they live. . . . It's another sort of a North Mexican kind of a thing, uh, very protesty. Very, very protesty. And, uh, one of the protestiest of all things I ever protested against in my protest years . . ."[1]

The Mamas & the Papas. The song is a history of how the band came to be formed.

"Creeque Alley." The area referred to is in St. Thomas, Virgin Islands, and is not pronounced as "creek" nor is it correctly spelled in the song title. Rather, it is pronounced "creaky" and it is spelled "creque." There is a website (creequealley.com) specifically devoted to explaining the historical meaning behind each line of this song. The song mentions various musicians (such as John Sebastian, Barry McGuire and Roger McGuinn), bands (The Mugwumps and the Lovin' Spoonful) and locations (The Night Owl—a café in Greenwich Village, New York) with which the band members intersected during their rise to the top. While the information in the song is mostly accurate (if the references are sometimes oblique), one exception is the line about Cass Elliot planning to go to Swarthmore College. Elliot had briefly attended American University as a provisional freshman, but never made it to her sophomore year and never intended to go to Swarthmore, outside of Philadelphia. So she never was a sophomore and she never planned to go to Swarthmore, but at least it's an interesting sort of rhyme.[2]

Queen. One of their biggest hits

"Bohemian Rhapsody"

Led Zeppelin. The song is on *Houses of the Holy* and the title is a pun.

"D'yer Mak'er." The name of the song is derived from an old joke, where two friends have the following exchange: "My wife's gone to the West Indies." "Jamaica? (which has a similar pronunciation as "D'you make her?")" "No, she went of her own accord." The Jamaican reference is because it is a reggae-infused song. This is one of the few Zeppelin songs in which all four band members share songwriting credit.

Neil Young. The song is from an album of the same name. One of its lines is unusual in that it references the Decade in which the song was written and performed, which happens to be the 1970s.

"After the Gold Rush." The references to "the 1970s" has been amended by Young in concert over the Decades, and currently is sung as "the twenty-first century." Dolly Parton wanted to include this song on *Trio II* with Emmylou Harris and Linda Ronstadt but she did not know what the song meant. So they called Young and asked him and, according to Parton, he said "Hell, I don't know. I just wrote it. It just depends on what I was taking at the time. I guess every verse has something different I'd taken."[3]

Loggins and Messina. The singer sings about being in love with his honey even though he has no money.

"Danny's Song." This was written by Kenny Loggins as a gift to his brother Danny for the birth of Danny's son Colin. **Incidentally, while their version of the song is now well remembered, it was another artist whose cover of the song was a far bigger hit, reaching #7 on the *Billboard* Hot 100 in 1973. Who was that artist?**

Anne Murray.

The Moody Blues. The song begins with a references to Timothy Leary being dead.

"Legend of a Mind." Written and sung by flautist Ray Thomas of the Moodies, this may be one of the few rock songs (with the possible exception of some Jethro Tull songs) which has a full two-minute flute solo in the middle of the six-minute song.

The Byrds: The song was written (like many of the Byrds' hit songs) by Bob Dylan, but the Byrds, had a bigger hit with it. It includes the line about being older then than he is now.

"My Back Pages"

David Bowie. The first line of the song references Major Tom.

"Space Oddity." In 2013, the song gained renewed popularity after it was covered by Canadian astronaut Chris Hadfield, who performed the song while aboard the International Space Station, and therefore became the first music video shot in space.

Donovan. The first line of the song references sunshine coming through his window.

"Sunshine Superman"

Simon and Garfunkel. The most successful version of this song was a cover by Harper's Bazaar.

"The 59th Street Bridge Song (Feelin' Groovy)."

The Righteous Brothers. Bobby Hatfield solos on the entire beautiful 1965 song.

"Unchained Melody." This song has an interesting history. In 1936, songwriter Alex North approached Bing Crosby with the still untitled song. Crosby turned the song down and it remained unrecorded for almost twenty years. In 1955, North and lyricist Hy Zaret were contracted to write a song as a theme for the prison film *Unchained*, and their song eventually became known as the "Unchained Melody." The song focuses on someone who pines for a lover he has not seen in a "long, lonely time." The 1955 film centers around a man who contemplates either escaping from prison to live life on the run, or completing his sentence and returning to his wife and family. The song was nominated for an Academy Award but did not win.

The song has become one of the most-recorded songs of the 20th century, by some estimates having spawned over 500 versions in many languages. Les Baxter released an instrumental version which reached #1. Then came song recordings by Al Hibbler, reaching #3 on the

Billboard charts; Jimmy Young, that hit #1 in the U.K. and Roy Hamilton, reaching #1 on the R&B chart and #6 on the pop chart. Although the Righteous Brothers' (or more accurately, Hatfield's) version of the song is the best remembered today, it only reached #4 on the *Billboard* Hot 100 in 1965. It also charted again in 1990 after it was used in the 1990 blockbuster *Ghost*.[4]

The Who. Many mistakenly believe the title is "Teenage Wasteland."

"Baba O'Riley." Some famous songs are created in the studio in such a way that they cannot be fully played live and this is one. ("Bohemian Rhapsody" by Queen is another.) The long intro is Pete Townshend playing on his Lowrey organ. He put it on a "marimba repeat" setting to create the repeating sound he was looking for, which cannot easily be reproduced live. Therefore, when the band plays the song in concert, they simply wait on stage until the long organ intro is completed. The song then "goes live" with the familiar bass line and the drums. This is one of those songs (like "(You Gotta) Fight for Your Right (To Party!)" by the Beastie Boys) that stands for the opposite of what some people think it does. The song is not intended celebrate youth, drinking, and drugs. Rather, as Townshend said in an interview, it was inspired by the "absolute desolation of teenagers at Woodstock, where the patrons were smacked out on acid and 20 people had brain damage. The dichotomy was that it became a celebration: 'Teenage Wasteland, yes! We're all wasted!'"[5]

Cat Stevens. The song is a conversation between a father and a son and appears on the album *Tea for the Tillerman*.

Because there are no specifically memorable lyrics in the song I basically gave away the title of the song in the hint: "Father and Son."

Mitch Ryder and the Detroit Wheels. This was a top 10 hit for the group in 1965 and the song sounds like it is about someone named C. C. Ryder.

"Jenny Take a Ride." The name Jenny is mentioned in the lyrics but the full title is not.

The Bee Gees. This song was their first international hit.

"New York Mining Disaster 1941," which reached #12 in the UK and #14 in the US.

Two questions regarding this song: First, what is the name of the man addressed in the song? Second, was there a mining disaster in the State of New York in 1941?

The answer to the first question is Mr. Jones. The song suggests a conversation between a trapped miner and a Mr. Jones (who is referenced on six occasions in the song) although the narrator's voice is the only one we hear. There are other miners trapped as well. The narrator shows them a photo of his wife, and indicates that he would like her to be informed of his fate if he should die but anyone else makes it out OK. The time passing is punctuated by the narrator's growing sense of panic. He twice warns Mr. Jones to lower his voice for fear that he might cause an avalanche. As the song progresses, the lyrics get slower and softer as if to indicate that time and air is running out for the doomed men.

In answer to the second question, there was no mining disaster in New York in 1941. Although there was one in 1939 in Pennsylvania in which six men were killed, it's not likely that the song's composers, Robin & Barry Gibb knew of this. Rather, the song took its inspiration from a different disaster, that which occurred in the Welsh village of Aberfan in 1966 when a coal slag heap fell onto a crowded and busy school killing 144 people died there including many teachers and children. That disaster occurred only a few months before the song was written in 1967. Barry and Robin actually wrote the song when they were sitting in a dim staircase at Polydor Records following a power outage.[6]

The Band. The song begins with the singer arriving in "Nazereth."

"The Weight." While the song lyrics do not contain the title, they do refer repeatedly to "the load." Because there are a number of apparent Biblical allusions in the song (Moses, Luke, the devil, no place for a weary traveler to sleep), people have often assumed that one of those references was in the first line of the song about pulling into Nazareth. However, according to songwriter Robbie Robertson, that is actually a reference to the small town of Nazareth, Pennsylvania, which is the home of C. F. Martin & Company, famous for its Martin guitars and other instruments. Although the song was written by Robertson, drummer Levon Helm sings the first three verses, bassist Rick Danko sings the fourth verse, and Helm and Danko share the fifth verse. They performed the song at Woodstock and during the 1976 concert at the Winterland Ballroom in San Francisco which was made into a documentary called *The Last Waltz* by Martin Scorsese. In the latter version, they are accompanied by the Staples Singers.

Although the song only peaked at #63 on the *Billboard* chart, *Pitchfork Media* named it the 13th best song of the Sixties, and the Rock and Roll Hall of Fame named it one of the 500 Songs that Shaped Rock and Roll. PBS called it "an essential part of the American songbook." After Helm died in 2012, Bruce Springsteen said, before doing a cover of "The Weight": "Levon's voice and drumming was so incredibly versatile. He had a feel on the drums . . . it comes from a certain place in the past and you can't replicate it."[7]

The Carpenters. Cowritten by Leon Russell, which is surprising, given the style of music for which he later became known. The song was one of the Carpenters biggest hits.

"Superstar." Richard Carpenter felt that the original words "and I can hardly wait to sleep with you again" were a bit risque for his sister Karen to sing, so he changed it to the somewhat less suggestive "and I can hardly wait to be with you again." The finished recording was done on the first take and was the first time Karen had ever sung the song. She read the (revised) lyrics off of a napkin.

Simon and Garfunkel. The song appears on *Bridge Over Troubled Water*.

"El Condor Pasa"

Brenton Woods was essentially a one-hit wonder. He had a song that reached #9 on the *Billboard* Hot 100 in 1967 that still receives airplay today. What is the title?

"Gimme Little Sign."

Finally, in Rod' Stewart's signature song "Maggie May," the word "May" (possibly her last name?) is never sung in the song.

CHAPTER 39

A Thanksgiving Tradition

A song released in 1967 by a 20-year old singer-songwriter song takes up the entire side of an album (18:34 to be exact) and relates the story of the arrest of the singer being arrested for littering just after Thanksgiving in 1965. This chapter relates to that song.

What is the song and who was the singer-songwriter? As a hint, it features more talking than singing.

"Alice's Restaurant" by Arlo Guthrie. While many of the songs discussed in this book have remained popular throughout the years and are re-learned by each new generation (think for example "Sweet Caroline" by Neil Diamond, "California Girls" by the Beach Boys or "Take It Easy by the Eagles"), the same cannot be said of "Alice's Restaurant." For one thing, for obvious reasons, it is rarely played on the radio (even in the era of commercial-free satellite radio) except on Thanksgiving. Nevertheless, for those old enough to have heard it when it first came out in 1967, it remains extremely popular. The album on which it appears (of the same name) rose to #17 on the *Billboard* chart. It was also made into a movie in 1969 starring Guthrie himself.

The day after Thanksgiving, 1965, Guthrie and a friend were arrested for littering. Two days later, they pleaded guilty in court before a blind judge, who entered the courtroom with a seeing-eye dog. They were fined $50 and told to pick up their garbage. Later, Guthrie was called for the draft. At a psychological examination, in an attempt to portray himself as insane, he indicates to the psychiatrist that he is homicidal. ("I want to kill!" says Guthrie repeatedly.) However, to Guthrie's disappointment, the examiner views this favorably. In the final line of questioning before induction, the officer asks Guthrie about any record of arrests. Guthrie tells the story of the littering incident, which proves significant enough a criminal offense to potentially disqualify him from military service. Guthrie questions why the officer wants to know if Guthrie is moral enough to join the Army (and do the horrible things that soldiers are sometimes asked to do) after being a litterbug. The officer rejects Guthrie for military service, declaring "we don't like your kind" and sends his fingerprints to the FBI.

While considered ultimately as an anti-war song (Guthrie talks at the end about "ending war and stuff"), Guthrie has said that it is also "celebrating idiocy."

The Alice in the song was restaurant-owner Alice M. Brock, who in 1964 used $2,000 to purchase a deconsecrated church in Great Barrington, Massachusetts, where Alice and her husband Ray would live. It was here rather than at the restaurant—which came later—where the song's Thanksgiving dinner was actually held. The church was also where the garbage came from that Guthrie tossed into the ditch. While Brock was a restaurateur, there is no reference to any restaurant in the story (other than the chorus). However, the former Alice's Restaurant is now known as Theresa's Stockbridge Cafe. In 1991, Guthrie bought the church that had served as Alice and Ray Brock's former home, at 4 Van Deusenville Road, Great Barrington, Massachusetts, and converted it to the Guthrie Center, a nondenominational, interfaith meeting place.

Guthrie was 18 when the events occurred and only 20 when he wrote the song. He debuted it at the 1967 Newport Folk Festival and the article which appeared in the *New York Times* the next day led off: "The most unlikely song hit since 'Yes, We Have No Bananas' or 'Flat Foot Floogee' swept triumphantly through the Newport Folk Festival yesterday, the festival's last day."

Ordinarily, musicians enjoy playing songs that their audiences recognize but, in an interview with NPR, Guthrie lamented the opposite: "The only thing I really miss about doing it these days is that there's maybe a few people in every crowd that haven't heard it, but it's nothing like having the few hundred or a few thousand people years and years ago—40 years ago—when nobody had heard it. Those moments can't be repeated."

Here are a few questions about the song:

What is the actual title of the song?

Despite the fact that the song begins "This song is called Alice's Restaurant," the actual title of the song is "Alice's Restaurant Massacree."

What is the name of the arresting officer?

In the song, he is referred to simply as Officer Obie, but his real name is William Obanhein. He was the police chief of Stockbridge, Massachusetts when the "crime" occurred. He played himself in the movie, telling *Newsweek* magazine (September 29, 1969, where his photo appears) that making himself look like a fool was preferable to having somebody else make him look like a fool. Obanhein had posed for Norman Rockwell (himself a resident of Stockbridge) for a handful of sketches, including a 1959 black-and-white sketch "Policeman With Boys."

What is the address of the military induction center in New York City?

39 Whitehall Street.

What is the name of the bench where Guthrie is told to sit at the induction center?

The Group W bench.[1] There is a store in New Haven, CT near the Yale campus called Group W Bench. It sells artwork, clothing, and handmade items and according to its sign, it has been "pleasing the senses in New Haven since 1968." In other words, the store opened almost immediately after the song came out and has been in business ever since.

CHAPTER 40

Accidental Hit Songs (Famous B-Sides)

Possibly, many millennials don't even know what A-sides and B-sides refer to (or for that matter turntables and 45 rpm record adapters or inserts). Back when record companies released 45s (and before that, 78s), the A-side of the disc featured the recording that the artist, record producer, or the record company intended to receive the initial promotional effort, hopefully leading to radio airplay, and thus becoming a hit record. The B-side (or "flip-side") was a song which was not considered as strong. Every so often however, the B-side surprises. In fact, "Rock Around the Clock" by Bill Haley and the Comets, the song that many say launched the modern rock and roll era in 1954, was a B-side to a song that virtually no one has heard of today called "Thirteen Women (and Only One Man in Town)." In the case of many of the songs discussed in this chapter, they were later re-released as A-sides once it was realized that it was the B-side that was the true hit song, but they were all originally released as B-sides.

The A-side was "Hung on You" by the Righteous Brothers, which went nowhere. The B-side reached #4 on the *Billboard* Hot 100 in 1965. (As a hint, the title is not mentioned in the lyrics.)

"Unchained Melody" by the Righteous Brothers (even though only Bobby Hatfield sings on the track).

The A-side was "Let's Spend the Night Together" by the Stones, released in 1967. However, radio programmers refused to play that track because it was considered too sexually suggestive, so they played the B-side instead. That song, which is notable for Brian Jones' recorder parts, was described by Richie Unterberger of AllMusic.com as "a good candidate for the most melodic Mick Jagger-Keith Richards composition ever . . . one of the few Rolling Stones songs that could be fairly said to be as melodic as any of the best Lennon-McCartney compositions." What is the B-side song?

"Ruby Tuesday." The lyrics and most of the music was written by Keith Richards, while Jones also assisted with music. Jones also played piano on the track, and the double bass was played jointly by bassist Bill Wyman (pressing the strings against the fingerboard) and Keith Richards (bowing the strings). Of the song, Mick Jagger said "It's just a nice melody, really. And a lovely lyric. Neither of which I wrote, but I always enjoy singing it."

In Richards' autobiography, he writes that he was inspired to write the song when his girlfriend at the time, Linda Keith, broke up with him, got into drugs, and started seeing Jimi Hendrix. "That's the first time I felt the deep cut. The thing about being a songwriter is, even if you've been fucked over, you can find consolation in writing about it, and pour it out. Basically, Linda is Ruby Tuesday." (Taylor Swift is a good recent example of a songwriter creating one hit sing after another based on the same theme.)

As for "Let's Spend the Night Together," when released in 1967, it only reached #55 on the U.S. chart, while "Ruby Tuesday" hit #1. Yet, today, it is certainly considered one of their classic recordings and in fact *Rolling Stone* ranks it ahead of "Ruby Tuesday" (14 vs. 19) on its list of the 100 Greatest *Rolling Stone* songs.[1]

This song was released by the Spinners in 1972. The A-side was "How Could I Let You Get Away," which only reached #77 on the *Billboard* Hot 100. However, the classic million-selling B-side reached #3 on the chart. The lead singer of the group for many of its songs (and the B-Side song) was Bobby Smith. The song was recorded at Philly's Sigma Sound Studios, and the house band MFSB provided the instrumentation. Who is the group and what is the song?

The group is the Spinners and the B-side song is "I'll Be Around," written by Thom Bell.

The song "Reason to Believe," written by Tim Hardin, was the A-side of this single by Rod Stewart off his breakout album *Every Picture Tells a Story*. However, some DJs in the Midwest flipped over the 45 and began playing the B-side instead, from the same album- What was that B-Side?

"Maggie May." About this song (cowritten by guitarist Martin Quittenden), he told *Q* Magazine: "'Maggie May' was more or less a true story, about the first woman I had sex with, at the Beaulieu Jazz Festival [in 1961]. It nearly got left off because the label said it didn't have a melody. I said, 'Well, we've run out of time now, these are all the tracks we've recorded.' They said, 'Alright, then, bring it on.'" Stewart's record company didn't think it would be a hit, so they released it as the B-side of "Reason to Believe." However, once "Maggie May" overtook "Reason to Believe" in popularity, it was reclassified as an A-side. Ron Wood, later of the Rolling Stones, plays guitars on the track. He had been with Stewart as a member of the Faces.[2]

Paul McCartney thought this 1967 song was not commercial enough and so it was relegated to the B-side of his song "Hello Goodbye." John Lennon, who wrote the B-side track, was none too pleased about the decision. What was the song?

"I Am the Walrus." While most Beatles songs are great songs, there are few which have lyrics as banal as "Hello Goodbye" (although one could argue that that was a more frequent hallmark of McCartney's songs after the Beatles broke up). It is also difficult to imagine two more diametrically opposed songs than these two, one being in some respects a quintessential McCartney song and the other being a quintessential Lennon song. On the *Rolling Stone* list of the 100 Greatest Beatles Songs, "Hello Goodbye" came in at #100. So one way of looking at it is that it made the list; another is that it is at the bottom of the list. "I Am the Walrus" came in at #33.

As for Lennon, he was incredulous that his song was the B-side while McCartney's was the A-side: In a 1970 interview with *Rolling Stone*, he took at a gratuitous dig at the song when discussing the fact that he wanted his song "Revolution" to be released as a single in 1968: "I had it all prepared, but they came by, and said it wasn't good enough. And we put out what? 'Hello Goodbye' or some shit like that? No, we put out 'Hey Jude,' which was worth it—I'm sorry—but we could have had both." Based on decisions such as this, he complained after the band's breakup that "I got sick and tired of being Paul's backup band."

Writing on the website *Pop Dose,* Jon Cummings also expressed incredulity about the fact that "Hello Goodbye" was made the A-side single: "C'mon, admit it—this is one dippy little piece of Paul-poo. Imagine: John shows up in the studio with frickin' 'I Am the Walrus,' and Paul says, 'Right, mate, I've got a perfect little A-side for that one,' and starts in on the 'hey-la, hey-ba hello-ah' bit. And John thinks, not for the last time, 'How do you sleep?'"[3]

The A-side of this was the novelty song "They're Coming to Take Me Away, Ha-Haaa!" by Napoleon XIV which reached #3 on the *Billboard* Hot 100 in August 1966. What was the B-side?

It was the A-side played in reverse, and called "!aaaH-aH ,yawA eM ekaT oT gnimoC er'yehT." In his *Book of Rock Lists*, rock music critic Dave Marsh called the B-side the "most obnoxious song ever to appear in a jukebox." What is surprising about that statement is that the song ever appeared in a jukebox at all. The song can be heard on YouTube.[4]

With some 45s, both the A-sides and B-sides are hits. However, with the exception of Elvis Presley and the Beatles (who did it routinely because they almost couldn't help

themselves), there are very few instances of this, especially after the Decade started. What was the B-side to "Wouldn't It Be Nice" by the Beach Boys in 1965?

"God Only Knows." Another Beach Boys combo (released before the Decade was "I Get Around" (A-side) and "Don't Worry Baby" (B-side).

A side: Proud Mary by Creedence Clearwater Revival. B-Side?

"Born on the Bayou."

This song by Chicago was released as a B-side twice. The song was initially released as the B-side to "Make Me Smile" in March 1970. It was re-released in June 1971 as the B-side to the re-release of "Beginnings." Although "Make Me Smile" reached #9, "Beginnings," backed with this song, reached #7 on the U.S. *Billboard* **Hot 100. The original lead vocalist of the song was Terry Kath. The song was a popular "slow-dance" song at high school proms and university dances during the 1970s. What is the title of the song?**

"Colour My World" (with British spelling)

In the A-side of this record by Simon and Garfunkel, writer Paul Simon "anthropomorphizes" the animals. That song reached #16. A cover of the B-side by Harpers Bizarre reached #13. What are the two sides?

"At the Zoo" and "The 59th Street Bridge Song (Feelin' Groovy)" respectively.

For those familiar with Manhattan, what is the actual name of the 59th Street Bridge?

The Queensboro Bridge, now called the Ed Koch Queensboro Bridge.

The original A-side was called "Another Park, Another Sunday," but it didn't receive much airplay, in part because of its line "radio just seems to bring me down."[5] The B-side became the only #1 song for the Doobie Brothers during the Decade and is famous for its a cappella ending. What was that song?

"Black Water." This was one of their relatively few hits written and composed by the only person who has been a member of the band through their entire career, which started in 1970. **Who is that person?**

Patrick Simmons. The band's other #1 came during the Michael McDonald era, "What a Fool Believes," in 1979.

This song was first released as the B-side of "Church Street Soul Revival" in 1970. Although people today think of this as a song by Tommy James and the Shondells, it was actually a Tommy James solo effort, written and recorded by him after the breakup of the band in 1970. It was also his most successful solo song, reaching #4 on the *Billboard* Hot 100. What was the song?

"Draggin' the Line."

This B-side song hit #7 on the *Billboard* Hot 100 in 1972. The lyrics consist of a single (intelligible) word, and that word is "hey" (or perhaps more accurately "hey!"). What is the song?

"Rock and Roll (Part Two)" by Gary Glitter. Naturally enough, the A-side was "Rock and Roll (Part One)," which does have lyrics.

The A-side of this song by this Canadian group was called "Hello Melinda Goodbye," which went nowhere. The B-side reached #3 on the *Billboard* Hot 100 and was ranked as the #24 song for 1971. The song hit the top 10 a second time in 1990, when it was covered by the group Tesla. What is the song and who is the band that recorded it?

"Signs" by Five Man Electrical Band.

Finally, for those Vanilla Ice fans out there, "Ice Ice Baby" was the B-side to his cover of the Wild Cherry song "Play That Funky Music." While the latter was initially unsuccessful, it was re-issued after the success of "Ice Ice Baby" and rose to #4 on the *Billboard* Hot 100 chart.

Endnotes

INTRODUCTION

1. http://www.huffingtonpost.com/wray-herbert/is-the-music-of-the-60s-r_b_3007514.html
2. http://rateyourmusic.com/list/AlRog/chock_full_o_hits
3. http://www.huffingtonpost.com/will-bunch/casey-kasem-and-the-death_b_5500648.html

CHAPTER 1

1. http://en.wikipedia.org/wiki/List_of_best-selling_albums
   David Hepworth, Never a Dull Moment, Henry Holt (2016).
2. David Browne, *Fire and Rain*, Da Capo Press (2011)
3. http://www.songfacts.com/detail.php?id=14611
4. David Leaf, *Celebrate: The Three Dog Night Story, 1965–1975* (CD liner)
5. http://blog.chron.com/40yearsafter/2010/07/for-tommy-james-the-past-is-the-future
   -part-2/
6. http://www.songfacts.com/detail.php?id=1626
   http://www.angelfire.com/mo/stephenlaug/articles/hitch199508.html
   David Dunlap, "No More Mony in Midtown Skyline," *The New York Times*, 2/4/2008.
7. https://rockhall.com/inductees/the-jackson-five/timeline/
8. http://www.locoloboevents.com/cgi-bin/locolobo/displaybio.pl?010
   http://web.archive.org/web/20041214155344/www.johnbsebastian.com/bio2.html
9. http://www.officialcharts.com/chart-news/the-official-top-10-biggest-selling-male
   -singles-artists-of-all-time-r__2470/
10. http://www.surfermoon.com/interviews/asher.html
    http://www.npr.org/2000/06/19/1075634/good-vibrations
11. http://www.billboard.com/artist/419428/who/chart?page=2&f=379
12. Kent Hartman, *The Wrecking Crew: The Inside Story of Rock and Roll's Best Kept Secret.* St.
    Martin's Press (2012)
    Anthony Summers, *Sinatra: The Life*, Random House Digital, Inc. (2006)
    http://www.thefranksinatra.com/songs/strangers-in-the-night

http://www.theoriginof.com/scooby-doo.html

13. http://en.wikipedia.org/wiki/Adult_Contemporary_(chart)

14. "Quotables," *Chicago Tribune*, 3/7/2000

    Thomas Dimopoulos, "Bye, Bye Local Legend: Don Mclean Refutes Tale Of Song's Origin," *The Post-Star*, 11-26-2011

    http://www.npr.org/2011/12/01/143009813/american-pie-doesnt-belong-to-saratoga-springs

    Clark DeLeon, *Memory Bank a Little Off But the Sentiment Still Holds*, The Philadelphia Inquirer, 8-13-2002

    http://www.bbc.com/news/entertainment-arts-32208584

15. http://www.pastemagazine.com/blogs/lists/2011/04/band-names-inspired-by-literature.html

    The Doors documentary *When You're Strange*

    Jeremy Simmonds, *The Encyclopedia of Dead Rock Stars: Heroin, Handguns, and Ham Sandwiches*, Chicago Review Press. (2008)

16. http://www.allmusic.com/artist/the-guess-who-mn0000061480/biography

    http://www.classicrockhereandnow.com/2013/07/burton-cummings-interview-guess-who.html

CHAPTER 2

1. http://neilwiki.wikispaces.com/Suite+Judy+Blue+Eyes

   http://www.thedailybeast.com/articles/2011/12/03/judy-collins-new-book-suicide-alcoholism-nude-photos-and-more.html

   Steve Silberman, *Singing Their Way Home: 35 years of Crosby Stills and Nash*; http://www.stevesilberman.com/csn/

   David Browne, *Fire and Rain*, Da Capo Press (2011)

2. NPR Interview 5/8/201

3. http://www.classicbands.com/JimWeatherlyInterview.html

4. http://www.songfacts.com/detail.php?id=799

   http://barrymcguire.com/index.php?page=bio4

5. http://www.songfacts.com/blog/interviews/sandy_chapin/

   http://www.harrychapin.com/circle/winter04/behind.htm

   Singer Chapin's Widow to give Lawsuit Funds to Hunger Battle, Wilmington Morning Star, 10-8–1986.

6. http://enthusiasmnoted.wordpress.com/2013/09/26/song-of-the-day-dont-call-us-well-call-you-sugarloaf/

   http://cmhof.org/inductees/sugarloaf

http://70spop.wordpress.com/2011/12/22/dont-call-us-well-call-you-by-sugarloaf
-claridge–1975/

7. http://countrymusictreasures.com/storybehindthesong/ruby-dont-take.html
   http://www.songfacts.com/detail.php?id=2113
   Ann Rule, *A Rage to Kill and Other True Cases*. Simon and Schuster (1999)

8. http://theboot.com/jeannie-c-riley-harper-valley-pta-lyrics/

9. Joel McIver, *Black Sabbath: Sabbath Bloody Sabbath* (2006).
   Robert Wasler, *Running with the Devil: Power, Gender and Madness in Heavy Metal*,
   Wesleyan University Press (1993)
   http://www.songfacts.com/detail.php?id=1284

10. https://www.youtube.com/watch?v=BD36EWh_1vE (Simon and Garfunkel on The
    Only Living Boy in New York—(BBC Imagine, January, 2012))
    Pete Fornatale, *Simon and Garfunkel's Bookends*, Rodale (2007).
    David Browne, *Fire and Rain*, Da Capo Press (2011).
    http://www.college.columbia.edu/cct_archive/jul_aug06/updates3.php
    http://c250.columbia.edu/c250_celebrates/remarkable_columbians/art_garfunkel.html
    http://www.songfacts.com/detail.php?id=2551

11. David Hinckley, "Legendary Singer Claude Jeter Dies," *New York Daily News*, 1-8-2009
    Jon Pareles, "Ambition Never Gets Old," *The New York Times*, 5-22-2016
    Ben Sisario, "Claude Jeter, Gospel Singer with Wide Influence, Dies at 94," *The New York
    Times*, 1-10-2009

12. http://www.musicianguide.com/biographies/1608000738/Jerry-Jeff-Walker.html
    Jerry Jeff Walker, *Gypsy Songman*. Woodford Press (2000)

13. http://www.songfacts.com/detail.php?id=2453

CHAPTER 3

1. https://web.archive.org/web/20060217012035/
   http://www.geocities.com/~beatleboy1/dba11road.html
   Michael Sullivan, *"His Magical, Mystical Tour"*, Time, *12-10-2001*
   http://oldies.about.com/od/thebeatlessongs/a/something_2.htm
   http://vegasblog.latimes.com/vegas/2006/12/sinatra_elvis_a.html

2. Mark Lewisohn, *The Beatles Recording Sessions*. Harmony Books. (1988).
   Bob Spitz, *The Beatles*, Little, Brown (2005)
   Ian McDonald, *Revolution in the Head: The Beatles' Records and the Sixties* (Third Revised
   ed.). Chicago Review Press) (2007)

David Sheff, *All We Are Saying: The Last Major Interview with John Lennon and Yoko Ono*, St. Martin's Press (2000).

3. http://www.beatlesbible.com/1967/06/04/mccartney-harrison-watch-jimi-hendrix-london/
    Barry Miles, *Paul McCartney: Many Years from Now*, Holt (1998).
    http://www.npr.org/player/v2/mediaPlayer.html?action=1&t=1&islist=false&id=10634329&m=10634334
    http://www.feelnumb.com/2010/03/22/jimi-hendrix-covered-sgt-pepper-days-after-its-release-in-front-of-the-beatles/

4. Brian Southall, *Northern Songs*.Omnibus (2007)
    Ian MacDonald, *Revolution in the Head: The Beatles' Records and the Sixties*, Pimlico (2005)
    Craig Cross, *Day-by-Day Song-by-Song Record-by-Record* (2005)
    Bill Harry, *The Beatles Encyclopedia: Revised and Updated*. Virgin (2005)
    Lynton Guest *The Trials of Michael Jackson*. Aureus Publishing. (2006)
    George Harrison, *I Me Mine*, Phoenix (1980)..

5. http://www.beatlesbible.com/1969/01/30/the-beatles-rooftop-concert-apple-building/2/

6. Martin Sandler, *How the Beatles Changed the World*, Walker (2014).
    http://www.beatlesbible.com/1969/01/30/the-beatles-rooftop-concert-apple-building/
    Chris O'Dell, *Miss O'Dell*, Touchstone (2009).

7. Ian MacDonald, *Revolution in the Head: The Beatles' Records and the Sixties*, Pimlico (2005)
    Bob Spitz, *The Beatles*, Little, Brown (2005)
    Mark Lewisohn, *The Beatles Recording Sessions*. Harmony Books (1988)

8. https://www.youtube.com/watch?v=xOZUKhkvLMQ (Sheila Bromberg and the harp solo on She's Leaving Home)

9. Ian MacDonald, *Revolution in the Head: The Beatles' Records and the Sixties*, Pimlico (2005)
    George Martin, *All You Need Is Ears*. St. Martin's Press (1994)
    Mark Lewisohn, *The Beatles Recording Sessions*. Harmony Books (1988)

10. Mark Lewisohn, *The Beatles Recording Sessions*. Harmony Books (1988)
    Ian MacDonald, *Revolution in the Head: The Beatles' Records and the Sixties*, Pimlico (2005)
    Barry Miles, *Paul McCartney: Many Years from Now*, Holt (1998)
    Walter Everett, *The Beatles as Musicians: Revolver Through the Anthology*. Oxford University Press (1999)

11. http://www.billboard.com/artist/365008/richie+havens/chart
     http://www.upvenue.com/music-news/blog-headline/1058/top-10-best-music-covers.html
     http://www.bbc.com/news/entertainment-arts-29791820

12. http://www.rollingstone.com/music/lists/100-greatest-beatles-songs-20110919/
     julia–19691231

13. Bob Spitz, The Beatles, Little, Brown (2005)
     Stephen J. Spignesi, Michael Lewis, *Here, There and Everywhere: The 100 Best Beatles
     Songs* Black Dog and Leventhal (2004).

14. Mark Lewisohn, *The Beatles Recording Sessions.* Harmony Books (1988)
     http://www.rollingstone.com/music/lists/100-greatest-beatles-songs-20110919/
     sexy-sadie–19691231
     Craig Cross, *The Beatles: Day-by-Day, Song-by-Song, Record-by-Record.* Lincoln, NE (2005)
     Jann Wenner. *Lennon Remembers.* W.W. Norton & Co. (1971)
     Barry Miles, *Paul McCartney: Many Years from Now*, Holt (1998)
     Geoff Emerick, *Here, There and Everywhere: My Life Recording the Music of the Beatles*
     (Gotham, 2007).
     Kevin Ryan and Brian Kehew, *Recording the Beatles: The Studio Equipment and Techniques
     Used to Create Their Classic Albums*, Curvebender Publishing (2006).

15. http://www.beatlesbible.com/1966/08/29/candlestick-park-san-francisco-final-concert
     Cary Schneider, "What The Critics Wrote About the Beatles In 1964," *The Los Angeles
     Times*, 2/9/2014.

16. http://www.livescience.com/32769-which-band-headlined-the-first-stadium-rock
     -concert.html
     http://liveforlivemusic.com/features/the-beatles-shea-stadium-dave-schwensen/
     http://www.beatlesbible.com/1966/08/23/live-shea-stadium-new-york-2/
     Lennon's comments about Jesus were actually published in a British magazine in March
     1966, but were not republished in America until July 1966.

17. Richard Harrington, "His Musical Notes Have Become TV Landmarks." *The Washington
     Post*, 11-24-2002.
     http://player.interactual.com/news/McCartney.htmhttp://www.telegraph.co.uk/news/
     uknews/1558117/Beatles-never-told-of-protests-at-satellite-show.html
     http://www.beatlesbible.com/1967/06/25/the-beatles-on-our-world-all-you-need-is
     -love/
     http://keithmoonmovie.com/keith-moon-records-with-the-beatles/

18. Barry *Miles, The Beatles Diary Volume 1: The Beatles Years. Omnibus Press. (2001).*
     http://www.beatlesource.com/TV/index.html
     Bob Spitz, *The Beatle*s, Little, Brown (2005)

19. "The Beach Boys' Mike Love: 'There are a lot of fallacies about me,'" *The Guardian*, July 4, 2013

20. Hunter Davies, *The Beatles*. McGraw-Hill (1968)
    http://www.beatlesinterviews.org/dbjypb.int3.html
    http://web.archive.org/web/20080419020720/http://www.applecorp.com/aditl/origins.htm
    http://web.archive.org/web/20090104230914/http://www.applecorp.com/aditl/notes3.htm
    http://web.archive.org/web/20090104160513/http://www.applecorp.com/aditl/notes4.htm
    http://www.allmusic.com/song/a-day-in-the-life-mt0011741643

21. Zoe Dare Hall, "She's Leaving Home (Again)," *The Daily Mail*, 5-17-2008 http://oldies.about.com/od/thebeatles/a/The-Beatles-Songs-Shes-Leaving-Home.htm
    http://listverse.com/2010/05/16/10-stories-behind-beatles-songs/

22. http://www.rollingstone.com/music/lists/100-greatest-beatles-songs-20110919

23. http://www.allmusic.com/album/live-peace-in-toronto–1969-mw0000653014

24. Mark Edmonds, "Here, There and Everywhere," *The Sunday Times* (3-20-2005)
    Maurice Chittenden, "McCartney wrote Sgt Pepper 'with a little help from his roadie friend," *The Sunday Times* (3-20-2005)
    Barry Miles, *Paul McCartney: Many Years from Now*, Holt (1998).
    http://www.hooksandharmony.com/decline-death-mal-evans/
    http://beatlesnumber9.com/mal.html
    http://news.bbc.co.uk/2/hi/entertainment/2029059.stm

25. http://www.youtube.com/watch?v=0yU0JuE1jTk (Give Peace A Chance (1969) - Official Video)

26. Mark Lewisohn, *The Beatles Recording Sessions*. Harmony Books (1988)
    Bill Harry, *The Beatles Encyclopedia: Revised and Updated*. Virgin (2005)

27. http://www.rollingstone.com/music/lists/100-greatest-beatles-songs-20110919/i-want-you-shes-so-heavy–19691231
    http://www.beatlesbible.com/1969/08/20/mixing-editing-i-want-you-shes-so-heavy/

28. Barry Miles, *Paul McCartney: Many Years from Now*, Henry Holt (1997)
    http://mentalfloss.com/article/30523/who-was-walrus-analyzing-strangest-beatles-song

29. Brant Mewborn, B*iography Tells Inside Story of Beatles*, *Anchorage Daily News*, 5-7–1983
    Peter Brown, *The Love You Make: An Insider's Story of the Beatles*, New American Library (2002)
    Bob Spitz, *The Beatles*, Little, Brown (2005)

30. http://curate.tumblr.com/post/406315807/the-essays-in-black-victorians-black-victoriana

https://ia700802.us.archive.org/27/items/JohnLennonInterview1972HitParader Magazine/1972JohnLennonHitParaderInterview.pdf

31. Ian MacDonald, *Revolution in the Head: The Beatles' Records and the Sixties*, Pimlico (2005)

Mark Lewisohn, *The Beatles Recording Sessions*. Harmony Books (1988)

32. http://abbeyrd.best.vwh.net/recdate.htm

33. Bruce Spizer, *The Beatles Solo on Apple Records*, 498 Productions (2005)

Robert Rodriguez, *Fab Four FAQ 2.0: The Beatles' Solo Years, 1970–1980*, Backbeat Books (2010).

34. Adam Gopnik, "Long Play," *The New Yorker*, 4-25-2016

35. *Dave Barry's Book of Bad Songs*, Andrews, McMeel (1997)

36. https://www.youtube.com/watch?v=kSwUzM_nTGM (Lennon or McCartney)

37. http://www.rollingstone.com/music/lists/100-greatest-rolling-stones-songs-20131015/sittin-on-a-fence–1967–19691231

CHAPTER 4

1. Peter Benjaminson, *The Lost Supreme: The Life of Dreamgirl Florence Ballard*, Chicago Review Press (2007)

http://www.history-of-rock.com/supremes.htm

Mary Wilson, *Dreamgirl: My Life as a Supreme*, Cooper Square Publishers (1986)

2. http://performingsongwriter.com/kris-kristofferson-bobby-mcgee/

Andy Langer, "Q and A with Kris Kristofferson," *Esquire*, 2/27/2006

http://www.esquire.com/features/qa/ESQ0306MUSIC_84_1

3. http://www.cracked.com/article_20423_5-mind-blowing-true-stories-behind-famous-songs.html

4. http://voices.yahoo.com/5-facts-didn't-know-otis-redding-dock-12131932.html

5. http://badfingerlinks.bravepages.com/features/rollingstone-pete.html

http://www.findagrave.com/cgi-bin/fg.cgi?page=gr&GRid=7471112

http://paul-mccartney.musicnewshq.com/news/discconnected-botb-without-you/show

http://www.bbc.co.uk/wales/music/sites/welsh-love-songs/pages/badfinger-without-you.shtml

http://lonesomebeehive.wordpress.com/2012/03/05/rock-n-roll-suicide-pete-ham-tom-evans-of-badfinger-cant-take-it-anymore/

http://badfinge.ipower.com/BadfingerLibraryNews.html

6. http://popdose.com/the-popdose-100-the-greatest-cover-songs-of-all-time/
7. http://www.snopes.com/music/artists/mamacass.asp
   https://www.themedicalbag.com/story/mama-cass-elliot
   Edi Fiegel, *Dream a Little Dream of Me: The Life of Cass Elliot*, Chicago Review Press (2005).
8. Brian Chin, Liner notes for *Marvin Gaye & Tammi Terrell: The Complete Duets* (2001)
9. Corbin Reiff, *Forgotten Heroes: Terry Kath*, Premier Guitar, 5-11-2013.
   http://www.premierguitar.com/articles/Forgotten_Heroes_Terry_Kath?page=3

CHAPTER 5

1. Ellen Sander, "Woodstock Music and Art Fair: The Ultimate Rock Experience," *Saturday Review* vol. 52, no. 39 (9-27–1969),
2. Elliot Tiber, "How Woodstock Happened. . . Part 2".
   http://www.woodstockstory.com/how-woodstock-happened-2.html http://web.archive.org/web/20100201054600/http://www.discoverynet.com/~barnes/wsrprnt2.htm
3. http://www.salon.com/2000/04/04/mitchell_2;
   Jim Farber, "Joni Come Lately," *New York Daily News*, 4-13–1998http://www.foxnews.com/entertainment/2009/08/29/secrets-woodstock-truth-joni-mitchell.html
4. http://www.woodstockstory.com/passingperformersbands.html
   http://www.11points.com/Music/11_Bands_That_Skipped_Woodstock_For_Incredibly_Lame_reasons
   http://archives.waiting-forthe-sun.net/Pages/Interviews/DoorsInterviews/hullabaloo_1968.html
   http://www.songfacts.com/blog/interviews/ian_anderson_of_jethro_tull/
   http://www.doors.com/ftp/intervws/july3.htm
   (Liner notes to *Tommy James and the Shondells: Anthology*).
   http://www.ledzeppelinnews.com/2009/08/at-woodstock-led-zeppelin-was-never.html
5. http://www.riverreporter.com/issues/08-10-30/news-attorney.html
   Fritz Mayer, "County Attorney Waxes Historic," *The River Reporter*, 11-5-2008.
   http://www.woodstockpreservation.org/Gallery/MaxYasgur/MaxYasgur.htm
6. JimFusilli, "Woodstock's Forgotten Man," *The Wall Street Journal*, 8-/6/2009
7. http://www.woodstockstory.com/artiekornfeld.html
8. http://www.creators.com/lifestylefeatures/books-and-music/pop-talk/taking-stock-two-veterans-of-sha-na-na-look-back-on-woodstock.html
   http://www.youtube.com/watch?v=XnpzsveBJdA&feature=kp (Richie Havens Interview About Woodstock Performance)

Douglas Martin, "Richie Havens, Folk Singer Who Riveted Woodstock, Dies at 72," *The New York Times*, 4-22-2013

http://www.news-journalonline.com/article/20130104/ENT/301039990

Hank Bordowitz, *Bad Moon Rising: The Unauthorized History of Creedence Clearwater Revival*. Chicago Review Press (2007)

Christian G. Appy, *Patriots: The Vietnam War Remembered from All Sides*, Penguin Books (2004)

http://www.countryjoe.com/cheer.htm

9. http://pantheonsongs.grigr.com/2012/07/canned-heat/

http://blog.mjmurphy.com/?p=374

https://www.youtube.com/watch?v=3Qo9R5kDZWY (Bull Doze Blues)

http://www.songfacts.com/detail.php?id=4209

10. http://www.superseventies.com/sw_laydown.html

http://consequenceofsound.net/2015/03/heres-how-much-each-artist-earned-from -playing-woodstock/

http://priceonomics.com/how-much-did-the-musicians-of-woodstock-get-paid/

http://www.dailymail.co.uk/tvshowbiz/article-1204849/Forty-far-facts-knew -Woodstock.html

11. http://www.cbsnews.com/pictures/acts-that-almost-made-it-to-woodstock/11

David Stampone, *No Helicopter, No Butterfly*, The San Diego Reader, 8-12-2009

Michael Lang, *The Road to Woodstock*, Ecco (2010)

Pete Fornatale, *Back to the Garden*, Touchstone (2010)

12. http://www.wpi.edu/news/20090/woodstock.html

http://www.superseventies.com/sw_laydown.html

"Rod Stewart: The Jeff Beck Band Could Have Played Woodstock," *Rolling Stone*, 10–19-2012

http://www.huffingtonpost.com/2013/11/25/woodstock-trivia_n_4334870.html

http://www.drumheadmag.com/web/feature.php?id=14

13. http://www.chronos-historical.org/rockfest/articles/WG1.html

Robert Santelli, *Aquarius Rising: The Rock Festival Years*, Delacorte Press (1980).

14. David White, "R-I-P Altamont Raceway," *San Francisco Chronicle*, 5-25-2009.

"The Rolling Stones Disaster At Altamont: Let It Bleed," *Rolling Stone*, 1-21–1970

http://web.archive.org/web/20080314073233/http://www.rollingstone.com/news/ story/5934386/rock__rolls_worst_day

https://www.youtube.com/watch?v=yQzNtYsf5D4 (The Story of the Altamont Rock Concert in December 1969)

Bill Osgerby, *Biker: Truth and Myth: How the Original Cowboy of the Road Became the Easy Rider of the Silver Screen*. Globe Pequot (2005).

Dennis McNally, *A Long Strange Trip: The Inside History of the Grateful Dead,* Broadway, (2002).
http://www.history.com/this-day-in-history/the-altamont-festival-brings-the–1960s-to-a-violent-end
http://www.morethings.com/music/rolling_stones/images/hells_angels/

15. http://www.thesun.co.uk/sol/homepage/features/4872320/The-Stones-on-legendary-Hyde-Park-gig-in–1969-and-2013.html

16. https://en.wikipedia.org/wiki/The_Concert_for_Bangladesh

17. Joshua M. Greene, *Here Comes the Sun: The Spiritual and Musical Journey of George Harrison,* John Wiley & Sons
    https://web.archive.org/web/20120303010643/http://www.gadflyonline.com/12-3-01/music-georgeharrison.html
    https://www.flickr.com/photos/yokoonoofficial/3385752173/
    Alan Clayson, *George Harrison,* Sanctuary (2003)
    Keith Badman, *The Beatles Diary Volume 2: After the Break-Up 1970–2001,* Omnibus Press (2001)

CHAPTER 6

1. http://en.wikipedia.org/wiki/Cathy_Smith
   Bob Woodward, *Wired: The Short Life and Fast Times of John Belushi* (1984)
   http://theband.hiof.no/articles/the_weight_viney.html
   http://www.reddit.com/r/IAmA/comments/2e8cjz/gordon_lightfoot_here_singersongwriter_for_over/
   Barney Hoskyns, *Across The Great Divide: The Band and America.* Hyperion (1993)
   http://www.corfid.com/gl/press/press14.htm
   Connie Hamzy interview with Howard Stern, December 8, 2010.
   Chris O'Dell, *Miss O'Dell,* Touchstone (2009).
   http://en.wikipedia.org/wiki/Cynthia_Plaster_Caster
   http://www.cynthiaplastercaster.com
   Pamela Des Barres, *I'm with the Band,* Chicago Review Press (2005)
   http://www.therichest.com/expensive-lifestyle/entertainment/the-10-most-famous-rock-groupies-of-all-time/10/
   Jada Yuan, "152 Minutes with Bebe Buell," *New York Magazine,* September 25, 2011
   Bebe Buell and Victor Bockris, *Rebel Heart: An American Rock and Roll Journey.* St. Martin's Press (2001)
   Pamela Des Barres, *Let's Spend the Night Together: Backstage Secrets of Rock Muses and Supergroupies.* Chicago Review Press. (2007)

CHAPTER 7

1. http://www.pandora.com/steam
   http://persephonemagazine.com/2013/12/record-machine-na-na-hey-hey-kiss-him
   -goodbye-by-steam/
   http://www.songfacts.com/detail.php?id=713
   Fred Bronson, *The Billboard Book of #1 Hits* (2003)
2. http://www.rollingstone.com/music/lists/the-top-25-teen-idol-breakout-moments
   -20120511/the-monkees–1967-20120511
3. http://www.rollingstone.com/music/lists/the-top-25-teen-idol-breakout-moments
   -20120511/the-monkees–1967-20120511
   Andrew Sandoval, "How Davy Jones and the Monkees Impacted Music, Hollywood—
   and Jack Nicholson," *The Hollywood Reporter*, 3/8/2012
   Glenn Baker, *Monkeemania: The True Story of the Monkees*. Plexus Publishing (1986, rev.
   2000)
   Eric Lefcowitz, *Monkee Business: The Revolutionary Made-For-TV Band*. Retrofuture
   (2010)
   http://listentotheband.weebly.com/beat-it-the-top-10-singing-drummers.html
   Andrew Sandoval, *The Monkees: The Day-by-Day Story of the 60s TV Pop Sensation*.
   Thunder Bay Press (2005)
4. http://www.billboard.com/articles/list/2155531/the-hot-100-all-time-top-songs?
   list_page=2
   https://www.youtube.com/watch?v=h9nE2spOw_o (The Archies—Sugar, Sugar
   (Original 1969 Music Video))
5. https://www.youtube.com/watch?v=VH0cBuOIkL4 (Don Kirshner explaining how the
   Archies were created)
6. http://www.songfacts.com/blog/interviews/toni_wine/
   Marti Smiley Childs, *Echos of the Sixties*. EditPros. (2011)
   Tony Orlando, *Halfway to Paradise*, Macmillan (2003).
7. http://www.allmusic.com/artist/new-vaudeville-band-mn0000891873/biography

CHAPTER 8

1. http://www.cnn.com/2006/SHOWBIZ/Music/04/25/worst.songs/index.html
   http://www.aolradioblog.com/2010/09/11/100-worst-songs-ever-part-three-of-five/
   http://www.loomia.com/?redir=frame&uid=www5479067aab3693.74590634 (People
   Magazine 9-9–1974)

Jerry Buck, "Singer sets sights off the road," *The Free Lance-Star* (2-20–1986)

Dave Barry's Book of Bad Songs, Andrews, McMeel (1997)

2. http://en.wikipedia.org/wiki/Feelings_(song)

3. http://www.rollingstone.com/music/pictures/readers-poll-the-10-worst-songs-of-the
    -1970s

    http://www.aolradioblog.com/2010/09/11/worst-songs

    Robert Plyler, "Practically Perfect in Every Way," *The Post Journal*, 6-30-2012

    http://en.wikipedia.org/wiki/Feelings_(song)

    http://www.leagle.com/decision/19881924863F2d1061_11763

4. "*Beatles classic voted worst song*"BBC, 11-10-2004

    Tom Rowley, *Poll: What is the worst Beatles song?* 10/5/2012

    http://www.today.com/id/4788104#.VHqLaWoo6Ul

    http://www.cnn.com/2006/SHOWBIZ/Music/04/25/worst.songs/

    http://blogs.houstonpress.com/rocks/2010/09/the_ten_worst_beatles_songs
    _of.php?page=2

    Jonathan Gould, *Can't Buy Me Love: The Beatles, Britain, and America.* Three Rivers Press (2007)

    Rob Sheffield et al. *The New Rolling Stone Album Guide* (4th ed.), Fireside (2004).

    http://www.thetoptens.com/worst-beatles-songs/

    http://ultimateclassicrock.com/worst-beatles-songs/

    http://myq105.cbslocal.com/2014/01/02/the-top-5-worst-beatles-songs-of-all-time/

    http://www.ranker.com/list/worst-beatles-songs/ranker-music

5. http://www.vanityfair.com/hollywood/2014/02/johnny-carson-the-tonight-show

6. http://www.rollingstone.com/music/pictures/readers-poll-the-worst-songs-of-the-sixties
    -20111116/2-bobby-goldsboro-honey-0035097

    http://www.cnn.com/2006/SHOWBIZ/04/19/eye.ent.worstsong/index.
    html?eref=sitesearch

7. Kayla Webley, *Top 10 Songs with Silly Lyrics*, Time, 3-15-2011

8. http://www.cnn.com/2006/SHOWBIZ/Music/04/25/worst.songs/index.html

    Joseph Murrells, *The Book of Golden Discs*,Barrie & Jenkins (1978)

    http://canadianmusichalloffame.ca/2012/03/page/3

    http://www.songfacts.com/detail.php?id=2112

    http://www.slate.com/articles/arts/music_box/2005/03/goodbye_papa_its_hard_to
    _die.html

9. http://patch.com/california/shermanoaks/qa-with-america-singer-gerry-beckley

10. Robert Windler, "Year of the Dragons," *People Magazine*, 10-18–1976.

11. http://www.songfacts.com/detail.php?id=2005

CHAPTER 9

1. DavidSimons, *Studio Stories – How the Great New York Records Were Made*, Backbeat Books (2004)
   http://www.rollingstone.com/music/lists/the-500-greatest-songs-of-all-time-20110407/simon-and-garfunkel-the-sounds-of-silence-20110526

2. http://www.npr.org/player/v2/mediaPlayer.html?action=1&t=1&islist=false&id=11604803&m=11604903&live=1

3. http://www.songfacts.com/detail.php?id=1422

4. http://www.allmusic.com/artist/grateful-dead-mn0000988440/awards

5. http://www.setlists.net/

6. http://www.billboard.com/bbcom/charts/yearend_chart_display.jsp?f=The+Billboard+200&g=Year-end+Albums&year=1972

7. http://www.edsullivan.com/artists/dave-clark-five
   Andrew Pierce, "Why I Turned Down a Gong from Harold Wilson,"*The Telegraph*, 12-10-2008

8. J.J. Colagrande,"Bob Marley's Ex-Girlfriend Brings Her Own Marley Documentary to Miami,"*Miami New Times*, 4–19-2012

9. http://riverising.tripod.com/john-bluemoonswamp/bmsinterviews.html?stop_mobi=yes
   Hank Bordowitz, *Bad Moon Rising: The Unauthorized History of Creedence Clearwater Revival*. Chicago Review Press (2007)
   http://digital.library.unt.edu/ark:/67531/metadc19837/m1/
   http://www.forgottenhits.com/creedence_clearwater_revival
   http://www.creedence-online.net/history/
   Jon Landau, "Mardi Gras," Rolling Stone, 5-26–1976

10. Kurt Loder, "Joan Baez: The *Rolling Stone* Interview," *Rolling Stone* 4-14–1983
    Greg Kot, "'Waltz' Bittersweet for Many, But Not for Robbie Robertson,"*The Chicago Tribune*, 4-7-2002
    Jon Pareles, "Richard Manuel, 40, Rock Singer and Pianist,"*The New York Times*, 3-6–1986
    http://www.memory.loc.gov/ammem/today/may10.html
    Bill Flangan, "Rick Danko on The Band—New Albums, Old Wounds," *Musician Magazine*, 12–1993
    http://articles.latimes.com/2008/feb/17/entertainment/ca-letters17.S1

11. http://www.harrynilsson.com/bio/
    Nick Talevski, *Knocking on Heaven's Door: Rock Obituaries*. Omnibus Press (2006)

James Bates, "In the End, Only Creditors Talked to Nilsson," *Los Angeles Times*, 11-7–1994 (the title of this piece being a somewhat unkind reference to Everybody's Talkin'). http://lifeofthebeatles.blogspot.com/2009/06/beatle-people-harry-nilsson.html

12. http://www.allmusic.com/artist/leonard-cohen-mn0000071209/biography
    Sylvie Simmons, *I'm Your Man: The Life of Leonard Cohen*, HarperCollins (2012)
    Dan Glaister, "Cohen Stay Calm as $5 million Pension Disappears," *The Guardian*, 10-7-2005
    Katherine Machlem, "Leonard Cohen Goes Broke," *MacLean's*, 8-22-2005
    http://www.nme.com/news/leonard-cohen/22406
    Liel Leibovitz, *A Broken Hallelujah: Rock and Roll, Redemption, and the Life of Leonard Cohen*, Norton (2014)
    Author not given, "Leonard Cohen's Ex-Manager Sentenced to 18 Months in Prison," *Rolling Stone*, 4–19-2012

13. https://www.youtube.com/watch?v=Xk7DOe5EGgM (Chelsea Hotel #2)
    David Hepworth, Never a Dull Moment, Henry Holt (2016)

14. http://www.songfacts.com/detail.php?id=13100
    http://web.archive.org/web/20050616181341/http://www.rockhall.com/hof/inductee.asp?id=66

15. Michael Bryan Kelly *The Beatle Myth: The British Invasion of American Popular Music, 1956–1969*. McFarland. (2014)
    http://www.allmusic.com/artist/the-beau-brummels-mn0000135032/biography
    http://www.goldminemag.com/article/beau-brummels-look-to-rewrite-history-with-greatest-hits-package

16. http://legendsrevealed.com/entertainment/2012/09/05/did-in-a-gadda-da-vida-come-about-because-of-a-misheard-lyric/
    http://www.drumheadmag.com/web/feature.php?id=14

17. http://www.songfacts.com/detail.php?id=2051
    http://popcultureaddict.com/interviews/marklindsay/

18. Rob Lowman, "Roll of a Lifetime Founding Bassist Bill Wyman Looks Back At the Stones," *Los Angeles Daily News*, 10-27-2002.
    Bill Wyman, *Rolling with The Stones*, DK Adult (2002)
    Rolling Stones, *According to the Rolling Stones*. Chronicle Books (2003)
    http://rockhall.com/inductees/the-rolling-stones/bio/
    Keith Richards, *Life*, Little Brown (2010)

19. http://www.brucespringsteen.it/e_streetx.htm
    http://www.rollingstone.com/music/news/the-band-on-bruce-their-springsteen-20090121

20. http://www.rodandcustommagazine.com/hotnews/0601rc_75_most_significant_1932
_fords/printer_friendly.html
http://www.songfacts.com/detail.php?id=964
http://kearth101.cbslocal.com/2013/09/11/not-fade-away-bruce-springsteens-the
-wild-the-innocent-and-the-e-street-shuffle-turns-40/
Kevin Cahillane, "Two Guys Left Behind in the E Street Shuffle," *The New York Times*,
5/1/2005.
http://www.rollingstone.com/music/lists/100-greatest-bruce-springsteen-songs-of-all
-time-20140116/tenth-avenue-freeze-out–19691231

21. http://www.allmusic.com/artist/bernie-taupin-mn0000378436/biography
http://www.berniejtaupin.com/biography.bt
http://www.examiner.com/article/great-musical-collaborations-elton-john-and-bernie
-taupin
James McKinley, "Still Making Music Together, Far Apart," *The New York Times*,
9-27-2013.
https://www.youtube.com/watch?v=rX6qiHjqzao (Elton John and Bernie Taupin on
The Arsenio Hall Show)

22. http://ultimateclassicrock.com/elton-john-first-american-concert/

23. Margalit Fox, "Dan Peek, of the Rock Band America, Dies at 60," *The New York Times*,
7-26-2011.

24. http://newsone.com/934515/teena-marie-interview-im-a-black-artist-with-white
-skin/
http://newsone.com/935925/the-life-legacy-and-yes-blackness-of-teena-marie/

CHAPTER 10

1. Jean Patterson, *Crazy About "Layla"; Eric Clapton Song Inspired by Nizami,
12th century Azerbaijani Poet*, Azerbaijan International, Autumn, 1998
http://www.iranicaonline.org/articles/leyli-o-majnun-narrative-poem
http://www.artarena.force9.co.uk/perlm.htm
Pattie Boyd, *Wonderful tonight: George Harrison, Eric Clapton and Me*, Crown Archetype
(2008)
http://www.eric-clapton.co.uk/interviewsandarticles/reptileinterview.html

2. http://www.roadsideamerica.com/story/12603

3. http://www.snopes.com/music/songs/motherchildreunion.asp
http://www.vh1.com/music/tuner/2014-10-15/the-whitest-moments-in-reggae/

4. http://www.songfacts.com/detail.php?id=536
5. http://www.metacafe.com/watch/1435187/carly_simon_meaning_of_gavotte/
    http://mentalfloss.com/article/32295/11-obscure-references-classic-songs-explained
    http://www.carlysimon.com/You're_So_Vain.html
    Daniel Kreps, "Carly Simon Refutes Theory That "So Vain" Target Is David Geffen," *Rolling Stone*, 3-1-2010
    Kathy Dowd, "Carly Simon Says 'You're So Vain' Is About Warren Beatty – Well, Only the Second Verse: 'He Thinks the Whole Thing Is About Him!'," *People*, 11-18-2015.
6. http://www.secondhandsongs.com/topic/34176
    Pierre Perone, "Gene Raskin—Singer, Songwriter and Architectural Scholar," *The Independent*, 6-18-2004
7. https://www.youtube.com/watch?v=XBXUP5GqYJs (Herbie Flowers)
    https://www.youtube.com/watch?v=GeSnzKZvxNE (*Jump Into the Fire*)
8. http://www.allmusic.com/song/brown-sugar-mt0010819670
    Tony Sanchez, *Up and Down with the Rolling Stones*, Da Capo Press (1996)
    http://www.superseventies.com/sw_brownsugar.html
    Keith Richards, *Life*, Little Brown (2010)
    http://www.iorr.org/talk/read.php?1,1600085,160008
9. https://www.youtube.com/watch?v=TLm9KX-LvMM (Garden Part—The Story of Ricky Nelson's Song)
10. Mark Kemp, "The Allman Brothers Band—At Fillmore East," *Rolling Stone*, 7-16-2002
    Jason Fry, "Rock's Oldest Joke: Yelling 'Freebird!' In a Crowded Theater," *The Wall Street Journal*, 3-17-2005
    Alan Paul, *One Way Out—The Inside History of the Allman Brothers Band*, St. Martin's Press (2014)
11. Richard Williams, *Phil Spector: Out of His Head*, Omnibus Press (2003).
    http://www.songfacts.com/detail.php?id=2822
    http://www.rollingstone.com/music/lists/the-500-greatest-songs-of-all-time-20110407/ike-and-tina-turner-river-deep-mountain-high-20110525
12. https://archive.org/details/HarryChampion
    Colin MacInnes, "The Old English Music Hall Songs Are New," *The New York Times*, 11-28–1965
    http://www.allmusic.com/artist/hermans-hermits-mn0000575051/biography
13. http://www.poemhunter.com/jose-marti/biography/

CHAPTER 11

1. Jeff Guinn, *Manson*, Simon & Schuster (2013)
2. Peter Ames Carlin, *Catch a Wave: The Rise, Fall, and Redemption of the Beach Boys' Brian Wilson*, Rodale (2006).
   George Will, "The Beach Boys Still Get Around, 50 Years Later," *The Washington Post*, June 20, 2012.
   http://www.brianwilson.com/news/2014/1/29/brian-answers-fans-questions-in-live-qa
   https://www.youtube.com/watch?v=_bxfR-Vuo8Y (The Beach Boys/Murry Wilson: Help Me Rhonda)
   http://www.albumlinernotes.com/Murry_Wilson.html
   Lynn Van Matre, *Child of Abuse, Beach Boy Brian Wilson Finally Tells His Story, And It Isn`t Pretty*, Chicago Tribune, 10/13/1991
   Karen Heller, *A Beach Boy's Blues for Brian Wilson, The Days of "Fun, Fun, Fun" Have Ebbed*,10/23/1991
   Richard Williams, "The Beach Boys Poison Pen Letter," *The Guardian*, 1/7/2010
3. David Hepworth, Never a Dull Moment, Henry Holt (2016).
4. http://digital.library.unt.edu/ark:/67531/metadc19772/m1/
   David Hinckley, Notes from*Phil Spector: Back to Mono (1958–1969)*boxed-set booklet (1991)
   http://albumlinernotes.com/Back_To_Mono__Songs_.html
   http://www.cbsnews.com/news/barry-mann-and-cynthia-weil-still-have-that-lovin-feelin/2/
   http://www.bbc.com/news/uk-northern-ireland-15186967
5. http://www.huffingtonpost.com/mike-ragogna/emsoul—inspirationem-a-c_b_1658056.html
6. David Browne, *Fire and Rain*, Da Capo Press (2011)
7. http://www.oldbuckeye.com/prox/jazz.html
   http://www.kissasylum.com/KissHell/pc_interview1.html
   http://www.rollingstone.com/music/news/the-devil-and-ginger-baker-20090820
   http://www.effingham.net/bishop/CopelandInterview.htm
   http://www.pinkfloydfan.net/threads/gilmour-mason-wright-the-30-year-technicolor-dream-mojo-magazine-july–1995.1484/#post23744
   http://wcbsfm.cbslocal.com/2013/01/24/revealed-ten-unanswered-questions-from-beware-of-mr-baker/
   http://www.allmusic.com/artist/ginger-baker-mn0000655273/biography
8. http://www.soulwalking.co.uk/Archie%20Bell%20&%20The%20Drells.html
   http://www.rollingstone.com/music/lists/the-500-greatest-songs-of-all-time-20110407/archie-bell-and-the-drells-tighten-up-20110526

9. Fred Bronson, *The Billboard Book of #1 Hits*, 5th Edition (Billboard Publications) (2003)
    Wesley Hyatt, *The Billboard Book of #1 Adult Contemporary Hits*. Billboard Publications, (1999)
    Barry Manilow, *Sweet Life: Adventures on the Way to Paradise*, McGraw-Hill (1987).

10. http://joelfrancis.com/tag/berry-gordy/page/2/

11. http://www.thebighousemuseum.com/the-band/

12. Bob Mersereau, *The Top 100 Canadian Albums*, Goose Lane editions (2008).
    http://www.huffingtonpost.com/entry/neil-young-more-barn_us_576927bae4b015db1
    bca809f?section=

13. Jayson Greene, *George Harrison: All Things Must Pass*, Pitchfork, 6–19-2016
    John Harris, *A Quiet Storm*, Mojo, July 2001

14. Dwight Garner, "Sex, Drugs and Southern Rock, in Success and Excess," *The New York Times*, 5-27-2012
    http://rulefortytwo.com/secret-rock-knowledge/chapter-8/foot-shootin-party/

15. Jon Savage, 1966, *The Year the Decade Exploded*, Faber and Faber (2016)

16. http://www.alkaseltzer.com/as/faqs.html

17. http://www.allmusic.com/artist/the-kinks-mn0000100160/biography
    Doug Hinman, *The Kinks: All Day and All of the Night*. Hal Leonard Corporation (2004)
    Thomas Kitts, *Ray Davies: Not Like Everybody Else*. Routledge (2007).
    Author not given, *The Night the Genius of the Kinks Almost Came to an End in Wales* (Western Mail (Wales), 6-25-2103.
    Jon Savage, *The Kinks: The Official Biography*. Faber and Faber (2004).
    Brawls and Bans: The History of the Kinks' Struggles in America| http://ultimateclassicrock.com/kinks-in-america

18. http://www.songfacts.com/facts-derek_%5E_the_dominos.php

19. http://www.feelnumb.com/2009/10/21/john-lennon-co-wrote-david-bowies-song-fame/

20. Mark Sutherland, "Party On: Queen's Brian May Remembers 'Bohemian Rhapsody' on 40th Anniversary," *Rolling Stone*, 10-30-2015
    Paul Fowles, *A Concise History of Rock Music*. Mel Bay Publications, Inc. (2009)
    http://www.officialcharts.com/chart-news/queen-s-bohemian-rhapsody-voted-the-nation-s-favourite-number-1-single__2258/

21. Dave Marsh, *Bruce Springsteen: Two Hearts: The Definitive Biography, 1972-2003*. Routledge (2004).

22. Bruce Lambert, "Bill Graham, Rock Impresario, Dies At 60 In Crash," *The New York Times*, 10000/27/1991

23. http://www.superseventies.com/sw_youaintseennothinyet.html
    Interview track on the album *King Biscuit: Bachman–Turner Overdrive* (King Biscuit Flower Hour Records, 1998)

24. http://mentalfloss.com/article/19005/music-7-songs-fewer-35-words
    http://www.songfacts.com/detail.php?id=8611
    http://louisianamusichalloffame.org/content/view/45/81/
25. http://www.bobdylan.com/us/songs/quinn-eskimo-mighty-quinn
    http://www.songfacts.com/detail.php?id=2399
26. file:/Downloads/SSRN-id2309742.pdf
27. Andrew Loog Oldham, *Stoned*. St. Martin's Griffin (2002)
    http://www.independent.co.uk/arts-entertainment/music/features/ian-stewart-the
    -sixth-rolling-stone-2236089.html
    Keith Richards, *Life*, Little Brown (2010), page 92.
    Peter Fornatale, *50 Licks: Myths and Stories from Half a Century of the Rolling Stones*,
    Bloomsbury (2013)
28. http://www.sonnycurtis.com/
29. http://www.averagewhiteband.com/_news/history.html
    http://www.70disco.com/awb.htm
30. http://freddiemercury4ever.wordpress.com/career/
31. http://rockhall.com/story-of-rock/features/all-featured/7734_willie-mae-big-mama
    -thornton-story-hound-dog/
32. http://en.wikipedia.org/wiki/Chris_Montez

CHAPTER 12

1. https://web.archive.org/web/20050406140935/http://www.doctorhook.com/interview.
   html
2. Johnny Cash, *Cash: The Autobiography*, HarperOne (2003)
   http://mentalfloss.com/article/30082/johnny-cashs-boy-named-sue-was-written-shel
   -silverstein
   Eugene Bergmann, *Excelsior, You Fathead! The Art and Enigma of Jean Shepherd*, Applause
   Theater (2005)
   "Johnny Cash is Indebted to a Judge named Sue," *New York Times*, July 11, 1970.
3. http://www.rollingstone.com/music/lists/the-500-greatest-songs-of-all-time
   -20110407/aretha-franklin-respect-20110516
4. http://www.abbaomnibus.net/years/articles/billboard_17081991.htm
5. This song was originally released by *The Undisputed Truth* in 1971, but their version is
   largely forgotten. The Temp's version on the other hand hit #1 and was ranked #168
   onRolling Stone's list of the500 Greatest Songs of All Time
6. http://www.allmusic.com/artist/disco-tex-and-the-sex-o-lettes-mn0001202301

CHAPTER 13

1. http://www.youtube.com/watch?v=yigd-aDV5uQ(Liza Minnelli "Sweet Blindness" on The Ed Sullivan Show
    Larry King:Liza Minnelli on marriage, her mother Judy Garland)
2. http://www.songfacts.com/detail.php?id=10541
3. http://www.superseventies.com/1972_4singles.html
    http://retrainyourbraintohappiness.blogspot.com/2014/06/melanie-safka-look-what
    -they-did-to-her.html
4. http://web.archive.org/web/20071011225301/ http://jazztimes.com/reviews/cd_reviews
    /detail.cfm?article_id=15185&section=CD+Reviews&issue=200412
    http://web.archive.org/web/20040717164311/http://www.dirtylinen.com/106
    /ronstexc.html
5. http://www.allmusic.com/artist/bobbie-gentry-mn0000065397/biography
    http://performingsongwriter.com/bobbie-gentry-ode-billie-joe/
6. http://performingsongwriter.com/bobbie-gentry-ode-billie-joe/
    http://www.songfacts.com/detail.php?id=1623
7. http://rulefortytwo.com/secret-rock-knowledge/chapter-15/tallahatchee-bridge/
    http://performingsongwriter.com/bobbie-gentry-ode-billie-joe
    http://www.rollingstone.com/music/lists/the-500-greatest-songs-of-all-time
    -20110407/bobbie-gentry-ode-to-billie-joe-20110526
8. http://www.songfacts.com/blog/interviews/janis_ian/
9. http://www.musicradar.com/news/drums/the-12-greatest-singing-drummers
    -ever-486045/6
10. http://www.artistdirect.com/artist/credits/bobbye-porter/518052
    http://en.wikipedia.org/wiki/Bobbye_Hall
11. Jon Kutner and Spencer Leigh, *1000 UK Hits*, Omnibus Press (2005)
    http://www.songfacts.com/detail.php?id=2578
12. http://www.allmusic.com/artist/dusty-springfield-mn0000159214/biography
    http://www.rockonthenet.com/artists-j/eltonjohn_main.htm
    http://www.cpinternet.com/~mbayly/article26.htm
    http://web.archive.org/web/20100407211250/http://www.rollingstone.com/news
    /story/6598132/89_dusty_in_memphis
    http://www.1000recordings.com/music/dusty-memphis/
    Chris Welch, *Led Zeppelin*, Orion Books (1994)
    Mick Wall, *No Way Out*, Bauer Media Group (2005).

CHAPTER 14

1. http://oldies.about.com/od/thebeatlessongs/a/foryoublue.htm
   Pattie Boyd, *Wonderful Tonight*, Harmony Books (2007)
   http://abbeyrd.net/harrison.htm
2. http://www.accessbackstage.com/america/song/song005.htm
   http://www.songfacts.com/detail.php?id=3019
   "Lennon–McCartney Songalog: Who Wrote What," *The Hit Parader Interview Magazine* (*Hit Parader*). Winter 1977
   David Sheff, *All We Are Saying: The Last Major Interview with John Lennon and Yoko Ono*, St. Martin's Press (2000)
   http://www.angelfire.com/mo/stephenlaug/articles/hitch199508.html
   http://www.songfacts.com/detail.php?id=1884
   Mark Teehan. "The Byrds, "Eight Miles High", the Gavin Report, and Media Censorship of Alleged 'Drug Songs' in 1966: An Assessment," *Popular Musicology Online* (2010).
   Johnny Rogan, *The Byrds: Timeless Flight Revisited* (2nd ed.). Rogan House. (1998).
   Hank Bordowitz, *Bad Moon Rising: The Unauthorized History of Credence Clearwater Revival*, Chicago Review Press (1998)
   http://www.straightdope.com/columns/read/2389/will-smoking-banana-peels-get-you-high
   Brooke Kroeger and Cary Abrams, *Anatomy of the Great Banana Smoking Hoax of 1967*, The The Local East Village, 2-28-2012.
   Holly George-Warren, ed. *The Rolling Stone Encyclopedia of Rock & Roll* (3rd ed). Fireside (2001).
   The Aftershow, *NME*: 66. 6-18-2011.
   Ballad in Plain D: An introduction to the Bob Dylan era (audio). *Pop Chronicles*. Digital. library.unt.edu. (Show 32, track 2)
   http://digital.library.unt.edu/ark:/67531/metadc19791/m1/
3. http://digital.library.unt.edu/ark:/67531/metadc19770/m1/
4. http://www.songfacts.com/detail.php?id=802
   http://www.classicbands.com/StrawberryAlarmClockInterview.html

CHAPTER 15

1. http://www.waybackattack.com/top100-noveltyhits.html
2. http://www.songfacts.com/detail.php?id=5353
3. http://www.digitaldreamdoor.com/pages/best_songs-novelty.html

CHAPTER 16

1. http://blogcritics.org/take-me-home-country-roads-she
    JohnRaby, "John Denver's Country Roads Becomes West Virginia State Song," *Las Vegas Review-Journal*, 3-18-14
    http://www.mprnews.org/story/npr/135150085
2. Jennifer Brown, *Lawmakers OK 'Rocky Mountain High'*, The Denver Post, 3-12-2007
    http://www.netstate.com/states/symb/song/co_rocky_mountain_high.htm
3. https://www.youtube.com/watch?v=jP55F_-SFoU (Ohio State Marching Band playing Hang On Sloopy at the 2012 Buckeye Invitational)
    https://www.youtube.com/watch?v=oh59FSzMiZg (OSU Halftime vs. Penn State-Hang On Sloopy)
    https://www.youtube.com/watch?v=nXrGmfISNBg (Hang On Sloopy at Indians Game)
    https://www.youtube.com/watch?v=fh0hHm-ckQw (The Vibrations—My Girl Sloopy)
    Sherrie Tucker, "Rocking the Cradle of Jazz: Women who changed the face of music," *Ms. Magazine* (2004).
    http://u.osu.edu/osualp/handbook/ohio-state-traditions/osu-songs/hang-on-sloopy/
    http://www.ohiohistorycentral.org/w/Ohio's_State_Rock_Song_-_Hang_On_Sloopy?rec=1878
    Sean Murphy,*Flaming Lips Tune Pulled as Oklahoma's Rock Song,*Associated Press, April 12, 2013.
4. Emily Gibson, "How 'Sweet Caroline' Became the Pitt Fans' Singalong," *Pittsburgh Post-Gazette*, 11-26-2010
    https://www.youtube.com/watch?v=o0GskeQs5V0 (Pitt Football Game Day)
5. Kurt Reighley, "The State I'm In," *The Seattle Times*, 10-27–1999
    http://www.soundandvision.com/content/international-louie-louie-day
6. http://www.welcometoasburypark.com/acr121.shtml
    Dave Marsh, *Bruce Springsteen" Two Hearts, the Story*, Routledge (2004).

CHAPTER 17

1. http://www.thefortunes.co.uk/history.html
2. http://lcweb2.loc.gov/ammem/ccmphtml/colaadv.html
    http://www.coca-colacompany.com/stories/coke-lore-hilltop-story
3. http://www.songfacts.com/detail.php?id=2410
4. "Thomas W. Dawes, 64, Musician, Wrote Alka-Seltzer, 7-Up Jingles," *The Boston Globe*, 11-4-2007.

CHAPTER 18

1. Eric Lacitis, "Herb Alpert's 'Whipped Cream Lady' Now 76," *The Seattle Times*, 8/26/2012
    Nick Paumgarten, "Whipped Again," *The New Yorker*, 4/10/2006
2. http://www.feelnumb.com/2010/01/24/adolf-hitler-did-not-make-the-cut-on-the
    -beatles-sgt-pepper-album-cover/
    Anthony Barnes, "Where's Adolf? The Mystery of Sgt. Pepper is Solved," *The Independent*, 2/3/2007
    Barry Miles, *The Beatles: A Diary*.Omnibus (1998)
3. Mick Wall, *When Giants Walked the Earth: A Biography of Led Zeppelin*. Orion (2008)
    http://ultimateclassicrock.com/10-things-you-didnt-know-about-led-zeppelin-four/
    Barney Hoskyns, *Led Zeppelin IV—Rock of Ages*, Rodale (2006)
    http://superhypeblog.com/marketing/the-marketing-genius-of-led-zeppelin-iv
4. https://music.yahoo.com/blogs/stop-the-presses/pink-floyd-dark-side-40-years
    -later-40-205227757.html
5. http://www.npr.org/player/v2/mediaPlayer.html?action=1&t=1&islist=false&id=
    10634329&m=10634334
6. MarkLewisohn, *The Beatles Recording Sessions*.Harmony (1988)
    Mark Lewisohn, *The Complete Beatles Chronicle:The Definitive Day-By-Day Guide To The Beatles' Entire Career*, Chicago Review Press. (2010 ed.)
7. http://www.alexandruvita.com/blog/2010/05/14/most-famous-album-covers-ever/
    http://www.nevermindthebuspass.com/happiness-archive/classic-album-covers
    /classic-album-covers-strange-days-the-doors/
    http://www.vh1.com/photos/gallery/?fid=1486056&page=1&thumbnails=true
8. http://mentalfloss.com/article/52066/stories-behind-22-classic-album-covers
    Andrew Neill, and Matthew Kent. *Anyway Anyhow Anywhere – The Complete Chronicle of The Who*, Virgin (2002)
    http://www.vh1.com/photos/gallery/?fid=1486056&page=1&thumbnails=true
9. https://www.discogs.com/release/451342-Sticky-Fingers/images
    Joe Coscarelli, "Art of the Rolling Stones: Behind That Zipper and That Tongue," *The New York Times*, 6-7-2015
10. David Beard, "Learn about The Beach Boys' 'Summer Days' Album Cover," *Goldmine*, 7-20-2010
11. David Hepworth, *Never a Dull Moment*, Henry Holt (2016).
12. David Sheff, *All We Are Saying: The Last Major Interview with John Lennon and Yoko Ono*. Macmillan (2000).
    http://www.rarebeatles.com/album2/butcher/butch$.htm

The Beatles Anthology, Chronicle Books LLC (2000).
http://entertainment.ha.com/itm/music-memorabilia/recordings/beatles-yesterday-and-today
http://www.whatsellsbest.com/news-stories/2016/02/beatles-butcher.html

CHAPTER 19

1. "Whiter Shade Most Played Song," BBC News, 4-13-2009(http://news.bbc.co.uk/2/hi/entertainment/7996979.stm)
2. *Procul Harum singer Gary Brooker wins A Whiter Shade of Pale royalty court battle*, The Mirror, 4-4-2008
   https://music.yahoo.com/blogs/yradish/singles-that-have-sold-over-10-million-copies.html
   http://www.brits.co.uk/history/shows/1977
   http://news.bbc.co.uk/2/hi/entertainment/8176352.stm
   http://www.publications.parliament.uk/pa/ld200809/ldjudgmt/jd090730/fisher-1.htm
3. http://www.afi.com/100Years/songs.aspx
4. http://en.wikipedia.org/wiki/Eurovision_Song_Contest
   BBC News, *Abba wins "Eurovision 50th" vote*, 10/23/2005 (http://news.bbc.co.uk/2/hi/entertainment/4366574.stm)
5. http://www.neatorama.com/2014/06/18/Yesterday-The-Most-Recorded-Song-of-All-Time (4,000 covers)
   http://www.guinnessworldrecords.com/content_pages/record.asp?recordid=50867 (1,600 covers)

CHAPTER 20

1. http://seventiesmusic.wordpress.com/2012/02/23/venus-shocking-blue–1970/
2. http://www.youtube.com/watch?v=ukhfhUHtD0g (Vicki Lawrence—The Night the Lights Went Out in Georgia—1973)
   http://www.wnyc.org/story/song-sequels/
3. http://www.songfacts.com/detail.php?id=3347
   http://www.leftlion.co.uk/articles.cfm/title/paper-lace-interview/id/621
4. http://www.bobborst.com/popculture/top-100-songs-of-the-year/?year=1966
   http://www.events-in-music.com/number-one-songs-the-ballad-of-the-green-berets.html
   http://articles.latimes.com/1989-11-06/news/mn-708_1_barry-sadler

5. http://www.allmusic.com/artist/every-mothers-son-mn0000129131/biography
https://www.youtube.com/watch?v=aTvUbAQIefA (Every Mother's Son—Come On Down to My Boat)
https://www.youtube.com/watch?v=-056FPxXTmI (The Rare Breed—Come On Down To My Boat)

6. http://www.rollingstone.com/music/news/big-brother-meets-twisted-sister –19851107?page=2
http://www.thepoisonreview.com/2014/04/27/tox-tunes-82-one-toke-over-the-line -lawrence-welk/
http://www.rockcellarmagazine.com/2012/12/03/one-toke-over-the-line-more-than -a-one-hit-wonder/#sthash.GbVkaWKD.dpbs
http://www.brewerandshipley.com/Misc/OneTokeWelk.htm

CHAPTER 21

1. http://www.hitquarters.com/index.php3?page=intrview/opar/intrview_Phil_Ek _Interview.html

2. Bruce Weber, "Jerry Wexler, R&B Impresario, Is Dead at 91." *The New York Times*, 8-15-2008.
Ashley Kahn, "Jerry Wexler, The Man Who Invented Rhythm and Blues," *Rolling Stone*, 8-15-2008

3. http://www.discogs.com/artist/17207-Jimmy-Miller

4. Sean Piccoli, "Tom Dowd, 77 Music Producer," *The Sun Sentinel*, 10-29-2002
http://www.thelanguageofmusic.com/discography.htm
http://www.soundonsound.com/sos/Oct04/articles/rocketscience.htm
http://www.thelanguageofmusic.com/bio_60.HTM

5. http://www.rollingstone.com/music/artists/elton-john/biography

6. Craig McGregor, *Bob Dylan: A Retrospective*, Morrow (1972)
David Simons, *Studio Stories: How the Great New York Records Were Made*, Backbeat Books (2004).
Chris Charlesworth "Sound of Silence". *The Complete Guide to the Music of Paul Simon and Simon & Garfunkel*, Omnibus Press (1996)
Marc Eliot, *Paul Simon: A Life*. John Wiley and Sons (2010)

7. http://www.nme.com/list/50-of-the-greatest-producers-ever/262849/page/5
http://www.joemeekpage.info/essay_07_E.htm
http://joemeekdoc.com/who-is-joe-meek/

http://arpjournal.com/668/take-the-last-train-from-meeksville-joe-meeks%E2%80%99s-holloway-road-recording-studio–1963-7/

http://en.wikipedia.org/wiki/Joe_Meek

8. http://www.earcandymag.com/normansmith-book.htm

    http://www.seth.com/stories/a_ticket_to_rye.html

    Mark Blake, *Comfortably Numb: The Inside Story of Pink Floyd*, Thunder's Mouth Press (2008)

9. Geoff Emerick, *Here, There and Everywhere: My Life Recording the Music of the Beatles* (Gotham, 2007)

10. http://www.georgiaencyclopedia.org/articles/arts-culture/chips-moman-b–1936

    http://www.allmusic.com/album/memphis-boys-the-story-of-american-studios-mw0002299112

    http://www.onthisveryspot.com/find/spot.php?spot_web_name=American_Sound_Studios

    Roben Jones, *The Story of American Studios*, University of Mississippi Press (2006)

    http://www.allmusic.com/artist/chips-moman-mn0000773669/biography

11. http://www.analogplanet.com/content/veteran-recording-engineer-roy-halee-recording-simon-and-garfunkel-and-otherspart

12. http://www.allmusic.com/artist/richard-perry-mn0000132751/biography

    Robert Adels, "Beatles to Blue Eyes," *The Village Voice*, 11-8–1973

    Stephen Holden, "Old Grandpa Who," *The New York Times*, 5-3–1989

13. Larry Rohter, "What He Saw in the Control Room," *The New York Times*, 12–19-2014

CHAPTER 22

1. http://jalopnik.com/5858239/remembering-the-wreck-of-the-edmund-fitzgerald-36-years-later

    James R. Gaines, "Great Lakes: The Cruelest Month,"*Newsweek*, 11-24–1975.

    http://www.hourdetroit.com/Hour-Detroit/November-2010/Mariners—Church-of-Detroit

    Jane Stevenson, "Lightfoot Chnages 'Edmund Fitzgerald' Lyric,"*The Toronto Sun*, 3-25-2010

    https://www.youtube.com/watch?v=rS1qXLLHmBg (The Wreck of the Edmund Fitzgerald - Gordon Lightfoot - Niagara Falls NY 11-7-2015)

2. http://www.slate.com/blogs/crime/2013/01/11/harry_chapin_sniper_the_bizarre_1970s_ballad_that_sympathizes_with_mass.html

CHAPTER 23

1. http://www.guitarworld.com/20-greatest-supergroups-all-time
2. Author not given, "Return of a Supergroup," *Time*, 8-5–1974
3. http://www.uncut.co.uk/eric-clapton/eric-clapton-on-cream-i-was-in-a-confrontational
   -situation-24-hours-a-day-feature
4. http://www.guitarworld.com/20-greatest-supergroups-all-time
   http://ultimateclassicrock.com/top-supergroups/
   Harry Shapiro, *Graham Bond: The Mighty Shadow*. Crossroads Press (2004)
5. George Forrester, *Emerson, Lake & Palmer: The Show That Never Ends*, Helter Skelter (2005)
6. Steve Hochman, "That 'Pretentious' Trio ELP Is Back on the Rock Scene," *Los Angeles Times*, 8-26–1992
7. http://www.robertchristgau.com/get_artist.php?name=emerson+lake+and+palmer
8. http://ladiesofthelake.com/cabinet/bssliner.html
9. http://www.bbc.co.uk/music/reviews/9bvr

CHAPTER 24

1. http://www.npr.org/2000/10/28/1113153/tammy-wynettes-stand-by-your-man
   http://www.loc.gov/rr/record/nrpb/registry/nrpb-2010reg.html
   https://www.youtube.com/watch?v=89Q2rpsjlUo (Tammy Wynette—Stand By Your Man Controversy)
2. http://www.countrymusicclassics.com/CMCStorySongDec.htm
3. Tom Roland, *The Billboard Book of #1 Country Hits* (Billboard Books, 1991)

CHAPTER 25

1. http://www.edsullivan.com/artists/the-rolling-stones/
   Christopher Sandford, *Mick Jagger: Primitive Cool*, St. Martins Press (1994)
   http://www.edsullivan.com/artists/the-doors
   Marie Korpe, *Shoot the singer!: Music Censorship Today*. Zed Books. (2004)
   Michael Hicks, *Sixties Rock: Garage, Psychedelic, and Other Satisfactions*. University of Illinois Press (2001)
2. http://www.bbc.co.uk/radio2/soldonsong/songlibrary/adayinthelife.shtml
3. https://www.youtube.com/watch?v=VAZAdhPXQ2w (John Lennon explaining Lucy in the Sky with Diamonds)

4. http://www.nzherald.co.nz/radio-industry/news/article.cfm?c_id=295&objectid=10483279&ref=rss
5. David Hepworth, *Never a Dull Moment*, Henry Holt (2016).
    http://www.npr.org/player/v2/mediaPlayer.html?action=1&t=1&islist=false&id=1115821&m=18674971
    http://en.wikipedia.org/wiki/List_of_black_Academy_Award_winners_and_nominees#Best_Original_Song
    http://en.wikipedia.org/wiki/Theme_from_Shaft
6. Jeff Amarakin, *Got a Revolution: The Turbulent Flight of Jefferson Airplane*. Simon and Schuster (2003)
7. Guy Raz, "Radio Free Georgetown," *Washington City Paper*, 1/29/1999.
8. http://top40.about.com/od/top10lists/tp/Bad-Words-In-Pop-Songs-10-Notorious-Examples.htm
9. http://www.thebeatles.com.hk/john/discography/details.php?diRecord=UnfinishedMusicNo.1

CHAPTER 26

1. http://articles.philly.com/1994-08-21/entertainment/25842000_1_top-rock-stars-jim-gordon-grammy
    Will Hermes, "All Rise for the National Anthem of Hip-Hop," *The New York Times*, 10/29/2006.
    Kent Hartman, *The Wrecking Crew: The Inside Story of Rock and Roll's Best Kept Secret*. St. Martin's Press (2012)
    http://www.drummerworld.com/drummers/Jim_Gordon.html
    Patrick Flanary, "Jailed Drummer Jim Gordon Denied Parole," *Rolling Stone*, 5-17-2013
2. http://rateyourmusic.com/list/mattymath/great_music_really_recorded_by_the_wrecking_crew
    David Goggin, *Hal Blaine and The Wrecking Crew*, Rebeats Press (2010)
    Kent Hartman, *The Wrecking Crew: The Inside Story of Rock and Roll's Best Kept Secret*. St. Martin's Press (2012)
    http://www.berklee.edu/news/4554/berklee-welcomes-carol-kaye-for-bassdayze
3. Peter Silverton, *Filthy English: The How, Why, When and What of Everyday Swearing*, Portobello Books (2011)
    John Jackson, *A House on Fire: The Rise and Fall of Philadelphia Soul*, Oxford University Press (2004)

Norm N. Nite, *Rock On: The Illustrated Encyclopedia of Rock N' Roll, 1964 - 1978*. Thomas Y. Crowell (1978)

4. http://seventiesmusic.wordpress.com/2012/05/17/my-baby-loves-lovin-white-plains–1970/
    http://en.wikipedia.org/wiki/Tony_Burrows
    https://www.youtube.com/watch?v=n9R7vlM_zbI (Tony Burrow—A One Hit Wonder Five Times)

5. C.S. Fuqua, *Music Fell onAlabama: The Muscle Shoals Sound That Shook the World*. New South Books (2006).
    http://www.alamhof.org/inductees/timeline/1995/muscle-shoals-rhythm-section/

6. http://www.npr.org/player/v2/mediaPlayer.html?action=1&t=1&islist=false&id=156482702&m=160879136
    http://www.allmusic.com/album/memphis-boys-the-story-of-american-studios-mw0002299112
    http://www.onthisveryspot.com/find/spot.php?spot_web_name=American_Sound_Studios
    Roben Jones, *The Story of American Studios*, University of Mississippi Press (2006)
    http://www.allmusic.com/artist/chips-moman-mn0000773669/biography

7. Don Snowden, "For Clayton, Gloom is Gone," *Los Angeles Times*, 3-13–1986
    http://www.npr.org/player/v2/mediaPlayer.html?action=1&t=1&islist=false&id=1883847378&m
    http://www.openculture.com/2013/06/mick_jagger_tells_the_story_behind_gimme_shelter.html
    http://www.bing.com/videos/search?q=20+feet+from+stardom+merry+clayton+video

CHAPTER 27

1. http://www.genemaclellan.com/?page_id=27
    Nick Talevski, *Knocking on Heaven's Door: Rock Obituaries*, Omnibus Press (2006).
    http://www.canoe.ca/MusicHistoryJanuary/january19.html

2. Scott Benarde, Stars of David: Rock 'n' Roll's Jewish Stories, Brandeis Univ. Press (2003)
    Tom McNichol, "A 'Spirit' From the '60s That Won't Die," *The New York Times*, 12-24-2006.
    http://www.examiner.com/article/exclusive-norman-greenbaum-reveals-the-true-origin-of-spirit-the-sky
    http://www.christianorder.com/editorials/editorials_2011/editorials_feb11.html

https://www.youtube.com/watch?v=TYqkoaA6ow8 (Los Angeles Angels of Anaheim Starting Lineup 8-24-2009)

3. http://www.songfacts.com/blog/interviews/tom_johnston_from_the_doobie_brothers/
   http://www.songfacts.com/detail.php?id=16882

4. http://www.songfacts.com/detail.php?id=2173
   http://www.wonderingsound.com/a-users-guide/muscle-shoals-musical-history/

5. http://www.youtube.com/watch?v=uLO-zuV4LrQ (Morning Has Broken)

6. http://www.allmusic.com/song/turn%21-turn%21-turn%21-to-everything-there-is-a
   -season-mt0002704305
   http://www.haaretz.com/news/pete-seeger-s-role-in-ending-israeli-house-demolitions
   -1.4618

7. http://www.milesago.com/Artists/janet-mead.htm

CHAPTER 28

1. http://www.rollingstone.com/music/artists/big-star
   http://www.allmusic.com/artist/big-star-mn0000051992
   http://www.nme.com/blogs/nme-blogs/alex-chilton-a-cult-hero-remembered

2. http://www.allmusic.com/artist/mc5-mn0000182598/biography
   http://www.rockonthenet.com/archive/2000/vh1hardrock.htm
   http://www.rollingstone.com/music/lists/500-greatest-albums-of-all-time-20120531
   /mc5-kick-out-the-jams–19691231

3. http://www.billboard.com/artist/419361/velvet-underground/chart?f=305
   https://web.archive.org/web/20090104131142/http://www.rollingstone.com/news
   /story/5938174/the_rs_500_greatest_albums_of_all_time/
   http://www.huffingtonpost.com/2013/10/28/velvet-underground-banana_n_4170126
   .html
   http://www.allmusic.com/artist/the-velvet-underground-mn0000840402/biography
   http://music.hyperreal.org/artists/brian_eno/interviews/musn82.htm

4. http://www.allmusic.com/artist/captain-beefheart-mn0000988638/biography
   Lester Bangs, "Mirror Man," *Rolling Stone*, 4/1/1971
   Pierre Perrone, "Captain Beefheart," *The Independent*, 12/192010
   http://www.npr.org/sections/therecord/2010/12/22/132147348/don-van-vliet
   -known-to-rock-fans-as-captain-beefheart-dies
   Will Hermes, "Ten Essential Captain Beefheart Songs," *Rolling Stone*, 12/20/2010
   http://www.beefheart.com/grow-fins-rarities–1965–1982
   http://www.rollingstone.com/music/artists/captain-beefheart

Ewen MacAskill, "Captain Beefheart, Who Has Died Aged 69, was Provocative and Unpredictable," *The Guardian*, 12/17/2010

CHAPTER 29

1. http://www.hoax-slayer.com/dueling-banjos-hoax.shtml
    http://media.gunaxin.com/tribute-banjo-player-deliverance-dueling-banjos/71240
2. http://news.bbc.co.uk/2/hi/uk_news/england/2816253.stm
    https://www.youtube.com/watch?v=1RqcL4QlAKA (Ray Jackson talking about *Maggie May*)
3. http://www.fanpop.com/clubs/101-most/articles/7894/title/101-most-unforgettable-snl-moments
    Paul Farhi, "Blue Öyster Cult, Playing Along With 'More Cowbell'," *The Washington Post*, 1-29-2005
4. https://www.youtube.com/watch?v=ahPumX-aIzw (Brian Auger Talks About the Yardbirds For Your Love)
    http://www.songfacts.com/detail.php?id=1093
    https://www.youtube.com/watch?v=XirG-qwMCMc (Lady Jane—Rolling Stones)
    http://www.songfacts.com/detail.php?id=462
    https://www.youtube.com/watch?v=-q4foLKDlcE (Joni Mitchell—California (BBC))
    https://www.youtube.com/watch?v=xpdhqljxhtQ (Whole Lotta Love Theramin solo)
    https://www.youtube.com/watch?v=R8ifTS5NEsI (Live! The Lovin' Spoonful—"Do You Believe in Magic")
    Paul Gambaccini, *Paul McCartney, In His Own Words*, Putnam (1983)
    http://www.nevilleyoung.co.uk/pennylane
    https://www.youtube.com/watch?v=mQyBRS8Nby8 (Penny Lane Piccolo Trumpeter)
    http://www.thewho.net/linernotes/ByNumbers.htm
    http://www.idrs.org/resources/whoswho/browserecord.php?-action=browse&-recid=12745
    Geoff Emerick, *Here, There and Everywhere: My Life Recording the Music of the Beatles* (Gotham, 2007)
    http://www.reuters.com/article/2009/08/10/us-beatles-idUSTRE5790IA20090810
    Author not given, *Penny Lane Was On His Mind*, Daily Post (Liverpool, 7/14/207)
    https://www.youtube.com/watch?v=wBBl7S08kbw (AC/DC—It's a Long Way to the Top (If You Wanna Rock 'n Roll))
    http://www.democraticunderground.com/101868299
    http://www.planetmellotron.com/toptens2.htm

https://www.youtube.com/watch?v=ajGdNTFxRy0 (Mike Pinder describes how the mellotron works)

CHAPTER 30

1. http://marshalltucker.com/
   http://www.procolharum.com/niels2.htm
   Roger Dopson, sleeve notes,*Manfred Mann: The E.P. Collection*, 1989
2. Michael Walker, *What You Want Is In the Limo*, Spiegel & Rau (2013).
   Susannah Cahalan, "Rock Stars' Wackiest Backstage Demands," *The New York Post*, 10-11-2014.
3. http://www.complex.com/pop-culture/2012/09/the-70-hottest-women-of-the-70s/
4. http://kearth101.cbslocal.com/2013/09/11/not-fade-away-bruce-springsteens-the-wild-the-innocent-and-the-e-street-shuffle-turns-40/
   Kevin Cahillane, "Two Guys Left Behind in the E Street Shuffle," *The New York Times*, 5/1/2005.
   http://www.rollingstone.com/music/lists/100-greatest-bruce-springsteen-songs-of-all-time-20140116/tenth-avenue-freeze-out-19691231
5. AP, "Obituary: Mary Travers, 72; Member of Folk Group Peter, Paul and Mary," *Washington Post*, 9-17-2009.
6. Sam Inglis,*Harvest*, The Continuum International Publishing Group (2003)
   Wesley Stace, "Old Man Takes a Look at His Life," *The Wall Street Journal*, 9/28/2012.
   Neil Young, *Waging Heavy Peace* Blue Rider Press (2012)
   "Lynyrd Skynyrd and Neil Young: Friends or Foes? An Analysis of*Sweet Home Alabama*and*Southern Man*". Thrasher's Wheat. http://www.thrasherswheat.org/jammin/lynyrd.htm
   http://www.lynyrdskynyrdhistory.com/less2.html
   Marley Brant,*Freebirds: The Lynyrd Skynyrd Story*. Billboard Books (2002)
   http://lynyrdskynyrd.com/bio

CHAPTER 31

1. http://www.accessbackstage.com/america/song/song005.htm
2. http://en.wikipedia.org/wiki/I'm_Easy_(song)
3. http://www.telegraph.co.uk/culture/music/rockandpopfeatures/8241127/Gerry-Rafferty-and-his-songs-of-alienation.html
4. http://en.wikipedia.org/wiki/Long_Cool_Woman_in_a_Black_Dress

5. http://www.allmusic.com/artist/the-knickerbockers-mn0000099888/biography
    http://en.wikipedia.org/wiki/The_Knickerbockers
    http://www.examiner.com/article/lies-and-she-s-the-one-among-best-of-british-invasion
    -sound-alikes
    "Land of a thousand laments - So far, 1119 letters and e-mails," *The Star-Ledger*,
    6-13-2005
6. http://www.independent.co.uk/news/obituaries/fontella-bass-singer-famed
    -for-her-powerful-interpretation-of-the-millionseller-rescue-me-8432763.html
    Ben Sisario, "Fontella Bass, 72, Singer of 'Rescue Me,' Is Dead."*The New York Times*,
    12/27/2102
    http://www.cbsnews.com/news/rescue-me-soul-singer-fontella-bass-dead-at-72/

CHAPTER 33

1. http://www.rollingstone.com/music/albumreviews/blue-ridge-rangers–19730705
    http://www.allmusic.com/album/the-blue-ridge-rangers-mw0000198528
2. http://www.popentertainment.com/toddrundgren.htm
    http://www.independent.co.uk/arts-entertainment/music/features/todd-rundgren
    -nothing-but-the-truth-6165625.html
    http://www.allmusic.com/album/something-anything-mw0000191577
    http://www.inthestudio.net/online-only-interviews/todd-rundgren
    -something-anything-pt1/
3. Robert Rodriguez,*Fab Four FAQ 2.0: The Beatles' Solo Years, 1970–1980*. Backbeat Books
    (2010)
    Chip Madinger and Mark Easter,*Eight Arms to Hold You: The Solo Beatles Compendium*.
    44.1 Productions (2000)
    Keith Badman, *The Beatles Diary Volume 2: After the Break-Up 1970–2001*. Omnibus
    Press (2011).
    http://www.rollingstone.com/music/albumreviews/mccartney–19700514
    http://www.allmusic.com/album/mccartney-mw0000194129

CHAPTER 34

1. http://ruthannfriedman.com/lyrics/
2. http://www.slate.com/articles/newsandpolitics/chatterbox/2001/09/itstheendof
    theworldasclearchannelknowsit.html

3. 41 Years Ago: Stevie Wonder Steals a #1 Song From Jeff Beck| http://ultimate
    classicrock.com/stevie-wonder-jeff-beck-superstition/?trackback=tsmclip
    http://dmme.net/interviews/appice.html
    http://en.wikipedia.org/wiki/Superstition_(song)
    Annette Carson, *Jeff Beck: Crazy Fingers*, Backbeat (2001)
    Ben Fong-Torres, *Not Fade Away*, Backbeat (1999)

CHAPTER 35

1. https://www.youtube.com/watch?v=HbWXJWWqaqQ (Dylan Klebold and Nate
    Dykeman going to Columbine)
2. Michele Kort, *Soul Picnic: The Music and Passion of Laura Nyro*, St. Martin's (2003)
    http://www.songfacts.com/detail.php?id=12772
3. http://vimeo.com/20137276
4. http://www.paul-simon.info/PHP/showarticle.php?id=13&kategorie=1
    Daniel Lewis, "Daniel J. Berrigan, Defiant Priest Who Preached Pacifism, Dies at
    94," *The New York Times*, 5/1/2016.
5. http://www.offbeat.com/2002/02/01/james-sugar-boy-crawford/
    http://www.offbeat.com/2009/04/01/iko-iko-in-search-of-jockomo/
    http://hereandnow.wbur.org/2014/06/04/dixie-cups-chapel-love
    http://mentalfloss.com/article/48862/iko-iko-wan-dey-what-do-words-mardi-gras
    -song-mean
    http://www.history-of-rock.com/dixie_cups.htm
    http://www.songfacts.com/detail.php?id=8955
    http://en.wikipedia.org/wiki/Iko_Iko
6. Liner notes for The Turtles' anthology *Solid Zinc*.
7. "LaBelle Says Didn't Know Meaning of 'Lady Marmalade,'" *Jet* 79(21). March 11, 1991.
    p.8
8. http://www.thestar.com/entertainment/music/2014/08/22/the_origins_of_the_ooga
    _chaka.html
9. http://www.songfacts.com/detail.php?id=9524
10. http://www.songfacts.com/blog/interviews/bill_withers/
11. *Reddy, Helen. The Woman I Am: A Memoir*. The Penguin Group (2006)
    http://www.troyrecord.com/general-news/20130320/helen-reddy-hear-her
    -roar-thursday-night
12. http://web.archive.org/web/20080730052332/http://www.cnn.com/2008/SHOWBIZ
    /TV/07/16/deaths.ap/index.html

Elaine Woo, "Former TV host also founded software firm," *The Los Angeles Times*, 7-16-2008

Bruce Weber, "Les Crane, Talk-Show Host, Dies at 74," *The New York Times*, 7/15/2008.

13. http://www.broadcasting-history.ca/index3.html?url=http%3A www.broadcasting-history.ca/news/unique/am_text.html

William Bordes, "Canadian Record Hailing U.S. A Hit; Journalist Tired of Hearing Americans 'Kicked Around'," *The New York Times*, 1-13–1974

CHAPTER 36

1. http://www.rollingstone.com/music/lists/the-500-greatest-songs-of-all-time-20110407/the-rolling-stones-i-cant-get-no-satisfaction-20110516

   Keith Richards, *Life*, Little Brown (2010)

2. http://www.history.com/this-day-in-history/john-lennon-writes-and-records-quotinstant-karmaquot-in-a-single-day

CHAPTER 37

1. Eriq Gardner, "Judge Asked to Order Jimmy Page and Robert Plant to Attend 'Stairway to Heaven' Trial," *The Hollywood Reporter*, 5–19-2016

   www.youtube.com/watch?v=zTz_iX_L0VA (Led Zeppelin Steals Songs)

   www.youtube.com/watch?v=tiiY4ciKFQA (Led Zeppelin Examples of Plagiarism)

2. https://www.theguardian.com/music/musicblog/2014/jun/23/bands-hate-songs-led-zeppelin-stairway-heaven-radiohead-creep

   https://emiliocogliani.wordpress.com/2014/05/17/robert-plant-the-lead-singer-of-led-zeppelin-hates-stairway-to-heaven-why/

3. www.bbc.com/news/entertainment-arts-28929167

4. Brad Tolinski, "Light and Shade," *Guitar World*, January 1998.

   Larry Lehmer, *The Day the Music Died: The Last Tour of Buddy Holly, the Big Bopper and Ritchie Valens*, Schirmer Trade (2003)

5. http://www.rollingstone.com/music/albumreviews/houses-of-the-holy-20030730

   Gavin Harrison, *Is Tiny Dancer Really Elton's Little John*, Three Rivers Press (2006).

   Austin Scaggs, "Q&A: Robert Plant," *Rolling Stone*, 5-5-2005

6. Peter Doggett, "The Apple Years," *Record Collector*, April 2001

   Chip Madinger & Mark Easter, *Eight Arms to Hold You: The Solo Beatles Compendium*, 44.1 Productions (2000)

7. *Bright Tunes Music Corp. v. Harrisongs Music, Ltd.*, 420 F. Supp. 177 (S.D.N.Y 1976).
   http://abbeyrd.best.vwh.net/mysweet.htm
8. Fogerty v. Fantasy, Inc., 510 U.S. 517 (1994).

CHAPTER 38

1. http://www.wikisearch.net/search?q=Marijuana+(song)&page=6
   http://www.americansongwriter.com/2009/04/the-30-greatest-bob-dylan
   -songs-18-rainy-day-women-12-35/
2. http://creequealley.com/
   http://www.songplaces.com/Creeque_Alley/Creeque_Alley_St_Thomas_Virgin
   _Islands
3. http://emmylou.net/triosong.html
   http://onesweetsong.blogspot.com/2010/06/neil-youngafter-goldrush.html
4. Gary Giddins, The Bing Crosby CBS Radio Recordings, 1954–1956 (liner notes) (2009)
   http://news.bbc.co.uk/2/hi/entertainment/3246887.stm
5. http://thewho.net/whotabs/gear/guitar/html
   http://guitarworld.com/pete-townshend-interview-the-who?page=2
6. http://musicouch.com/instruments/brass/the-story-in-the-song-the-bee-gees-new
   -york-mining-disaster–1941/
   http://www.brothersgibb.org/history-part-4.html
7. http://theband.hiof.no/history/part_5.html
   http://pitchfork.com/features/staff-lists/6405-the-200-greatest-songs-of-the–1960s/\
   http://www.infoplease.com/ipea/A0150472.html
   http://www.pbs.org/arts/gallery/quick-hits-levon-helm-theweight/quick-hits
   -levon-helm-theweight/

CHAPTER 39

1. John Wilson, "Newport Is His Just For A Song; Arlo Guthrie Festival Hero With 'Alice's
   Restaurant,'"*The New York Times*, 7-18–1967.
   http://www.bsnpubs.com/warner/reprise/reprise6200.html
   http://www.npr.org/templates/story/story.php?storyId=5028273
   http://www.massmoments.org/moment.cfm?mid=342
   http://www.arlo.net/
   http://www.alicebrock.com/alice.html

CHAPTER 40

1. http://www.allmusic.com/song/lets-spend-the-night-together-mt0004277604
   http://www.allmusic.com/song/ruby-tuesday-mt0018040606
   http://www.rollingstone.com/music/lists/100-greatest-rolling-stones-songs
   Bill Wyman, *Rolling with the Stones*, DK Adult (2002)
   Keith Richards, *Life*, Little Brown (2010)
2. http://www.songfacts.com/detail.php?id=1304
3. http://www.rollingstone.com/music/lists/100-greatest-beatles-songs-20110919
   /hello-goodbye–19691231
   http://www.beatlesbible.com/songs/i-am-the-walrus/
   Jann Wenner, *The Rolling Stone Interview: JohnLennon*, 1/21/1971
   http://imaginepeace.com/archives/4385
   http://popdose.com/jesus-of-cool-the-worst-number-one-hits-of-the-sixties/
4. https://www.youtube.com/watch?v=bRAs5rs54z4 (VIX Noelopan- !Aaah- ah yawa em
   ekat ot gnimoc're yeht)
   Dave Marsh, *Book of Rock Lists*, Dell Books (1982).
5. Tim Morse, *Classic Rock Stories: The Stories Behind the Greatest Songs of All Time*. St.
   Martin's (1998).10cc, 189

Index